Life Could Be a Dream

Life Could Be a Dream

*African American Blues,
R&B, Gospel and Doo Wop,
1946–1956*

Jerry Wasserman

McFarland & Company, Inc., Publishers
Jefferson, North Carolina

LIBRARY OF CONGRESS CATALOGING-IN-PUBLICATION DATA

Names: Wasserman, Jerry, 1945– author.
Title: Life could be a dream : African American blues, R&B, gospel and doo wop, 1946–1956 / Jerry Wasserman.
Description: Jefferson, North Carolina : McFarland & Company, Inc., Publishers, 2025. | Includes bibliographical references and index.
Identifiers: LCCN 2025015623 | ISBN 9781476697116 (paperback : acid free paper) ∞
ISBN 9781476655307 (ebook)
Subjects: LCSH: African Americans—Music—20th century—History and criticism. | Blues (Music)—1941–1950—History and criticism. | Blues (Music)—1951–1960—History and criticism. | Rhythm and blues music—History and criticism. | Gospel music—History and criticism. | Doo-wop (Music)—History and criticism | Popular music—United States—1941–1950—History and criticism. | Popular music—United States—1951–1960—History and criticism. | BISAC: MUSIC / Genres & Styles / Soul & R 'n B | HISTORY / African American & Black
Classification: LCC ML3479 .W406 2025 | DDC 780.89/96073—dc23/eng/20250404
LC record available at https://lccn.loc.gov/2025015623

ISBN (print) 978-1-4766-9711-6
ISBN (ebook) 978-1-4766-5530-7

© 2025 Jerry Wasserman. All rights reserved

No part of this book may be reproduced or transmitted in any form or by any means, electronic or mechanical, including photocopying or recording, or by any information storage and retrieval system, without permission in writing from the publisher.

Front cover: (clockwise from upper left) Mahalia Jackson (ETH Library, Switzerland), B. B. King (University of Houston Libraries Special Collections), Sister Rosetta Tharpe and Ray Charles (both photographs by James J. Kriegsmann)

Printed in the United States of America

McFarland & Company, Inc., Publishers
Box 611, Jefferson, North Carolina 28640
www.mcfarlandpub.com

Table of Contents

Preface   1
Introduction: Standing at the Crossroads, 1946–56   5

Chapter One—Blues: Can't Be Satisfied   23
   Texas, Oklahoma, California: Pioneers (T-Bone Walker, Lightnin' Hopkins, Lowell Fulson)   25
   Going to Chicago: Mississippi Pioneers (Big Bill Broonzy, Memphis Minnie, Robert Nighthawk, Big Boy Crudup)   30
   Going to Chicago: Muddy and After (Muddy Waters, Jimmy Rogers, Floyd Jones, JB Lenoir, Eddie Boyd, Otis Rush)   35
   Going to Chicago: Wolf and Elmo (Howlin' Wolf, Elmore James)   42
   Going to Chicago: The Harp Masters (Sonny Boy Williamson II, Little Walter, Junior Wells, James Cotton)   46
   Ladies Sing the (Rhythm &) Blues (Big Mama Thornton, Faye Adams, Big Maybelle, Etta James)   52
   Don't Forget the Motor City (John Lee Hooker)   58
   Blues in New Orleans (Guitar Slim)   61
   Beale Street Blues (B.B. King and Bobby Blue Bland)   62

Chapter Two—Rhythm & Blues: Let the Good Times Roll   66
   The Pioneers: Rhythm & Joy (Louis Jordan, Helen Humes, Dinah Washington)   70
   Sing Us a Song, You're the Piano (Wo)Man (Julia Lee, Bull Moose Jackson, Camille Howard, Nellie Lutcher, Roosevelt Sykes, Memphis Slim, Amos Milburn, Little Willie Littlefield)   79
   Leaders of the Pack (Roy Milton, Tiny Bradshaw)   87
   Shouters (Big Joe Turner, Wynonie Harris, Roy Brown, Jimmy Witherspoon)   89
   Balladeers (Percy Mayfield, Johnny Ace, Little Willie John)   99
   Mama, He Treats Your Daughters Mean (Little Esther, Ruth Brown, LaVern Baker)   103
   Laissez les bons temps rouler (Fats Domino, Lloyd Price, Shirley & Lee)   109
   Rock the Joint (Wild Bill Moore, Jimmy Preston, Chris Powell, Goree Carter, H-Bomb Ferguson, Jimmy Liggins, Jackie Brenston, Sonny Parker, The Treniers)   112

Chapter Three—Gospel: Too Close to Heaven 117
    Mahalia Jackson and the Big Bang 121
    Madame, Sister, Mother, Professor, Reverend (Edna Gallmon Cooke,
        Rosetta Tharpe, Jesse Mae Renfro, Alex Bradford, Rev. Kelsey) 122
    Jubilee to Gospel: How Sweet the Quartet Sound (Golden Gate Quartet,
        Trumpeteers, Bells of Joy, Radio Four, Violinaires, Highway QCs,
        Staple Singers) 128
    A Little Bit Harder Now (Pilgrim Travelers, Golden Echoes, Spirit of Memphis,
        Harmonizing Four, Angelic Gospel Singers) 132
    What Then: Hard Gospel Voices of Salvation and Doubt (Dixie Hummingbirds,
        Ward Singers, Soul Stirrers with R.H. Harris, Soul Stirrers with Sam Cooke,
        Dorothy Love Coates & the Original Gospel Harmonettes, Blind Boys
        of Alabama, Five Blind Boys of Mississippi, Famous Davis Sisters,
        Swan Silvertones, Sensational Nightingales, Meditation Singers,
        Chosen Gospel Singers, Jackson Gospel Singers, Kansas City
        Soul Revivers) 138

Chapter Four—Doo Wop: The Glory of Love 163
    Birds Take Flight (Ravens and Orioles) 167
    Gospel Goes Doo Wop (Dominoes, Larks, "5" Royales, Five Keys, Drifters) 170
    Where Were You in '52? (Cardinals, Swallows, Clovers, Five Crowns, Harptones,
        Willows, Spaniels, Flamingos, Blue Jays) 177
    1954: The Revolution Will Not (Yet) Be Televised (Crows, Chords, Charms,
        Royals/Midnighters, Moonglows, Penguins) 186
    More from '54 (Cadillacs, Solitaires, Diablos, Honey Bears) 192
    A Rare Species: Women in Doo Wop (Shirley Gunter and the Queens, Hearts,
        Lillian Leach and the Mellows, Shirley Haven and the Jacks) 194
    Rolling on the R&B Tide (Platters, Turbans, El Dorados, Five Satins,
        Del-Vikings, Cleftones, Heartbeats, Dells, Channels) 196
    Teenagers in Love: Schoolboy Doo Wop (Mello-Moods, Schoolboys,
        Frankie Lymon and the Teenagers, Lewis Lymon and the Teenchords,
        Ruth McFadden and the Harptones) 203
    The Best of the Rest (Nutmegs, Meadowlarks, Jaguars, Wheels, Chips) 209

Chapter Five—Roots of a Revolution 212
    The Blues Had a Baby (Aretha Franklin, Ray Charles, Little Richard,
        James Brown) 212

Chapter Notes 225
Bibliography 237
Index 245

Preface

The tumultuous decade following the end of World War II saw the civil rights movement begin transforming Black lives and American society. The era also proved momentous for African American popular music: new record labels, new styles, and exciting new sounds in the form of electrified blues combos, rhythm and blues shouters, gospel and doo wop quartets and more. By the middle to late 1950s, rock 'n' roll would dominate the American soundscape and soul music would be born out of gospel's marriage with rhythm & blues. As the Black music of the postwar decade gradually faded from radio and jukeboxes, much of it also drifted into relative obscurity.

Equal parts scholarly study, popular survey, and fanboy tribute, *Life Could Be a Dream* aims to bring this phenomenal body of music back into general awareness, to reanimate its excitement for a new audience, and to explore connections between the socio-political dreams of Black America and the scintillating music it created during that period of great expectations and frustrated hopes. This book examines the African American expression of four musical genres during the years 1946–56: blues, rhythm & blues, gospel, and doo wop. I omit jazz, a huge, complex category on its own, and instrumental music generally. I discuss those four distinct but linked genres in separate chapters, ending with an additional short chapter exploring the root recordings of four seminal African American artists whose work helped define soul and rock 'n' roll. I discuss more than a hundred singers and groups, many of the musicians who played with them, and almost 500 songs.

As a white American music lover growing up in the 1950s and '60s, I heard few of these songs. Well into my forties I listened to the usual Boomer suspects: Dylan and the Beatles, the Doors and Stones, Al Green, Joni Mitchell, Wilson Pickett, the great girl groups, Motown, and the like—classic rock and soul—along with some doo wop and lots of rock 'n' roll. As records gave way to cassettes, then CDs, then online libraries, I gradually discovered more of the earlier material, beginning with doo wop. Those dreamy, yearning love ballads with their amazing harmonies and fast, danceable jump numbers on the records' flip side shaped my earliest musical tastes. I got hooked on blues sometime later, when so-called classic rock started feeling stale. Mesmerizing and exciting, joyous and menacing, the blues, I came to realize, was not just complex, sophisticated music but a deep cultural mode, a prism through which parts of twentieth-century African American life might be viewed. Foundational to the Black music of the 1940s and '50s, the blues itself significantly evolved during the postwar era, profoundly affecting African American writers, too: Ralph Ellison, Alice Walker, Toni Morrison, August Wilson, Walter Mosley and more, as well as Black and Indigenous Canadian novelists and playwrights. I began integrating blues into my university research and teaching in the 1990s.

Postwar rhythm & blues and gospel entered my musical consciousness via iTunes, Spotify, and YouTube. Across these platforms you can easily hear every song discussed in this book. I knew some of the R&B, filed in my mind under rock 'n' roll ("Rocket '88'"; "Shake, Rattle and Roll"), but much of it I was hearing for the first time. I knew none of the gospel. Some of the music I loved best from the 1960s and '70s was gospel-like: The Impressions' "People Get Ready," Al Green's "Jesus Is Waiting," Pacific Gas & Electric's "Are You Ready?" When I stumbled upon the earlier, classic gospel, it knocked me out. With little patience for organized religion but an insatiable appetite for religious art, I recognize that the enormous power of these songs and singers has as much to do with their religious passion as their musical genius.

Life Could Be a Dream began as an attempt to share my playlist of African American music from the 1940s and '50s with my music-savvy friends, some of them musicians themselves, who had never heard many of these artists or their songs. I have continued to expand that list but this book makes no attempt to be encyclopedic or exhaustive. You won't necessarily find the artists' most popular, best-selling hits here. And some of the major names of this period in Black music will be missing. I employ only four criteria: the songs were recorded, released, or charted between 1946 and 1956; they fall into one or more of my four generic categories; they have lyrics; they move me. These song titles appear in **boldface** type in my text.

I have been as rigorous and wide-ranging as possible in my research, building on the work of earlier and contemporary critics to understand the origins, meanings, and impacts of African American music of this era. My discussions aim to appreciate the music in all its details and illuminate the ways it engaged with the postwar issues that affected African American life, to honor the remarkable array of Black artists who created this extraordinary body of music, and to share my observations and enthusiasms with you. Thanks for listening.

Dates and identifications: I have tried my best to identify dates and to name singers and musicians accurately. But hard data are not always available. Inaccurate and contradictory sources proliferate, particularly in the case of photos. I take full responsibility for any errors in this book.

Acknowledgments: I could never have accomplished this project without the encouragement and feedback of friends and family. Thanks to Glenn Wasserman, Peter Anderson, the late Tony Dawson, and Rueben Gurr for their questions and comments on the work in progress; Gage Averill for his advice on organization; Ira Nadel for his publishing suggestions; Scott Low, Tim Hunt, Valerie Gruson, and all who took my Zoom course during the Covid lockdown on the music of this era; musician friends Jane Mortifee, John Mitchell, Shari Ulrich, and Chris King for their inspiration; my blues brothers John Cooper and the late, great Dave Mackinlay for sharing my musical passions; and the amazing Adam Gussow, harp monster, scholar, friend. Many thanks to Laurie C. Matheson for believing in this book, to my fine editor Gary Mitchem, and to all the terrific folks at McFarland as they continue to recover from the carnage of Hurricane Helene. And as always, to my wife Sue for her generous critical eye and for always believing in me.

Introduction

Standing at the Crossroads, 1946–56

"The music grew out of the African American way of life. The way … Sister Williams sang in the choir, the way the old brother down the street played the slide guitar and crooned the blues, the very special way the people danced, walked, laughed, cried, joked, got happy, shouted in church."
—Johnny Otis, *Upside Your Head!*
Rhythm and Blues on Central Avenue

"In my generation we came up with the rise of rhythm and blues, the big city blues of screaming horns and endless riffs. … We needed quartets like the Ravens and the Orioles to translate our real funk…. Dinah and Ruth B. were gospel sounds inside the blues. And the gospel itself was an urban spiritual that wanted to bring blues right on into the church and forget the devil sposed to have something to do with it."
—Amiri Baraka, *The Autobiography of LeRoi Jones*

"That was my entire motivation. I wanted to tell the world something about the inimitable nature of Skip James' music, I wanted to proclaim Muddy Waters' and Bo Diddley's genius…."
—Peter Guralnick, *Looking to Get Lost:*
Adventures in Music & Writing

"*How* music works—the theory, the practice—is learnable. … *Why* it works, God only knows. Maybe not even God."
—David Mitchell, *Utopia Avenue*[1]

In the summer of 1957 my cousin Stanley from the Bronx, three years older than me, slept over at our house on Long Island. That night Stanley talked to almost–12-year-old Jerry about doo wop music and sex, subjects that would remain intertwined for me into adulthood. A few months later I bought my first 45 rpm record: not doo wop but a wailing instrumental called "Raunchy." I didn't know what the title meant but the music moved me. The record appeared in September 1957. The light blue Phillips label credited Bill Justis and His Orchestra. A Memphis songwriter and sax player, Justis turned out to be a one-hit wonder but "Raunchy" was huge. In January

1958, the record went to #1 on *Billboard*'s Rhythm & Blues chart. A note-for-note cover version by pianist Ernie Freeman, released two months later, reached #4 on *Billboard*'s Hot 100 Pop chart and #1 R&B, where it remained for two weeks longer than Justis' original. In a reversal of the 1950s musical default whereby white artists covered and outsold Black hits, Justis was white, Freeman Black.[2]

I didn't know or care about any of this, nor that Phillips Records was a subsidiary of Sam Phillips' Sun Records, the pioneering outfit that first recorded B.B. King, Howlin' Wolf, Elvis Presley, Jerry Lee Lewis, and Johnny Cash. I savored the physical object: holding the record in my hand, pasting the number "1" on the label, filing it in the first of my boxes that would eventually hold fifty 45s each, putting the yellow plastic adapter in the hole, and playing it on my tinny record player. I cared most about the tune, which I realize now was a relatively tame distillation of African American rhythm & blues: a repetitious bass guitar riff alternating with the restrained squawk and wail of Justis' tenor sax. At the time it rocked me and I loved it.

This book serves as a prelude of sorts to "Raunchy." It analyzes and celebrates African American music at a crossroads in the decade before 1957, an underappreciated and underexamined musical era. Recorded from 1946 through 1956, from the first year after the Second World War to the mid-1950s ascension of rock 'n' roll, Black popular music of this period increasingly crossed over from the rhythm & blues category—the coded term for all Black music well into the 1950s—onto the white pop charts. Some of it was genuinely raunchy, some of it powerfully moving, much of it hugely entertaining. A handful of the great singers of the era have filtered into the broad musical pantheon. But most of this decade's songs came and often went before even the Baby Boomers began listening to or collecting music. To most listeners today, the African American songbook of the postwar decade remains obscure, largely invisible and inaudible. This book aims to reintroduce these great songs and artists into the contemporary listening experience and explore the place of this dynamic decade in the evolution of American music.

For organizational purposes I divide the music into four sometimes overlapping, sometimes problematic genres: blues, rhythm & blues (R&B), gospel, and secular harmony, aka doo wop. I omit jazz, a huge category that often overlaps with blues and rhythm & blues. African American jazz artists produced superlative music during this decade. Miles Davis, John Coltrane, Billie Holiday, Ella Fitzgerald, Sarah Vaughan … a full list would warrant a large book on its own. In fact, many large books have been devoted to the jazz of this era. Having chosen to discuss only songs with lyrics, I omit instrumentals but not instrumentalists. Lester Young, Dexter Gordon, Milt Jackson, Charles Mingus, Benny Carter, and Ben Webster are a few of the great jazz players who appear in this book as accompanists on R&B songs I discuss. But by and large, the great jazz singers drew their repertoire from the standards of the Great American Songbook, very different material from what most of the artists in this book were singing. Helen Humes, Dinah Washington, Jimmy Witherspoon and a few others certainly also sang jazz, but I have tried to make clear the reasons I categorize them under rhythm & blues. The blurring of categories is an unavoidable fact of musical life.

Introduction: Standing at the Crossroads, 1946–56

The Second World War ended in late 1945. By 1946, changes in Black music were becoming evident: the evolution of blues from rural to urban, the postwar spin-off of rhythm & blues, the beginning of the golden age of gospel, and the formation of the first R&B-based secular harmony groups that would later be called doo wop. Unofficially, rock 'n' roll first appears around 1954. Black popular music, as it crossed the color bar, overlapped with white pop and rock 'n' roll but retained a distinct identity.

On April 24, 1954, less than a month before the Supreme Court's landmark *Brown v. Board of Education* ruling, a headline in the music industry bible *Billboard* screamed, "Teen-Agers Demand Music with a Beat, Spur Rhythm-Blues." *Teen-Agers* meant white teens. "The teenage tide has swept down the old barriers which kept this music restricted to a segment of the population," the article continued circumspectly, letting the long racial history of American music remain subtext, choosing not to elaborate on what those barriers and restrictions might be. Just eighteen months later, *Billboard* proclaimed, "1955 was the year rhythm and blues virtually took over the pop field." By February 4, 1956, a *Billboard* editorial recognized "the mass acceptance of rhythm and blues—its emergence from narrow confines and its impact on the broad field of pop music," again using the coded *narrow confines* to reference the African American audience. In *Big Beat Heat*, his biography of influential disc jockey Alan Freed, John Jackson argues that rhythm & blues and rock 'n' roll were interchangeable until late 1956. "By the end of the year, white America would be claiming rock & roll as its own." Significantly, in February 1957, *Billboard* re-named its "Rhythm-Blues Notes" column "On the Beat: Rhythm & Blues-Rock & Roll." By the fall of '57, *Billboard* reported that all but one of the top fifteen songs on the R&B chart—including "Raunchy"—also appeared on the Pop chart. African American blues, rhythm & blues, gospel, and doo wop lived on beyond 1956, but musical borders had by then blurred so significantly as to make that year a logical endpoint for this study.[3]

The crossover phenomenon—the infiltration and transformation of Black rhythm & blues into rock 'n' roll—interests me less than the music itself. In the first years of the postwar era this music played almost exclusively to African American audiences and listeners. As segregated as the rest of American life, its hits appeared on *Billboard*'s Harlem Hit Parade from 1942 to 1945. *Billboard* then renamed that chart Race Records, separate from the charts for Popular Records and Country & Western. The magazine replaced the term *Race* with *Rhythm & Blues* in 1949 as the signifier of African American music. But that didn't fool Black artists. To singer Ruth Brown, R&B stood for "race and black." To Bo Diddley it meant "rip-off an' bullshit."[4] In 1955, *Billboard* instituted a Top 100 list, which in 1958 became the Hot 100, in addition to its segregated categories. The R&B chart disappeared in 1963, only to be revived in 1965. In many ways the musical history of the era mirrors its social history.

⁓⁓⁓

This book does not purport to be a formal history of postwar Black popular music, only a dip into its deep waters with a careful eye on the larger historical contexts. Among the most important and well-known music-historical facts:

the effects of the Great Migration on African American music. In the early twentieth century the majority of African Americans lived in the strictly segregated agrarian South, many working as sharecroppers in a system resembling serfdom. Racist policies formalized inequality, enforced in part by lynching. As a result, African Americans began moving from the South to northern industrial cities where wages were much better and racism somewhat less toxic. Accelerated by the mechanization of the plantations on which so many Black men and women toiled, this enormous demographic shift gained speed after World War II. Between 1940 and 1960, another three million African Americans moved from the rural South to the urban North. Through the Great Migration, "African Americans *reinvented* themselves," Henry Louis Gates, Jr., writes, leading to "the exchange of traditional southern and northern black cultures and the resulting synthesis of the two."[5]

African American music reinvented itself in a similar synthesis, as the waves of migration rolled north and west after World War II. Black singers and musicians from Mississippi, Arkansas, Tennessee, and Louisiana often made Memphis their first stop, then headed up Highway 61 or hopped the Illinois Central Railroad to St. Louis and Chicago, or detoured to Detroit; blues men and women from Texas and Oklahoma went west to Los Angeles; from Florida, Alabama, Georgia, and the Carolinas they migrated to New York and Philadelphia. The change in environment led to changes in the music, transforming southern acoustic to northern electric. Blues trios and the pre-war lone bluesman with guitar or piano morphed into a new blues band configuration, some combination of guitar(s), bass, piano, drums, harmonica, and singer. The new sound, Ed Ward writes, was amplified and aggressive.

> The music howled, it moaned, it brought the spirit of the most haunting and elegant Delta blues into the city, electrified it, and turned its boasting sexual power loose among people who were simultaneously homesick for the old land and trying hard to forge a new life in a place that allowed a black man lots of opportunity—within bounds, of course.[6]

The postwar Black audience wanted music that reminded them of down home but also reflected their new socio-economic realities.

Another crucial factor was the mid–1940s break-up of Black swing orchestras, a key segment of the big bands that toured the country. Too expensive to sustain and musically too rigid to adapt to evolving tastes, they succumbed on the one hand to rhythm & blues bands: smaller, more efficient, musically more limber outfits with piano, bass, drums, a horn section of up to four pieces, and a vocalist. Louis Jordan and His Tympany Five (often seven musicians) led the way on this paradigm shift with their big city, good-time music, up-tempo, upbeat, and self-assured. "Let the Good Times Roll," sang Jordan. Out in Los Angeles, Johnny Otis remarked on "[t]he high-spirited exuberance of the African-American church tradition and of the little honky-tonk clubs.... They were demonstrating that artistry, energy, and fun could coexist in Black music without sacrificing artistic integrity." At the same time, musicians wanting the improvisational, exploratory freedom of jazz also split from the big bands, leading to the rise of complex forms like bebop. As jazz became more arcane, Black popular music you could dance to—rhythm & blues—gained public favor.[7]

Most of the artists in the vanguard of the new gospel sound had Southern roots but brought their energetic bluesy styles to the urban congregations up North. Scholars date 1932 as the start of the shift from Black spirituals to gospel blues, when former bluesman Thomas A. Dorsey wrote "Precious Lord, Take My Hand" and began converting Chicago's Black church choirs to the new highly animated gospel style. By the mid-1940s, traditional hymns and jubilee-style spirituals were giving way to a "new wave of youthful black worship ... the sweet sounds of heaven thrown together with the noise of hell."[8] This bluesy, often hard-rocking sound—gospelers called it house-wrecking or church-wrecking—consisted of solo singers and quartets (often five or six voices), male and female, in elaborate call-and-response arrangements, *a cappella* or with sparse instrumental accompaniment.

Louis Jordan, backstage at the Paramount Theater (?), New York City, c. July 1946. William P. Gottlieb/Ira and Leonore S. Gershwin Fund Collection, Music Division, Library of Congress.

Secular Black harmony groups sang *a cappella* on the street corners of northern and a few southern cities, forming quartets with a call-and-response dynamic between the lead and background similar to that of the gospel groups. They created music with a gospel feel, concerned with worldly love rather than the love of a transcendent God. Christened *doo wop* in the early 1960s and applied ex post facto to the harmony groups of the previous decades, their sometimes saccharine, sometimes silly music could be, at its best, intense and beautiful. It grew out of a communal need for self-expression in cities where segregation severely limited the social and physical mobility of young African Americans. Lead singer Herman Denby of Baltimore's The Swallows told an interviewer: "[W]e used to go out on the street and sing. What else, what else did we have? Nothing. I mean, there were places that we wanted to go, you couldn't even go. We weren't allowed in there."[9]

The music business itself changed significantly during this period. A new performing rights organization, Broadcast Music, Inc. (BMI), appeared in 1940, challenging the monopoly that the American Society of Composers, Authors, and Publishers (ASCAP) held on music publishing. ASCAP's restricted membership severely limited the diversity of music played on radio. BMI proved a game-changer for African American songwriters and musical artists: "Not only did BMI accept all kinds of music; it paid royalties on all aired performances, whether live or recorded, on networks or independent stations. All writers now had a conduit into the mainstream industry...." The disc jockey soon emerged as a radio phenomenon. White DJs and a growing number of Blacks could play what they wanted, reflecting and influencing musical tastes. Down South, bluesmen Sonny Boy Williamson II, Little Walter, Robert Nighthawk, and Howlin' Wolf all had regular segments on white stations KFFA and KWEM in Arkansas. A few influential Black stations emerged in the late 1940s, particularly WDIA in Memphis, whose disc jockeys included B.B. King and Rufus Thomas.[10]

The public appetite for music increased substantially during the war. Radio and juke box plays grew exponentially and record sales exploded. After the introduction of the 45 rpm format in 1948, many singles were released as both 45s and 78s for several years until the 78 got phased out. The 33⅓ rpm LP also appeared in 1948. Record buyers had more choices than ever. Yet the major labels continued to ignore the African American market. To fill that void, small independent labels appeared in urban hubs across the country to record the vital new Black music: Sun in Memphis; Specialty, Aladdin, and Modern in Los Angeles; King/Federal in Cincinnati; Chess and Vee-Jay in Chicago; Duke/Peacock in Houston; Savoy in Newark; Atlantic in New York; and many more, all attuned to the local tastes of Black audiences.[11] Although crucial to the development and distribution of the new sound, they often ripped off their artists, many of whom still struggled decades later to recoup the royalties they were owed.

Framing this musical metamorphosis were the profound changes experienced by African Americans themselves at this historical crossroads. My title, *Life Could Be a Dream*, comes from a line in the 1954 doo wop hit "Sh-Boom" by the Chords. Its title and refrain have been linked to H-bomb testing and fears of nuclear warfare, a nightmarish element of the postwar dream. The Cold War cast some dark shadows, as did postwar inflation, recessions, and the hot war in Korea. But on balance the postwar era proved more positive. The momentous victories of World War II meant that the survivors of that war and of the Depression could dream of a new era of peace and prosperity. Unlike much of the rest of the world, North America had emerged physically unscathed, richer and stronger than ever. Modernity promised new inventions and consumer goods to make life easier and better.[12]

For African Americans the times potentially held even more promise: the dream of social, political, and economic equality, the dream Martin Luther King, Jr., would go on to articulate so eloquently. The postwar decade marked the beginning of the modern civil rights era. A few years after the war ended, President Harry Truman ordered the desegregation of the U.S. military. Black heroes like Rosa Parks and Dr. King led a bold new push for voting rights and the desegregation of public transportation. The seminal *Brown v. Board of Education* decision, ruling so-called "separate but equal" segregated public schools unconstitutional, offered further hope that, as Sam Cooke would sing a few years later, a change was gonna come. African Americans could dream of a new world of equality and opportunity.[13]

On the flip side, the Black men and women who had fought in a war to preserve freedom and human dignity came home to a United States that still denied them dignity and freedom. What had they been fighting for? Listen to Big Joe Turner's **"I Got My Discharge Papers,"** recorded in January 1946 at the very dawn of our postwar decade. In this 12-bar blues, accompanied by Al Williams' honky-tonk piano and Warren Brocken's squealing trumpet, Turner assumes the role of a recently discharged GI who sings to his baby about the three, or was it two, years he spent in the war. He can't seem to recall. (Big Joe himself avoided the service.) When he started fighting, he sings, he didn't give a damn. The refrain repeats that he didn't mind fighting as long as he knew what it was for: the woman he loves and his "dear old Uncle Sam." The glaring cynicism in both the lyrics and vocal led, not surprisingly, to Turner's label, Savoy, failing to release the song.

For all the postwar optimism and gradual political advances, the movement towards equality continued to be slow and grudging. Civil rights protesters faced violence and sometimes death. Economic advancement stalled. Racism and discrimination remained alive in the South and the ghettos of the North. Black musicians themselves, traveling around the country, experienced those indignities every day: third-rate segregated accommodations, harassment, humiliation. Postwar life could be a very bad dream for African Americans, a nightmare of failed hopes and continued oppression—at the very least "a dream deferred," as Langston Hughes wrote in his 1951 poem "Harlem." Deferred too long, such dreams could dry up or explode. Sh-boom! The music reflected similar feelings in downbeat blues like Jimmy Witherspoon's **"Ain't Nobody's Business"** (1948) or Eddie Boyd's **"Third Degree"** (1953), the coded protests of R&B like "I Got My Discharge Papers" and doo wop like Frankie Lymon and the Teenagers' **"I'm Not a Juvenile Delinquent"** (1956) or the Chips' **"Rubber Biscuit"** (1956), and the vocal anxiety of some hard gospel, posing musical question marks amid the usual unequivocal faith.

Postwar Black popular music reflects the socio-political situation of African Americans at that time in complex and often sublimated ways. Anger, hope, joy, frustration, fear, the gamut of emotions, intensified by the possibilities the postwar decade seemed to open—and close—for African Americans, the songs contain them all. The lyrics rarely make the connections explicit. For the most part, protest songs like those of the folk revival and soul era that link directly to the civil rights movement do not appear in the body of music explored here. But social history and the changing times always provide the context within which the music was created, performed, and originally received. Great art can contain multiple referents, have diverse and sundry meanings.

In an essay titled "Jazz and the White Critic" from 1963 (when he still called himself LeRoi Jones and used the term *Negro*), Amiri Baraka writes, "Negro music is essentially the expression of an attitude, or a collection of attitudes, about the world, and only secondarily about the way music is made." This book attempts to link those attitudes to the ways Black music was made in the decade following World War II. "Say It Loud–I'm Black and I'm Proud," James Brown would sing in 1968. African American musicians and singers were already cranking it up in the postwar decade. Chicago's heavily amplified electrified blues bands; the rhythm & blues shouters with their pounding pianos and howling saxophones; the screaming, growling, percussive gospel quartets whose songs of salvation burst out of the churches into the streets—the volume and power of this distinctive Black music expressed the pride of the artists and the communities in which and for which it played. Its lyrics spoke of Black manhood, agency for both women and men, sexual potency, the dream of freedom. Doo woppers sang more softly on one side of their records, but with harmonic solidarity and collectivity. Even their love songs carried a message. Ann Powers observes,

> at a time when national attention turned to atrocities like the killing of fourteen-year-old Emmett Till, falsely accused of flirting with a white woman, [doo wop] was the sound of young black men being amorous, openly and innocently. In a way, it was a form of protest. If conventional language had no room for these voices, they'd make up their own.[14]

Terminology and categorization are vexing issues. Trying to classify blues, rhythm & blues, gospel, and doo wop as distinct genres can be a frustrating exercise. African American musicians and singers themselves rarely distinguished among blues forms. B.B. King spoke for many: "I don't feel that I am a country blues singer or a blues musician or an urban blues musician or city blues. … I think one thing: I'm B.B. King and I play what I feel." But some broad distinctions can apply. Rhythm & blues, Richard Ripani argues, developed a more "emotional and declamatory" vocal style than blues generally, and R&B rhythm manifested itself in a strong emphasis on the second and fourth beats: "The raw and aggressive, backbeat-driven twelve-bar blues song designed for dancing was one of the most important stylistic innovations of the late 1940s and early 1950s." Sometimes called *jump blues* (check out Big Joe Turner's **"Jumpin' Tonight"** [1950] or the Flamingos' **"Jump Children"** [1954]), rhythm & blues uses more horns than blues tunes, and uses them more fully. "See, that was the one thing that made rhythm and blues different from the old-fashioned blues," Johnny Otis explained. "The singer is singing and instead of just guitars twanging, the horns played whole notes, rolling those riffs near the end of the choruses, you know, whole notes with melodies attached to them."[15] Blues singers tended to play an instrument—guitar, piano, harmonica, bass—whereas many R&B performers simply sang in front of a band. The guitar is the key instrument in most blues of this era, the saxophone dominant in R&B. Blues guitarists like T-Bone Walker and Guitar Slim made showmanship key to their live acts. Johnny "Guitar" Watson would stand on his hands and pick the strings with his teeth. Not to be outdone, a sax god like Big Jay McNeely, aka Big Jay McSquealy, King of the Honkers, squealed and honked his rhythm & blues, "blowing freakish notes and wowing audiences with extreme, often bizarre showmanship," playing while leaping across the top of a bar or lying on his back, legs kicking in the air. The tenor sax in rhythm & blues may be often as dominant a voice as the singer.[16]

Rhythm & blues generally—but not always—sounds more upbeat and up-tempo than blues, good-humored and celebratory compared to the darker view of the world and personal relations that blues often takes. One of the signature rhythm & blues songs that opens the era, Helen Humes' **"Be-Baba-Leba"** (1945/46), begins with a line expressing just how fine she feels. That feel-good exhilaration runs through the lyrics, vocal tone, and music of so many of these songs. R&B frequently adopted the common 12-bar blues verse form: three lines of four bars each, the second line repeating the first; two bars of vocals followed by two bars of instrumental response in each line. At the same time, those songs typically changed the blues mood, utilizing quicker rhythm and a lighter, breezier vocal tone. In a riposte to this generalization Albert Murray makes the important argument that the purpose and effect of *all* blues song is "stomping the blues," "*playing with* the blues" or "riffing-the-blues." Murray astutely insists that "blues music regardless of its lyrics almost always induces dance movement that is the direct opposite of resignation, retreat, or defeat."[17]

Popular musical categories frequently overlap. Helen Humes said, "I've been called a blues singer and a jazz singer and a ballad singer—well, I'm all three, which means I'm just a singer." Did T-Bone Walker play rhythm & blues or blues guitar? Did Clyde McPhatter sing rhythm & blues or doo wop? LeRoi Jones (Amiri Baraka) sensibly proposes a *blues continuum* that connects all these genres. In his book on soul music, Peter Guralnick examines his own terminology and the relationship of soul to rhythm & blues. "The designations were in a sense the invention of critics and anthologists," he concludes. Subjective they may be, but separate designations along the blues continuum nevertheless provide useful definitional markers and organizational tools. As Black music scholar Samuel A. Floyd, Jr., argued, "The defining of such terms as jazz, blues, ragtime, spiritual, jubilee, gospel, funk, stomp and others is immensely important if we are to conduct research in these areas with any degree of precision, reliability, or validity...."[18]

The African American community maintained a strict distinction between gospel and *the devil's music* in theory. But in practice many of these artists worked both ends of that continuum. Early bluesmen like Son House went back and forth from the blues to the church, the secular to the sacred, as did Sister Rosetta Tharpe during the postwar decade, as Little Richard and Al Green would later do. Thomas A. Dorsey, the sometime blues songwriter and musician who initiated the modern gospel sound, felt that blues and gospel were intimately related: "Blues is as important to a person feeling bad as 'Nearer My God to Thee.'" Both blues and gospel, Dorsey argued, evoke "the same feeling, a grasping of the heart." This became something of a commonplace among blues singers, echoed, for example, by John Lee Hooker: "I used to be a spiritual singer. But I get just as deep a feeling from the blues as I would from the spirituals.... I get that real deep down

Helen Humes at the Avery Willard Studio, New York City, 1940s. Helen Humes Photograph and Print Collection, The Filson Historical Society, Louisville, KY.

sad feelin'." Some gospel artists felt the same. Lead singer Ira Tucker of the powerhouse Dixie Hummingbirds explained:

> Just like when you hear all these blues, these guys from the Delta and the lower part of the South. They worked. They were out in the fields. They sung what they felt. Same is true with gospel. Gospel came from loneliness, bewilderedness and shortchanged in life, cursed out and knocked down and everything.[19]

A few gospel hits made the *Billboard* charts in the 1940s and '50s, and the so-called Gospel Highway became a lucrative touring route for Black musical artists. But not nearly as lucrative as commercially-driven secular music. Many gospel artists tip-toed along that border, even Mahalia Jackson, the biggest gospel star and one of the most insistently devout, "trying to have it both ways: holding onto the capital of devout integrity ... even as she pursued the prestige of recognition by singing love songs on a radio show." Most blues, rhythm & blues, and doo wop artists first sang in church. Some who belonged to gospel groups crossed over, even before Sam Cooke's groundbreaking move from gospel star to pop star in 1957. Crossing over was not just about money: "It was a passage from the segregated past into an integrated future, the passage from a religious life focus to a humanistic mindset, and the passage from economic limitations to seemingly infinite economic possibilities."[20] *Seemingly* is the operative word here. Though fame sometimes followed, fortune rarely did.

The term *doo wop*, invented in the 1960s, was applied retroactively to harmony group tunes from the 1940s and '50s, a time when most still considered that music a sub-set of rhythm & blues. Except for its harmonies, fast doo wop is indistinguishable from up-tempo R&B. In their *Complete Book of Doo-Wop*, Anthony Gribin and Matthew Schiff suggest that the harmony group style could have been named "doo-wop rhythm and blues." Another critic calls doo wop a "'sweeter' strain of r&b" that had become so toothless by 1956 that *Cash Box* labelled the doo wop sound of groups like The Platters "rhythm and happies."[21] But Black doo wop was not just R&B without the bite, even in its mid–1950s adolescent phase. Despite often banal lyrics, the best doo wop songs can be emotionally devastating. In many cases the singers' gospel roots inform the emotive power of their song. Modelled on gospel, doo wop's quartet format uses bass and falsetto extensively in counterpoint, an evolution from gospel, and many doo wop recordings utilize gospel's innovation of switching leads, introducing a second lead voice mid-song for dramatic effect.

Rhythm & blues also overlaps with *rock 'n' roll*. "They put me in the Hall of Fame for cutting the first rock 'n' roll record," Ike Turner said about his role in the song "Rocket '88.'" "But I was playing rhythm and blues. That was all I was playing."[22] Rhythm & bluesman turned rock 'n' roll star Chuck Berry recorded "Roll Over Beethoven" for Chess Records in the transitional year 1956. Celebrating the musical triumph of rock 'n' roll, Berry sings the words *rock* or *rockin'*, *roll* or *rolling* seventeen times. But he also sings *rhythm & blues*, *rhythm*, or *blues* six times. Berry used the same Chess rhythm section as bluesman Muddy Waters: Willie Dixon bass, Fred Below drums. At that point the transition remained incomplete.

White disc jockey Alan Freed appropriated the phrase *rock and roll* in the early

1950s to make the music he played on his radio show and the rhythm & blues concerts he organized more palatable to the young white audiences who had started to cross over, listening and dancing to Black music and further blurring categories. The terms *rock* and *roll* in African American recorded music date back to 1922 and a lascivious blues by Trixie Smith, "My Man Rocks Me with One Steady Roll." Rocking and rolling were transparently coded blues terms for having sex. By 1950, rocking also meant dancing, but always with double entendre implied. Both words appear frequently in the R&B songs in this book.

An important part of my approach to understanding these songs involves listening carefully to lyrics: *hearing* this music holistically. You can hear most of them in full on Spotify or Apple Music if you have an account. Searching iTunes will get you about a minute's sample of each song; to hear the entire song you have to buy it. Nearly every song mentioned in this book is available free on YouTube, though who knows what royalties, if any, the artists receive. Be sure to input artist, song title, and year, since you will often find multiple versions of the song, even by the same artist, recorded at different times. (Dates in parentheses after song titles in this book represent the year the song was originally recorded or released.) I almost always discuss original releases here rather than re-recordings or later live performances. But performance videos will give you an idea of the artists' looks and style, and they sometimes sound better than the original. Googling the artist and song title will usually take you to a useful Wikipedia entry and get you not only YouTube recordings but multiple websites offering the lyrics. Many of the pages turn out to be empty and those that provide transcriptions are almost inevitably inaccurate. *Always* compare lyrical transcriptions with what you hear in the song.

The notion of *satisfaction*, along with its objects or absence, provides one important common denominator to help distinguish elements of blues, rhythm & blues, gospel, and doo wop. Accompanied only by his electrified slide guitar and Big Crawford's stand-up bass, Muddy Waters' breakthrough blues recording, **"I Can't Be Satisfied"** (1948), tells his woman how he's troubled and worried. He just can't be satisfied or stop crying—the tears a rarity in blues. He repeats both confessions in the four choruses. Muddy's song speaks of essential blues subjects: travel and the permutations of love. It also reflects the dissatisfactions some in his community felt about life in the industrial North, and their homesickness for the agrarian South. On both the personal and communal levels, blues validated African American lives: "The blues insisted that the fate of the individual black man or woman, what happened in their everyday 'trivial' affairs, what took place within them—their yearnings, their problems, their frustrations, their dreams—were important, were worth taking note of and sharing in song."[23]

Unhappy with his situation in Chicago, Muddy imagines catching a train and heading back down South for good. He asks his woman if she wants to go with him, feels like shooting her, has a troubling dream that she left him, then envisions being greeted with joy when the train reaches its destination. You frequently hear this note of optimism in even the darkest blues—a variant of the traditional verse, "The sun's gonna shine on my back door someday, / Wind's gonna rise and blow my blues away." In contrast to his threat of violence, Muddy injects a note of what sounds like self-mockery when he sings that he can *never* be satisfied, letting his voice rise up in a kind of vocal wink. Anything but grim, the bouncy music itself illustrates Albert Murray's dictum that blues music often tells a different story than its lyrics. Still, the song ends with its choral refrain, reiterating the singer's worry, trouble, and dissatisfaction. One line suggests that his woman shares his blues, which may be the African American condition: no way, he sings, could *we* be satisfied. In the final line he still can't help crying.

Contrast that with the Dixie Hummingbirds' **"I'll Be Satisfied"** (1949), one of the most popular gospel songs of the era, written by turn-of-the-century composer Charles Albert Tindley. Several other quartets covered it including the Highway QC's, Spirit of Memphis, and Swan Silvertones. Dorothy Love Coates and the Gospel Harmonettes sang a different song with the same title and similar sentiment, and the Blind Boys of Alabama and Pilgrim Travelers each recorded a song called "Satisfied with Jesus." As opposed to the bluesman who can't get no satisfaction in this life, the gospel singer awaits certain satisfaction in the life beyond when, as the Hummingbirds sing, his soul will rest with the Lord. The gospeler's nearly absolute faith contrasts with the blues singer's radical skepticism, having to contend with intrinsic human faithlessness in the form of a lover or ex-lover. The bluesman sings only of this life's pleasures and pain, even when anticipating his own death. In "Goin' Down Slow" (1941), later recorded by Howlin' Wolf and Bobby "Blue" Bland, St. Louis Jimmy Oden consoles himself in the face of mortality: at least he has had his fun. "Unlike gospel," Greil Marcus writes, "blues was not a music of transcendence; its equivalence to God's Grace was sex and love."[24]

In the Hummingbirds' jaunty *a cappella* arrangement, Ira Tucker's tenor soars over background harmonies that drive home the title phrase, "I'll be satisfied," repeated more than forty times during the record's 2:18. The song also contains a traditional blues couplet, "One of these mornings and it won't be long/You'll look for me but I'll be gone." It appears as well in the Soul Stirrers' **"I'm Gonna Move in the Room with the Lord"** (1950), the Harmonizing Four's **"Say a Word"** (1952), and the Blind Boys of Alabama's **"I'll Fly Away"** (1953). Though key elements in both blues and gospel, movement and travel differ in their directions. The blues traveler usually *escapes from*. The blues train takes the singer or his/her baby away. Heading in the opposite direction, the gospeler *journeys to*: death, the Lord, salvation. The gospel train is bound for glory. The Harmonizing Four change the end of the second line of that couplet from the blues' escapist "I'll be gone" to gospel's afterlife-directed "I'm going on home." Death in gospel is a consummation devoutly to be wished. But in the postwar era of hope for a better home on this American earth, gospel voices sometimes strain with ambivalence.

Conversely, worldly love gives rhythm & blues life its meaning. In Billy Ward and His Dominoes' upbeat **"I'd Be Satisfied"** (1952), lead singer Clyde McPhatter requires only a little of his estranged lover, even her smile alone, to be satisfied. He appeals to heaven, but only to send him more of her love to satisfy him, and a swinging, sensual saxophone solo seconds his desire. Or step slightly outside our postwar decade and listen to Jackie Wilson's "I'll Be Satisfied" (1957). A member of the Dominoes, then its lead singer after McPhatter left the group in 1953, Wilson launched his solo career with a string of R&B hits, including this mid-tempo rocker on which his soulful voice declares to his lover that she need only kiss him, smile, and hold his hand. That's enough to make his life worth living. Unlike the blues singer who can't be satisfied and the gospeler who finds satisfaction only in the beyond, the rhythm-and-blues man or woman finds this life of secular pleasure extremely satisfying. Rhythm & blues songs *embrace* life, love, sex, and the complexity of relationships with rhythm and joy. "Let the Good Times Roll," Louis Jordan advises, because you live only once. "Snatch and Grab It," sings Julia Lee, before it gets away. "It's Later Than You Think," Roy Milton warns. Seize the day, because nothing else matters but this life.

Up-tempo doo wop shares the rhythm & blues sentiment, but doo wop balladeers can only wish for the worldly consumption found in most R&B. The doo wopper almost always finds satisfaction deferred or frustrated in ballads. Two of the genre's iconic songs, the Orioles' **"Too Soon to Know"** (1948) and the Penguins' **"Earth Angel"** (1954), begin with questions: Does she love me? Will she be mine? The doo wop lover lives in a state of suspended yearning, his agony exquisite, the outcome of his passion uncertain. He *could* be satisfied if only she *would* satisfy him. The male doo wop persona (almost all secular harmony groups in this period are male) has more in common with the gospelers than with his blues brothers. He fills the ballads with secularized religious language: she's divine, I adore her. The singer desires transcendent love, prays for an earth angel. His self-deprecating, often tearful masculinity is sensitive and vulnerable. The Penguins' Cleveland Duncan calls himself a fool. The Orioles' Sonny Til dreamily intones about the tears he'll shed when she leaves, his vow to go on living more sigh than self-assertion.

This book aims to historicize and contextualize the extraordinary African American music and musical artists of the postwar decade, and to introduce or reintroduce them to anyone who cares about popular music but lacks familiarity with the work of Wynonie Harris or Amos Milburn, Dorothy Love Coates or Nellie Lutcher. Like Robert Santelli's *The Best of the Blues: The 101 Essential Albums*, Dave Marsh's *The Heart of Rock & Soul: The 1001 Greatest Singles Ever Made*, or Jim Dawson and Steve Propes' *What Was the First Rock 'n' Roll Record?* I have not based my choice of these songs and artists on any objective metrics. But unlike those authors, I make no claim for the primacy, superiority, or essentiality of these songs. This is not a *Best of* book. I take an approach more appreciative than evaluative; something like Bob Dylan's in *The Philosophy of Modern Song*, though not as freewheeling. Discussing the aesthetics of popular music, Theodore Gracyk writes that "appreciation aims at discovering whatever is to be found in experiencing a particular work.... [It] does not inspect an object in light of its ability to satisfy fixed criteria or some standard...." At the same time, I'm always listening for the music's engagement with its specific postwar contexts, aspiring like Questlove, in his *Music Is History*, "to chart history through music and to trace music through history, all the while trying to look more closely and more critically, trying to unpeel and uncover...." If I overuse the word *great* in showcasing, historicizing, and disinterring songs of this era, I make no apologies. In the latest volume by perhaps the best living critic of this kind of music, Peter Guralnick states his personal motivation for what he does: "I started writing about the blues with one idea and one idea only. To tell people about this music that I thought was so great."[25]

Despite the rich textual archive—books and essays on these artists and genres—this music has been critically neglected and underrated. Critics and historians tend to value the secular songs of this era primarily as early avatars of the rock 'n' roll revolution to come. As well, most of the key books about the period were published in the last century. Still the best book on R&B, Arnold Shaw's *Honkers and Shouters: The Golden Years of Rhythm & Blues* dates from 1978. Anthony Heilbut's *The Gospel Sound* remains the most comprehensive study of gospel, though it first appeared fifty years ago. Robert Palmer's *Deep Blues* (1981) set the standard for all blues studies. A few more recent books range across genres, including Brian Ward's *Just My Soul Responding: Rhythm and Blues, Black Consciousness, and Race Relations* and Preston Lauterbach's *The Chitlin' Circuit and the Road to Rock 'n' Roll*. Both make some effort to address the corpus of postwar, pre-rock 'n' roll Black music, sacred and secular, as a continuum rooted in its time and place. But neither focuses strictly on the postwar decade. And few books look closely, as this one does, at a broad range of African American popular songs from this era to understand what they say and how they say it.

I am not a musician nor a musicologist. My expertise in textual and performance analysis derives from long experience as both a professor of English and Theater and a stage-and-screen performer—understanding how dialogue works in concert with other elements of a scene, much like the way song lyrics work with other elements of performance. I am very aware of my musicological limitations. Books like Allan Moore's edited collection *Analyzing Popular Music* provide detailed technical explanations for how recorded songs work. I appreciate the technical detail, but as a musical layman listening to and reassessing the postwar body of African American popular song, I use only the tools with which I'm comfortable, and with which the broadest possible range of music lovers should be comfortable. "We murder to dissect," poet William Wordsworth warned against the dangers of over-intellectualizing. I believe in staying attuned to both the semantics and the visceral, emotional impact that makes the best music so powerful and meaningful. My practice consists of what Moore refers to as "close analytical listening." Musicologist Richard Crawford calls it "the literary approach to black music research," working "outside the realm of formal musical scholarship" to "make a reader or listener understand and *feel* the special qualities of black experience as it is reflected in black music." Explaining how he approached writing about music while "almost entirely lacking in musical training or knowledge," Guralnick says, "what I was trying to capture ... was the *feeling*...." Bob Dylan writes, "It's what a song makes you feel about your own life that's important."[26]

My approach to individual songs depends on what I hear, feel, and understand in each. I use the acronym *VOCAL* as my methodological template. *V* stands for

Voice: its quality, pitch, elasticity, what the singer does with the words and melody. O for Orchestration: the musical elements in the recorded performance, the sounds of the accompanying instruments, and wherever possible, names and information about the key musicians. *A* represents Arrangement: how the song is sung, its tempos and emphases, the relationship of the voices to the lyrics and music, and to each other in the case of groups. *L* stands for Lyrics: the words sung. In some cases, especially doo wop, conventional or banal lyrics feel less important than voice and arrangement. But each song invites its own application of this template. All these elements rest on the fulcrum *C*. In my formulation C can stand for Context: the social, musical, and historical conditions within which the recording took place. Or Count: the number of times a key line or phrase repeats for thematic emphasis. Or Composition: the overall relation of the parts to one another. Or Charisma: that ineffable something that distinguishes great vocal recordings from the rest.

In *The Creativity Code: Art and Innovation in the Age of AI*, Marcus Du Sautoy writes about the ways computers can absorb huge databases of information about music, writing, and painting, and create their own versions of those arts with their own creative twists. He also discusses the limitations of artificial intelligence in those areas, its inability—so far—to sustain musical, literary, or artistic ideas to the point where they become creatively distinctive works (although that is changing rapidly). This led me to think about my own attempts to decode the music at the heart of this book. Exactly what creative elements make up these songs? How do music and lyrics, vocal textures and arrangements combine to become meaningfully unique? What is their particular alchemy? What social, political, economic, and biographical imperatives helped shape them? And why do they continue to move me in the ways they do?

AI software could undoubtedly come up with reasonable facsimiles of blues, gospel, rhythm & blues, and doo wop songs. The 12-bar blues pattern can be easily replicated. So much doo wop relies on the same four-chord progression (C-major, A-minor, F-major, G-major or G^7) that musicians refer to it as the Ice Cream Changes, because "using them is as easy as eating ice cream."[27] But could artificial intelligence re-create the transcendent power of Muddy Waters' "Rolling Stone"? Could it replicate the individual signature of the great R&B artists or gospel quartets at the height of their powers—the sweet seductions of Clyde McPhatter, the tear-down-the-house call to worship of the Gospel Harmonettes' Dorothy Love Coates or the Alabama Blind Boys' Clarence Fountain, the soulful yearning of a first-rate doo wop harmony group? I doubt it. Even when written and performed within formulaic structures, the songs and performances in this book have been transformed by their artists, made unique, personal, powerful, inimitable. That's the C for Charisma. Introducing *Just My Soul Responding*, his study of rhythm & blues and race in the 1950s and '60s, Brian Ward writes, "if there are places in what follows where the prose turns a little more purple than might be seemly, it is only a doomed attempt to convey just a little of the music's enormous emotional and sensual power; its bright wit, intelligence and integrity."[28] I say amen to that.

A note on gendered violence. Blues and rhythm & blues lyrics can be grossly misogynistic, sometimes threatening direct violence against women. One common scenario dramatizes the paranoid, jealous, swaggering man who feels the need to control his cheating or unruly woman. In **"Honey Hush"** (1953) Big Joe Turner threatens his woman with a baseball bat unless she stops her yakety yak. In **"I'm Gonna Murder My Baby"** (1954), a lyric that goes back to Doctor Clayton's "Cheating and Lying Blues" (1941) and reappears in Robert Nighthawk's "Goin' Down to Eli's" (1964), one of the most thrilling and disturbing live blues ever recorded, Pat Hare sings that he would rather kill his baby and go to prison than constantly worry about her cheating and lying. In a chilling irony, Hare actually murdered his girlfriend and died in prison.

Blues critics address this issue in various ways. Through "intimate violence," Adam Gussow asserts, "black blues people reclaimed their own and each other's bodies from the depredations of wage labor, conjured with the spiritual wounds that had been bequeathed to them by slave-born parents and inflicted on them by Jim Crow, rediscovered their pride and agency...." Angela Davis argues that women's blues song made "oppositional stances to male violence" possible by publicizing the violence in lyrics and performance: "Through the blues, menacing problems are ferreted out from the isolated individual experience and restructured as problems shared by the community."[29] Neither critic excuses blues violence; both see it as compensatory and performative, transformed by song into something culturally more manageable. Still, to a twenty-first-century listener the misogyny remains appalling.

Many of the songs included in this book take a relatively reasoned approach to romantic disappointment. But examining blues and rhythm & blues song in any detail means inevitably dealing with misogyny and vocalized violence. Turner's driving dance beat and Hare's ravaged vocal and revolutionarily distorted electric guitar make both "Honey Hush" and "I'm Gonna Murder My Baby" musically compelling performances. I pass on them both. At the same time, I include Muddy Waters' "I Can't Be Satisfied" because its articulated threat, though disturbing, seems a function of the song's complex blues psychology, a symptom of the singer's worried mind, deeply troubling him. Waters originally titled this song, in a 1941 field recording by Alan Lomax, "I Be's Troubled." I understand that not all readers will agree with my neither fully ethical nor consistent position.

Domestic violence is not the only gendered issue in postwar blues and R&B. As defense industries ramped up during the war and men were drafted, more and more women went to work. The west coast shipyards attracted numerous Black men and women from the southwest, part of the great rhythm & blues migration westward. But when the war ended, many men—Black and white—expected women to return to domestic roles. In **"Shipyard Woman Blues"** (1946) Jimmy Witherspoon and the Jay McShann Sextet make their postwar anxieties explicit. With the war now over, Witherspoon complains, we can see how defense-working women made fools of us men, how they got ornery when making more money than us. They should go back to the kitchen with their pots and pans (a line echoed almost a decade later in Big Joe Turner's "Shake, Rattle and Roll"). After a whining trumpet solo, the song ends with

Witherspoon's demand that the shipyard woman hang up her pants, put on a dress, and give men back their privilege.

On the other side of the gender divide, postwar blues and R&B announced a generation of bold and unapologetic women asserting their right to satisfy their appetites, live and work whatever way they chose. Women in blues and R&B songs unashamedly trumpeted their sexuality in an era when female sexuality was still publicly taboo. And when dealing with a cheating or otherwise inadequate lover, they gave as good as they got. From Memphis Minnie to Helen Humes, Dinah Washington and Ruth Brown to Big Mama Thornton and Big Maybelle, Black women in the postwar era performed their agency. They growled and shouted and purred, took their pleasure and left when they wanted.

Female artists are relatively rare in the blues chapter and virtually absent in the first decade of postwar doo wop. Big Mama Thornton, Big Maybelle, Faye Adams, and Etta James certainly sang the blues, but they also cross over into rhythm & blues in one or more of the songs discussed here. Many of the blues and rhythm & blues offerings could go either way. As for doo wop, only a scattering of female African American singers and groups performed secular harmony before 1957. The golden age of girl groups followed soon after: the Chantels, Marvelettes, Shirelles (my top three), Ronettes, Supremes, Crystals, Martha and the Vandellas, and more.[30]

Three notes on race. First, a number of catchy, novelty-style doo wops of this era stereotyped Asians and Africans. Racially insensitive or offensive lyrics that may have been taken for granted or found comical seventy years ago cannot be today. I don't believe they should be "cancelled," but they will not appear in this book. Second, I do not base my selections and discussions on an assumption that only Black people can play and sing certain kinds of music. Some African American critics have made the essentialist argument that others may be able to sing and play blues, but "only a black American can *be* a bluesperson."[31] I am in no position to agree or disagree with that statement. This book encompasses only African American music because so much of this material is culturally determined, and with few exceptions African American artists sing my favorite songs of this period. Many important producers, writers, and arrangers were white: Jerry Wexler, Ralph Bass, Sam Phillips, the Chess brothers, Leiber & Stoller, and others. But only one song *performed* by white artists made my final list: "The House of Blue Lights," a great 1946 tune sung by Ella Mae Morse with boogie-woogie piano by Freddie Slack. As the single exception, this song got dropped.

Finally, as a white man standing outside African American culture and writing about Black music, I represent it from my own privileged racial perspective, just as I write from my position as a heterosexual middle-class male. Any claims I make about what it might have felt like to be in the skin of those Black artists I have filtered through my own understanding of the era and what I hear in the songs. I claim no objective validity for my analyses or conclusions. I hope my enthusiasm for these remarkable artists and their work will be contagious, and that my analyses will help anyone interested in the music to experience it more richly. In my case, the act of criticism is absolutely a labor of love.

George Floyd's murder occurred while I was writing this book, followed by the tide of demand for change and support for Black Lives Matter that swept across the continent, producing its own backlash. Black lives made all the music here, rooted in conditions of inequality, injustice, and racialized violence as acute as or worse than those that play out today. Yet at the same time, these men and women partook of the postwar dream that things could get better, even in the face of another fierce backlash. In the wake of the George Floyd moment, I would like this book to be a small contribution to the good dream, a reminder of the immense riches these great African American singers and musicians left for us, a tribute to their extraordinary legacy and the culture that produced it. I remain deeply grateful and indebted to them all.

Chapter One

Blues
Can't Be Satisfied

"Blues is our father and our mother, our grandparents, our history, plus our daily black soulful lives as brothers and sisters against and within the reality and the idea of this place. Blues is the basic pulse and song, the fundamental description and reaction."
—Amiri Baraka, *The Autobiography of LeRoi Jones*

"The blues is an impulse to keep the painful details and episodes of a brutal experience alive in one's aching consciousness, to finger its jagged grain, and to transcend it, not by the consolation of philosophy but by squeezing from it a near-tragic, near-comic lyricism."
—Ralph Ellison, *Shadow and Act*

"But the most astonishing aspect of the blues is that, although replete with a sense of defeat and downheartedness, they are not intrinsically pessimistic; their burden of woe and melancholy is dialectically redeemed through sheer force of sensuality, into an almost exultant affirmation of life, of love, of sex, of movement, of hope."
—Richard Wright in Paul Oliver, *Blues Fell This Morning: Meaning in the Blues*[1]

Robert Johnson may have had a wonky sense of geography when he called Chicago *that land of California* in "Sweet Home Chicago" (1937). But he correctly identified California and Chicago as the sweetest destinations for music makers in the Great Blues Migration. Postwar blues is nearly synonymous with Chicago blues. Most of the great blues singers of the era who ended up in the Windy City came from Mississippi. In the early part of the twentieth century a rich blues culture developed in the Mississippi Delta—the flat, fertile cotton-growing area between the Mississippi and Yazoo rivers—boasting artists like Charlie Patton, Son House, Willie Brown, Tommy Johnson, and Robert Johnson. Many of the singers and musicians who would dominate mid-century Chicago blues heard those masters and learned from them. Some even played with them. Their music was what Robert Palmer calls *deep blues*, "created not just by black people but by the poorest, most marginal black people," most of them illiterate, living "in virtual serfdom" in the nation's poorest state. In separate interviews in the 1970s, bluesmen Eddie Boyd, Muddy Waters, and

John Lee Hooker, all Delta born-and-raised, were asked if they ever went back there to play after establishing themselves in the North. "Not to Mississippi," said Boyd. "I hated that place." Muddy's answer: "I wanted to get out of Mississippi in the worst way. Go back? What I want to go back for?" Said Hooker, "I went to my hometown, what used to be the worstest state in the world years ago—Mississippi."[2]

Before leaving the South, many of this second generation of Mississippi blues greats played together in juke joints in the Delta, in Memphis, and in the wide-open Arkansas towns of Helena and West Memphis across the river: Sonny Boy Williamson II, Robert Nighthawk, Elmore James, Jimmy Rogers, Arthur "Big Boy" Crudup, and Louisiana-born Little Walter Jacobs. Together, individually, or with small, dynamic bands, they would become the bright stars of Chicago blues. Along with Muddy Waters and Howlin' Wolf they brought the deep Delta blues style to the urban North. Mississippi blues pioneers Big Bill Broonzy, Memphis Minnie, and others whose musical careers stretched back to the 1920s also contributed some wonderful music to postwar Chicago. Not all Mississippi musicians made Chicago their destination. John Lee Hooker took his inimitable style to Detroit. B.B. King developed a horn-heavy big band sound in Memphis to complement his soulful singing and marvelous guitar work. Guitar Slim settled in New Orleans and picked up some of its swampy blues sounds.

Other rich sources of postwar blues were the Southeast and Southwest. I have omitted the great East Coast Piedmont bluesmen, including Blind Willie McTell, whose enormous talent peaked before the postwar decade, and Sonny Terry and Brownie McGhee, who starred in the folk and blues revivals that followed our era. The Southwestern artists mostly headed farther west to Los Angeles, including Texan T-Bone Walker, father of the electric blues guitar. Oklahoman Lowell Fulson joined him, as did many of the singers and musicians who led the rhythm & blues revolution. Lightnin' Hopkins briefly tasted L.A., where he made his first recordings, but spent the bulk of his career back home in Houston. Texas blues generally sounds different than deep Mississippi blues. Charles Keil summarizes: "drones, moans, the bottleneck guitar techniques ... a heavy sound and rough intensity" characterize Delta blues, whereas the Texas tradition "emphasized a somewhat lighter touch: guitar playing ... with an emphasis on single-string melodic dexterity; more relaxed vocal qualities and an open rather than a dense accompaniment texture...." Keil goes on to list another half-page of distinctions, then points out some of the many exceptions.[3]

We begin with blues pioneers T-Bone and Lightnin', Big Bill and Minnie, Nighthawk and Big Boy. Then Muddy and Sonny Boy and Wolf. Their colorful professional pseudonyms suggest a secret society, a world elsewhere.[4] But the musical world they created did not remain secret for long. Of the four genres in this book, blues is most widely known, the form that developed the greatest international reach. Playing to largely African American blues audiences in the postwar decade, these artists exploded into broader public view during the British invasion of the 1960s, when bands like the Rolling Stones covered their records and reintroduced the blues to a white America that had undervalued it, to a wider world, and to a new audience raised on rock 'n' roll.

The full fascinating history of the blues from the late nineteenth century to the present lies outside the scope of this book, but blues has been more than just the 12-bar structure, the call-and-response between voice and instrument, or the sounds of *blue notes* flattened in pitch. Blues is a way of viewing, approaching, and enduring the world through anger, humor, resilience and, of course, music. Evolved during the darkest days of Jim Crow, it became part of African Americans' strategy for dealing with the trials and tribulations, the 'bukes and scorns, of their "daily black soulful lives," as Amiri Baraka put it.[5] Formalized in the 1910s and made broadly popular in the 1920s when first put on records, African American blues songs are sometimes called *secular spirituals* for good reason. Like Baraka, other Black writers of the twentieth century have provided eloquent definitions. I defer again to Albert Murray's *Stomping the Blues*, a wise and entertaining book that sees blues music as incantation and affirmation intended to drive the blues away. In the epigraphs at the top of this chapter two of the last century's finest authors, Ralph Ellison and Richard Wright, saw the blues as an acknowledgment, even embrace, of brutal experience: pain and defeat counterbalanced by transcendence; affirmation and redemption brought about by the sensual lyricism of the music and its performance.

An illuminating approach to blues can be found in the conclusion to William Barlow's *Looking Up at Down: The Emergence of Blues Culture*. Barlow makes a four-part argument for blues as a form of "African American cultural resistance to white domination." *The blues sound*—weird, visceral, off-key by European musical standards—gives it "a subversive character." *Blues lyrics and texts,* "focused on the everyday lives of the black masses," offer lessons on self-assertion and survival. The improvisational element of *blues performance* affirms individual freedom, and audience participation makes it communal. Finally, *blues sensibility*: the artists' lifestyles, their ways of seeing the world, and especially the personas they adopted—hoodoo doctors, wild women, voodoo queens—constitute "a black pantheon ... in sharp contrast to the one-dimensional, docile black stereotypes created by and for the dominant white culture."[6] The postwar blues upped the ante on all these elements.

Texas, Oklahoma, California: Pioneers

The unquestioned innovator of electric blues guitar and the blues guitar king for at least half the postwar decade, Aaron Thibodeaux **T-Bone Walker** (1910–75) "is the fundamental source of the modern urban style of playing and singing blues." B.B. King idolized him. Jimmy Witherspoon called him "the Charlie Parker of guitars when it comes to blues." For Johnny Otis, T-Bone "single-handedly defined what rhythm and blues guitar was all about." Along with his early adoption of the electric guitar, the jazzy swing he put to his blues, and the single-string magic and dynamic rhythms of his playing, he inspired T-Bonemania in performance: "He did the splits without missing a beat, played the leads behind his head.... He repeatedly excited crowds, whose women reacted by throwing purses, clothing and even their husbands' pay-checks onto the stage."[7]

Born to the blues, T-Bone grew up in Dallas with his guitar-playing mother.

He led around Blind Lemon Jefferson, the most influential male blues singer and guitarist of the 1920s. Touring with bandleader Cab Calloway and legendary blueswoman Ma Rainey, Walker made his first record in 1929, then moved to Los Angeles where he played with bandleaders Les Hite and Freddie Slack. In 1946, he signed with L.A.'s Black & White Records. Produced by the legendary Ralph Bass, Walker recorded more than three dozen great tunes in 1946–47, fronting five-piece combos that crossed blues with rhythm & blues: piano, bass, drum, trumpet, and tenor sax along with his guitar. Los Angeles boasted many underemployed big band and jazz musicians. The tight ensembles Bass put together for T-Bone included some of the best session players on the coast. His entire extensive repertoire of 12-bar blues songs is well worth hearing.

T-Bone's first hit on Black & White, the ballad **"Bobby Sox Blues"** (1947), aka "Bobby Sox Baby," climbed to #3 on *Billboard*'s Race chart, the highest any of his recordings would achieve. The song's writer, Dootsie Williams, went on to found Dootone Records and record the Penguins' "Earth Angel." Jack McVea and His All Stars provide a low-key backdrop to Walker's bluesy guitar, with McVea's moody tenor sax and Tommy Kahn's piano responding to Walker's lyric. T-Bone opens the song with a beautiful forty-second-long single-string solo that sounds as contemporary today as it did more than 75 years ago. Recorded a decade before Chuck Berry's "Sweet Little Sixteen," the lyrics signal the proto-cultural integration that would characterize the immediate postwar era. The singer will let his baby go because she thinks about nothing but stage, radio, and movies. He complains that she traded her cookbooks for scrapbooks and spends too much time on fan mail to take care of him. When he asks if she loves him, she wonders what Frankie would say. That would be Sinatra, the bobby-soxers' teen idol of the day.[8] Bass's classy arrangement and Walker's bluesy playing and singing give depth and weight to a frothy musical subject—the new youth audience that would embrace R&B, doo wop, and ultimately rock 'n' roll. An uptempo 12-bar romp from the same band, **"Don't Leave Me Baby"** (1947) showcases Walker's single-string magic and relaxed, unfussy vocals. The title says everything you need to know about the lyrics. The label calls it "low down blues" but this record rocks. McVea's rhythm section (Frank Clarke bass, Rabon Tarrant drums) leads

T-Bone Walker as member of Freddie Slack's band, in rehearsal or a recording studio with his Charlie Christian electric guitar, c. 1942. Pictorial Press Ltd./Alamy Stock Photo.

the way for a series of brief, rapid-fire T-Bone solos plus a nice trumpet break from Red Kelly.

"Call It Stormy Monday" (1947) cemented Walker's reputation as the most important and influential blues artist of the era. T-Bone wrote this gorgeous 12-bar slow-burner, featuring some of the best lyrics in blues history. His sterling performance inspired future masters B.B. King and Albert King to take up electric guitar and it generated many cover versions, including Bobby Bland's superb "Stormy Monday Blues" (1961). Walker himself re-recorded it for Atlantic Records in 1955. The lyrics chronicle a very bad week, every day worse than the one before, until Friday brings payday, Saturday play day, and Sunday pray day when the singer falls to his knees and asks the Lord for mercy. These are Black working-class blues, both intensely personal and communal. The song's opening word, "they," takes until Saturday to revert to the first-person "I." Lloyd Glenn on piano and tenor saxman Bumps Myers quietly complement Walker's subtle guitar work. Teddy Buckner's trumpet blows an ambiguous note of celebration on Friday when the week's pay flies in. Trumpet and sax add dramatic emphasis to Walker's prayer for mercy. The record vividly evokes for me a scene in Walter Mosley's novel *Devil in a Blue Dress*. In a Los Angeles tavern, circa 1948, Black private eye Easy Rawlins observes: "[H]alf the people in that crowded room had migrated from Houston after the war, and some before that. California was like heaven for the southern Negro." But postwar reality could be very different from the dream. "Life was still hard in L.A. and if you worked every day you still found yourself on the bottom."[9]

John W. Davis' bass kicks off the introduction to **"T-Bone Shuffle"** (1947) with its relaxed shuffle rhythm, written by bass man Shifty Henry and released on Black & White's Comet subsidiary. Walker's guitar takes over, then gives way to Myers' sax. After a single verse T-Bone takes a long guitar solo, and in the second break he riffs against George Orendorff's restrained trumpet. The carpe diem lyric implores his baby to let her hair down and have fun while she can, an existential position that becomes more commonplace in rhythm & blues. A good shuffle boogie can bring her the satisfaction she needs. All this with a vocal "so smooth and silky," writes Robert Santelli, "that it's hard to say if his voice is complementing his guitar work, or vice versa."[10]

Willard McDaniels' boogie-woogie piano and Billy Hadnott on bass pump out the rhythm to introduce **"Hypin' Woman Blues"** (1949), another Shifty Henry composition. Capitol Records, which bought Walker's masters when Black & White went bust in 1949, released this exciting recording, an up-tempo 12-bar blues with oddly elliptical lyrics. The singer sees women everywhere on the street, but says a guy has no chance if he has no money. In the second verse he picks up a destitute, drunken woman, penniless, hungry, and nearly blind. Something mysterious then happens as Walker reverts to the standard blues complaint that women are nothing but trouble, and the standard blues strategy: a man just has to keep moving. The first instrumental break finds T-Bone fully in charge. The second features Bumps Myers' tenor solo and McDaniels' rockin' piano. Then the entire band, with Teddy Buckner's trumpet and Oscar Lee Bradley on drums, brings it home.

Our final selection comes with a new band as T-Bone signed with L.A.'s

Imperial label, where he recorded a lot of fine R&B in the early 1950s. **"The Hustle Is On"** (1950) has a beat similar to "T-Bone Shuffle," but three saxophones and a trumpet make the band louder and the sound more amplified. Walker almost shouts the vocal. The rhythm section opens the song again, followed by a T-Bone solo. The American economy went into recession in 1949 and the road to fulfilling the dream got that much bumpier. Times are hard, Walker sings to his woman, taxes high, and the good jobs all gone. You have to hustle to make it. But what does the music say? Eddie "Lockjaw" Davis' squealing tenor sax solo sounds like the "almost exultant affirmation" that Richard Wright says redeems the melancholy and woe of the blues.

Texan Sam **Lightnin' Hopkins** (1912–82) carved out a prolific postwar career with a discography of around 1000 songs, most self-penned, on more than twenty labels. He learned his throwback country blues style from pioneers Blind Lemon Jefferson and Texas Alexander in the 1920s. When he joined up with pianist Wilson "Thunder" Smith for his first recording session in 1946, a producer nicknamed him Lightnin.' The name stuck. Traveling only to perform or record, Hopkins hardly ever left East Texas, geographically or musically. He went out of style in the heavier Chicago blues era and stopped recording for a while until his country blues authenticity and virtuoso guitar playing made him a star of the 1960s folk revival.

Hopkins took an idiosyncratic musical approach. "There should be an element of uncertainty to the music," Santelli observes. "The lyrics should be pulled from the sky and made to fit into the confines of an improvised tune." His legendary orneriness at recording sessions meant that "He might play and sing something fierce and new, but just as likely he'd redo a song he'd done the day before, changing a line or two because he felt like it. Or he'd record a song by one of his peers and call it his own," writes Michael Hall. Hall locates Hopkins' irresistible sound in his "deep drawl that was so lonely and sad it seemed to come from another existence—and his loping, finger-picking guitar style...."[11] Many of his recordings sound similar, but he could write lyrics on just about anything and change the music, too, when he felt like it.

The hits that Hopkins scored on the *Billboard* charts encompassed cars (**"T-Model Blues"** [1949]), guns (**"Shotgun Blues"** [1950]), and coffee (**"Coffee Blues"** [1952]). But for quirkiness, none compares with the slow-paced **"Short Haired Woman"** (1947), one of the best of his early solo blues records for Houston's Gold Star label. An original take on the male blues complaint, the song begins with Hopkins grumbling about a woman whose hair is no longer than his. This short-haired woman means trouble; he has to keep buying *rats*—wigs—for her. A complex issue in the Black community back then, hair remains so today as schools ban Black kids because of their hair style. But the song is delightful with its slightly showy guitar work, as Hopkins goes electric here for the first time. Typically, he crams many words into a line, stretching 12 bars to 13 or 14, and his singing has a talking blues quality, especially in the stop-time verse. Despite the lyrics, Hopkins sings this moody 12-bar blues straight-faced without a hint of humor.[12]

The same can't be said for his recording of Tampa Red's **"(Let Me) Play**

with Your Poodle" (1947) on Aladdin. Prefacing his dive into this raucous, fast, single-entendre romp, Lightnin' implores us not to get mad because he means no harm. He can hardly keep from laughing when he sings each permutation of the title line, always followed by his tongue-in-cheek clarification: of course, I mean I want to play with your little *dog*. Thunder Smith's piano and a drummer accompany Hopkins' ringing guitar on this rockin' party tune.

But Hopkins was not just a novelty act. He switches gears again for **"Tim Moore's Farm"** (aka "Tom Moore Blues") (1948). Recorded on Gold Star and released nationally on L.A.'s Modern Records, it stayed on *Billboard's* Race chart for 13 weeks and went to #1. Like many of his songs, it sounds autobiographical. Blues is truth, blues artists often say. Though truthful, the song didn't tell Hopkins' own story. The brutal, violent Moore plantation in central Texas—"a Texas version of a feudalist indentured-servitude/prison farm"—had generated a blues titled "Tom Moore's Farm" that was sung around the region in the 1930s. Texas bluesman Mance Lipscomb, the co-writer, didn't record it until 1960 when he released it anonymously, fearing reprisals from Tom Moore, who still ruled his domain: "If he knew I put out a song like that," said Lipscomb, "I couldn't live here no more. I wouldn't live six months if he knowed that."[13]

Hopkins rewrote the song and released his version under his own name twelve years *before* Lipscomb's. A Black sharecropper named Sam made the mistake, he sings, of moving his family onto Tim Moore's farm. (Changing Tom to Tim would hardly have put Hopkins in less danger.) The miserable, threatening white boss compounds the usual hard work. When his wife dies, Sam asks permission to bury her. Moore's response: Sure, n—, but remember you have to plow, so bury her some dinner time. Sam stands up to him but gains no ground and the narrative ends in stalemate. Hopkins' edgy acoustic guitar does some of the arguing for him. It speaks of regret and suppressed anger. That a Black man in Texas, in Jim Crow times, wrote and sang this brave, chilling song about standing up to a powerful white man says something profound about Hopkins and the Black audience that made it a best-seller. Surely they could hope that the times were a-changing. Listen to the words and music. You'll leave shaken.

The early career of **Lowell Fulson** (1921–99) represents the best of both traditional Texas-Oklahoma rural acoustic blues and the new swinging west coast style. Raised on an Indian reservation near Tulsa, Fulson landed in Oakland after the war where he made his first recordings, accompanied by his brother Martin on second guitar. With his slow laments and precise guitar work, Fulson sounds like he could have grown up next door to Hopkins, both of them heavily influenced by Texas Alexander. Around 1950 he moved to Los Angeles, leading a band that, for a while, included Ray Charles on piano. Once Fulson came under the spell of T-Bone Walker, his style changed.

Fulson's first success, **"Three O'Clock Blues"** (1948), briefly hit the *Billboard* charts and later became a blues standard. B.B. King's 1951 breakthrough version soon overshadowed Fulson's original. **Johnny "Guitar" Watson** had another terrific rendition titled **"Three Hours Past Midnight"** (1956), and Larry Davis scored with "Three O'Clock Blues" in 1968. Colin James made one of the all-time best Canadian blues recordings with "Three Hours Past Midnight" (1993). Those performances all owe a clear debt to T-Bone Walker's guitar sound. Fulson plays in a more old-school style and sings lyrics as blue as they get. At three in the morning he can't sleep. He can't find his baby and can't be satisfied. He gives himself twenty-four hours. If he still can't find her, he'll drown himself. In the final verse he says goodbye and asks God's forgiveness. Analyzing B.B. King's recording, Ted Gioia claims the lyrics "start out as an insomniac's lament, but end with a weepy farewell more suited to a suicide note."[14] Not here. Fulson's insomnia resembles Muddy Waters' troubles in "I Can't Be Satisfied," both symptoms of larger dissatisfactions. And this suicidal farewell sounds anything but weepy. Fulson sings slowly and mournfully in a high, forceful voice, his Oklahoma twang slightly slurred as if he might have been drinking to dull the pain. Strumming back-up, brother Martin provides a bottom for Fulson's beautiful acoustic guitar work, his high notes tolling a blues eulogy for love lost. A superb underrated record.

"Reconsider Baby" (1954), one of Fulson's most successful recordings, remained on *Billboard*'s Rhythm & Blues chart for 15 weeks and reached #3. Elvis covered it. So did Eric Clapton. A relaxed 12-bar shuffle, it features sensitive-blues-guy lyrics and killer T-Bone-style electric guitar. Fulson had signed with the Checker subsidiary of Chicago's Chess Records but recorded "Reconsider Baby" on tour in Dallas with his big R&B-style band: seven or eight players plus Fulson, three or four saxes, a trumpet, and trombone. The record sounds more Texas-L.A. than Mississippi-Chicago. His baby is leaving, they've been together a long time, and he hates to see her go. He hopes she'll come back someday and asks her to reconsider. No blues swagger or compulsion, just a reasonable request from a disappointed lover. The fat horn section responds, but at the heart of the song beats Fulson's lengthy guitar solo, reinforced by Paul Blake's tinkling piano. T-Bone should have been proud.

Going to Chicago: Mississippi Pioneers

The great postwar blues migration made Chicago the promised land for many expatriate Mississippi musicians. African American clubs on the South Side and the Maxwell Street outdoor market bred some of the best music of the American twentieth century. Many of these artists jammed together and played on one another's records. From 1932 until the end of the war, the major label for Chicago blues was Bluebird, a low-budget subsidiary of RCA-Victor. Producer Lester Melrose created *the Bluebird sound*, carefully arranged acoustic blues with a rhythm section and sometimes horns. Important pre-war Bluebird artists included Tampa Red, Memphis Minnie, Big Bill Broonzy, Robert Nighthawk, and Big Boy Crudup. Chess Records became the primary label for postwar blues in Chicago, founded by brothers Phil and Leonard Chess in 1946. A dozen or more smaller companies also played important roles.[15] The following represents only the tip of the Chicago blues iceberg.

Big Bill Broonzy (1893–1958) belongs to the earliest generation of recorded bluesmen. He made his first record in 1927 and joined Georgia Tom and the Famous Hokum Boys in the early 1930s. (When Georgia Tom left the blues for the church, he reassumed his real name, Thomas A. Dorsey.) During his long career Broonzy wrote, recorded, and played guitar on hundreds of songs, comfortably moving across styles from jug band music and lighthearted sexual hokum, to a five-piece T-Bone-style blues band with trumpet and saxophone, to a solo act with just his acoustic guitar. Arriving in Chicago in 1921, he became a central figure in the city's blues scene. Many of the postwar blues stars who migrated to Chicago from Mississippi acknowledged Broonzy's help in getting them oriented to the city and connected to the clubs that would employ them. ("Big Bill," said Muddy Waters, "that's the nicest guy I ever met in my life." The year after Broonzy's death, Muddy recorded a tribute album, *Muddy Waters Sings Big Bill Broonzy*.) In 1946, Broonzy performed in a series of People's Songs concerts with Lead Belly, Woody Guthrie, and Pete Seeger, and soon became a mainstay on the folk revival circuit. In 1951–52, he toured France, Germany, and England, one of the first to bring the gospel of blues to Europe in person.[16]

These tours presented Broonzy in a variety of personas: as a forerunner of American jazz, as urban bluesman Big Bill, and as a folk-blues artist. In the latter guise his European repertoire favored old-style country blues. In Paris, he recorded **"Baby, Please Don't Go"** (1952), a traditional blues first put on record by Big Joe Williams in 1935 and subsequently covered by everyone from Muddy Waters and Van Morrison to AC/DC and Aerosmith. Accompanied only by his crystal-clear acoustic guitar, Broonzy sings a deep Mississippi blues, begging his woman not to go back to New Orleans and leave him here on Parchman Farm, Mississippi's infamous state penitentiary. In contrast to the relatively upbeat tune and tempo, the dozen repetitions of the title line plus Broonzy's reference to Parchman Farm suggest the anxiety behind the singer's pleading. Notorious for its brutality and exploitation of African American prisoners, Parchman leased them out to neighboring plantations where they worked under appalling conditions.[17]

Broonzy could be fearlessly outspoken. In 1947, he joined a freewheeling conversation with Memphis Slim and John Lee "Sonny Boy" Williamson about the origins of the blues, recorded by ethnographer Alan Lomax. The three bluesmen talked candidly about life in the South: the poverty, brutal levee camps, chain gangs, and prison farms; the value white men placed on Black lives (less than that of a mule); and lynching. Lomax waited until 1957 to release it on record, and made sure to protect the three with pseudonyms. Not until 1990 were their true identities revealed. But Broonzy had no qualms about going public with his feelings about racial oppression when he recorded **"Black, Brown and White"** (1951) in Paris. He had written it as early as 1939. The major American record companies all turned it down but France's Vogue label snapped it up. Again, Broonzy sings and plays unaccompanied. The tempo may be quicker than "Baby, Please Don't Go," the tone lighter and free of bitterness, but the lyrics are unequivocal in their critique of American racism and color prejudice. Refused service in a bar, ignored on the unemployment line, paid half what another man was paid for the same work, the singer explains in the chorus the hierarchy of color in postwar America: white is up, brown down, but if you're black, brother, get back! In the final verse he asks another brother what he will do about Jim Crow. Packing a strong political punch, this tune became one of the most important protest songs of the era.[18]

Our final Big Bill selection shows the flip side of his versatile postwar musical persona. An R&B-style jump shuffle recorded in Chicago for Mercury Records, **"You've Been Mistreatin' Me"** (1949) credits Big Bill Broonzy and His Fat Four: alto sax, piano, bass, and drums. In this classic 12-bar you-done-me-wrong blues, Broonzy tells his woman he's tired of her mistreating him and she'll be sorry when he leaves her to ease his worried mind. Antonio Cosey's howling sax makes way for Broonzy's shouting vocal and brisk guitar work. A fine effort from a veteran bluesman able to adapt to changing times.

Robert Santelli considers **Memphis Minnie** (1897–1973) "the most important female blues artist from the end of the classic period in the late 1920s until the arrival of Big Mama Thornton, Big Maybelle, and the other blues belters in the early 1950s." Broonzy played with Minnie in a 1930s foursome and she vanquished him in a head-to-head musical contest. He testified that she could "pick a guitar and sing as good as any man I ever heard." A tobacco-chewing, snuff-dipping woman who looked and dressed "like an old-maid schoolteacher," according to Langston Hughes, she more than held her own in the rough-and-tumble of juke joints and blues clubs.[19] Like Broonzy, she wrote and recorded hundreds of songs, was among the first blues guitarists to use an amplifier, and adapted her country blues to urban styles in the postwar period. Born Lizzie Douglas, she left her Mississippi home for Memphis at age thirteen, married three different bluesmen, and made her best records in the 1930s with her second husband, singer/guitarist Joe McCoy. Their record company christened them Memphis Minnie and Kansas Joe. Her third husband, Ernest Lawler, aka Little Son Joe, played guitar on her last recordings in mid-century Chicago along with some of the city's best bluesmen.

In her earlier blues Minnie often sang about the things that satisfied her sexual desire: the sting of her bumble bee ("Bumble Bee"), the chauffeur who gives her rides ("Me and My Chauffeur Blues"). In her fifties, she still sounds very much her own woman on these postwar songs, singing upbeat blues of female liberation. **"Down Home Girl"** (1949), a slow 12-bar blues recorded for Regal Records but unissued at the time, features a strong shouting vocal by Minnie, moody guitars from her and Little Son Joe, and the barrelhouse piano of Sunnyland Slim (Albert Luandrew), another key figure in the Chicago blues scene. She plans to leave Chicago and her lover simply because she's tired of him. His inadequacy gives her the downhome blues. She'll find herself a man back home in Memphis who knows what to do.

"Kissing in the Dark" (1953), for J.O.B. Records, finds Minnie in fine form, a born lover and kisser. It's her birthmark, she tells us. Bouncing along in this mid-tempo romp behind her and Joe's best guitar work of the period and Little Brother Montgomery's honkytonk piano, thoroughly modern Minnie embraces the hipster gospel of the time. She sings of a woman who ditches a date with a square when she meets a hep cat, and urges us to get hip to the crazy jive. A delightful last encore from the final recording session of a true giant of the blues.

The slide or bottleneck guitar produced one of the signature deep blues sounds that Mississippi artists brought to Chicago. No one in the postwar era played slide better than **Robert Nighthawk** (1909–67). Born Robert Lee McCollum in Helena, Arkansas, Nighthawk had deep roots and multiple connections in the Mississippi blues scene. He learned slide guitar from his cousin, Delta bluesman Houston Stackhouse, who had learned it from the great Tommy Johnson. Nighthawk played at Muddy Waters' Clarksdale wedding in 1932 and with nearly all the musicians who gigged around Helena and the Delta, including John Lee Hooker and John Lee "Sonny Boy" Williamson, who revolutionized the blues harp. He had a regional hit in 1937 with "Prowling Nighthawk," which gave him his stage name. Arriving in Chicago in 1940, Nighthawk came under the tutelage of guitarist Tampa Red (Hudson Whittaker), another important character in the Chicago blues story. Red's slide technique strongly influenced both Nighthawk and Muddy Waters, Nighthawk's friend and admirer, who convinced the Chess brothers to record Nighthawk on their Aristocrat label, the precursor to Chess Records.[20]

His first record on Aristocrat, a two-sided masterpiece produced by Willie Dixon, who would become central to the Chess sound, "Annie Lee Blues" and "Black Angel Blues" have low-key accompaniment by Ernest Lane on piano and Dixon on bass. These slow 12-bar blues showcase Nighthawk's slide work and vocals. On **"Annie Lee Blues"** (1949) his warm voice has an unurgent, almost lazy quality as he explains his dilemma to the reluctant Annie. She promised herself to him. He wants her. If she refuses, he'll say goodbye for the last time. He cries her name, as if to say, "C'mon! Can't you see why you have to be my woman?!" Then he lets his guitar talk for him. The aching music speaks more loudly than his words. If she doesn't stick around after hearing that, she doesn't deserve him.

Lucille Bogan wrote and first recorded "Black Angel Blues" in 1930 with solo piano. Tampa Red's 1946 remake featured his slide. Later, B.B. King de-racialized the song as "Sweet Little Angel" (1956) and made it a centerpiece of his repertoire. Bogan's Black angel was a man. Nighthawk's **"Black Angel Blues"** (1949) has a different sexual flavor, sung by a man in celebration of his sweet Black woman: he likes how she spreads her wings. But nothing in the lyrics or performance sounds lascivious. Nighthawk sings with absolute conviction that he'll die if she leaves him. He expresses her generosity as a lover in a traditional floating verse. When he asks her for a nickel, she gives him ten dollars. When he asks her for whiskey, she buys him a still. Compared to "Annie Lee," the guitar is less prominent, Lane's piano and Dixon's bass more audible in support of Nighthawk's restrained, classy slide. Leading into the break he calls out, "Well, all right man!" What man wouldn't be enthusiastic about an angel like her?

Nighthawk could jump the blues, too, in his recordings for Chicago's United Records. His cover of Bumble Bee Slim's 1935 **"Bricks in My Pillow"** (1952) was unreleased at the time but included on Delmark Records' 1999 reissue of Nighthawk's

United sides. He discards his slide solos on this jazzy, upbeat shuffle, playing rhythm guitar and giving the pianist equal prominence. Remarkable for the stark contrast between its bright musical tone, pace, relaxed vocal, and the lyrics, this record practically defines what it means to have the blues. Its lyrics lack only a mistreating woman. The singer has bricks in his pillow, spiders and snakes in his room, mud in his water, holes in the pockets of his patched pants, and he can't pay the rent. He hears a train whistle and feels like leaving but has nowhere to go. He wants to drink but has no whiskey. Not entirely alone, he addresses nearly every line to "mama." He calls "All right" before the lighthearted piano solo, a vocal shrug at the absurdity of it all and an invocation of the blues truism, "I laugh to keep from crying." I may be the unluckiest man living, he and the music seem to say, but I'm glad to be alive in 1952.

Interviewed in 1956, Elvis Presley said, "Down in Tupelo, Mississippi, I used to hear old Arthur Crudup bang his box like I do now, and I said if I ever get to the place where I could feel all old Arthur felt, I'd be a music man like no one ever saw." The model for three of Elvis's records including his first, "That's All Right," **Arthur "Big Boy" Crudup** (1905–74) deserved the compliment. But he also deserves better than just a footnote in rock 'n' roll history. Crudup began recording blues in Chicago in 1941 but Big Boy never really took to the big city. He remained in Mississippi his whole life, working as a sharecropper while making the occasional journey North to record, so his sound never developed like that of the Mississippi expats who stayed in Chicago. Receiving no royalties for his songwriting, he quit recording in 1955, his story a parable of the Black musician's blues life at mid-century:

> I wasn't getting enough out of it to live. I'd had to go make some records, then go back South, go on the farm, work railroad, cut pulp wood, work for the city, play music Friday night and Saturday night to try to take care of my family, and was supposed to be a musician and a record star. And so I just quit it. I found out all the money was going the other way and I wasn't getting any.[21]

Crudup recorded **"That's All Right"** (1946) for RCA-Victor, a she-done-me-wrong-but-I-can't-make-up-my-mind-what-to-do-about-it blues that rocks like R&B and twangs like country. His mama and papa warned him about women and, sure enough, his woman doesn't want him anymore. He loves her but has to let her go. That's all right—whatever she wants to do. And he sounds like he means it. The situational ambiguity of the title phrase, repeated eighteen times, makes the song more interesting than traditional blues complaints. Is it all right that she's leaving? All right that she's doing what she wants at his expense? The ambiguity does nothing to diminish the energy of this up-tempo dance tune. "Yeah, man!" Crudup calls out, introducing the break, which he fills with his rockin' guitar while bassist Ransom Knowling and Judge Riley on drums rock along with him. His dynamic performance, much like Nighthawk's, preaches acceptance with a blues shrug: My baby's leaving, but what the hell. Let's party!

Using the same romping tune and accompaniment, Crudup's **"I'm Gonna Dig Myself a Hole"** (1951) offers a blues response to the Korean War, one of many similar recordings of the period. Sometimes called "Build Myself a Cave," sometimes "The World's in a Tangle," the song also appeared on records by John Lee Hooker, Honeyboy Edwards, Jimmy Rogers, and Robert Jr. Lockwood.[22] Driven by Knowling's bouncy bass, Crudup's version explains that the singer has gotten his draft notice. His baby worries about him. But no problem: he has no intention of going into the army. Instead, he'll dig a hole and move underground with her. He hopes they'll come out to a world with no more wars to worry about. (In some versions *Reds* substitutes for *wars*.) A form of blues resistance, the song reflects the treatment of Black soldiers during and after World War II. No wonder some of these guys would hesitate to put their lives on the line for their country again.

Going to Chicago: Muddy and After

We can divide postwar Chicago blues into before and after Muddy Waters. All the blues artists discussed above cut records before 1948, the year Muddy's recordings for the Chess brothers on Aristocrat began to revolutionize Chicago blues. That process accelerated as Muddy began gathering his quintessential Chicago blues band, players like Jimmy Rogers, Otis Spann, Little Walter, Fred Below, and Willie Dixon. Though never as broadly popular a blues ambassador as B.B. King would become, **Muddy Waters** (McKinley Morganfield) (1915–83) was The Man in mid-century Chicago: the Hoochie Coochie Man, the Manish Boy, the Mojo Man, the Rolling Stone, the face and voice of Chicago blues for more than three decades. Which bluesman did the Rolling Stones want to meet first when they came to America? Muddy Waters. His deep, powerful sound and blues dignity kept his boasting machismo in check. He also played terrific slide guitar and wrote some of the blues' most memorable anthems. The great Howlin' Wolf competed with him for Chicago blues supremacy but Muddy's sound proved more influential, prolific, and long-lasting.

Growing up in a family of sharecroppers on the Stovall plantation near Clarksdale, Mississippi, he got his nickname roaming the muddy cotton fields. He learned guitar by watching and listening to Delta masters Son House and Robert Johnson. While still on the plantation, Muddy made field recordings for folklorist Alan Lomax in 1941–42. Lomax released two of his songs, "I Be's Troubled" and "Country Blues," in a

Muddy Waters on tour in Paris with the American Folk Blues Festival, 1963, recorded by French public radio and television agency ORTF. Philippe Gras/Alamy Stock Photo.

Library of Congress collection. (Muddy would re-record them for Aristocrat in 1948 as "I Can't Be Satisfied" and "I Feel Like Going Home.") When he heard himself on record in 1943, he packed his things, took the train from Clarksdale to Memphis, then another straight to Chicago.[23]

During his early years in Chicago Muddy gigged at South Side clubs with other transplanted Mississippi bluesmen: guitarists Jimmy Rogers and Baby Face Leroy Foster, pianists Eddie Boyd and Sunnyland Slim, and Little Walter Jacobs, who would soon become Chicago's blues harp god. Playing slide guitar, Muddy settled into a groove with Rogers and Walter. The three of them, amplified, went to musical war together, challenging house bands to duels. "We used to go around calling ourselves the Headhunters," Muddy recalled.[24] He signed with Aristocrat but none of his records went anywhere until the 1948 session where he re-did the two songs Lomax had earlier produced. From then until his death in 1983, Muddy Waters defined the Chicago blues sound. You can't go wrong listening to any of his many great songs.

The flip side of "I Can't Be Satisfied," **"I Feel Like Going Home"** (1948) showcases a powerful blend of voice and guitar, and the title reflects the homesickness many of his compatriots felt for the South they had left. Accompanied by Big Crawford's rhythmic bass, Muddy opens with 37 seconds of hypnotic amplified slide. He runs the gamut from single-string notes to dense chords, almost as if he were auditioning. His rich voice resonates with urgency despite the slow tempo, but his vocal has a sly trickster quality. Listen to what he does with the word "Well!" Tapping into his deep Delta roots, Muddy borrows the melody and second verse of Robert Johnson's "Walking Blues" (1937). Comprising three verses of two lengthy repeated lines each, Muddy's lyrics tell a story of frustrated love in well-worn country blues tropes. Echoing Johnson, he wants to blow his horn—have sex. But, like Johnson, Muddy sings that when he got up that morning, she had gone, and if he doesn't find her he'll die or endure in pain until she stops her evil ways. "This was the old deep Delta blues, no doubt about that," Robert Palmer writes, "but it was also something new. It stood out amid the glut of r&b releases by sax-led jump combos and blues balladeers because of its simplicity, its passion, and its hypnotic one-chord droning."[25]

In an auspicious February 1950 session for Aristocrat/Chess, Muddy made his second recording of "Rollin' and Tumblin'" in two months. Leonard Chess had wanted Muddy to re-create an old-timey blues sound and insisted he keep recording with only sparse support. But just back from a successful tour down South, Muddy's band was tearing up Chicago clubs. Muddy wanted to put *that* sound on record. In January 1950, he joined bandmates Little Walter and Baby Face Leroy in a surreptitious session for tiny Parkway Records. "Wired, fired and inspired," according to Muddy's biographer Robert Gordon, the band felt the session to be "a victory whoop, a collision between the thrill of visiting a former life and the rush of resuming a contemporary one."[26] Among their recordings: a six-minute, two-sided version of Hambone Willie Newbern's 12-bar "Roll and Tumble Blues" from 1929. They called theirs **"Rollin' and Tumblin'"** (1950) and themselves the Baby Face Leroy Trio.

An orgiastic postwar musical celebration, this astonishing record belies its downbeat blues lyrics. On side one the singer tells of his sleepless nights, rolling around in bed and crying. He again repeats Robert Johnson's line: he wakes up in the morning bereft. The second stanza echoes "I Can't Be Satisfied": his baby celebrates as a train rolls in. As the train leaves again, he regrets not saying goodbye. Who is leaving and why? It hardly matters because the riotous performance overwhelms the lyrics. Muddy plays slide, Walter harp, and Leroy drums, a single pulsing riff driving the song. Leroy sings lead but they all moan and shout over each other. Side two consists of three minutes of wordless humming and moaning over the howling instruments. In his classic study of gospel, Anthony Heilbut describes how worshippers in Black churches hum, moan, and scream "the spirit into presence by wailing lines that predict the blues." Muddy and friends go house-wrecking here:

> The sounds are pugilistic and sexual. Someone yelps. Someone else responds. The randomness of the interjections is frightening, the rapid-fire drumming disorienting. Muddy's slide rings like loose spokes on an iron wheel, haywire. The harp is hypnotic. Chant and hum, chant and hum. Violence hangs everywhere, the sex heated and raw.

Sandra Tooze adds, "Muddy and Walter's slide guitar and harp duel still ranks among the most inspirational Chicago blues ever recorded."[27]

When angry Leonard Chess learned that Muddy had gone rogue, and that the Parkway recording was selling well, he immediately brought his blues star back into the studio to re-record the song. On the Chess version of **"Rollin' and Tumblin'"** (1950) Big Crawford's unamplified bass and a drum back Muddy's vocal and slide. Retaining the opening line about sleepless nights, Muddy rewrote the other lyrics, dipping into the blues' collective repository for traditional floating verses. He tells his baby not to let anyone tear down his barrelhouse (a verse from Newbern's original), imagines himself a duck diving into a river of whiskey, and regrets that he gave up religion for women and drink. He hums and moans through the break. For Jim Dawson and Steve Propes, this version "set the standard of the rockin' Chicago blues of the '50s."[28] I consider this excellent record a pale imitation of the Leroy Trio's masterpiece.

At that same session, singing solo and playing without a slide, Muddy recorded **"Rollin' Stone"** (1950), his signature number that generated the name of the band and music magazine, and great songs by Bob Dylan and the Temptations, the latter a critique of the rolling stone mystique. (Being a rolling stone might have been fun for papa but was not very good for his family.) Muddy's powerful declaration of selfhood inaugurated a string of what Ted Gioia describes as "Whitmanesque songs of himself, full of attitude, celebrating his life force and increasingly his libido...." Not subject to the whims of a fickle woman or tormented by anxiety and sleepless nights, he presents himself here as an archetype: the strong, free, sexually magnetic Black man in full control of his destiny. The "I" in this song is unequivocally Muddy; he names himself in the lyric. The melody and verse about wanting to be a catfish that good-looking women would try to catch, Muddy took from Robert Petway's 1941 Delta standard, "Catfish Blues."[29]

But "Rollin' Stone" is an entirely different beast. Muddy slows the tempo, plucks his guitar aggressively, and sings with menacing confidence. Not a man to be messed with, he visits (*ho-oh!*) a married woman who tells him her husband just left the house. Sure enough. The third verse recounts his near-mythic birth, his mother's prediction that her boychild will grow up to be a rolling stone. Sure enough. In the final verse he touches base with the origins of his destiny, heading back down the road to Rolling Fork, his Mississippi birthplace. This blues travel doesn't translate as *running away from* but as *rambling*, the bluesman going where he wants, doing what he wants, in full control of his environment and his life.

Muddy was just warming up. In 1951, he cut three of his best records for Chess, with some of his best slide work. The supplicant in **"Long Distance Call," "Honey Bee,"** and **"She Moves Me,"** he sings slowly and methodically, as though he needs to construct a woman as powerful as the man he himself had been in "Rollin' Stone." In "Long Distance Call" he asks her to *please* call him and offers her a Cadillac. His honey bee rambles, on the move all over the world, and he has to wait for her to come home. In "She Moves Me" she finds her apotheosis as a black magic woman. She has her own money, gets herself drunk, calls him dumb and square. He takes it, wondering how she manages to move him. The answer comes in the final verse: she can make the dumb speak, the blind see, even raise the dead. (A few months earlier, Rice Miller aka Sonny Boy Williamson II had recorded "Eyesight to the Blind" about a woman with similar powers.) Little Walter, finally allowed into the studio with Muddy, plays an amplified harp. Unhappy with the session drummer, Leonard Chess slams the bass drum himself, establishing an insistent rhythm. Muddy's vocal, with his amp cranked up near max, expresses the power of his manhood along with his lyrical appreciation of potent Black womanhood.[30]

"Hoochie Coochie Man" (1954) represents Muddy at the top of his sexual and musical game. Written by Willie Dixon, who penned two other macho anthems Muddy recorded that year, **"I Just Want to Make Love to You"** and **"I'm Ready,"** the song became Muddy's biggest hit, reaching #3 R&B. The recording features what may be the ultimate Chicago blues band: Jimmy Rogers on second guitar, magnificent Otis Spann on piano, Dixon on bass, Fred Below playing drums, and Little Walter on harp, giving the song an almost orchestral blues sound. Utilizing a dramatic stop-time rhythm following each verse line—da-*da*-da-da-*dum*—the song employs the imagery of hoodoo, black folk magic, to mythologize Muddy. At the scene of his birth a gypsy woman tells his mother that the boychild she has coming will be special. The auspicious signs include multiple sevens that promise he'll be a good luck child. In case those omens aren't enough, he gathers a variety of hoodoo charms conferring strength, good fortune, and sexual power: a black cat's bone, a mojo, and a John the Conqueror root. Pretty women will crave him. Muddy's vocal emphases drive the point home. He'll *make* them jump with pleasure. You best not mess with him because *every*body knows who he is. I am what I am, the song declares: the hoochie coochie man.[31]

Not just Muddy's sideman and master of second guitar, **Jimmy Rogers** (1924–97) was an excellent songwriter, singer, and lead guitarist in his own right with an "irresistible, buttery-smooth vocal quality." Santelli calls him "the great unsung artist of Chicago blues."[32] Playing guitar behind Robert Nighthawk's slide in Helena helped prepare him for seconding Muddy in Chicago. At Chess he wrote and cut a few excellent sides with Muddy's band, which became his own. A 1950 session with Little Walter and Big Crawford produced a double-sided gem, **"That's All Right"** b/w **"Ludella."** A relaxed shuffle, "That's All Right" shares both Big Boy Crudup's title and the way the phrase presents the singer as a model of reasonable male behavior, but with a slower tempo and different lyrics. She told him she loved him but she doesn't anymore. He knows she loves another man and he spends his nights wondering who it might be. But that's all right, he sings over and over. No snapping pistols or threats. He just sounds disappointed. The dominant musical voice, Little Walter's trilling harp duets with Rogers' guitar while Big Crawford provides the rhythm.

Rogers recorded **"Chicago Bound"** (1954) at the same session as Muddy's "Hoochie Coochie Man" with the same great band, Rogers and Muddy switching places. This straight-up jump blues relocates Memphis Slim's rockin' migration anthem, **"Harlem Bound"** (1948), to Chicago. (We'll listen to "Harlem Bound" in the next chapter.) Accompanied by his own boogie woogie piano, Slim sang about going from Memphis to East St. Louis in 1932 and from there to Chicago. From Chicago he intends to go to Harlem. Rogers appropriates Slim's tune (they received co-writing credit) and leaves for Memphis in 1934, then off to St. Louis, and finally to Chicago. Rogers' version involves more women than Slim's. His Georgia baby begs him not to go but he leaves anyway. His Memphis woman dumps him. His love life improves in St. Louis but he also leaves that town—the phrase repeated most often. Unlike Slim, Rogers will stay in Chicago, the greatest place. Rogers' guitar and Walter's harp replace Slim's piano and two saxes with the rest of the band providing rhythm. On this travelling song the music really moves. Rogers swings the vocal, sounding genuinely happy to have made the journey. The first instrumental break features Walter's dynamic harp solo. The second lets Otis Spann strut his stuff, his sensational piano boogie referencing Slim's original. All in all, a joyous record that captures the excitement of the decade's movement north.

In contrast, **Floyd Jones** (1917–89) brought some of the deepest, darkest Mississippi blues to mid-century Chicago. His first recording of **"Dark Road"** (1951) on J.O.B. featured Sunnyland Slim on piano. Chess re-recorded the song later that year, dropping Slim's piano along with bass and trumpet in favor of Jimmy Rogers' guitar and Little Walter's harp with stunning results. On Chess's **"Dark Road"** Jones channels Tommy Johnson's 1928 classic, "Big Road Blues." Rambling in the Delta in the 1930s, Jones might have learned the song directly from Johnson himself, or from Howlin' Wolf.[33] The spooky musical performance and existential lyrics evoke all the dark roads, literal and metaphoric, that Black men and women faced in the Jim Crow South—and in northern cities like Chicago. In the pre-dawn opening verses the singer eyes a dark, lonesome road that he just can't go down alone. In the two middle verses, traditional blues scenarios, his mother died when he was young, leaving her wicked son with only a blessing. He asks a conductor to stop the train and let him ride, but to no avail. Terror, death, loneliness, and failure haunt the song, along with blues resilience: in the final verse he faces his fear and walks down the road, crying. The guitars, harp, and drums join in an ominous drone that repeats over and over as

Jones howls and moans, sometimes in falsetto à la Howlin' Wolf. The blues doesn't get deeper than this.

Jones's recording of "Hard Times" (1949), on the short-lived Tempo-Tone label, credits Sunny Land Slim and His Sunnyland Boys. With Muddy Waters on second guitar behind Jones, Slim's vaudeville-style piano dominates the record. He plays at too quick a tempo for the subject and for Jones's thin, mournful voice. The same song re-recorded for Chicago's Black-owned Vee-Jay Records, retitled **"Ain't Times Hard"** (1954) and credited to Floyd Jones and His Band, nails it. Sunnyland slows things down and his piano is farther back in the mix. Jones's voice sounds much stronger, and Eddie Taylor's guitar and especially Snooky Pryor on harp give the song a modern Chicago blues sound. Jones's lyrics remain gloomily the same, this time in the wake of the 1953–54 recession. Times are hard. The union tells him his work week has been cut back to four days. If things don't get better, he'll have to leave town. How graphically this song expresses these economic blues.

J.B. Lenoir (1929–67) came to Chicago in 1949. Another Mississippi bluesman who had little use for his home state ("The way they do's you down there in Mississippi," he told Paul Oliver, "it ain't what a man should suffer, what a man should go through"), he had his biggest hit with the romping **"Mamma Talk to Your Daughter"** (1955). His **"Eisenhower Blues"** (1954), on Chicago's Parrot label, arose from the same recessionary conditions as Jones's "Ain't Times Hard." Lenoir played with some of the city's top bluesmen, but on this mid-tempo shuffle a nondescript band backs his vocal and guitar. His high voice barking out the proto-protest lyrics makes it a keeper. Eisenhower's presidency gives him the blues. Taxes are high, he has no money, no shoes for his baby, and no fun. This song addresses the listener directly: What are *we* gonna do? In a sign of the times, it proved so controversial that the label made Lenoir re-record the song, dropping all references to Eisenhower and changing the title to "Tax Payer Blues."[34]

Eddie Boyd (1914–94) grew up in Clarksdale, a Delta town of fewer than 20,000, famous for its blues pedigree and notorious for its racism.[35] Muddy Waters, John Lee Hooker, Sam Cooke, and Ike Turner all hailed from within a few miles of there. Boyd came to Chicago in 1941 and struck gold in 1952–53 with three of the biggest blues hits of those years: **"Five Long Years," "24 Hours,"** and **"Third Degree."** An excellent songwriter, he sang and played piano on his records.

"Five Long Years" (1952) became a classic, #1 on *Billboard*'s Rhythm & Blues chart for seven weeks. Among its many fine covers, Buddy Guy's studio and live versions take the prize for me. No one ever wrote a better blues complaint about the domestic economy. The singer feels badly mistreated. He worked hard for his wife, slaved in a steel mill (where Boyd himself worked), and brought home his pay every week. But after five years she threw him out. The singer addresses a male *you* and wonders if you've been mistreated. The last stanza proposes that you learn from him: his next wife will be a working woman who brings home the dough. The slow 12-bar blues opens with Boyd's mournful piano. Ernest Cotton's equally dolorous tenor sax responds to each lyrical line. The bass and drums lay down a steady dirge-like beat. Muddy Waters plays inconspicuous guitar. Boyd sings with great conviction, sad and frustrated by his woman's betrayal. The precarious status of relationships in the blues world means even a once happily married man can't be satisfied for long.

Boyd recorded "Five Long Years" on the small J.O.B. label. Once it hit big, Chess snapped him up and released **"Third Degree"** (1953) by Eddie Boyd and His Chess Men, one of the most powerfully gloomy blues ever recorded. Always sensitive to racism, Boyd eventually left the United States to live in Europe. "Third Degree" (Miriam-Webster defines it as "the subjection of a prisoner to mental or physical torture to extract a confession") catalogues the injustices that would drive a Black man from America. Boyd copped some of the lyrics—the accusations of forgery and murder—from Texas Alexander's "Levee Camp Moan Blues" (1927) and great Georgia bluesman Blind Willie McTell's "Death Cell Blues" (1933). Even though McTell's singer is locked in a cell and condemned to death, Boyd manages to be darker and gloomier. The melody here resembles "Five Long Years," only slower, with a funereal tenor sax and strong guitar work from Lee Cooper accompanying Boyd's piano. His melancholy vocals articulate his misery. Accused of a series of crimes he could not have committed because, he sings, he's blind, crippled, and illiterate, he concludes that bad luck is killing him. It's more than he can bear. Though a blues constant, bad luck seems metaphorical here: the (in)justice system that persecutes and overwhelms him. Black lives, the song says, really don't matter in 1950s Chicago.

If you knew Boyd's songs only from those somber 1950s hits, you might be surprised to learn that in the late 1940s he cut some of the best, most upbeat jump blues Chicago ever produced. He recorded a slower, duller version for Chess in 1952, but his original **"Rosa Lee Swing"** (1947) for RCA-Victor, an infectious 12-bar boogie, doesn't just swing, it rocks. The label credits Little Eddie Boyd, Blues Singer and his Boogie Band. Boyd wrote the song and pounds the piano. Rosa Lee has her big legs all over him in this lively blues complaint, but he wants her gone. Stop jiving him, he sings, playing him for a fool. The label may emphasize *Blues Singer,* but Boyd surely doesn't have the blues here, whatever the lyrics say. He blasts the vocal, telling Rosa Lee to get hip to the situation while bass man Ellsworth Liggett and Booker T. Washington's drums lay down a heavy rhythm. Boyd yells, "Blow saxman!" and the delirious squealing riff that follows comes from "Sax" Mallard on clarinet, very unusual in R&B. Clapping and shouting, Boyd bellows, "Blow Bill," and tenor saxman Bill Casimir blows a brilliant solo without the honking tricks R&B sax players tended to perform. The slick arrangement varies the instrumental responses to Boyd's lyrics, and the song is an absolute joy, an unjustly obscure jump masterpiece.

When teenage **Otis Rush** (1934–2018) left his Mississippi home to visit his sister in Chicago, she took him to a club to see Muddy Waters: "I'd just arrived, and I don't know nothin' about guitar. … I heard Muddy, and I said, 'Give me a guitar!'" Rush would go on to become one of the most influential blues artists of the next generation. "With its visceral attack, beautiful phrasing, shimmering vibrato, and elastic bends," Jas Obrecht writes, "Otis' guitar approach was soon inspiring a generation of rock and blues guitarists," including Eric Clapton, Jimmy Page, Carlos Santana, and Stevie Ray Vaughan. Rush's ferocious singing style stunned Robert Palmer: "His grainy, gospelish singing carried the weight of so much passion and frustration, it sounded like the words were being torn from his throat...."[36] Rush initiated a new phase in Chicago blues, dubbed the West Side sound, a thoroughly modern sound rooted in tradition, that soon included Buddy Guy and Magic Sam. He cut his first records in 1956 so just squeezes in at the end of our decade.

Willie Dixon brought him into Eli Toscano's new Cobra Records studio for both Rush's and the label's first session. Dixon recalls: "Eli didn't even have enough money to buy Otis Rush an amplifier. I jumped up and bought the amplifier with $75 of my own money...."[37] Dixon wrote the songs and played bass on them, including **"I Can't Quit You Baby"** (1956). From the opening chords you know this 12-bar blues is special. Rush's guitar starts the song slowly with a reverb effect that gives it depth and weight. The first cry of his highly emotional vocal sets up the rest of the song. She's destroying his family life and has even caused him to mistreat his child but he can't quit her. Obsessed, he can't help desiring her, crying over her. Howling with love and frustration, he vocalizes gospel-style *we-e-e-e-l* and *ye-e-e-s*, falsetto *ohhh* and *ooooh*. As though he can't stop talking about her, the song has no instrumental break. Rush's guitar shows more restraint than his vocal, and the excellent band provides a thick blues wall of sound. Lafayette Leake on piano, Big Walter Horton's subtle harp, and Wayne Bennett on second guitar help Rush express the depths of an illicit love rich and terrible. Led Zeppelin covered the song on their first album.

Rush's next release, **"My Love Will Never Die"** (1956), tells a similar story in only two verses with the same band, an additional sax, and more anguished vocals. Al Duncan's slow, ominous drumbeat sets the rhythm. Still avoiding elaborate guitar-god solos, Rush lets his voice do the work, worrying key words, utilizing melisma, rare in Chicago blues. Again, the singer feels trapped in an overwhelming passion he can't resist or consummate. She continues to do him wrong but he can only beg her to try to love him—*plea-e-e-e-ease*, he cries twice in falsetto, answering himself with short guitar bursts—because he'll *ne-e-e-e-ver* change his mind: his love for her will never die. With the instrumental mix less dense here, you can clearly hear the piano and drums. Red Holloway's short, lonely sax solo separates the verses. Dixon indulged in some psychological poetry in the second verse. The singer asks his beloved to hold flowers that grow from his grief—or his grave? Rush, in falsetto, knows they represent his mind breaking down from the stress of his immortal love. The song ends with an instrumental crescendo and diminuendo: great love and deep disappointment in a fabulous record.

Going to Chicago: Wolf and Elmo

Muddy Waters and Chester Burnett aka **Howlin' Wolf** (1910–76) were the top dogs in Chicago blues. At over 6'3" and 300 pounds with size 17 shoes and hands so large they made his guitar seem small and his harmonica disappear, Wolf had a voice like industrial sandpaper on a bass drum. He emitted a strange, deep, hoarse sound that could morph into a hum, moan, or falsetto howl. Arnold Shaw describes "a wolflike growl compounded of agony and aggression, but not without moments of pain and hurt." To top it off he had extraordinary showmanship. Robert Palmer recalls seeing Wolf live in 1965, steaming across the stage, blowing harp as if having an epileptic fit; playing guitar while on his back or doing somersaults; leaping onto the side curtain and climbing it while he sang, microphone under his arm.[38]

Wolf had deep roots in the Delta. He lived on a plantation near Charlie Patton, the father of Delta blues, who taught him guitar. He played alongside Robert Johnson, learned harp from Rice Miller (Sonny Boy Williamson II), and by 1950 he had his own West Memphis radio show and the hottest band in the region. Sam Phillips brought Wolf into his recently opened Memphis Recording Studio in 1951. Stunned by Wolf's raw power and talent, Phillips told Palmer, "When I heard Howlin' Wolf, I said, 'This is for me. This is where the soul of man never dies.'" Phillips would go on to record B.B. King, Elvis Presley, Jerry Lee Lewis, and Johnny Cash. But his biographer Peter Guralnick attests that Phillips considered Howlin' Wolf "the greatest talent, the most profound artist he had ever encountered."[39]

Because his Sun Records was not yet up and running, Phillips sold Wolf's initial recordings to Chess, where Wolf's first record appeared. Critics reach for hyperbole trying to describe **"Moanin' at Midnight"** (1951): "Two minutes, fifty-six seconds of pure anxiety"; "an auditory fever dream"; a "throbbing paean to bipolar disorder." Guitarist Willie Johnson "sounded as if he was twanging baling wire with a six-inch nail ... [in] counterpoint to Wolf's mournful vocal, which sounded as if he might swallow the microphone and jump out of the jukebox speaker at any moment." The extraordinary wordless first forty seconds of the song open with what both Palmer and Guralnick call Wolf's "unearthly moan." Palmer continues, "Willie Johnson's overamplified guitar and Willie Steel's drums came crashing in together and then Wolf switched to harp, getting a massive, brutish sound and pushing the rhythm hard."[40]

Only those three instruments accompany the vocal, laying down a single rhythmic chord that runs through the entire song, responding multiple times to each of Wolf's short vocal lines. The inexplicably ominous situation finds somebody knocking on his door: a debt collector? a threatening white man? or maybe the devil. The singer worries but doesn't know how he can escape. When the phone

Howlin' Wolf performing on the British TV show *Ready, Steady, Go,* Dec. 1964. Pictorial Press Ltd./Alamy Stock Photo.

rings he pretends he's not there. Only a single line constitutes the third verse, preceded by Wolf's ethereal moan and howl. That line, spoken to his child, his woman, or himself, says not to worry, daddy will be there in the bed. But the five repetitions of the violent instrumental riff immediately preceding the line might be saying something else: the musical equivalent of his terrified moan, or perhaps chest-beating in the face of the song's nameless existential, racial, or personal threat. Delta blues doesn't get any deeper than this. Wolf re-recorded the song on RPM Records in a less potent version called, somewhat ludicrously, **"Morning at Midnight"** (1951).

A more conventional blues complaint but a fine song and Wolf's biggest hit, the flip side, **"How Many More Years"** (1951), rose to #4 on the *Billboard* chart where it remained for eleven weeks. In a strangely constricted voice Wolf wonders how much longer to let her screw him around. He'll go down on his knees to make her understand. But finally, he will have to pack his things and walk out the door. Nothing seems mournful about the musical presentation. The pianist—possibly Ike Turner—plays hard-driving boogie woogie. After each verse Wolf blasts his harp, wailing out a different story than the lyrics tell. This performance makes you understand why the harp was called the Mississippi saxophone. Between Willie Johnson's "thunderous power chords" on guitar and the sound of Wolf's rasping voice, Palmer writes, "this music was heavy metal, years before the term was coined."[41]

Wolf came up to Chicago in 1953 and signed with Chess. Muddy and Wolf's styles and sounds differed greatly, but Chess' two stars developed a heated competition for blues primacy on the label and in the city's clubs, sometimes poaching each other's players. The mid–1950s found Willie Dixon writing for both Wolf and Muddy, and Wolf recording in the Chess studio with a band comparable to Muddy's. A Dixon composition, **"Evil Is Goin' On"** (1954) complements Wolf's vocal and harp with Otis Spann's piano, Dixon's bass, drummer Earl Phillips, and guitarists Jody Williams and Hubert Sumlin, the latter a key to Wolf's sound for the next decade. The song turns the paranoia of a jealous man into warnings and advice to other men. If you're away from home and can't sleep, you can be sure something evil is going on. Dixon uses traditional blues tropes to elaborate: mules kicking in stalls, first trains smokin', backdoor men leaving. That's evil! Wolf expresses the evil vocally, shouting each verse and singing the chorus in a different demonically constricted voice. Dixon built stop-time into the song as he did with "Hoochie Coochie Man," the guitars and drum pounding out the rhythm. Spann's piano dominates the instrumental mix, laying out a series of right-hand high notes that sound to me like the mocking voice of the woman accused of cheating. In the two breaks the piano collides with the lamentation of Wolf's harp. Show me some proof, jealous man, says the piano. I don't need to prove your evildoing, woman, the harp responds—just listen to how upset you've made me.

Howlin' Wolf reached far back into his Mississippi past for **"Smokestack Lightning"** (1956), a hypnotic one-chord trip into the deepest blues. A song Charley Patton might have sung, it sounds primitive and strangely poetic, a series of strobing verses about loneliness and infidelity lit by the sparks from a locomotive. Wolf half-shouts, half-growls the six stanzas, ending each by asking if you hear him crying. *You* could be his woman or us, his listeners. His cry follows each of those lines, a howling *Whoo-hoo, whoo-hoo, whoo*. Most of the verses repeat standard blues infidelity suspicions: Where did you stay last night? Who was here while I was away? But two verses about trains add another dimension to his lamentation. To the awe-struck singer, what comes out of the smokestack looks like lightning and shines like gold. A traditional trope comprises the fourth verse: conductor, please let a poor boy ride. That phrase resonates with the final verse, where Wolf casts himself as a little boy who loved trains and still thinks of sparks from the smokestack as golden lightning. Wolf recorded the song "Poor Boy" (1957) the next year, his version of the blues standard "Poor Boy Long Ways from Home." That poignant sense of personal desolation turns what might be a stock blues complaint into a superb existential lament. The hypnotic music foregrounds Wolf's eerie, pained vocal—the band playing just that single chord, the guitars restrained, the drumbeat prominent. Wolf joins the band in the two breaks, blowing the same chord on his harp. The big man mesmerizes.

Elmore James (1918–63) was a monster on the amplified slide guitar. Having worked as a radio repairman, he adjusted his equipment to get a stinging, reverberant guitar sound. His amplifier always cranked up high, he sang louder than almost any of his peers. And his music, writes Santelli, "remains some of the most incendiary, brutally honest blues that's ever been made."[42] Like Wolf, James recorded in the South before making his way to Chicago. In 1951, he went into the tiny Trumpet Records studio in Jackson, Mississippi, to accompany his long-time friend and musical companion, harpist Rice Miller—Sonny Boy Williamson II. There, the story goes, someone surreptitiously recorded James's first record, **"Dust My Broom"** (1951) (credited to Elmo James), while he and his band rehearsed. In the 1930s, James may have played with Robert Johnson. "Dust My Broom" borrows freely from "I Believe I'll Dust My Broom" (1936), one of Johnson's signature songs. The success of James's version led to a recording contract with L.A.'s Bihari brothers—rivals of Chicago's Chess brothers—who released his disks on two of their Modern Records affiliates, Meteor and Flair. James did his best-known recording of the song in 1959 for Fire Records.

When "Dust My Broom" made the *Billboard* charts, James knew he was onto a good thing. He defined himself by the song. Calling all his bands The Broomdusters, he made four variations of "Dust My Broom" over the next four years: **"I Believe"** (1952), **"Please Find My Baby"** (1953), **"Standing at the Crossroads"** (1954), and **"Dust My Blues"** (1955). The bands on all four were significantly different, from the stripped down "Please Find My Baby" (just Ike Turner's piano and a drum) to the overloaded "Standing at the Crossroads" (trumpet, two saxophones, piano, bass, and drums). "Dust My Broom" got a very full sound from James's slide, a bass, drums, and Sonny Boy Williamson's melodic harp that makes the already addictive beat even more danceable. All these fine records had in common James's distinctive, forceful voice; what Palmer calls "the heavily amplified electric banshee-wail" of his guitar; and The Riff: "a machine-gun triplet beat that would become a defining sound of the early rockers": *da-da-da da-da-da da-da-da da-da-da DUM*.[43]

The four follow-up songs further varied and responded to James's original variation of Johnson's song. A 12-bar blues shuffle, "Dust My Broom" (slang: to leave in a hurry) opens when the singer awakens, vows to hit the road, and let his friends have his room. His best girl has strayed. He writes and phones every town from West Helena, Arkansas, to East Monroe, Louisiana, to try to find her. (Robert Johnson goes much further, looking for her in China, the Philippines, and Ethiopia.) Because she wants every man she meets, he'll leave his home. In contrast, James is contrite on his other best version of the song, "I Believe." He gets up in the morning and decides to return home, find his baby, and tell her he was wrong. He doesn't want a misbehaving woman or a drunk, but he was wrong to leave her. James's vocal is wilder and more emotional here, and the song swings a little more than "Dust My Broom." These Broomdusters "rocked harder than any other Chicago blues band," according to Palmer, who cites James's slashing slide, Johnny Jones's rockin' piano, J.T. Brown's honking sax, and Odie Payne, Jr.'s, propulsive drumming.[44]

"**Sunny Land**" (1954), the flip side of "Standing at the Crossroads" and another song of contrition, shows how James could utilize emotional vocals with slower, less propulsive music, a combination central to his later hits, "It Hurts Me Too" (1957) and "The Sky is Crying" (1960). "Sunny Land," sometimes called "Sunnyland Train," is a plangent 12-bar blues lament. The lonesome sound of the omnipresent train whistle makes him feel so bad he wants to cry because his baby left on the Sunnyland train this morning. She says she's coming home but he waits and waits. He knows he has to change but is certain she will need him someday. Even with excellent L.A. session players Willard McDaniel on piano and Maxwell Davis on tenor sax, the single repetitive riff sounds clunky, and James's slide is nearly inaudible. Still, I love this song for its vocal attack, James's voice nearly breaking in a soulful cry when he sings about how bad he feels or wails *Yeah*, a sorry affirmation of his wrong choices and their consequences.

Going to Chicago: The Harp Masters

The harmonica has been a mainstay of blues and folk performance since at least the 1920s, when musicians used the inexpensive, portable, easily learned instrument to imitate train whistles and complement the deeper sound of jug bands. **John Lee "Sonny Boy" Williamson** (1914–48) revolutionized the blues harp, sometimes called the Mississippi saxophone because of its versatility and ability to sound like a horn. The Tennessee native moved to Chicago in 1934, began recording for Lester Melrose, and soon became a mainstay of the Bluebird sound. Many of the songs from his first session, especially "Good Morning, School Girl" (1937), became classics, and more followed. (For a special treat listen to Big Mama Thornton's gender-reversed "School Boy" [1965], accompanied only by Mississippi Fred McDowell's slide guitar.) Williamson did for harmonica what T-Bone Walker did for electric guitar: made it an essential blues instrument. At various times his sidemen included Robert Nighthawk, Big Bill Broonzy, and Eddie Boyd. The premier blues musician in Chicago for a decade until his murder in 1948, Williamson inspired a new generation of Chicago blues harp players. These four postwar-era masters all became accomplished accompanists, but they also built outstanding careers leading their own groups.

A fascinating, secretive, chameleon-like character, **Aleck "Rice" Miller** (c.1910–65) wrote some of the most striking blues lyrics of the era and played great amplified harp. In the early 1940s, he had a radio show on Helena's KFFA with guitarist Robert Jr. Lockwood. Titled *King Biscuit Time* after the flour he advertised, his show

Sonny Boy Williamson II (Rice Miller) on harp, center, with Willie Nix (drum) and Robert Jr. Lockwood, Memphis, c. 1950. Pictorial Press Ltd./Alamy Stock Photo.

broadcast live blues across the Delta, Arkansas, and Tennessee. He became so popular that the company named a brand of corn meal after him. An extraordinary showman, he played "with the harmonica in his mouth sideways, like a cigar. Sometimes he played a harmonica that was entirely hidden inside his mouth, smiling a sly, enigmatic smile." After touring England in the 1960s, he performed in a three-piece suit and bowler hat. He was an absolute original except for one thing: the name he took around 1941, Sonny Boy Williamson, already belonged to the great harp player John Lee Williamson, still actively performing and recording. For clarity's sake, critics and blues historians have taken to calling them Sonny Boy Williamson I and II. For this discussion I will refer to Sonny Boy II—Rice Miller—simply by the name he used, **Sonny Boy Williamson**.[45]

At the Trumpet studio in Jackson, where he accompanied Elmore James on "Dust My Broom," Sonny Boy's initial session yielded one of his most lyrically inventive songs, **"Eyesight to the Blind"** (1951). A swinging 12-bar shuffle, the song celebrates his woman who walks as if her daddy were a millionaire, and whose loving brings eyesight to the blind, speech to the deaf and dumb, and resuscitation to a dying man who says the entire state knows how fine she is. Williamson's bluesy harp and Willie Love's piano answer his expressive vocals and adept phrasing on this musically joyful number. This record announces a unique blues talent.

Another Trumpet session later in the year gave rise to two songs I'll always associate with Canada. In the musically rather pedestrian **"Nine Below Zero"** (1951) Sonny Boy sings about being rejected by his woman and thrown out in the cold— colder than Mississippi usually ever gets. I prefer **"Mr. Down Child"** (1951), the song from which Canada's Downchild Blues Band took its name. (Don't mistake this for Sonny Boy's 1963 recording with Eric Clapton's Yardbirds or his remake called "Down Child.") With a livelier band and Sonny Boy's superb harp, the song proffers advice to other men. Watch out, buddy, a woman will tell you she loves you when she doesn't. Just don't let her mistreat you twice. Nothing novel about the sentiment or lyrics except for their specific address to the peculiarly named Mr. Down Child. But what a delightful performance. Joe Willie Wilkins on guitar and bassist Cliff Bivens set up Sonny Boy's rocking harp. He snaps his fingers, launches into falsetto, and loads up before the final instrumental sequence.

Williamson joined the Chess stable in 1955. Chicago made his songs a little more formal, a little less improvisational. But he had the benefit of Chess's premier studio band: Waters, Rogers, Spann, Dixon, and Below. Everything came together on **"Don't Start Me Talkin'"** (1955). He never blew his harp harder or better, and the elite musicians behind him, especially the guitars, give this stop-time shuffle a classic Chicago sound. Sonny Boy's lyrics, unique in the blues, have him playing the part of an ironically self-important observer here, a neighborhood busybody. On his way to Rosie's he stops to tell Fanny Mae what he overheard her boyfriend say. He reports that a married woman met a man downtown who gave her a black eye; then she lied to her husband about it. Possibly the same woman, on her way to the beauty shop (with borrowed money), gets in another man's car and asks him to take her around the block. In the chorus the singer warns that if he starts talking, he'll tell everything he knows because he can't stand the bad behavior and game-playing, the lying, the *signifyin'*. What brilliant, detailed, original, musically addictive storytelling.

At the same session with the same band, Williamson recorded **"Work with Me"** (1955), a dynamite 12-bar blues shuffle with solid backing from Waters and Rogers on guitar. Sonny Boy's wah-wah harp celebrates the joy of sex. Lyrically, this may be the most one-dimensional song he ever wrote, but he finds originality in the conventions. In four verses Sonny Boy repeats his seduction mantra in a peculiar vibrato: his baby, mama, little girl should do it with him because he can satisfy her. He'll teach her how to work with him and he'll work with her, drive her crazy, make her happy. He can work all night, his stamina coming from the training he did as a kid! The year before, Hank Ballard and the Midnighters had released the R&B rocker "Work with Me, Annie," a record that caused a scandal and sold a million copies. Anyone listening to Black music would have known that Sonny Boy was singing about a kind of work way more fun than picking cotton or trucking steel.

Robert Santelli writes of "a long-standing debate in blues circles": was the more accomplished harmonica player **Little Walter Jacobs** (1930–68) or Sonny Boy II? I favor Sonny Boy by a whisker. I prefer his rougher, more countrified sound on both harp and vocals to the slicker, technically brilliant Little Walter. But the consensus goes with Walter, the virtuoso who followed his idol, John Lee Williamson, in revolutionizing blues harp. Santelli explains one of the things that set him apart: "Cupping his hands around both the harp and mike and controlling the amount of air that flowed through the connection made the notes Little Walter blew sound richer and more poignant…."[46]

Born in Louisiana, Walter left home at twelve or thirteen and made his way to Chicago via New Orleans and Helena, where he crossed paths with Sonny Boy II, Robert Jr. Lockwood, and Jimmy Rogers. In addition to the musicians he met and played with, Walter's influences included the records of Sonny Boy I and Louis Jordan's saxophone solos. In Chicago, Rogers introduced him to Muddy Waters. Walter joined Muddy's band, playing harp on some of Muddy's and Rogers' best records. In 1952, Walter recorded a harp instrumental for Chess with the two guitar masters backing him. "Juke" rocketed up the *Billboard* charts to #1, where it stayed for eight weeks. Convinced that he was not just a sideman but a star, Walter left Muddy and formed his own band with guitarist brothers Louis and Dave Myers and drummer Fred Below, christening them The Jukes. They recorded a string of hits on Checker. "With the Myers brothers and Below the sound was much more jazz-based, and so big was the sound of Walter's amplified harp and so revolutionary his phrasing that it seemed at times as if he was blowing a sax."[47] The Myers brothers' previous band, the Aces, had Junior Wells on harp. When Walter left Muddy, Muddy grabbed Junior for his band.

Little Walter and His Night Caps released **"Mean Old World"** (1952) on the B-side of "Sad Hours," Walter's instrumental follow-up to "Juke." The slow 12-bar shuffle had previously been recorded by guitarists Broonzy and T-Bone Walker. Leading with his harp, Little Walter turns the song on its head. With the Myers brothers' guitars reduced to "a simple 'lumpety-lump' bass line ... Walter shows off a sound rarely heard before on amplified harp: he hits a chord, then adds a warble by rapidly moving the harp back and forth over his lips.... The effect is a powerful, plaintive trill that adds greatly to the intensity level."[48] Walter's mournful harp opens the song, his voice picks up the mood, and the harp trills in response to every vocal line. The guitars and Below's drums offer persistent downbeat commentary as does Walter's heartbreakingly beautiful harp solo. The otherwise conventional blues lyrics, addressed to a cold woman who he says doesn't love him, gain an existential dimension by the title phrase: he has a problem not just with a woman but with the world. The singer explicitly tells us what the music says: he has the blues. No doubt about it.

"Blues with a Feeling" (1953), another hit for Little Walter, reached #2. Drummer Rabon Tarrant wrote it and originally recorded it as a jump blues with Jack McVea's band in 1947. Walter turns it into a song in the same vein as "Mean Old World" but without the weary resignation. It feels stronger, more assertive. You can hear it in Walter's aggressive harp solos, his vocal that attacks the lyrics rather than succumbs to them, especially in the stop-time verse, with Jimmy Rogers' guitar accompaniment taking Louis Myers' spot and Dixon's bass added to the mix. Lyrically, he's crying, trying to find his baby who left him. But the second verse transforms that straightforward quest into something once again broader and more profound. Being left all alone is worse than rejection by a woman. That's the blues he's feeling.

More often, Little Walter characteristically sounded upbeat, rhythm & bluesy. On the face of it, **"Tell Me Mama"** (1953) laments. His mama has been boogying without him and she has a boyfriend. The singer insists that she tell him the truth. Who was that guy running out our back door carrying his overcoat and hat when I came home? Once again, Walter transforms an older song, Washboard Sam's "Back Door" (1937). As if going over the scene in his mind, he repeats the image of the backdoor man running past him, except now the guy smells like whiskey and carries *Walter's* overcoat and hat. The ironic lyric, vocal tone, and quick tempo undercut any sense of anger or remorse. Dixon's bass leads the way, racing off like the backdoor man himself. Below's drum clips along with it while Walter's harp and vocals run to catch up. Walter's first harp solo starts with a howl, then goes quiet, as if sneaking up on the guy or questioning his lover more intimately. In the second break the harp is more persistent: C'mon, mama, tell me!

Little Walter's most popular and commercially successful song, and one of his most mellow, **"My Babe"** (1955) charted for nineteen weeks and stayed at #1 for five. After the Myers brothers left the band, Walter brought in Robert Jr. Lockwood on guitar. Willie Dixon jazzed up the melody of the spiritual "This Train" and changed the lyrics. Instead of this train bound for glory, the singer celebrates the glory of this woman, his babe. Tough and principled, she puts up with no cheating or fooling from him, and stays true. "From the opening drum hit and walking bass guitar line ... Walter sings with energy and conviction, and his lively, swinging two-chorus harp solo is a nice controlled power surge."[49] A great talent, Little Walter burned out young, dying in a fight at age 37.

As much a prodigy as Little Walter, Amos Wells Blakemore, Jr., aka **Junior Wells** (1934–98), was only 18 and had not yet recorded when he and 22-year-old Walter switched places in 1952. Born in Memphis, Junior arrived in Chicago as an adolescent. When the precocious kid got a little older, he challenged his idols, especially Walter, in Chicago's blues clubs. At 16, he was playing harp in The Aces. Junior had a couple of sessions backing Muddy and one with Floyd Jones before recording his own records in 1953. He became a regular on Chicago's blues A-list for the next four decades, and a certified star after finding superb chemistry with Buddy Guy in the 1960s. If I had to rank my favorites among the blues harp masters of this era, I would put Junior Wells first. Though not as accomplished a harmonica player as Sonny Boy or Walter, Junior had easily the most expressive, adventurous voice of them all, often adding a little laugh as if he were just having a ball. Add his always enthusiastic, full-throated, and contagious harp attack. And "his timing was incredible. His rhythm was so ingrained that he was often mistaken for James Brown's brother."[50]

Anticipating his later recordings with guitar greats Earl Hooker and Buddy Guy, Junior fortunately had the best guitarists in the city behind him on his sessions for Chicago's States label. Junior re-recorded most of these songs in later years but would never reproduce the raw early-'50s blues that he sang and played here. For his first release, **"Cut That Out"** (1953), Junior re-made a song by Bill Broonzy ("You Better Cut That Out," 1940), also recorded by Sonny Boy I. The Aces rejoined him on guitar, bass guitar, and drums, plus Johnny Jones on piano, producing a supremely rollicking sound. Broonzy and Sonny Boy sing this to another man. A misbehaving woman hears Junior's admonition. He warns her to cut it out—stop getting drunk because it makes her fuss and fight—and stop cheating on him, too. *YEAH*, she'd better follow his advice *be–FORE* it's too late. He tries various gambits in the stop-time vocal to get her to change her ways, the tone always neutralizing anything resembling a threat. Musically, the up-tempo number suggests a party. Junior's lengthy harp solo, emphasizing the high notes, sounds celebratory. This first recording absolutely requires a second listen.

That same first session produced **"Hoodoo Man"** (1953), a 1947 Sonny Boy I original, its punchline taken from a Louis Jordan song, "Somebody Done Hoodooed the Hoodoo Man" (1940). When Junior re-recorded it in 1965 as "Hoodoo Man Blues" on the album of that title, the song became his signature. The 1953 version appeared on the States label misspelled as "Hodo Man" and attributed to Junior Wells and his Eagle Rockers, the same band that played on "Cut That Out" (flip side: "Eagle Rock") with Elmore James replacing Louis Myers on guitar. In this lyrically and musically superb performance, Fred Below's drum pounds out the slow, almost lazy downbeat shuffle rhythm as Junior tries to make his woman understand how he feels about her cheating. He even went to Louisiana to get a mojo hand (shades of Muddy Waters) that might give him the power to end her infidelity. But in the chorus, his friends keep telling little Junior that his unfaithful woman has out-hoodooed the hoodoo man. In the final verse, deep blues and hoodoo meet in the big city. Instead of coming home to find another man going out his back door, Junior buzzes the elevator to take him to her third-floor apartment, but she somehow delays it—probably long enough to give her backdoor man time to get down the back stairs. Blues poetry replaces the clichéd cheating-woman complaint. Musically sublime, Elmore's biting slide and Junior's harp take turns responding to his vocals and filling the break. The harp howls with melancholy, the sound of a man confused, defeated, and seriously out-hoodooed.

Louis Myers and Below along with Muddy Waters, Otis Spann, and Willie Dixon, another dream band, backed Junior at his next session. Junior's' **"'Bout the Break of Day"** (1954) makes significant changes to Sonny Boy's 1937 "Early in the Morning." The first verse suggests something lascivious as Junior introduces an 18-year-old girl who considers herself grown up. (Sonny Boy's girl was 12!) The final three verses revert to the misbehaving woman and hard-done-by guy formula. She does him wrong and drives him to drink. The final insult: she boogies without him in the juke joint. In the chorus he asks her to come to him at the break of day, then laments that he holds an empty pillow. The tight band opens with Spann's piano, quickly joined by the guitars and harp. Junior's timbre and phrasing, more interesting than ever, underline the singer's strength and resilience even as he worries key words (*wi-i-i-ne, ea-ea-ea-rly*). He introduces his thrilling harp solo by calling out, "Let's go down South, man," recalling Muddy's "I Can't Be Satisfied." Whether retreating from the pain and frustration of life in the Northern city to return to his first home, or embracing the song's Southern roots, it reminds us of the synthesis of Black cultures that produced the brilliance of Chicago blues.

The fourth postwar harp master, Mississippian **James Cotton** (1935–2017) learned the instrument from Sonny Boy Williamson II in Helena, played in Howlin' Wolf's West Memphis band, recorded his own songs in Memphis, then moved to Chicago to join Muddy Waters' band after both Walter and Junior had left. Cotton wrote and sang **"Cotton Crop Blues"** (1954) but, unusually, doesn't play harp on the Sun Records release. It vividly describes the sharecropper's lot and explains why Mississippi cotton fields held so little promise for African Americans. In the three verses of this 12-bar blues complaint the singer insists that he will no longer gamble on raising cotton, a crapshoot. He works all summer, then finds the price too low come fall. The poor farmer breaks his back plowing and has nothing to show for it in the end. Cotton sings with weary resignation while John Bowers' drum beats out a death march. But Pat Hare's violent, distorted guitar highlights this record. He plays "intense and climactic fills around Cotton's vocal before exploding into a solo of extraordinary violence and passion."[51] An entire history and culture, rooted in the blood and sweat of Mississippi's cotton fields, can be heard in that blues explosion.

Ladies Sing the (Rhythm &) Blues

Despite the great female singers who defined the Classic Blues of the 1920s, and the many women who sang with swing orchestras in the prewar years, men overwhelmingly dominated the postwar era. *Blues* became a label attached primarily to artists who sang and played an instrument. With the exceptions of Memphis Minnie and Big Mama Thornton, that combination was rare among blueswomen of the postwar decade. In contrast, the big rhythm & blues tent had no trouble accommodating male and female artists who sang without playing. Blues and rhythm & blues consistently overlap. All the female blues singers of the postwar era could conceivably come under the rhythm & blues rubric because so much of their notable pre–1957 output leans towards R&B. In the end I decided against moving them to that chapter, not just to avoid the impression that every postwar blues artist except Memphis Minnie was male, but also because these women truly sang the blues.

While Minnie was ending her distinguished career when she recorded in Chicago at mid-century, these four women were just establishing themselves. All four sang in church as youngsters, mixing gospel into their blues and utilizing the guttural vocalisms that became a hallmark of hard gospel in the postwar years. Contrary to the concentration of postwar male blues in Chicago, only one of these women—Etta James—migrated there, and then only in 1960 when she began recording for Chess. Big Mama toured Europe with Muddy Waters and other Chicago bluesmen in the 1960s. But in the postwar decade these women came from or headed to Los Angeles, Houston, New Jersey, and New York to make records for companies that wanted to turn them into rhythm & blueswomen.

Alabama-born Willie Mae **Big Mama Thornton** (1926–84) left home at fourteen, toured with the Hot Harlem Revue, then moved to Houston where she was signed by Don Robey, the Black owner of Peacock Records who, according to his own assistant, "didn't know a record from a hubcap." Though Thornton also played harmonica and drums, Robey never let her record with them: "All they wanted was for me to just sing," she complained.[52] To Robey's credit he recognized her vocal talent and sent her to producer Johnny Otis, who asked a young L.A. songwriting team, Jerry Leiber and Mike Stoller, to come up with something for big-voiced Thornton. Their **"Hound Dog"** (1952) became a huge hit for Big Mama, spending seven weeks at #1 R&B, and an even bigger hit for Elvis Presley in 1956. After "Hound Dog," Thornton toured with Otis' band, making an outstanding debut at Harlem's Apollo Theater, the ultimate testing ground for Black entertainers.

Presley's version of "Hound Dog" makes little sense. The 12-bar blues conjures an angry woman verbally whipping her no-good man, vociferously countering those male blues complaints about misbehaving women. In the three choruses she calls him a hound dog, tells him to stop sniffing around her door, and in a wonderful sexual metaphor insists he stop wagging his tail because she's not feeding him anymore. In the verses she tells him she can see through his high-class pose, accuses him of making her miserable, and hits him with another put-down: you don't want a real woman, just a home. She has his number.[53]

"Hound Dog" introduces a great female blues shouter. "I don't sing like nobody but myself," Big Mama told an interviewer, and you can hear it in this song. She growls the first words, *Y-o-o-o a-y-y-y-nt*, letting us know we're in the presence of a formidable woman firmly in control, completely at home in her own skin. She shouts the lyrics as if trying to shoo away a hound who just won't go, and outgrowls him at every turn. She even howls a little during the instrumental break while kibitzing with the guitar player. Maureen Mahon calls Thornton's performance "sassy and subversive," bringing "the blues tradition of outspoken women into the rhythm and blues context, putting sexuality and play with gender expectations in the foreground." *Cash Box* described it this way: "The tune is a rhythmic Latin tempo middle beat and the thrush belts it dramatically and expressively. Easy when she should be easy and driving when she has to bang it home. The rhythmic handclapping has just enough of the spiritual feel to stir up the emotions and raise the blood pressure."[54] Thornton's musicians, including Pete Lewis on guitar, deliver the handclapping and barking. Bassman Mario Delgarde provides the funky Latin rhythm. The label calls them Kansas City Bill & Orch—actually Johnny Otis' band, named for his drummer, Leard "Kansas City" Bell. Otis, contracted to another label, had to fudge it. He took the drums himself when Bell couldn't get the time right. A great performance of a supremely witty song.

Big Mama had not only a big voice but a big body. She unabashedly celebrates her size and sexual attractiveness in **"They Call Me Big Mama"** (1953), credited to Thornton and Robey. The blues aesthetic has long appreciated female fleshliness. Male blues singers long for "a big legged woman" or "a heavy hipped woman." A trope from Tommy Johnson's oft-covered "Big Fat Mama Blues" (1929) appears in many subsequent blues songs: whenever a fat mama shakes the meat on her bones, a skinny woman loses her home. Louis Jordan recorded "I Like 'Em Fat Like That" (1944) and Roy Milton joyously celebrates the **"Big Fat Mama"** (1947) he desires. Women's blues and R&B don't feature many big fat papas, Dinah Washington's **"Fat Daddy"** (1953) an exception. Fats Domino in **"The Fat Man"** (1950) and Big John Greer in **"I'm the Fat Man"** (1952) celebrate their own seductive bulk. In Thornton's song they call her Big Mama because she weighs 300 pounds. She knows just what to do with that body to rock and roll him— that phrase repeated six times. This time the label calls her band Kansas City Bell. The horns and drums drive the song, rocking and rolling with an extended honking tenor sax solo from James Von Streeter. Great rhythm & blues.

But Big Mama shows herself a blueswoman at heart on one of her best early records, **"Every Time I**

Willie Mae "Big Mama" Thornton with her Hohner Marine Band harmonica, mid to late 1950s. Hohner publicity photograph. Pictorial Press Ltd./Alamy Stock Photo

Think of You" (1952), recorded in Houston. With a persona in this lyrically conventional lover's complaint the opposite of the Big Mama we've heard so far, the wronged woman sings a catalogue of woes and begs her man to return. All day she thinks about him and cries, all night she's sleepless and in pain. She will forgive him if he comes back because she loves him so. Big Mama's plaintive vocal in this slow blues retains some of the shouting quality that would dominate her later, more upbeat records. You can hear it in the *We-e-ell* she tacks onto the beginning of a line. The horn-heavy Joe Scott Orchestra, Peacock's house band, accompanies her with Bill Harvey blowing a beautifully melancholy tenor sax solo. The arrangement has a few nice touches, including a stop-time opening and a pleading last line where she worries the words *please, please*—an abjection that seems entirely out of character for the Big Mama who would sing "Hound Dog." She returned to the inconsolable lover theme in 1968 when she wrote, and Janis Joplin heard her sing, "Ball and Chain."

Faye Adams (1923–2016?), born Fanny Tuell in Newark, grew up singing gospel before going secular. Bandleader Joe Morris renamed her and signed her to New Jersey's Herald Records. With Morris writing her songs and his orchestra behind her, Adams had three #1 records in 1953–54. Her first and best, **"Shake a Hand"** (1953), stayed atop *Billboard*'s Rhythm & Blues chart for ten weeks and crossed over to #22 Pop. This rich gospel-tinged recording has the rare synergy that comes from an ideal combination of singer, song, and orchestration. The band sets an almost funereal tempo with a slow, gospel-style piano leading the way. The horns come in later to raise the emotional temperature.

With her precise diction and deep, soulful, tearful voice, Adams tries to preserve a relationship: Leave things to me, I'll share your troubles and take care of everything. Let's be truthful to each other, my love. Near the end things take a turn: I don't know what to do, she sings, we should go our separate ways. Just remember to pray every day and shake a hand. The choruses repeat the title phrase twelve times, the musicians singing in harmony with Adams. "A common greeting among followers of spiritual and gospel music," *Billboard* explained, the phrase "shake a hand" expressed faith and fellowship. Peter Guralnick considers the song one of the most important of the era because its fervent emotional approach "muddied the distinctions—stylistic, harmonic, and lyrical—between gospel and r&b," anticipating soul.[55] Tina Turner recorded a great funked-up soul version in 1985.

Another big, fabulous, soulful blues/R&B singer with a huge voice, Mabel **Big Maybelle** Smith (1924–72) has been largely forgotten. She grew up in Memphis, touring the South with swing bands in the 1930s. In the '40s she sang with Tiny Bradshaw and Jimmy Witherspoon (we'll meet them both in Chapter Two). Her career blossomed when a producer gave her the stage name Big Maybelle and brought her to New York to record for Columbia's rhythm & blues label, Okeh, with some of the best session men in the city. Lillian Leach, lead singer of New York doo wop group

The Mellows, recalls seeing Maybelle perform in a Bronx club: "She really shook the house. She'd stand up on top of the bar and dance barefoot. She was really exciting. And that voice! That was a thrill." Another fan, Aretha Franklin, called Maybelle "one of the baddest singers ever."[56]

Maybelle's own composition, **"Maybelle's Blues"** (1953), "a slow blues grind with strong gospel undertones," makes an excellent introduction to "the voice that loosened the putty on church windows."[57] A blues shouter extraordinaire, she shouts, growls, and takes her voice down to the bottom as she sings this abandoned lover's lament with a surprise ending. He left her at midnight and she can't sleep, tossing and weeping in her misery. Speechless with grief, she cries and moans, *Oh oh-oh-oh-oh*. She'll die without him. Leroy Kirkland's band, with three horns and Brownie McGhee on guitar, gives the record an old-fashioned sound. Without an instrumental break, Sam "The Man" Taylor on tenor sax gets only a few bars to strut his stuff. The song works because of Maybelle's powerful vocal and the turnabout in the final verse. Spoiler alert! After flagellating herself over the guy, she suddenly changes tactics, playing the sexy size card: your other woman don't have big legs like mine. With her mojo back, she goes on the attack. Shame on you, she sings, shouting *HEY!* as in "Hey, asshole!" Do not trifle with this woman.

On the blues ballad **"No More Trouble Out of Me"** (1954) Maybelle works with an Okeh eight-piece band including trumpet and three saxes. A slow, dull drumbeat marks the time and the big horn section makes the record sound ten years out of date, though it provides strong crescendos when Maybelle raises the stakes. Only the addition of Mickey Baker's ringing guitar drags the orchestration forward into the 1950s. The singer admits her faithlessness. Daddy, she vows, things are different now. She promises to give him no more trouble. She has learned her lesson and prays every night that he'll give her another chance. But Maybelle's vocal blows the lyric to pieces. Quietly repentant in the first stanza, she starts growling a few words, adding exclamations in the second. By the chorus she's shouting *and* growling, and offering an ironic, defiant laugh at the end of each of the lines assuring him that she prays every night. By the final stanza she sounds like her old self. Dominant "daddy" becomes subordinate "baby," and she works key words (*I-I-I; more—more—more*) as if to say, I have done more than enough groveling. Now it's time for *self*-affirmation. Literally yelling the title phrase in the final line, she no longer sounds repentant. She sounds like she's out of there.

"One Monkey Don't Stop No Show" (1954) reveals Big Maybelle in full R&B shouter mode. Putting shrinking violet Maybelle behind her, she sounds ironic, confident, dominant. She also boasts her best band yet: seven pieces (no trumpet) including tenor saxman Sam "The Man" Taylor, Mickey Baker on guitar, fine session pianist Ernie Hayes, and drummer Panama Francis. The band's almost vaudevillian intro finds Maybelle using a curious little slurred voice to tell her story. Her man gets out of bed and tells her he's leaving. I can't make you stay, she says, but you should know something. She then blasts into the chorus and the title line. An old blues expression, it has a clear meaning here: the monkey is him, the show hers. He leaves at three a.m. By four she has herself another man. A woman who has learned from experience, she advises other women: don't be chicken-hearted when a man who has gotten too big for his pants walks out the door, because you can always find another to take his place. Try it yourself, she suggests, then tell me I was right. The drunken little girl voice Maybelle uses in the verses sets up her ferociously shouted guttural choruses. Sam the Man gets to blow his fine sax, and Maybelle the Woman takes no crap.

One of the world's truly great blues and soul ballad divas for more than a half-century, **Etta James** (1938–2012) starred in R&B before that. Born Jamesetta Hawkins in Los Angeles, she became the protégée of L.A. rhythm & bluesman-of-all-trades Johnny Otis. He dubbed her Miss Peaches (she sang with a female trio called The Peaches), then Etta James. Her first record, produced by Otis, rocketed to the top of *Billboard*'s R&B charts, #1 for four weeks, when she was just fifteen. Her song answered "Work with Me, Annie" by Hank Ballard and the Midnighters, which had become a huge hit and *success de scandale* the year before. One of the most sexually explicit records of the 1950s, "Annie" made no attempt to hide what Ballard meant by *work*. Its popularity generated multiple sequels, from "Annie's Aunt Fanny" to "I'm the Father of Annie's Baby." Etta James's "pushy little jiveass reply to Hank," as she called it in her autobiography, was the best of them. Modern Records originally titled it "Roll with Me, Henry," but released it as **"The Wallflower"** (1955).[58]

Oh, those dirty words again: work, rock, roll. "Roll with Me Henry" / "The Wallflower" uses the same melody as "Work with Me, Annie" and clearly appropriates that song's male propositioning for a woman. Even though *roll* was as sexually coded as *work*, Modern hoped to get itself a hit and avoid the condemnation "Annie" faced by presenting "Henry" as a song about dancing. So far so good until Georgia Gibbs's whitewashed cover, "Dance with Me, Henry," which literally replaced all the rolling with dancing, steamrolled James's version off the pop charts.

"The Wallflower" denotes a partner who won't dance. She keeps demanding that he *roll* with her. She mentions ballin' cats, which may suggest a band at a dance—or pussy cats having sex (kidding). She refers to a boogie beat and his leaden feet, and says he needs to learn to dance. But she also repeats the phrase *roll with me* 21 times, *roll on* 14 times, and I lost track of how often the two other Peaches, backing her, sing *roll, roll, roll*. The man who answers sounds more like an eager lover than a wallflower. Richard Berry (composer of "Louie, Louie"), with what James called "that down-in-the-hole bass of his," sings call-and-response with her, answering all her demands in the affirmative. Berry also plays seductive boogie woogie piano with Otis on drums banging out a rock 'n' roll beat, and Maxwell Davis blowing brilliant tenor sax. First, Berry asks what he has to do to make her love him, then Etta tears in, "her fifteen-year-old voice gritty with experience beyond her years."[59] During her final "roll with me" riffs, she lets out a breathy squeal, "Oh, Oh, Henry!" And she doesn't mean the candy bar, Hank.

James followed "The Wallflower" with **"Good Rockin' Daddy"** (1955), a similar song more explicitly about dancing, though the rollin' and boogyin' she does with her good rockin' daddy must certainly be heard both ways. In a better song, **"Tough

Lover" (1956), a high velocity, unabashed Little Richard tribute, James eerily imitates his voice, his *yeah yeah* and *whooo*, and shows off her rock 'n' roll chops. Davis' rockin' sax break highlights both records. A few years later, Etta James headed for Chicago where Chess turned her in an entirely different musical direction. In 1960–62 she recorded a series of genius soul ballads and blues: "All I Could Do Was Cry," "At Last," "Trust in Me," "Fool That I Am," "A Sunday Kind of Love," "Stop the Wedding." Using her vocal strength and texture, and the lessons she learned singing about those tough lovin', rockin' and rollin' men, she transformed these lyrically more traditional subordinate-woman songs into anthems of female strength and soul-blues ambivalence.

Don't Forget the Motor City

Another original from deep in the Delta, **John Lee Hooker** (c. 1917–2001) had a sound as distinctive as any in the blues. Like Sonny Boy Williamson II, he mythologized his past, changed his date of birth when it suited him, and like both Sonny Boy and Lightnin' Hopkins, he recorded under a variety of pseudonyms for a multitude of labels. Like Wolf and Muddy, Hooker excavated the roots of the Delta blues and brought them North where he combined a primitive sound with modern amplification techniques and rhythms to create a unique hybrid. You can't mistake Hooker on record for anyone else. On guitar he often utilized a single chord. His expressive vocals had an extremely limited range. His eccentric timing and phrasing complemented his improvisational approach to blues recording. For Hooker, "no 'song' was ever actually completed.... Each piece was a platform for improvisation, a loose framework of lyrical and instrumental motifs into which he poured the emotions of the moment."[60] After kicking around Memphis and Cincinnati, Hooker landed in Detroit unlike most of his Chicago-bound Mississippi blues peers. He worked at Ford Motors and a steel mill until producer Bernard Besman began recording him in 1948, leasing the songs to Modern Records. Hooker would spend the next half-century as one of the world's most famous bluesmen.

John Lee Hooker, Chess Records publicity photograph early 1950s. Pictorial Press Ltd./Alamy Stock Photo.

Like many of our other artists, his first session delivered breakthrough results. More than 75 years later, **"Boogie Chillen"** (1948) remains a revelation. I don't know anything like it. John Milward calls it "a mesmerizing performance that nailed the gritty ruminative style that would become his musical signature ... the insistent beat conjur[ing] a kind of urbane Delta trance." Hooker's biographer, Charles Shaar Murray, describes it as having "the pared-down eloquence of a Delta haiku." It scored #1 R&B, stayed on the chart for 18 weeks in 1949, and had a powerful influence on aspiring bluesmen B.B. King, 12-year-old Bo Diddley, and 13-year-old Buddy Guy.[61] Recorded solo with an amplified acoustic guitar, a speaker and second mike in a toilet bowl to create echo, and a wooden plank that Hooker foot-stomped for added rhythm, "Boogie Chillen" opens with a compelling boogie-woogie pattern. Hooker's guitar does most of the talking: two of the song's three minutes are instrumental with little variation from its single hypnotic, droning riff.

In the mostly spoken vocal Hooker tells a vivid Proustian story, a semi-autobiographical Remembrance of Things Past, beginning with a flashback to nascent adolescent rebellion. Because his mother didn't allow him to stay out all night ("O Lord!"), he boogied in the house. In the second verse he arrives in Detroit and heads down Hastings Street, where he checks out the Henry Swing Club. People are dancing, having a ball—exactly what he wanted to do when he was a child. Projecting onto them, he excitedly calls out, "boogie chillen!" The flashback final verse finds him home again in his Mississippi bed, where he overhears his father tell his mother to let him boogie because what's in him will surely come out. It felt *so* good, he sings. In real time Hooker left home at about fourteen and came to Detroit in his mid-thirties, five years before he made the record. Chronological sophistication, psychological depth, and complex family dynamics create a rich thematic panorama with an irresistible boogie rhythm.

"Hobo Blues" (1949) has the most primitive sound Hooker ever attained on record and some of his bleakest existential lyrics. More a field holler than a structured song, it lacks verses and rhymes. Hooker plays guitar with a few more variations than on "Boogie Chillen" but a single droning riff drives the song again. The lyric consists of six sentences sung in a desolate voice, each followed by a cry and/or moan: *oh lord, mmmm*. The narrative: I hobo'd on freight trains, traveled far from home, left my old mother crying. Hopping a freight, "riding the blinds" to get from one place to another, was common among bluesmen in the South: fast, efficient, free transportation, though dangerous. But nothing here suggests movement as escape or freedom. This lonely kid treats a freight train as if it were a rare friend. Hoboing a long way from home but not reaching any destination, his experience recalls the "poor boy long ways from home" blues trope. Half the lyrics concern his mother's grief at his leaving. "He's gone," she wails five times in one sentence. If "Hobo Blues" were autobiographical, it would be a prequel to "Boogie Chillen," a dark night of the soul between his feel-good memories of childhood and the thrilling revelations of Detroit.

The amazing **"Burnin' Hell"** (1949) marked yet another direction for Hooker. Neither innocent child, excited big-city newbie, nor desolate solitary drifter, he presents himself here as a defiant nay-sayer, a rebel against the powerful communal force of doctrinaire Christianity. Murray calls the song "a devastating repudiation of

Christian notions of the afterlife." Don't confuse it with Hooker's 1959 re-recording on his album of the same title, or his very good 1970 version with Canned Heat. The relentless sound of this record reminds me of the Baby Face Leroy Trio's "Rollin' and Tumblin'" or Howlin' Wolf's roaring otherworldly songs. With Eddie Burns, another of Detroit's Mississippi expats, aggressively reinforcing the beat on harp and alternating instrumental breaks with Hooker's surprisingly ringing guitar, Hooker pounds out a single chord at twice the tempo of his other songs. He wastes no time declaring his apostasy: Everyone talks about burning hell but there's no such thing; no one knows where you go when you die. His mama and papa appear again, telling him to go to church and ask Deacon Jones to pray for him. When the deacon does, Adam Gussow observes, "words cease and the guitar and harp ride along for the next eighteen seconds. The ritual space of fervent evangelical prayer has been reclaimed by, supplanted by, the rowdiest of blues dance grooves."[62] The singer gets off his knees even more adamant. He reiterates his rejection of an afterlife and vows to pray no more.

This extreme example of blues as *the devil's music* argues, ironically, for the fictional nature of the devil's reputed home. Other blues songs take skeptical positions on religion but none so ferociously. Often, the blues singer tries to pray but women and whiskey get in his way. This differs from those blues and also from the carpe diem rhythm & blues songs discussed in the next chapter that *assume* that this world is all we have. Hooker tests his faith in an afterlife and explicitly rejects it. Deacon Jones, a generic Black clergyman, appears in numerous R&B songs. Often satirized as "a womanizing, dice-throwing, closet drunk," he represents the religious doctrine that "Burnin' Hell" rejects.[63] Bernie Besman chose not to release this Hooker song on Modern Records.

Hooker's originality shows on the songs he recorded but didn't write. He made them uniquely Hookeresque. Both his **"Queen Bee"** (1951) and **"Sugar Mama"** (1952) had long blues pedigrees. Tampa Red and Sonny Boy Williamson I recorded "Sugar Mama" in the mid–1930s, followed a few years later by Peetie Wheatstraw and Tommy McClennan. In every male singer's version, sugar stands metaphorically for female sexuality, the sweet love she brings him. Sugar as metaphor for *male* sexuality appears earlier in songs by Ma Rainey and Bessie Smith, notably Smith's "Need a Little Sugar in My Bowl." Hooker sticks to "Sugar Mama's" original lyrics in the first and last verse but takes liberties with the rest. He sings slowly with a strong beat amplified by his stomping foot and shows off some fancy licks on his electric guitar that we haven't heard before, as if he wants to impress mama so she'll be sure to bring him that sugar.

"Queen Bee" also has a compelling history. First recorded as "Bumble Bee" by Memphis Minnie in 1930, the song proved so popular that Minnie recorded four more versions the same year and bluesman Amos Easton took the stage name Bumble Bee Slim. In Minnie's versions the male bee sexually satisfies her with his stinger all day long. Hooker turns the male bumble bee into a female queen bee and sings three of Minnie's verses from her first release at a slow but jaunty, sultry, foot-stomping pace, punctuated by long moans of desire or satisfaction. He asks the queen bee to please come back to him because her stinger is the best, and when she stung him that morning she got him to "the place." *Mmmmmm*. The gender reversal makes sense in a blues context. Stephen Galt's *Barrelhouse Words* defines the term *stingaree* as "an unlikely but not uncommon blues or barrelhouse term for *pussy*." Hooker avoids stingaree but takes from Minnie the most outrageous image in her song and attributes it to his queen bee: "stinger long as my right arm." Sung about a male, this may be a woman's complimentary phallic exaggeration. Sung by a man about his female lover, it makes no sense at all. But what a great metaphor.[64]

Blues in New Orleans

A long-time jazz town, New Orleans at mid-century became a pretty jumpin' rhythm & blues town. But despite the relative proximity of the Mississippi Delta, straight-up blues was more of a rarity with notable exceptions like Mississippi-born guitarist Eddie Jones, aka **Guitar Slim** (1926–59). Another bluesman who flamed brightly and burnt out much too soon, he moved to New Orleans in the late 1940s and quickly developed a reputation as a showman. With his 300-foot-long amp cord, he would start playing in the street outside the club, then appear in the doorway riding on the shoulders of a huge assistant. Dressed in a bright red, blue, or purple suit with matching shoes and hair dyed the same color, he hit the stage running. Buddy Guy recalls, "Guitar Slim never sat down. He played his guitar between his legs, played it behind his back, played it jumping off the stage, played it hanging from the rafters." Fellow guitarist Earl King testified, "No one could outperform Slim. He was about the performinest man I've ever seen." He played, according to Robert Palmer, in an "almost frighteningly intense version of the T-Bone Walker style and an individual way of wresting screaming high-note sustains from his overworked amplifier." And he sang "the way sanctified preachers preached—groaning, screaming, torturing almost every syllable…."[65]

Slim made some unremarkable records for the Imperial and Bullet labels in the early 1950s. But his first session in New Orleans for Specialty Records proved explosive. Ray Charles, on piano, arranged Slim's self-penned **"The Things That I Used to Do"** (1953). It spent fourteen weeks at #1, became the best-selling R&B record of 1954, and an instant blues classic. This slow, methodical 12-bar blues talks about giving up on his baby. He will stop begging her to stay and searching for her all night. To end this unbearable disruption to his life he'll send her back to her mother and retreat to his own family. The pain in his soulful vocal gives the title line an existential weight common to many of the best blues. Slim claimed the devil gave him the lyrics in a dream, and the song almost feels otherworldly. Somehow, he's not just singing about the things he used to do concerning her but as if *nothing* he can do now will be the same: Lord, he just won't do those things no more. Charles's arrangement, with three saxes and a trumpet, gives the song a modern R&B sound. And what Santelli calls Slim's "slithering" single-string guitar work, with both treble and volume cranked up to create his signature distorted sound, joins with his pained vocal to form a brilliant hybrid Mississippi/New Orleans deep blues.[66]

At that same session Slim recorded another devastating tune, **"The Story of My**

Life" (1953), a slow-burning, agonized blues featuring his searing guitar in a spectacular solo. Slim makes explicit in this song the sense of general emptiness and loss implicit in "The Things That I Used to Do"—though "The Story of My Life" assuredly does not tell the story of Slim's life. Unlike the song's persona, Eddie Jones was not born in Alabama or raised in Tennessee (a reminder that a first-person blues may not necessarily be confessional, but sung from the perspective of a *character*). Anyway, in this very sad story a dead mother and absent father equal loneliness and misery. Wherever he goes, people try to hurt him. His life is hell. He'd rather be dead. Slim digs deep into his gospel roots and sings with a conviction that keeps the lyrical content from becoming morbid. He opens with a long moan, seconded by the horns and Charles's piano, then launches into his prayerful vocal, interjecting the word *Lord* six times. His guitar responds to each line as if crying over his fate, while the horns and bass play mournful fills. In the exquisite solo you can hear future echoes of Buddy Guy, Jimi Hendrix, and especially Stevie Ray Vaughan in this blues guitar god of New Orleans.

Beale Street Blues

Many blues artists who eventually made their way north stopped temporarily in Memphis, the closest big city to the Mississippi Delta, a Southern crossroads where Arkansas, Mississippi, and Tennessee converge. As early as 1912, W.C. Handy had written "Memphis Blues," and the city remains a blues mecca. Beale Street—once called Black America's Main Street—was the center of blues life and performance in Memphis. "Beale Street was heaven to the black man," said Memphis funkmaster Rufus Thomas. "I told a white fella on Beale Street one night, I said, 'If you were black for one Saturday night on Beale Street, you never would wanna be white anymore.'"[67] Riley **B.B. King** (1925–2015) landed there when he left the Mississippi Delta.

B.B. King is the best known of all blues singers—even better known than Muddy Waters because his career stretched well into the twenty-first century and his blues became more modern and mainstream: "Where Waters' blues was jagged and fierce," Santelli writes, "King's was smooth and soulful. Waters kept the raw, primitive strains of his Mississippi Delta roots out front in his music. King kept his under the weight of his band."[68] King recorded prolifically and toured exhaustively: 200–300 days a year with his B.B. King Orchestra for over four decades. A wonderful singer and spectacular guitarist, King also had a personable, relaxed demeanor that made him a popular ambassador of the blues. He first played and sang with a gospel group in the Delta and developed his single-string blues technique emulating T-Bone Walker. In 1946, King left his job driving tractor on a Mississippi plantation to live off his music in Memphis, where Sonny Boy Williamson II got him his first gigs.

Sonny Boy had a radio show on West Memphis station KWEM advertising Hadacol health tonic. When King pitched himself to Memphis' WDIA, they hired him to advertise rival Pepticon tonic. He played, sang live, pushed Pepticon, and spun blues, rhythm & blues, and pop records. He also joined the local Black musicians who plied the Beale Street strip. Soon Riley King became the Beale Street Blues Boy, then Blues Boy King, then just B.B. By 1951, he had his own radio shows, *Sepia Swing Club* and *Bee Bee's Jeebies*. He also played in the Beale Streeters band that variously included Johnny Ace, Bobby Bland, Junior Parker, Roscoe Gordon, and Willie Nix, who would all attain some musical success. King made a couple of records for Sam Phillips that went nowhere. But the Bihari brothers hit pay dirt with him at a 1951 session for their Modern Records subsidiary, RPM. (All the songs below appeared on RPM.) It yielded King's first hit, "Three O'Clock Blues," which spent five weeks at #1. In 1952, a booking agency sent him on the road with a thirteen-piece band for the first of his many long odysseys touring chitlin' circuit clubs and theaters across the country, the start of a sterling sixty-year-long career.[69]

Horns—soon to be a trademark—and Ike Turner's piano backed King's vocal and stellar single-string guitar work on **"Three O'Clock Blues"** (1951), his take on Lowell Fulson's 1948 hit. He sings soulfully and urgently in his dynamic tenor as the trumpet and saxes blow a mournful sound. King practically cries in despair at finding his woman gone. But at the same time—the beautiful paradox of the blues—he never really appears beaten down. So miserable he may consider suicide, he nevertheless makes a joke of it. During the instrumental break you can hear him shout— to himself, his bandmates, or his guitar. He named his guitar Lucille and she would be truer to him than any woman. The song ends with the singer saying goodbye to the world, but King doesn't ask God for forgiveness the way Fulson does; he urges us to tell his *baby* to forgive him for his sins. Despite his gospel roots, King's repertoire proved intensely secular throughout his career, often concerning women who let him down.

The self-penned **"My Own Fault, Darlin'"** (1952) represents a rare exception in the B.B. King canon: a song in which he takes full responsibility for the failure of a relationship. King's most recent biographer, Daniel de Visé, calls it "a muddle of regret, anger, and self-blame." The repentant lover admits it's his fault she treats him badly,

B.B. King, promotional photograph for his radio show *Sepia Swing Club* on WDIA, Memphis, c. 1948. Pictorial Press Ltd./Alamy Stock Photo.

because when she loved him he didn't love her back. She would bring her pay home to him but he just went out and cheated. Now she runs around with other guys and he's on his knees, promising to do better but admitting he still doesn't know why he acted that way. Simpler orchestration accompanies King's crying, pleading falsetto: a piano, vibraphone, and rhythm section but no muscular horns. He plays his aching guitar solo more gently, lighter on the strings, emphasizing the high end of the scale (de Visé hears "a ringing vibrato that channeled all the anger and pain of broken love").[70] It seems that a broken heart is just the way of the blues world.

King also wrote **"You Upset Me, Baby"** (1954), celebrating a special woman. It spent twelve weeks on the *Billboard* charts, two at #1. The earlier records had established King as a virtuoso blues guitarist. This record, de Visé argues, "seems to mark the emergence of his unique voice as a blues stylist."[71] The Bihari brothers had brought King to their Los Angeles studio where Maxwell Davis did the arrangement. The horn section returns in this stop-time shuffle, helping B.B. proclaim his appreciation for a woman so overwhelming that her presence hits him like a falling tree. At one point he says he can't even describe her, but most of the song does just that. He rattles off her voluptuous measurements, cites her crazy legs, perfect height, delicious hair style, and fair skin. (A preference for light skin over dark, colorism is a long-standing issue in African American culture.) Davis' tenor sax and the rest of the brass join King's guitar in the break to proclaim just how fine he feels to be upset this way.

In 1956, B.B. King set his own personal record for chitlin' circuit performances: a remarkable 342 shows. Yet he somehow managed to find time to record and release two of his best songs. **"Crying Won't Help You"** (1956) later appeared in a great six-minute version alongside his highest pop-charting song, "The Thrill Is Gone," on King's 1969 album, *Completely Well*. Equally stunning in its own way, this first incarnation of the song, another Tampa Red original, finds King singing at the high end of his range, almost breaking into falsetto. B.B. delivers his most expressive vocal yet in this cryin' shuffle, with the big band beautifully mixed so that horns, piano, bass, and drums are all distinctly present. His guitar sounds characteristically sublime. This *is* a blame song, a musical lecture to a woman getting what he thinks she deserves. She has treated him badly so he's leaving, and her crying won't bring him back. Yet despite how mean she has been to him, he'll generously wish her luck finding a new man. The song's addictive musical and vocal chemistry trumps its not particularly admirable lyric *Schadenfreude*. King punctuates his guitar solo with exclamations of joy. "Look out!" he whoops, a free man on his way to finding another woman.

"Sweet Little Angel" (1956), another classic tune King cut between chitlin' circuit gigs, contrasts with the Louise Bogan, Tampa Red, and Robert Nighthawk recordings. King's sweet angel is little rather than Black. He gives the song a significantly different sound with horns prominent in his band where Nighthawk had none, and substitutes for Nighthawk's memorable slide on "Black Angel Blues" his own typically gorgeous single-string work. "B.B.'s note-bends are spectacular," Colin Escott comments, "sounding almost like a lap steel in places." The sunny, soulful vocal also has a lot more energy; you believe him when he sings that she gives him joy in everything. Listen to his melismatic five-syllable falsetto articulation of *be-lie-ie-ie-ieve*. And note the inflationary change in the final verse. In previous versions the singer asks her for a nickel and gets a ten-dollar bill, asks for a drink and she buys him an entire still. When B.B. asks *his* woman for a nickel, she gives him a twenty. And nothing as banal as whiskey for them. When B.B. suggests they go out for a good time, she buys him a Cadillac Seville. Is this just blues hyperbole, a fantasy like the grotesquely long stinger of Hooker's queen bee? Or was King's little angel actually his manager, Maurice Merritt, who bought him his first Caddy? Sweet, either way.[72]

Bobby "Blue" Bland (1930–2013) came to Memphis from rural Tennessee in 1947 and soon became a Beale Streeter. He played no instrument but his soulful voice fronted the band. By his own admission he served a musical apprenticeship, traveling with B.B., Roscoe Gordon, and Junior Parker to chitlin' circuit clubs they headlined. Bland drove the car, hauled the instruments, watched and listened. He first recorded in 1952 for Modern. After spending a couple of years in the army, he found success in Houston on Don Robey's Duke label, where he broke out in 1957 with "Farther on Up the Road." During the next five years Bland proved himself a master of jump blues and ballads with classics like "I Pity the Fool," "Turn On Your Love Light," and "Stormy Monday Blues." Over his career he landed 63 records on the *Billboard* charts, the last nine from two albums he recorded with B.B. King. But between 1952 and 1957 he was finding his musical way.

Bland recorded **"Lovin' Blues"** (1952) in Memphis, backed by his buddies, the Beale Streeters: the first record Duke released with Bobby's new middle name, "Blue." Bland had left school in third grade, his biographer explains, and "embarrassed by his inability to read, had hesitantly enlisted some of the band members to help him with the lyrics." Whatever help they gave didn't improve things much. Lyrically, the song couldn't be more generic except for the final line. He loves her and wants no one else. One evening she declares she doesn't want him anymore, and walks out the door, saying Bobby, I still love you but—here the lyrics are difficult to understand—she'll blow her top (?) if she stays. The song works despite the lyrics. A doleful 12-bar blues with drummer Earl Forest thumping a death march beat while Billy Duncan's mournful tenor sax and B.B's downbeat guitar reinforce the mood, it showcases Bland's voice. You can hear the acknowledged gospel influence of Ira Tucker, great lead singer of the Dixie Hummingbirds.[73] Bland's phrasing, his worrying of certain words, and a technique he would repeat in other songs of this era announce the voice that will have such success later: instead of repeating the first half of a line in the final verse, he simply howls two bars of grief: *Ohhhh-OH-oh-oh-oh-oh-oh*.

He does something similar in **"I Can't Put You Down, Baby"** (1956), recorded in Houston with the backing of Bill Harvey's seven-piece orchestra, including three horns and Roy Gaines's hot guitar. The songwriting here, credited to Don Robey, also suffers from conventional lyrics—I can't put you down, I love you too much, and so on. But twice Bland replaces the first two bars of a repeated line with *YEAH, YE-eah-eah-eah, baby*, an exclamation much more expressive than the lyrics. This marriage of blues and gospel portends the sound of what would soon be called soul.

Chapter Two

Rhythm & Blues
Let the Good Times Roll

"If any description of me comes close, it's the tag 'rhythm-and-blues.' I've fooled around in the same way that blacks have been doing for years—playing the blues to different rhythms."
—Ray Charles, *Brother Ray: Ray Charles' Own Story*

"There was a kind of frenzy and extra-local vulgarity to rhythm & blues that had never been present in older blues forms. ... And somehow the louder the instrumental accompaniment and the more harshly screamed the singing, the more expressive the music was."
—LeRoi Jones [Amiri Baraka], *Blues People*

"To many Americans, rhythm and blues was the Kinsey Report set to music, a manifesto in the movement to repeal sexual reticence."
—Glenn C. Altschuler, *All Shook Up: How Rock 'n' Roll Changed America*[1]

Trying to pin down a single definition of rhythm & blues is a mug's game. Numerous blues songs might just as easily be labeled R&B. The same with much of doo wop. When *Billboard* re-named its Race chart Rhythm & Blues in 1949, it used the term to cover *all* Black popular music, including gospel. Without getting religious about it, I will suggest some parameters for defining, but not confining, postwar R&B. It will always overflow its boundaries. One critic broadly defines rhythm & blues as "popular music that arose in black communities after the swing era and before the arrival of the Beatles, roughly between 1945 and 1960."[2] Beatlemania didn't arrive in North America until 1964 but let's not quibble. R&B crystallized sometime around the end of the war, evolving from pre-war big band swing music, and was either absorbed into rock 'n' roll or morphed into soul in the late 1950s and early '60s, only to re-emerge in a new contemporary form in the 1970s and '80s.

Multiple factors caused the demise of the big bands and swing orchestras. Costs became prohibitive for large touring organizations. Logistical issues—wartime gas rationing, travel restrictions, and the loss of musicians to the military—made touring and maintaining the bands more difficult. In 1942, the American Federation of Musicians union, led by its president, James Petrillo, had gone on strike against record companies over the issue of royalties. The Petrillo strike lasted for two years, during which none of the large unionized swing bands could record, removing a significant source of their income. The strike ended in 1944 but the damage had been done. Independent labels arose to fill the void and record non-union musicians. These artists played and sang blues, gospel, country, and the evolving rhythm & blues. The majors showed little interest in this music or the audiences who listened to it. Now record buyers had a chance to discover it for themselves.

In another repercussion, the orchestral model began shifting away to smaller bands utilizing anywhere from five to nine players. In August 1946, *Billboard* observed, in its usual telegraphic prose, the "switch from big band policy to cocktail-type combos for vaude houses throuout (sic) the country," with Louis Jordan leading the way "in the small org field." In December of that year, no fewer than eight "top swing bands"—led by big names like Benny Goodman, Woody Herman, Harry James, and Tommy Dorsey—went bust. White bands mostly but some large African American bands also succumbed. Recognizing the new reality, bandleaders like Billy Eckstine and Johnny Otis reduced the size of their groups.[3]

The shift away from swing also had an aesthetic rationale. The music itself had begun to ossify. LeRoi Jones considered the transition from swing to R&B, or jump blues, a postwar response by African Americans to the mainstreaming of their music. "It was almost as if the blues people were reacting against the softness and 'legitimacy' that had crept into black instrumental music with the advent of swing … and for this reason, rhythm & blues sat as completely outside the mainstream as earlier blues forms." If rhythm & blues existed on the margins, what distinguished it from established popular music? Listen to Etta James's "The Wallflower" aka "Roll with Me, Henry," then Georgia Gibbs's cover version, "Dance with Me, Henry." Rock critic Charlie Gillett explains, "In almost every respect, the sounds of rhythm and blues contradicted those of popular music. The vocal styles were harsh, the songs explicit, the dominant instruments—saxophone, piano, guitar, drums—were played loudly and with an emphatic dance rhythm, the production of the records was crude. The prevailing emotion was excitement." Swing was essentially dance music. Exciting new times called for exciting new music and new styles on the dance floor. "The hot new style was jump," James Miller writes, "a simplified and superheated version of old-fashioned swing, often boogie-woogie based, usually played by a small combo of piano, bass and drums, with saxophone and trumpet."[4]

The new style of music may have been simplified but the musicians who performed it were highly trained professionals, many with long experience in the big bands alongside the Dizzy Gillespies and Charlie Parkers who left swing orchestras to pioneer the new bebop sound in jazz. Many of the singers and musicians we will meet in this chapter sang or played for Black bandleaders like Lucky Millinder, Jay McShann, Tiny Bradshaw, Cootie Williams, and Count Basie. The rhythm component of rhythm & blues was in excellent musical hands.

Black musical artists saw little distinction between blues and rhythm & blues. But the transformation of African American society from rural to urban affected its musical tastes in significant ways. We saw some of those changes reflected in the postwar urban blues, but for many African Americans blues itself had become anachronistic music, a throwback to the bad old days. The dreams of a new postwar world meant leaving that past behind. Brian Ward elaborates: "After the Second World War it was this increasingly urbanized, increasingly non-southern black audience—especially its youth—which first began to reject the gritty, rural, downhome sounds of the old blues in favor of the eclectic mixture of ineffable dance beats, sweet harmonies, bustling good humor, romance and ribaldry, which characterized r&b." The cosmopolitan R&B movement reflected "the post–World War II mood of confidence, progress, sophistication, and growing assertiveness in black urban America."[5] The specifics of geography proved less important than they were for blues. Parts of the great rhythm & blues migration began in the deep South, but much of it originated in places like Omaha and Kansas City, and could as likely end up in Cincinnati as in Chicago or Los Angeles.

African American responses to the music—especially its good-humored "ribaldry"—were not always so cosmopolitan. As rhythm & blues records became bolder and more explicit in exploring sexual themes, a backlash developed in Black communities. In 1952, when Black teens nearly caused a riot trying to get into Alan Freed's Moondog Coronation Ball rhythm & blues concert in Cleveland, the local African American newspaper criticized the event for "exploit[ing] the Negro teensters" with "low-brow, cheap [and] frequently obscene" music. In 1954, Memphis' WDIA, the nation's leading Black radio station, banned all records with "suggestive" lyrics, and the foremost African American newspaper, *The Pittsburgh Courier*, came out in opposition to "smutty" rhythm & blues records. Resistance came from the Black middle class, intelligentsia, and church, and even from jazz musicians who felt that R&B was merely commercial "entertainment, not self-expression."[6]

A much greater backlash to R&B grew among whites. As more and more white kids began listening and dancing to the records and attending rhythm & blues concerts, fears about the dissolution of the color line developed into "a domino theory of music in which it appeared that white youths were falling one by one into the abyss of Black culture." In 1954–55, white disc jockeys across the country announced that they were banning dirty R&B records, "smut," "suggestive trash." *Variety* published a panicky editorial about R&B *leer-ics* in 1955:

> [M]usic "leer-ics" are touching new lows. ... We're talking about "rock and roll," about "hug," and "squeeze," and kindred euphemisms which are attempting a total breakdown of reticences (sic) about sex. ... Our teenagers are already setting something of a record in delinquency without this raw musical idiom to smell up the environment still more.

Hug and *squeeze* and delinquent teenagers smelling up the environment—yikes! In what would prove a last-ditch effort to alter the trajectory of popular music in the 1950s, to maintain white hegemony even as Black rhythm & blues was giving birth to racially integrated rock 'n' roll, major label Columbia Records launched its 1955 catalogue of popular music with the slogan "Rhythm without the Blues."[7]

New Black music has always been perceived as a threat to (white) morality, good taste, and public order: jazz and blues in the 1920s, rhythm & blues and rock 'n' roll in the 1950s, rap and hip hop in the 1990s. In a 1955 issue of *Down Beat*, Alan Freed called out the racism at the heart of the censorship project. The campaign, he wrote, "smells of discrimination of the worst kind against the great and accomplished Negro writers, musicians, and singers...."[8] But the sexual squeamishness, hypocritical as it might have been, had a real basis. R&B acts often sang *about* sex in ways that blues usually did not and white pop simply refused to. Even rock 'n' roll, in its early days, circumvented the overt sexuality of R&B. Listen to Big Joe Turner's "Shake, Rattle and Roll," then Bill Haley and the Comets' bowdlerized recording.

Instrumentally, rhythm & blues distinguished itself from both blues and rock 'n' roll by subordinating their lead instrument, the guitar, and almost entirely eliminating the blues harmonica. Guitars frequently make up part of the overall sound on R&B records, but only two of the more than thirty artists featured in this chapter sang *and* played guitar. Vocalists singing alone or accompanying themselves on boogie woogie piano, saxophone, or drums front the rest of these songs. The boogie woogie style emerged from the "barrelhouse" blues culture of the 1920s and '30s. It entered the mainstream in 1938–39 when John Hammond produced two *From Spirituals to Swing* concerts at New York's Carnegie Hall to showcase African American music. Among the performers, pianists Albert Ammons, Pete Johnson, and Meade Lux Lewis caused a sensation with their fast-paced boogie woogie. At speed, the pianists played a three-chord bass pattern with the left hand while the right improvised with "short repeated phrases, runs, sharply struck chords, repeated single notes and trills which emphasized rhythm at the expense of melody." Pete Johnson had a long, productive partnership with vocalist Big Joe Turner. He explained, "Boogie is really a blues fugue. You play something with the left hand and then you play the same thing with the right, and then you play them against each other, like counterpoint."[9] Boogie woogie piano became a key component of R&B.

The tenor sax is rhythm & blues' most prominent instrument along with the piano. Extraordinarily expressive, the saxophone can sound sad and mournful or joyous and celebratory, as we hear in many blues songs. The rhythm and blues sax (usually tenor but sometimes alto or baritone) differed from the instrument's use in blues or in the first couple of years of rock 'n' roll. Often extravagantly wild, it called attention to the Dionysian revelry of R&B music and the Africanness of its African American sound. LeRoi Jones writes of "the uncommonly weird sounds" coming out of the R&B sax, and the tendency of the player to repeat a riff "past any useful musical context." The point, he claims, is "to make the instruments sound as unmusical, or as *non-Western*, as possible." Jim Dawson compares honking tenor sax players to Black preachers. "The honker who shrieked the same piercing note over and over ... was in effect preaching his own blissed-out, rapturous, propulsive, secular gospel of psychic tension and release." So many of the artists in this book were steeped in the rituals, emotions, and rhythms of the Black church, where they got their start in music. The honkers seemed to be preaching the R&B truth of body and spirit. Amiri Baraka (aka LeRoi Jones) recalls listening to saxmen Big Jay McNeely, Illinois Jacquet, Gene "Jug" Ammons, and Willis "Gator Tail" Jackson: "When Big Jay, and Illinois, Jug and Gatortail, the honkers and screamers of our day, came on, it was blues church we groaned and stomped to. Those screams were like black folks in sanctification, brown folks when they quit bullshittin' and let the full spirit take 'em."[10]

The honking, screaming horns, boogie woogie pianos, and electric guitars made rhythm & blues especially loud. Some of the most successful R&B singers, especially on the men's side, became known as *shouters,* cranking up the vocal volume to be heard above the instruments. Some of the best women shouted, too. Another group of *rockers*, mid-century wild men (and a few women), anticipated rock 'n' roll with their loud, fast R&B attack. The importance of showmanship in rhythm & blues did not mean that shouting, honking, and over-the-top stage routines excluded everything else. Smoky-smooth R&B balladeers made an impact, too. Although Arnold Shaw titled his authoritative survey of rhythm & blues *Honkers and Shouters*, he surprisingly prefers the balladeers: "Monotonous and repetitive as R&B tends to be as up-tempo jump music, so it becomes subtly and richly chorded in the ballads, with moody inner voicing and blues-rooted harmonies." I personally prefer the up-tempo jump tunes, wildly expressive at best and rarely monotonous. Nelson George avoids hierarchical assessments, distinguishing rhythm & blues holistically from rock 'n' roll: "Rock & roll was young music; R&B managed to be young and old, filled both with references to the past and with fresh interpretations, all at the same time."[11]

The most eclectic category in this book, rhythm & blues sported a wide range of musical sounds, vocal styles, and lyrical themes. I have tried to organize this chapter logically without pigeonholing anyone too tightly, since the singers were capable of great variation within their own styles and musical approaches. Look for a changing of the R&B guard between the first half of the postwar decade and the second. The blues shouters lost some ground as smoother vocal groups and raucous rockers gained popularity. Of the fifty top rhythm & blues artists of 1950, only three still made the top fifty list in 1955.[12] Whatever the context, the quality of the individual work remains most important: the ability of these songs to move you, soothe you, rock you, or make you laugh.

The Pioneers: Rhythm & Joy

We begin with pioneers of the genre whose musical experience pre-dated the postwar decade. Altering their styles and musical approaches to accommodate changing times and audience tastes, they heavily influenced the golden age of rhythm & blues. Many of them had sung and played with big jazz and swing bands. Accomplished musicians, they took to rhythm & blues with enthusiasm and renewed energy, embracing the opportunity to bust out, to explore new rhythms and upbeat lyrical messages. The times were a-changin', apparently for the better. Who would want to be left behind?

Louis Jordan (1908–75), the father of rhythm & blues, fundamentally influenced artists as varied as Chuck Berry, James Brown, and B.B. King. The latter covered 18 Jordan tunes in his 1999 tribute album, *Let the Good Times Roll*. A bandleader, vocalist, alto saxophonist, and entertainer supreme, Jordan established the template for much of what was to come. Born in Arkansas, he traveled and performed with a minstrel troupe as a teen. In the early 1930s, he moved north to join jazz bands in

Philadelphia and New York. In Chick Webb's orchestra Jordan played alto sax and took turns on vocals with Ella Fitzgerald. In 1938, he formed his own pared-down combo. All his records would be credited to Louis Jordan and His Tympany Five, a band that ranged from five to nine musicians with Jordan on alto sax and vocals. It became the most popular Black musical act of the era. By 1951, when he hit the charts for the final time, Jordan and his band had scored 54 *Billboard* top tens, 18 at #1, all on Decca. In 1946 alone, thirteen of his songs made the Race chart, six reached number one, and six crossed over onto the Pop chart. He also appeared in a series of feature films and musical shorts that cemented his pop-cultural dominance.

Jordan appealed to African American audiences for reasons similar to the popularity of postwar blues artists. Like them, he combined urban sensibility with familiar Southern rural tropes, embellishing it all with energetic, good-humored flamboyance. One critic commented, "He refuses to keep the ghetto in its place. He exploits the styles of sophisticated blues for entertainment, laughing at the boogie, refining the blues shout, parodying the solidarity of call-and-response…." For Nick Tosches, Jordan was "the crowning glory of postwar hep," revolutionizing the way popular music was delivered: "[W]ith my little band," Jordan explained to Arnold Shaw, "I did everything they did with a big band. *I made the blues jump.*"[13]

African American musical artists acknowledged his enormous influence, and he involved himself early in the civil rights movement, publicly denouncing the segregation of a New Orleans concert in 1948. Not unlike Louis Armstrong, whose wide-eyed expression he shared, Jordan had immense crossover appeal but vociferously objected to any suggestion of pandering to whites. He argued that he had developed his act playing to Black audiences, including at the Apollo where he got great responses. And if white audiences also found him entertaining, so be it. "His minstrel-show moves evoked home," Preston Lauterbach observes, "but his dazzling word play and lavender suit let everyone know it was okay to grow into something else. … [H]e embraced the funny, confusing, violent reality of farm folk in the city."[14]

In January 1946, Jordan kicked off the postwar decade with **"Choo Choo Ch'Boogie."** It became his biggest ever hit, #1 for eighteen weeks, and sold over two million records. The song concerns a different kind of train than the one that carried blues lovers away, headed for the promised land, or transported soldiers to and from military bases. White country musicians wrote it but Jordan made it jump. The lyrics played to one of his strengths as a singer: rhyming. The three six-line verses all end on the same rhyme sound. The record conveys the sheer joy of someone who loves trains—a Black GI, let's say, just demobilized, with his pack still on his back, starting the postwar era by pursuing a desert island fantasy down by the railroad. He has run out of money and can't find a job so can't afford to ride the rails. But if you take him back to the track, Jack, he'll happily live in a shack, listen to the clickety-clack rhythm and watch the trains roll along. The song opens with horns (Jordan alto, Josh Jackson tenor sax, Aaron Izenhall trumpet) replicating the *woo woo* of a train whistle, then clips along with a boogie beat driven by Jesse Simpkins' bass, Eddie Byrd on drums, and Wild Bill Davis' sterling piano.

A few months later, with the same band, Jordan recorded a huge two-sided hit, "Ain't Nobody Here but Us Chickens" b/w "Let the Good Times Roll." Sam Theard's

Louis Jordan and the Tympany Five on stage in New York City, 1946. From left: Wild Bill Davis (p), Carl Hogan (g), Jesse Simpkins (b), Aaron Izenhall (tp), Josh Jackson (ts), Eddie Byrd (d), Louis Jordan (as). William P. Gottlieb/Ira and Leonore S. Gershwin Fund Collection, Music Division, Library of Congress.

"Let the Good Times Roll" (1946) sums up the postwar optimism that generated rhythm & blues. (The label credits Spo-de-ode, Theard's stage name, and Fleecie Moore, Jordan's wife. Crediting his wife would backfire badly on Jordan. After they divorced, she received his royalties.) The record hung around the charts for 23 weeks, reached #2, and became an R&B standard. Jordan and the band reprise it, with bad lip synching, in Jordan's 1947 film *Caldonia*. "Let the Good Times Roll" doesn't roar down the tracks like "Choo Choo Ch'Boogie." A mid-tempo number without instrumental breaks, it opens and closes with horns and features a strong rhythm section. Davis' piano rolls along, quietly promising a good time.

Jordan mellows through the choruses, repeating the title in a matter-of-fact, isn't-it-obvious way. The verses are a different story, a call to R&B arms. He grabs our attention with a shout, then urges us to have fun. You have only this life; when you're dead, it's over. Each verse reiterates the message with minor variations. Stop wasting time and don't be afraid to lay down your cash to get things rolling. He's ready to spend what it takes to have a good time and tells the landlord: Hey, we're having a ball here. If the cops come, don't let them in. The final verse re-emphasizes the importance of doing this together, as articulated in the opening verse and repeated in the choruses. If this life is all we have, we had better help each other enjoy it. Finally, he insists, play this right and we won't need cops or anyone else to police our behavior. The civilized communal project of *letting* the good times roll means taking full advantage of the joys this life offers.

Written by a Canadian husband-wife team, **"Ain't Nobody Here but Us Chickens"** (1946) proved another Jordan blockbuster. Jordan and the Tympany Five also performed it in his 1947 film *Reet, Petite and Gone*. The #1 R&B record of 1947 spent seventeen weeks at the top of the Race chart and reached #6 Pop. Here, citified Mr. Jordan's rural Arkansas alter ego takes over. He transports his listeners back to the country, into the barnyard for the perspective of the chickens themselves. When farmer Brown hears a noise one night from the hen house, he grabs his gun. Who's there? The title provides the answer. These sassy chickens don't appreciate the farmer's disturbing them. Keep calm, they tell him. We have important things to do: dig up worms, hatch our eggs. Go back to sleep—and point your gun elsewhere. The Decca label calls it a fox trot. But these busy hens keep the song zipping along at a pace that ensures there will be no fox trotting in this chicken house. The horns are busy, too. Josh Jackson's lengthy, rockin' solo comes as close as any Tympany Five tenor ever came to the voguish squealing and honking of the postwar sax. Jordan didn't favor that style. "The tenor sax isn't supposed to be played that way," he insisted. The success of "Ain't Nobody Here but Us Chickens" led to **"Barnyard Boogie"** (1948), another witty hit from the farm animals' perspective. That one rocks even harder with the sax blowing just the way it was supposed to.[15]

Jordan's genius gave him the ability to move with ease and originality from country to city and back, covering all his listeners' bases. Another of his most popular records and a critical favorite, **"Saturday Night Fish Fry, Parts 1 & 2"** (1949), written by drummer Ellis Walsh, ticked every box. Once more Jordan plays the urbane partygoer, letting the good times roll. But here he heads south to New Orleans' Rampart Street, a crucible of African American jazz and blues. The occasion: a Saturday night fish fry. With its roots in slavery-time plantation culture, this ritual remained popular in the South but also moved north with the Great Migration.[16] In an earlier Jordan record, "They Raided the House" (1945), the police break up a rent party. In "Let the Good Times Roll" the singer asks the landlord to prevent the cops from messing up his good time. In this song the party gets busted for no evident reason. In addition to its infectious boogie tune and detailed evocation of African American tradition, "Saturday Night Fish Fry" comments on racism and the fraught relationship between Black communities and law enforcement. Sound familiar? *Plus ça change*, as they say in New Orleans. So much goes on here that even without an instrumental break the song clocks in at 5:24, too long for one side of a 78 RPM record. Decca released it as double-sided Parts 1 & 2. It spent twelve weeks at #1.

With two trumpets added to the usual Tympany Five configuration, a fanfare of five horns opens and closes the song. Bill Doggett's boogie woogie piano and Billy Hadnott's bass deliver the up-tempo drive. As catchy a hook as in any R&B record before or since, the choral refrain breaks into the lengthy narrative seven times. The gist: the place was really rockin', the folks dancing and having rowdy good fun through the night. The word *rockin'* appears 28 times. New Orleans *did* rock in 1949 with rhythm & bluesmen like Roy Brown, Dave Bartholomew, and Fats Domino burning up the clubs and cutting hit records.[17]

Good musicians get into fish fries for free, the song says. Maybe Jordan flashed his union card. He and a buddy went into a house on Rampart Street where a party was in full swing. A man was jiving with someone else's wife as a fat guy (Domino?) played piano. Women ranged from bobbysoxers to elegant dressers, and everyone was high. Suddenly, people ran screaming for the door. A raid! Cops blocked the exits and threw the partygoers into the paddy wagon like potato sacks. Jordan tried to hide but was arrested along with his buddy and jailed until his woman came to bail him out. In the closing verse he feels so shaken that he never wants to hear the word *fish* again. As in many blues songs, words and music operate in tension, the lyrics providing a dark real-life subtext to all that rockin' musical fun.

In the early 1930s, novice musician Louis Jordan toured with trumpet master Louis Armstrong and made his first recording as a member of Armstrong's band. By 1950, Jordan had become as popular as the legendary Satchmo. The two primo entertainers got together with the Tympany Five, waxing **"(I'll Be Glad When You're Dead), You Rascal You"** (1950). Written by Sam Theard, the song had been a staple of Armstrong's repertoire since 1930. Despite the violence that the lyrics suggest—the singer threatens to kill the rascal who stole his wife—the jocular music and vocal performances render the threat more rhetorical than real. "If the lyric laments but the music mocks," Albert Murray asserts, "the statement is not one of lamentation but of mockery."[18]

These mockers alternate verses, each playing over the other's vocal—Armstrong trumpet, Jordan alto—supported by a classic Tympany Five lineup: piano, guitar, bass, drums, trumpet, and tenor sax. Lyrically, they let the good times roll, egging each other on. Armstrong, especially playful, laughs and performs witty vocal gymnastics. Listen to what he does with the final verse, wondering what makes his wife think the rascal is so hot. They push each other, joyfully setting up the final minute when the band rocks out under Satchmo's improv. One Armstrong aficionado writes: "What a hot group! But of course, highest props go to Pops for the way he soars over the insistent riffing of Jordan, tenor saxophonist Josh Jackson and trumpeter Aaron Izenhall. Louis sounds so inspired he almost blows his chops through his horn."[19] This spectacular performance embodies an entire history of great African American music. The giant of New Orleans jazz meets the father of rhythm & blues.

Helen Humes (1913–81) might be called the mother of rhythm & blues. With a career dating from the 1920s and a distinguished resumé in blues and jazz, Humes celebrated the war's end by singing about liberation and sex with joy and plenty of rhythm. She led a parade of great women vocalists who helped define R&B in the late 1940s. Born in Louisville, Humes learned music in the church and cut her first blues records when she was just thirteen. By the late 1930s, she had established herself as a premier swing vocalist. When Billie Holiday left Count Basie's orchestra, Basie invited Humes to replace her. Jazz critic Will Friedwald asserts, "In 1927, Humes was very nearly in the same class as Bessie Smith and Ethel Waters; by 1938, she's worthy of being mentioned in the same breath as Billie Holiday and Ella Fitzgerald."[20] After spending four years with Basie, Humes went solo in 1942, playing at New York's Café Society along with the great boogie woogie pianists, then moving to Los Angeles, diving headfirst into its rhythm & blues world. Though a fine balladeer, she carved out the new R&B sound primarily as an up-tempo female shouter.

In September 1945, the month Japan's surrender officially ended the war, LA's Philo Records (soon to change its name to Aladdin) released a song Humes had written that begins with the celebratory line, "I feel so fine today." Millions of North Americans shared her sentiment. Recorded in late 1945, **"Be-Baba-Leba"** spent six weeks on the *Billboard* charts in 1946, beginning the postwar decade with a bang, so to speak. The war is over so let's party! A speedy, ecstatic, infectious ode to liberation, the song foregrounds a woman's freedom to enjoy her sexuality. Imagine the restaurant scene in *When Harry Met Sally* put to R&B music. After fronting big bands like Basie's for a decade, Humes sang here with the Bill Doggett Octet, also transitioning from orchestral swing to R&B. Pianist Doggett, who had arranged for Basie's band, led a classic rhythm & blues assembly: piano, guitar, bass, drums, and four horns. The tenor sax player's honking acrobatic performances gave him his nickname: Wild Bill Moore.

The singer feels so fine because the war has ended and her man is coming home. She has other men, but this one ... OOOOH-WEE! Built for speed, he has everything she needs. He thrills her morning and night, *comes in* like a tiger and makes her scream and holler: *oo oo oo baba-leba baba-leba baba-leba!!!* The title's euphemistic choral nonsense sounds at times like *bla bla bla*, suggesting sly mockery of the sexual content. But it feels genuinely, joyously sexy. Humes' vocal quality has something to do with that. "She had a delicate squeak of a voice," writes Friedwald, "yet far from tiptoeing through a song, she practically belts it out, making her understated and overstated, introverted and extroverted, subtle and in-your-face all at the same time."[21] And enjoying every moment.

The 12-bar arrangement opens with Chizz Harris' snare. An instrumental solo follows each verse: Wild Bill's superb tenor along with pounding drums gets the first two breaks, John Brown's alto solo the third, Alfred Moore's bass takes the fourth, and on the outro the whole band launches Humes' final orgasmic chorus into the cosmos. Her equally great live version, retitled **"E-Baba-Leba"** (1950), accompanied by Roy Milton's first-class band, further ups the tempo as Humes and the excited audience push each other. Recorded at Frank Bull and Gene Norman's Blues Jubilee in L.A.'s Shrine Auditorium before 5,000 zealous fans, it clocks in a minute shorter than the original, omitting instrumental breaks. Humes treats the verses a little more lasciviously, and the audience screams with as much delight as she gets from her man when he makes her holler.

Humes continued playing the good-time girl with her own uniquely liberated twists. A follow-up to "Be-Baba-Leba" on Philo/Aladdin, **"Pleasing Man Blues"** (1946) finds her setting a high bar for her man either to satisfy her or get lost. An all-star horn section backs her on this swinging 12-bar ballad with Snooky Young trumpet, Maxwell Davis and Lester Young on tenor sax, and Willie Smith on alto. Following her insistence that he control his love for her, Snooky blows a beautifully controlled trumpet solo. When she threatens to ditch him for jivin' her, Prez answers with an ultra-mellow, reassuring tenor solo. These guys want to please. Humes ends with a witty stop-time verse explaining that she requires lovin' moves from her man as precise as a Gruen watch.

Louis Jordan had written and recorded "They Raided the House" in 1945. The next year trumpeter Hot Lips Page covered it as "They Raided the Joint**.**" Humes did her version of **"They Raided the Joint"** (1947) for Mercury, presenting herself as a party girl observing a police raid. This song focuses less on the cops than on the ways other partygoers ostracize the singer. They wouldn't let her play their card games, eat their food, or drink their whiskey. But ironically, she was the only one *not* arrested, and she managed to get high anyway. Humes ends in a burst of *Schadenfreude,* standing in the corner laughing as everyone else gets busted. Buck Clayton, who had arranged and played trumpet on Page's recording, backs Humes here with his own veteran seven-piece group. Drummer Jo Jones opens on his hi-hats, Ram Ramirez's piano establishes the boogie woogie beat, then Humes sings her story in stop-time rhythm as the horns answer in the background. Humes increasingly toys with words and phrases in the chorus. Jazz critic Whitney Balliett describes her as a master of rhythm, and you can clearly hear that here. "When it pleases her, she drags behind the beat, passes it and falls back on it, and unerringly finds those infinitesimal cracks that exist between beats."[22] Rarely does she seem displeased.

At the same 1945 session that produced "Be-Baba-Leba," Humes cut another record with Bill Doggett's Octet, her own composition, "He May Be Your Man." In 1950, she recorded a louder, brassier version as **"He May Be Yours"** (1950). Later that year, she made the lyrics more explicit, added a boogie beat, and recorded it in a palpably exciting live performance at the Blues Jubilee, retitled **"I'm Gonna Let Him Ride"** (1950). These upbeat 12-bar blues, on L.A. labels Discovery and Modern, show two different sides of this liberated Ms. "He May Be Yours" is remarkably ecumenical. In a big band-style arrangement, Marshall Royal and his group accompany Humes as she addresses the other woman and accepts the fact that they share their man with a third lover. He may be yours, she sings, but no more exclusively than a telephone party line. So let's be friends and thank God he belongs to us all. A couple of fine sax solos alternate with Humes' ever-dynamic vocal and bracingly original lyrics. No one need be sad, no one gets blamed. They get together and let the good times roll.

"I'm Gonna Let Him Ride," like the live "E-Baba-Leba," takes a minute off the tune by dropping the sax breaks. With Roy Milton's band again in command, this live version really rocks. Camille Howard's boogie woogie piano and Jimmy Jackson's tenor sax drive it. But blunt sexual possessiveness replaces the singer's generous sharing impulse. Instead of the inclusiveness suggested by the party-line phone, she declares that his coming so much (to see her) has made her think he may be hers exclusively. From here on, think survival of the sexually fittest: three of us currently share him, but I'm taking him away from you. Humes throws in the lascivious 1920s blues line, "That man rocks me with one steady roll." He satisfies me, so if you want him, tie him up. Because if he's flagging my train, I'm gonna let him ride. *Rock* and *roll*, *come*, *ride*, and *drive* are standard blues/R&B double entendres. Listen, for example, to Humes asking her daddy to keep on driving her in **"Hard Driving Mama"** (1950). But *train* rarely appears as metaphor for the female body. Humes never hesitated to stretch the traditions of blues lyricism to accommodate her original, sexually liberated ideas.

The A-side of "I'm Gonna Let Him Ride," also recorded live, became one of her biggest records. **"Million Dollar Secret"** (1950), with Roy Milton and his crew on Modern Records, advises younger women to get themselves a rich old man. A few months later she went into the studio and cut **"Helen's Advice"** (1950) with Dexter Gordon's orchestra on the Discovery label. It advises older women to get themselves a hot young man. The two songs make a matched set and the records are R&B jewels.

She slows things down for the 12-bar "Million Dollar Secret," but shouts the lyrics in her usual effervescent way. Adapted from Wynonie Harris' "Young Man's Blues" (1945), advising young men to get themselves rich old women, and redone as **Young Man's Blues, Pts 1 & 2** (1946) by Claude Trenier, whom we'll meet at the end of this chapter, Humes' version opens with Camille Howard's leisurely triplets on piano. With Jimmy Jackson's sexy tenor, Junior Rogers on guitar, and Milton on drums, the seven players provide a fine musical analogue to her vocals. She'll tell you girls a million-dollar secret: if you're young and you want to hit the jackpot, find an old man. In a series of stop-time verses she explains. He'll have sexual experience so will be fine in bed. And along with his loving he'll give you lots of money. He's 78, she's 23. Her friends make fun of her but she gets the last laugh: he made his will out to her. Audience roars indicate they're onside with Humes' liberated, if mercenary, non-ageist approach to loving.

In the standard version of the *carpe diem* romance trope, a blues tradition, a man tells a woman to give it up before she's too old. Humes alters that model slightly in "Helen's Advice," another 12-bar ballad, in which *she* forcefully urges older women to get a young man. He may spend your money, work you like a slave, but the sex will make it all worthwhile. He'll get an old hen feeling like a young chick again. As usual, Humes presents herself as no blushing violet. She guarantees her advice for 69 years, but warns women not to get too … umm … orally ambitious. Another first-class crew of musicians works with her, led by tenor colossus Dexter Gordon who, Friedwald observes, "spotlights the singer at her loudest—and most exuberant."[23] Loud and exuberant would be one definition of this rhythm & blues diva, plus an attitude that says, I am woman: let the good times roll!

Born Ruth Jones in Alabama, the singer who became more famous than anyone else in this chapter moved to Chicago while still a child. Like so many R&B artists-to-be, she first sang gospel, in her case with the influential Sallie Martin Singers. Switching to secular music as a teen, she changed her name to **Dinah Washington** (1924–63) and became, in the words of Linda Dahl, "the outstanding vocal proponent of the union of gospel's lofty, soaring lilt with the earthy, salty quality of the blues." Performing with Lionel Hampton's band, Washington began recording in 1943, then had thirty top ten *Billboard* hits as a solo act with Mercury Records, 1948–55. Critics hold her in high esteem. Arnold Shaw cites her "flutelike voice, sinuous, caressing, and penetrating. Master of all the devices of blues and gospel shading—the bent notes, the broken notes, the slides, the anticipations, and the behind-the-beat notes—she handled them with an intensity that came from her early church training."[24] I love Washington's voice and her supreme phrasing even when her records suffer from over-arranged horns and, later in her career, schlocky strings.

In December 1945, she cut a series of fine records on Apollo in Los Angeles. One of those early sides, the mid-tempo **"No Voot No Boot"** (1946), offers a taste of what she could do in rhythm & blues. Washington's biographer dismisses it as a novelty. But *Billboard*'s more discriminating reviewer declares in his hipster prose: "It's crystal clear chirping ... typical Harlemese guttural spinning at a lively clip as she promises not to give it away if she can't get what she wants. Lucky Thompson's small jam band provides the proper musical spirit for Miss Dinah's song." The record reveals a cocky, self-possessed young woman. Within the next few years, Eddie "Cleanhead" Vinson would lament the waste of a woman's sexual youth in **"Old Maid Boogie"** (1947) and Wynonie Harris would warn a young woman not to keep **"Sittin' on It All the Time"** (1950)—just what Washington insists she *will* do here. Until she finds what she wants, she'll sit on it indefinitely. If she can't get her voot, no man will get her boot(y).[25] If a man isn't built for speed, too bad. Lucky Thompson's terrific eight-piece All Stars ensemble features his own mellow tenor sax swinging along with the vocal, Milt Jackson on vibes, and the great Charles Mingus on bass. In the stop-time verses Ms. D adamantly says forget it if you can't give her what

Dinah Washington performing at a Cavalcade of Jazz concert, Wrigley Field, Los Angeles, June 1950. Album/Alamy Stock Photo.

she wants. Karl George's trumpet and a sax share the first break, Wilbert Baranco's piano rides along with the vocal in verse two, followed by Jackson and Mingus. In the final verse Washington's voice dances around the deep groove the guys have established. The relaxed, assertive performance announces a special talent.

In 1949, two recording sessions for Mercury with a band led by Dizzy Gillespie's drummer, Teddy Stewart, yielded my other top two Lady Di R&B tunes. In **"Good Daddy Blues"** (1949), the kind of song she did best—a 12-bar boogie that rocks a little—Washington shouts in her high range about a no-good man and the guy who satisfies her soul. Ernie Wilkins' jazzy sax nudges Washington along quietly enough to allow her vocal instrument to rip. She had a no-'count man whose clowning gave her the blues. When she wanted loving, he would be out drinking, spending so much money he couldn't pay the rent or buy her clothes. So she got herself a new daddy, *ooooh*, a cool, kind papa who takes good care of her in every way. She enthusiastically stretches out that impressively elastic voice to let us know just how much she values him.

On **"Baby Get Lost"** (1949), from the same session, one of her only two #1 hits until her duets with Brook Benton in 1960, Stewart's anachronistic big band sound almost overwhelms the vocal in places. But Washington comes through, shouting her complaints with authority to another disappointing man in this stop-time ballad. He's a good lover but a rambler who cheats. She warns him that she can tell him to get lost anytime she chooses, and insists that she has to be the boss. Then she turns on the melisma. If you're not willing to play by my rules, *ba-a-aby, get lost*. In case he hasn't gotten the message, the final verse administers the coup: she has no time for his cheating because so many men are standing in line for her. A great stylist, a self-possessed woman who takes no crap, wielding a brilliant vocal instrument, that's the Dinah Washington I love.

Sing Us a Song, You're the Piano (Wo)Man

In their early years Helen Humes and Dinah Washington both played piano, the respectable instrument of choice for young African American women. A number of other rhythm & blueswomen and men put their piano skills to use in bands and on records. **Julia Lee** (1902–58), one of the most successful, charted ten times between 1946 and 1949. A talented musician and stylish singer known for her "risqué" songs, she grew up in Kansas City, a hotbed of jazz and R&B. She began performing in her brother George Lee's band in 1920 and cut her first record in 1927. After a long hiatus, she started recording again in 1944 for Capitol Records, scoring her string of top tens.

All her bands were called Julia Lee and Her Boyfriends. The one playing on **"Gotta Gimme Whatcha' Got"** (1946) rocked the hardest. Personnel unknown, except for Sam "Baby" Lovett on drums. An excellent tenor sax and squealing trumpet solo fill the breaks. Lee leads the way with pounding boogie woogie piano. The tune recalls the *hokum* of the 1920s and '30s: lighthearted, rhythmic double entendre songs. Its most famous practitioners, Tampa Red and Georgia Tom, sang "It's Tight Like That" and "You Can't Get That Stuff No More." This also sounds something like

Lightnin' Hopkins' "Let Me Play with Your Poodle." Lee sings with little variety but complete authority, sometimes dropping her voice in a mock-sexy purr. The verses, variations on how much she wants her man, how his sexiness thrills her, just provide an excuse for the many repetitions of the title phrase, three times in each of the six choruses, followed by exclamations of affirmation. Here's another woman—refreshingly, in her forties—who knows exactly what she wants and isn't shy about demanding it.

"Snatch and Grab It" (1947), her biggest hit, spent 28 weeks on the chart, twelve at #1. Another infectious boogie with limited lyrical range but a catchy hook, it epitomizes the postwar optimism that many African Americans embraced. The song never makes the *it* of the title explicit, but when opportunity knocks you better take it when you can. Snatch it, grab it, and hold it tight before it gets away. *It* might be the day to be seized, or the economic, political, or sexual moment. (One slang meaning of *snatch*, after all, is sexual.) Lee sings with a sly vocal smile, so who knows. No matter, it's a winner. Her Boy Friends do her proud in the terrific arrangement: Ernie Royal's trumpet and Dave Cavanaugh's tenor sax playing call-and-response in the first break, Lee's boogie woogie piano trading licks with Jack Marshall's guitar in the second, while bassman Harry Babasin keeps time.

"King Size Papa" (1948) also charted for 28 weeks R&B, nine at #1, and reached #15 on the pop chart. That important last statistic fed the growing hysteria over "leer-ics" as Black R&B started crossing over to young white audiences. The song's unsubtle hyperbolic double entendre says size matters. Over eight feet tall, her big, strong, extraordinary lover has shoulders four feet wide. She takes her door off the hinges when he comes, and he carries all she needs in his extra-large pack. Lee's slightly cartoonish piano intro and outro establish the tone. She introduces no irony into her vocal; the lyrics do the work. Benny Carter lends a touch of class to the mid-tempo shuffle, taking his alto sax solo in the same understated way as Lee sings. Surprisingly charming, this woman modestly snatches and grabs, appreciating her lover's gimme and what he's got.

Before continuing with the R&B pianist-vocalists, let's stick with "dirty" records for a minute. Cleveland's Benjamin **Bull Moose Jackson** (1919–89) sang and played tenor sax in Lucky Millinder's band before going solo with Cincinnati's King Records in 1946. He had a string of hit ballads in the late 1940s that have dated badly. "Benjamin Jackson was a Crosby-style crooner," Arnold Shaw writes, "though his heady baritone was closer to Vaughan Monroe and the styling of his records was imitative of Tommy Dorsey's sentimental balladry."[26] Not great press for a rhythm & bluesman. But Bull Moose also had a raunchy side that reached its apogee with **"Big Ten-Inch Record"** (1952). He plays the king-size papa himself on this novelty rocker, explaining all the ways his baby goes for his big ten-inch … blues record. His ten-inch (pause) record really gets her going. A strong vocal performance and Tiny Bradshaw's rockin' band make the tongue-in-cheek machismo musically exciting, with Jimmy Robinson's boogie woogie piano and a great sax solo by Red Prysock leading the way. Crosby and Dorsey would not have approved.

As the pianist in Roy Milton's Solid Senders, Texan **Camille Howard** (1914–93) played on some of Helen Humes' best records. Howard joined Milton's Los Angeles band in 1943 and her stylings played a big part in his success. Milton showcases her fast, versatile right hand and sings about her tall, tan, easy-on-the-eyes appearance in **"Camille's Boogie"** (1947). After **"Thrill Me"** (1947), with Howard on vocals, became a #5 hit for Milton's band on L.A.'s Specialty label, she more or less cloned it as **"Rock Me Daddy"** (1950) for her own group. Despite the similarly banal lyrics—thrill me, rock me, she sings to her man—the musical contrasts prove fascinating. Both performances are well worth a listen. A slow, smoky 12-bar boogie, "Thrill Me" features Howard's sultry vocal, William Gaither's lazy tenor sax, and Hosea Sapp's trumpet. Howard sings slightly off the beat, creating a jazzy disjunction with the music. Leading her own group on "Rock Me Daddy," she makes her piano more conspicuous, doodling adventurous arpeggios. Tenor saxman Earl Sumner Jackson responds with some serious squeals.

Born in Louisiana, her father a well-known bassist, **Nellie Lutcher** (1912–2007) played piano for Ma Rainey in her early teens. In 1935, she moved to Los Angeles where she became a popular club act. A series of 1947 sessions for Capitol produced three jazzy #2 R&B hits that also made the Pop chart, with Lutcher on vocals and piano backed by trios of guitar, bass, and drums, unusual orchestration for rhythm & blues. Though little known today, she is undoubtedly one of the best female R&B vocalists of the era. Linda Dahl praises "her effervescent voice and subtly inflected phrasing," and a piano style that "lifted the melody with a pleasant, swinging effect." Whitney Balliett calls her "a master of dynamics: whispers and shouts and crooning continually surprise one another. … She steadily garnishes her melodic flow with squeaks, falsetto, mock-operatic arias, yodels, and patches of talking."[27]

Nellie Lutcher playing piano and singing in New York City, 1946. William P. Gottlieb/Ira and Leonore S. Gershwin Fund Collection, Music Division, Library of Congress.

Her first session produced up-tempo, effervescent

"Hurry on Down" (1947), written by Lutcher and attributed awkwardly, like her other two hits, to Nellie Lutcher and Her Rhythm. But what a record! Ulysses Livingston on guitar, bassist Billy Hadnott (who played on some of Louis Jordan's best records), and Lee Young on drums provide subtle support. Her piano and Hadnott's bass take the lead but Lutcher's voice stars. Lyrically, she runs through a series of variations on one simple theme: I'm home alone, baby, so hurry over quick as you can. Hurry, she repeats with mock-urgency. Mama is gone all day so we'll have lots of time to play. The vocal dynamics and garnishes that Balliett describes appear everywhere in the performance. Each line has a unique quality. She squeals, squeaks, coos, changes the rhythms, and scats along to her sensational piano solo. An exciting record about a woman super-excited to get what she wants.

Lutcher also wrote **"He's a Real Gone Guy"** (1947). A quick-paced boogie, the song celebrates a jive-talking guy and all the reasons she loves him. Again, Lutcher's joyful performance transcends her lyrics. Hadnott's bass and Young's brushes bop along with her, and Lutcher accompanies her piano solo with even more scatting. She repeats the hipster phrase "real gone" thirty times, in twenty-five of them pronouncing the word *gawn* in a way I find crazily appealing. "Nellie was perfect for spreading the hipster gospel," Billy Vera writes of this "lighthearted Princess of Hep." Another signature performance by an artist with an unmistakable personal sound.[28]

Buddy Johnson and orchestra had recorded "Fine Brown Frame" in 1944. Lutcher transforms it. She switches genders—the title subject is now a man—eliminates the instrumental break, and adds two wicked verses to her **"Fine Brown Frame"** (1947), recorded with a new trio: Hurley Ramey guitar, Truck Parham bass, Alvin Burroughs drums. This explicit celebration of the Black/brown body reminds us again that rhythm & blues songs were aimed directly at African Americans. A few years later, singing for a primarily white rock 'n' roll audience, Chuck Berry could only obliquely celebrate his physical attractiveness as a Black man. His eyes had to stand in for his fine brown frame in "Brown Eyed Handsome Man" (1956).

In Lutcher's bouncy, swinging ballad she ogles a new guy in town whose body obsesses her. She doesn't even know his name: she can see only his fine brown frame and it makes her want to scream. Lutcher sings the first verses uncharacteristically straight. She goes to work on the next four, altering her phrasing, letting out a literal scream and an appreciative *oooweeee*. Then she adds two baroque verses, name-checking heartthrob actors and Hercules. All pale in comparison to Mr. Fine Brown Frame. Our hep princess drops into a Satchmo-esque guttural whisper to tell him that he may not be hip to the jive or all-reet, but *oh whoa whoa whoa whoa* she's crazy mad about his you-know-what. Whoa, Nellie!

Born near Helena, Arkansas, **Roosevelt Sykes** (1906–83), one of the most important early blues pianists to reinvent himself as a rhythm & bluesman, played the organ in church and learned to play piano in local barrelhouses. ("He sang in high bursts," Preston Lauterbach says, "as if shouting over a sawmill.") Based in St. Louis, Sykes cut his first records in 1929 and recorded prolifically in the '30s. "The most extrovert and technically capable pianist who came out of St. Louis," Sykes was much admired by his peers, according to David Evans; his "rumbling, churning bass patterns" even influenced Robert Johnson.[29] He wrote and recorded soon-to-be classic "44 Blues," "Driving Wheel," and "Night Time is the Right Time" before arriving in Chicago in 1941. In 1945–46, Sykes had three records in *Billboard*'s top three, including "The Honeydripper," which became his nickname.

Recorded on the Bluebird label, **"Anytime is the Right Time"** (1946) has the same tune as "Night Time is the Right Time" with different lyrics. Sykes, his piano, and backing trio (Jimmy Lacey guitar, J.T. Brown alto sax, Jump Jackson drums) stand at the crossroads where the earlier Bluebird sound meets the new rhythm & blues. This record shows what a budding R&B man and a small group of musicians could do with a blues ballad. Sykes's warm, expressive voice sounds a little like Fats Domino's. He takes the distinctive lyrics slowly, rolling out the piano chords as he tells his baby how anytime is the right time for them to be together. The modern sound comes from Brown's yearning sax, forward in the mix, responding to every vocal phrase. "Look out there, Jimmy boy," Sykes calls, introducing Lacey's guitar solo, soon joined by sax and piano in dynamic synergy.

A few months later Sykes made the blues jump in **"Flames of Jive"** (1946), a 12-bar boogie on RCA, one of the rockin'est records of the year. With a trumpet, two saxophones, guitar, bass, and drums, Sykes fronted a classic R&B band: his Original Honeydrippers. Witty lyrics abound. His baby has a new kind of loving, those flames of jive that can keep a man alive. Turn out the lights, he sings excitedly, and don't call the law. Musically, things jump from the start as Sykes issues shout-outs to the band. He has drummer Jump Jackson set the beat. Then all the horns announce the riff they'll repeat after the first verse and again at the outro. "Blow, Johnny Morton, blow!" introduces the trumpet solo after the second verse, followed by Bill Casimir honking his tenor sax, and Sax Mallard's alto solo after verse three. This is potent ensemble rhythm & blues in its early days.

Another important R&B pianist/vocalist, **Memphis Slim** (1915–88) was born John Chatman in Memphis. He cut his musical teeth on Beale Street and in Helena, then took his musician father's name, Peter Chatman, for his first recordings. Settling in Chicago in 1939, he re-christened himself Memphis Slim. From 1940–44, Slim played piano for Bill Broonzy. According to Big Bill, "When I first told Slim that he was playing like Roosevelt Sykes he got mad at me, but he found out what I meant; he changed and went to playing like Memphis Slim." Playing like Memphis Slim meant being "one of the fastest technicians in Chicago, second only to Pete Johnson."[30] Along with bluesmen Broonzy and Sonny Boy Williamson I, Alan Lomax recorded Slim's candid recollections of life in the Jim Crow South as *Blues in the Mississippi Night*. Sick of American racism, Slim moved permanently to Paris in 1962.

For Miracle Records he recorded **"Rockin' the House"** (1946), a fast 12-bar boogie that does exactly what its title says. He called his subsequent bands the House Rockers, slimmed-down Slim with only his piano, two saxophones, and a bass. But they rocked like a group twice the size and the song makes great use of every player. The minimal lyrics explain that my baby's in town, I'm feeling all right, so let's rock the house. She's fine, built for speed, and we're gonna jump tonight. Slim opens the song with fifteen seconds of intense boogie. After the first verse he hollers, "Look out, bass!" and Willie Dixon launches into an extended solo. "I was using it as a drum by slapping it at the same time to give it a beat," Dixon explained. "Everybody from all over everywhere wanted to know who was playing that bass because they didn't know a bass could make triplets like that."[31] Alex Atkins' vamping alto solo follows the second verse, and the song goes out with Ernest Cotton's tenor followed by another strong boogie run from Slim. This song didn't make Dawson and Propes' *What Was the First Rock 'n' Roll Record?* but easily could have.

For **"Harlem Bound"** (1946) on Miracle, Slim used the same House Rockers, with Charles Jenkins replacing Dixon on bass. Jimmy Rogers turned this song into "Chicago Bound" in 1954, and this is just as hot. Maybe hotter. Instead of the Chicago blues sound of guitars and harp, Slim's piano and two saxes create R&B excitement. Slim sings a little louder and more emphatically than Rogers, and his boogie woogie piano rocks. As in "Rockin' the House," an instrumental solo follows each verse. After a piano intro and a flourish of horns Slim begins his musical journey. He played blues and boogie in Memphis in 1932, but left, bound ultimately for the Black Mecca, Harlem. Atkins' alto sax follows. Next, Slim is in East St. Louis in 1934, where he has plenty of female admirers, but he leaves them and the city because he's Harlem bound. Cotton's wild squealing tenor solo reflects Slim's building excitement as he closes in on his goal. In the final verse he's doing very well in Chicago but still plans to leave. The piano and horns send him out. Does he actually get there? No matter. Only the journey counts.[32]

Nick Tosches calls **Amos Milburn** (1927–80) "the first great rock 'n' roll piano man."[33] One listen to any of the records discussed here will tell you why. Born in Houston, Milburn moved to Los Angeles in 1946 and struck up a productive relationship with Aladdin Records, where Maxwell Davis arranged Milburn's songs and played superb tenor sax on most of his early hits. Today, we recognize Milburn, if at all, for his string of good-natured but turgid drinking songs—"Bad, Bad Whiskey"; "Let Me Go Home Whiskey"; "One Scotch, One Bourbon, One Beer"—all hits between 1950 and 1953. For the record, Sam Phillips recorded my #1 R&B drinking song, **"Juiced"** (1951) by Billy Love, released on Chess and incorrectly attributed to Jackie Brenston, whom we'll meet shortly.

Fast boogie woogie party records, Milburn's best songs don't concern drinking but Milburn and Davis, voice, piano, and sax, celebrating their own good time. **"Amos' Blues"** (1946), from his first Aladdin session, will get your heart racing from the opening drum riff. Milburn's single boogie phrase, repeated over and over at top speed, kicks off the 12-bar lyrics. They convey a frustrated lover's complaint to his no-good baby in vivid blues imagery. She doesn't give him what she should, but he's a tough guy and can live alone if she can't get it together. Ironically, he blames booze for her behavior. If she doesn't stop drinking, she'll be dead. He'll take her shoes down to her in the bottom (low-lying land along a river but also what she has hit because of her drinking. Is she barefoot in a swamp somewhere?) and give her an ultimatum. She has heard his blues. He has to leave her. What will she do?

Okay, it isn't Shakespeare but this lover's complaint sparks with originality. And the music, wow! Milburn doesn't shout exactly, but his fine R&B voice lays out his argument with lyrical vehemence and comfortably keeps up with the torrid pace of his piano. The thrilling call-and-response between his vocal and Davis' sax precedes the 70-second-long instrumental break. Milburn pounds the keys for the first thirty. You'd have to be tone deaf not to hear in that solo where Jerry Lee Lewis came from. Then Davis' sublime tenor takes over. Ever wondered why boogie woogie piano and tenor sax are R&B's instruments of choice? Just listen to this glorious record.

Another sensational recording, Milburn's **"Down the Road Apiece"** (1946), a funky boogie woogie piano showcase from that same first session, rocks, rolls, races, and rumbles. The song invites us to head down to an all-night roadhouse with the singer—not to drink but to hear boogie so good it's better than fried chicken. Written by Don Raye, the original recording by the all-white Will Bradley Trio had Raye sharing vocals with drummer Ray McKinley, Doc Goldberg on bass, and R&B pianist Freddie Slack. In their excellent version they invite us to hear *them* play at that roadhouse. The lyric mentions their nicknames from their performances on the boogie woogie hit, "Beat Me Daddy Eight to the Bar."

Adopting the lyrics verbatim, Milburn makes the song his homage to those boogie woogie pioneers. Raye and McKinley opened their song with spoken dialogue: they want to hear some good boogie. Milburn uses the same exchange, speaking both parts himself. He turns the already up-tempo pace torrid and changes the color of the song. His Black Texan accent and delivery transform the Bradley Trio's hillbilly-sounding anthem. But his record still delivers the boogie—the *great* boogie—that he invites us to hear. After the introduction and the first name-checking verse, Milburn launches into a breathtaking solo that lasts a full 1:15 before giving the anonymous bass man a fifteen second showcase. (The vocal insists that only piano and bass play at this boogie rave.) Then Milburn allows his piano another fifteen rockin' seconds before returning to the verse. The piano boogies down the road for another twenty seconds for the outro, a total of more than two minutes of pure instrumental joy in a delirious three-minute celebration of the boogie he's singing about.

Milburn first hit the charts with his self-penned **"Chicken Shack Boogie"** (1948). It hung in at #1 for five weeks. This Louis Jordan *homage*, a raucous Saturday Night Chicken Fry without cops, has him heading to another little joint down the road. He invites us only in the last verse. He's looking for the Chicken Shack, an underground hole-in-the-wall with a dangerous reputation, wild parties, and finger-lickin' chicken. Have a drink, you cats, then let the good times roll! Milburn speaks rather than sings the lyrics. The excellent critic Sampson on the *Spontaneous Lunacy* website writes, "Though not as explosive a sound as you might expect, it's an addicting groove that acts like a degenerate pied piper, leading the head-bobbing followers to a wonderful life of sinful depravity."[34] Milburn's piano duets with Davis' tenor, but the sax dominates, four solos to one. Apart from a short bleating passage,

Davis maintains a classy restraint, and Milburn too. Maybe they don't want to call the bad cats' attention to themselves.

The success of "Chicken Shack Boogie" led to Milburn's groups getting an embarrassing moniker: Amos Milburn and the Aladdin Chickenshackers. It also motivated Milburn to write and record a couple of fine Chicken Shack clones with the same tune: **"Roomin' House Boogie"** (1949) and **"Sax Shack Boogie"** (1950). The former reached #1, and *Billboard* named Milburn "Top R&B Artist" those two years in a row. He's having a rent party in the rooming house, playing boogie and low-down blues. The noise makes his landlady mad but he doesn't care. Milburn's piano and Davis' sax go wild. The landlady is obviously less dangerous than those bad cats at the chicken shack. Another hole-in-the-wall down by the tracks, the sax shack features three saxes. Don Wilkerson's tenor gets pride of place with Milburn's piano. To add to the vivid storytelling, Milburn has fun with surreal, offbeat rhymed lyrics. And he wasn't done yet. In 1956, he re-recorded **"Chicken Shack Boogie"** in New Orleans at a smoking tempo and louder volume. Except for a brief solo, Milburn's piano gets out of the way to let saxman Lee Allen scream and wail, while drummer Earl Palmer slams the backbeat. In the year rock 'n' roll basically ingested rhythm & blues, what better locale than a chicken shack for this tasty treat.

R&B pianist **Little Willie Littlefield** (1931–2013) grew up in Houston where he formed a band with Don Wilkerson, soon to be Amos Milburn's tenor saxman and later a key member of Ray Charles's orchestra. Influenced by Milburn, Littlefield made his first records in 1949. Like so many Houston rhythm & bluesmen, he then headed for Los Angeles, where he scored a few top ten hits for Modern Records. Moving to King Records' Federal subsidiary, Littlefield recorded a new song by Jerry Leiber and Mike Stoller: **"K.C. Loving"** (1952), later called "Kansas City," a #1 hit for Wilbert Harrison in 1959. Big Joe Turner and Pete Johnson's **"Kansas City Blues"** (1947) probably influenced Leiber and Stoller. "Stoller composed a mellifluous, flowing melody," James Miller writes. "Leiber responded in kind, taking pains to craft a plain-spoken lyric full of picaresque detail, evoking Kansas City as a timeless utopia of wine, women and song." As a kid growing up in the rock 'n' roll age, Robert Palmer remembers how the song "promised us everything we ever wanted—movement, sex and satisfaction."[35]

Littlefield's melodious vocal amplifies the feeling of liberation that the swinging mid-tempo shuffle celebrates. The lyrics unfold in reverse. The opening verses mark K.C. as a dream-space where he might do anything, like the Detroit of Hooker's "Boogie Chillen." He's going to Kansas City to get some of its crazy loving. If he can't get there by train or plane, he'll walk. Littlefield cranks up the vocal in the verse about travel. It may be a long way from Houston or Los Angeles, but in his fantasy it's just down the road a piece. Only in the final two verses does the blues kick in. Why does he want to go so badly? Because if he stays where he is, he feels like he'll die. The blues impulse to get away combines with the R&B tendency to fulfill the wish, to find that utopian chicken shack. He imagines standing at 12th and Vine (Joe Turner stands at 18th and Vine in "Kansas City Blues") with a K.C. woman and some fine wine. Movement, sex, and satisfaction come together at a magical crossroads in an iconic city. Maxwell Davis, a presence on so much of the great R&B out of L.A., swings his dreamy tenor in response to the vocal lines. Drummer Jesse Sailes, the other lead player here, makes sure more rhythm than blues informs this dream boogie of yearning and desire.

Leaders of the Pack

Some of the best R&B vocalists who led their own bands, Louis Jordan among them, played instruments other than piano. Like the pianists, they underwent significant musical apprenticeships, learning their trade in an orchestra, spending time on the road, getting to know what audiences wanted, playing alongside some of the best musicians of the age. That experience paid off when they entered the recording studio. We met drummer **Roy Milton** (1907–83) earlier, playing with Camille Howard and Helen Humes. A native Oklahoman, Milton first joined Tulsa's Ernie Fields Orchestra as a singer and drummer. Moving to Los Angeles in 1933, he formed his own band, The Solid Senders, with Howard on piano, three horns, and a bass. Later, he would add a guitarist. They toured widely for more than a decade before making their first records. Milton's **"R.M. Blues"** (1946), a huge hit for Art Rupe's new Juke Box label, spent 25 weeks near the top of the rhythm & blues chart. In 1947, Juke Box became Specialty Records. By 1953, Milton and his band had charted nineteen songs, establishing Specialty as L.A.'s premier R&B label and themselves as one of the west coast's finest assemblages. Widely imitated by other L.A. rhythm & bluesmen, Milton had "one of the strongest claims to be called 'the inventor of the rock 'n' roll beat,'" according to Charlie Gillett.[36]

From the same December 1945 session that produced "R.M. Blues" came **"Milton's Boogie"** (1946). Although it charted for only a week, this dynamic 12-bar boogie with that inventive beat clearly illustrates how Milton molded an ensemble that showed all his players to their best advantage. He took Count Basie's big band jazz number "Boogie Woogie (I May Be Wrong)" (1937), with vocal by Jimmy Rushing, and turned it into an R&B anthem. In its conventionally frustrating love affair scenario his woman blames him for something and is going her own way. He loves her, she loves someone else, but that's all right. We've heard that sentiment before. The lyrics get a twist when he compares her to both the devil and a frog, and admits that her loving makes him shout.[37] Lyrically, the song ends with an echo-effect call-and-response between the singer and band that harkens back to the big band novelty style of Cab Calloway. Big Joe Turner continued this effect into the 1950s.

We hear Milton's drums only briefly in the first few bars of his boogie while the riffing horns carry on an exciting call-and-response with Howard's rocking piano. Milton has a much stronger vocal drive than Rushing, singing the devil/frog verse in stop time. The music paces more quickly with a much more modern sound. Whereas Basie's piano gets the only solo in his recording, Milton spreads the joy around. With Howard's piano driving the boogie beat, Buddy Floyd's tenor sax takes over. Then the entire band gets a workout, followed by Hosea Sapp's trumpet solo. The song vividly illustrates how a six-piece rhythm & blues band could match the sound of a full orchestra and ramp up the excitement big time.

By 1949, Milton had added Junior Rogers' guitar to his Solid Senders sextet, but Rogers has only a minor role in **"It's Later Than You Think"** (1950). I want this song played at my funeral: classic 12-bar carpe diem R&B with lyrics that underline the facts of mortality. You can't live forever. When you're dead, the end. So better not wait until tomorrow to have your fun. I love Milton's passionate vocal and his unusual rhythmic scanning of the title line: "It's later *than* you think." The conjunction emphasizes the difference between the lateness of the moment and the time you think you have left. In the space between what actually is and your illusion of it, you need to crank up the intensity and reinvent your life. And what does the motoring, up-tempo music say? Life can be fantastically joyful and thrilling, but it zips by so quickly that you have to live every moment to the max. Snatch and grab it. After each of the first two verses Jackie Kelso's tenor sax and Benjamin Waters' alto outdo each other in their exhilarating celebrations of life, while Dallas Bartley's bass beats like a heart at full tilt. After the final verse, Milton shouts the Senders into their triumphant sendoff with riffing horns and Howard's enthusiastic piano. What a way to go.

Portrait of Tiny Bradshaw by Carl Van Vechten, 1942. Library of Congress, Prints & Photographs Division, Carl Van Vechten Collection, [reproduction number, e.g., LC-USZ62-54231].

Myron **Tiny Bradshaw** (1905–58) made another record I want played when I shuffle off that mortal coil. A native of Youngstown, Ohio, with a degree in psychology, Bradshaw moved to New York in the early 1930s to sing and play drums in a variety of swing orchestras. In 1934, he put together his own big band and toured prolifically, playing for American troops occupying Japan in 1945. A musician's musician, Bradshaw was known for cultivating great tenor sax players. For a while in the late '30s Ella Fitzgerald sang with his band. Artists ranging from Louis Jordan to Buddy Holly admired him. After the war, Bradshaw stripped his band down to eight or fewer players and reinvented himself as a rhythm & bluesman. He charted five times in the early 1950s with King Records, his songs produced, arranged, and co-written by King's A&R man, Henry Glover.

"I'm Going to Have Myself a Ball" (1950), like "It's Later Than You

Think," aims to rock you straight into the hereafter. Bradshaw's lyrics are a little more complex than Milton's. He values money more than women because it provides the means to enjoy life. Put some away for a rainy day, then have yourself a ball. You're crazy if all you do is work. Death may come unexpectedly so make sure you can afford to treat every day like a holiday. Towards the end of the song Bradshaw riffs on the imperative, insisting that we "*HA-AVE* a ball!" He emphasizes the verb because the ball itself, like the money, is secondary to the having, the doing, the being. *Let* the good times *roll*. Along with his emphatic vocal, the sax wails the gospel of life-embracing hedonism, as it does in so many rhythm & blues classics. What Nick Tosches calls "the ceaseless saxophones of salvation" announce the truths of mortality as eloquently as any lyric. Rufus Gore on tenor "specialized in vivid, Technicolor screaming saxophone solos during which a listener with a good imagination might think they are being splattered with droplets of the performer's saliva, if not his blood and soul."[38] The soul is an R&B abstraction. Let your body *have* its ball before it's too late.

"Mailman's Sack" (1952), Bradshaw's hardest-rocking tune, features Gore blowing his brains out in an almost seventy second solo. The unusual lyrics, sung almost entirely in stop-time, describe the singer receiving a letter from his baby. Instead of writing back to her, he sticks a stamp on himself and jumps into the mailman's sack. Being in the sack suggests sex but the song values the journey more than the destination. Gore drives the mail truck urgently, honking and squealing for everyone to get out of his way while Calvin "Eagle Eye" Shields pounds the drums. Bradshaw shares the adrenaline, encouraging them with shouts: "Go! Rock it, rock it!!" And do they ever.[39]

Shouters

On their records they probably don't shout any louder than many other R&B singers. And as rhythm & blues began to morph into rock 'n' roll, yelling sometimes overtook shouting. Still, a group of singers who shouted their blues emerged in the postwar era as a major force in the rhythm & blues revolution. The de facto leader of this pack was Big Joe Turner. His shouting style, rooted in the rich Kansas City blues tradition, provided the template for other great male shouters of the era, including Wynonie Harris, Roy Brown, Jimmy Witherspoon, and Eddie "Cleanhead" Vinson. Albert Murray writes that Turner, along with his peers, "shouts the blues away and shouts a church-rocking-stomping-jumping-shimmying good time into being in the process." For Arnold Shaw, Turner "shouted his independence. He was the new black man."[40] The shouters were loud and proud singers, but except for Cleanhead, not instrumentalists. Their synergy with the great players, producers, and arrangers gathered in New York, Los Angeles, Chicago, New Orleans, Cincinnati, and Houston generated some of the best music of the postwar years. The songs below represent only a small sampling.

Born in the musical hotbed of Kansas City, **Big Joe Turner** (1911–85) had a big voice. Nick Tosches describes it as "oceanic and commanding, resonant with that rumbling deep down ... a voice of power." Whitney Balliett calls him "probably the greatest of blues singers."[41] Turner learned his trade in the city's jazz clubs and honkytonks where he tended bar, shouting to be heard over the bands and the crowds. At nineteen, he joined forces with K.C. pianist Pete Johnson. Their success at John Hammond's 1938 *Spirituals to Swing* concert and subsequent popularity helped fire up the boogie woogie phenomenon. After a residency in New York, Turner and Johnson moved to Los Angeles where Turner sang with Duke Ellington's orchestra and later with Count Basie. From 1945–47, Herb Abramson produced his songs for the National Records label, then co-founded New York's Atlantic Records with Ahmet Ertegun. Turner's career took off when he joined Atlantic in 1951, churning out hit after hit in the early 1950s, rockin' and rollin'. But when rock 'n' roll really took over, it left Turner—a big Black man in his mid-forties—behind. Best known as a good-time blues shouter, Big Joe also wrote lyrics among the most fascinating in the rhythm & blues canon.

Turner cut his own composition, the 12-bar **"My Gal's a Jockey"** (1946), with Bill Moore's Lucky Seven Band. Saxman Wild Bill Moore, who played on Humes' "Be-Baba-Leba," performs a classic squealing tenor solo here. Turner's lyrics present an ambivalent lover who can't decide whether to get back in the saddle or take a

Big Joe Turner with Pete Johnson on piano at Café Society, New York City, 1940. Dave. E. Dexter, Jr. Collection, LaBudde Special Collections, UMKC University Libraries.

walk. To *ride* is an R&B commonplace for sex. Normally, the man initiates the riding in these songs. Here, his gal is the jockey, and the woman on top makes him anxious. He might have to leave this big woman who rides him to exhaustion. Besides, he wants no kinky mane, but one that is smooth and straight, a 1930s blues verse that evokes the politics of hair.[42] Then he pivots. Everything's all right. He will see his baby tonight. She's teaching him how to ride, and he loves the way her shimmy moves him. The horn section shouts as enthusiastically as Turner as they gallop along together. Warren Brocken gets a trumpet solo while bass man Shifty Henry marks the time. The musical highlight, Moore's tenor solo, at one point suggests the fanfare that begins a horse race. I'll put my money on the big stallion with the girl in the saddle.

"Low Down Dog" (1947) entered Turner's repertoire after he and Pete Johnson performed it at *Spirituals to Swing*, and Turner went on to record it multiple times. His 1947 version for Aladdin is a 12-bar rocker with a tune similar to "My Gal's a Jockey." This time Turner wrote conventional lyrics. You mistreated me though I worked hard and brought you my pay. You're on top now but one day it will be my turn. I won't be your low-down dog anymore. He handles the sentiment with equanimity, referring to himself without self-pity, singing *Oo-oo-oo-oo-oo-wee* more in self-mockery than anguish. Johnson's lighthearted piano intro sets the tone and the three horn solos, topped by Jack McVea's sax in the lengthy break, positively proclaim "the buoyant sound of *freedom*—the steady shuffle rhythm behind him symbolizing his walking out…."[43]

The cult of the teenager was well underway when Atlantic's Ahmet Ertegun, using the pen name A. Nugetre, wrote **"Sweet Sixteen"** (1952) for Big Joe. By the end of the decade male pop singers would have an absolute fetish for sixteen-year-old girls: Chuck Berry's "Sweet Little Sixteen," the Crests' "16 Candles," Sam Cooke's "Only Sixteen," Johnny Burnett's "You're 16, You're Beautiful, and You're Mine." Young women in blues and R&B songs, courted by older men, generally lack the innocence of those rock and pop teens. Listen to the Du Droppers' **"Bambalam"** (1953), the Robins' **"School Girl Blues"** (1951), or Muddy Waters' "She's Nineteen Years Old" (1958). Muddy was 45 when he sang of his frustrations trying to please his teen squeeze. Joe Turner had turned 41 when he recorded "Sweet Sixteen" with Van "Piano Man" Walls and His Orchestra.

Atypically for Turner, his persona *does* feel sorry for himself in this song. The poignant blues ballad addresses a young woman who ran away from home at sixteen. The singer explains his feelings: You're the sweetest, I loved you from the moment we met, but you led me on and now you want to run away again. You can hear the regret and sorrow in his powerful voice, reflected in Walls's melancholy piano. Even the four horns, after blasting a note of hopefulness, fall back into quiet despair. The singer amplifies his desperation when he cries out "sweet sixteen" four times in the final verse. When he shifts from talking to her about their relationship to appealing for an understanding of how alone he is in the world—his brother fighting in Korea, his sister in New Orleans, his mother dead—poet Sherley Anne Williams hears the collective experience of deep, historically rooted African American trauma: "ruptured family relationships caused by the oppressive and repressive system of the country," reflecting "the audience['s] private pains…."[44]

From the sublime to the surreal. In 1953, Atlantic teamed Big Joe with Elmore James and a band they called His Blues Kings to record **"T.V. Mama"** (1953). Songwriter Turner was either inspired or on some otherworldly drug. Musically exceptional, the mid-tempo shuffle nicely melds Turner's booming voice and James's instantly identifiable slide guitar. His signature "Dust My Broom" riff responds to Turner's vocal, Little Johnny Jones subtly works his classy piano into the mix, Red Saunders' drumming provides the slow-rockin' rhythm. And the lyrics, oh my. Blues songs have compared women to horses and cows, cars and fruit trees. But what other songwriter cast a woman in the metaphor of a TV set? She of the strange anatomy appears to him in a dream, like a Magritte painting, with huge eyes, tiny feet, slim waist, and a wide screen. (Wide-screen TVs wouldn't appear in real life for another fifty years.) The final verse finds him rollin' and tumblin' (a tribute to James's blues pedigree) and mumbling in his sleep until his woman shakes him and he falls out of bed.

Life could be a dream. In a psychoanalytic discussion of the blues, Paul Garon argues that dreams represent the gratification of repressed desires and the aspiration for freedom. "New modes of poetic action, new networks of analogy, new possibilities of expression all help formulate ... the transformation of everyday life as it encumbers us today...."[45] Think of all those blues and R&B songs in which the man complains of his baby's unruliness or infidelity and how conveniently a sexed-up, robotic, electronic woman would transform his life and free him of those encumbrances. Ultimately, Turner's baby won't stand for his dream, waking him back to reality.

"Shake, Rattle and Roll" (1954) became Turner's best-known and most successful record, spending 32 weeks on the R&B chart, three at #1. Selling over a million copies, as did Bill Haley and the Comets' cleaned-up cover, the song became one of the avatars of rock 'n' roll. Written by Atlantic's brilliant African American A&R man, Jesse Stone, under the pseudonym Charles Calhoun, it features vivid imagery, a hook in the title line perfectly made for Turner's shouting, and another complex rhythm & blues relationship. The title phrase originally referred to throwing dice in craps, but here it takes on multifaceted meanings: behavioral, sexual, musical.

Another group of A-list Atlantic session men drives the up-tempo 12-bar blues: Stone on piano, Sam "The Man" Taylor tenor sax, Mickey Baker guitar, and Connie Kay drums. Dawson and Propes describe the song "propelled by Stone's distinctive piano triplets, the sinewy riff of the three-man horn section, the drummer playing on the offbeat and a steady, multiple hand-clapping brought up high in the balance—with Heywood Henry's baritone sax solo in the middle...." (Nick Tosches identifies that soloist as Taylor.) The arrangement complements Turner's aggressive vocal and lyrics: "lascivious," Tosches writes, "but not quite dirty enough to stop it from getting airplay."[46] The singer begins with macho demands—get out of bed, wash up, get in the kitchen and start cooking—and the familiar trope about how hard he works and how quickly she spends his money. He calls her a devil, complaining that she does nothing to save her soul. Yet, this devil's temptation is irresistible. His eyes linger on the way the sun shines through her thin dresses, he looks at her like a cat eyeing seafood. Then, going over and under, he has what sounds like an orgasm. All those images clean up or disappear in Bill Haley's bowdlerized version. At the same time, the action in the kitchen feels like a dance party. You can shake, rattle, and roll or save your soul. For kids in the mid-1950s it was no contest.

Turner's born-again popularity derived from the joy his best records delivered, connecting him with a decades-younger teen audience. A straight-ahead rockin' dance tune, **"Boogie Woogie Country Girl"** (1955) incorporates the older R&B boogie traditions that Turner never gave up. The clever lyrics by Doc Pomus, one of rock's best songwriters, conjure a country girl who fishes and milks cows but also digs rock 'n' roll, dislikes squares, and dances her ass off. Turner celebrates her without macho posturing. Fully engaged in the party, he shouts, "Let 'em roll," the phrase connecting this song to "Roll 'Em, Pete," the signature tune he and Pete Johnson first recorded in 1938. Referencing Johnson, Piano Man Walls's boogie woogie eighty-eights share center-stage with Turner's vocals, and drummer Connie Kay hits the back beat hard. A thoroughly modern old bluesman, Big Joe rocked 'til he dropped.

Joe Turner had the moniker Boss of the Blues. Not to be outdone, **Wynonie Harris** (1915–69) called himself Mr. Blues. With a big voice, sexual swagger, and shouting style similar to Big Joe's, Harris waxed dozens of rhythm & blues classics. He made one of the era's most important proto-rock recordings, "Good Rockin' Tonight," but there's a lot more to Mr. Blues. From Omaha, Nebraska, not exactly a blues capital, Harris regularly visited Kansas City clubs where he came to idolize Turner. As the vocalist for Lucky Millinder's orchestra in 1944, he had a hit with his first record, "Who Threw the Whiskey in the Well." His major successes as a solo act came with King Records from 1947 to 1952, landing thirteen songs on the R&B chart.

Not modest about his nickname, Harris included "Mr. Blues" in at least four of his records, all worth a listen: **"Mr. Blues Jumped the Rabbit"** (1946), **"Good Morning Mr. Blues"** (1947), **"Rock Mr. Blues"** (1950), and **"Mr. Blues Is Coming to Town"** (1950). But like Amos Milburn's odes to drinking, Harris' outrageous double entendre songs generated much of his fame: **"I Like My Baby's Pudding"** (1950), **"Keep on Churnin' (Till the Butter Comes)"** (1952), and more. His biographer, Tony Collins, attributes Harris' success partly to his ability to sing songs like that "with such disarmingly cheerful vulgarity." He turned even the most unlikely material into good-time dance music. Nearly all his records have at least a touch of the lascivious, but the way he radiated postwar optimism, his sheer raffish pleasure at being alive, strikes me as the seminal aspect of his music. More than just a dream, the good life in Wynonie-land permeates every scene. Mr. Blues he may have been. But as Collins writes, "His was a new style of blues for a new post-war era, slick and urban. His blues bemoaned the problems or, more frequently, celebrated the joys of life in the big city."[47] His most characteristic line occurs in the repeated refrain of **"Around the Clock"** (1946), a two-sided ballad Harris recorded with Johnny Otis' All Stars, in which a woman, making love with her man all night, keeps saying, "I'm so glad I'm living." And why not, if she's hanging with Mr. Blues.

Backed by Hot Lips Page's band, Harris cut three superb records for King in

December 1947. A 12-bar boogie, **"Lollipop Mama"** (1948) was written and recorded a couple of months earlier in Dixieland style as **"Lolly Pop Mama"** (1947) by fellow shouter Roy Brown, whom we'll meet next. The unsubtly obvious lyrical theme has his woman calling him her lollipop, wanting him to hurry up and bring it. But more than just a one-trick pony, she's a hard-loving mama who dominates him in the sack, rocking him day and night. Scared to complain because she has a heart like a bear and is strong enough to tote railroad steel, Wynonie squeals in pleasurable pain, it hurts so good. And the music is terrific. Superb tenor saxmen Tom Archia and Hal "Oklahoma" Singer trade musical responses to the vocal, and Singer gets a short, sweet solo, while the tight rhythm section of Joe Knight piano, Bobby Donaldson drums, and especially Carl "Flat Top" Wilson on bass drives the boogie beat. **"Lolly Pop Mama"** (1947) by Clarence Samuels, a New Orleans protégé of Roy Brown, also rocks hard.

Wynonie Harris promotional photograph, c. 1948–52. Everett Collection Inc./Alamy Stock Photo.

Released as the B-side of "Lollipop Mama," **"Blow Your Brains Out"** (1948) is my number one Wynonie song and one of my all-time rhythm & blues favorites. In Harris' tribute to the tenor sax, Tom Archia and Hal Singer do battle in one of the classiest exchanges you'll ever hear. It has the feel of a late-night jam session performed for fellow musicians as they hand off solos to each other. With the same rhythm section laying down the beat as on "Lollipop Mama," Harris plays MC, calling out "Tom Archia!" or "Oklahoma!" He appears to improvise some of the lyrics, then gets out of the way to let these two tenor giants blow their brains out because they *know* what a saxophone can do. A dream record for tenor sax connoisseurs and anyone else with musical taste.

Heard the news? **"Good Rockin' Tonight"** (1948), Harris' most iconic and successful song, spent 25 weeks on the R&B chart and anticipated rock 'n' roll. Written and first recorded by Roy Brown, it was then covered by Harris and later made famous by Elvis. To James Miller, "Harris and his combo transformed the song into a celebration of everything dance music can be: an incantation, an escape, an irrepressibly joyous expression of sheer physical existence." Brown's imaginative lyrics and Harris' perfectly phrased, raucous delivery join with "'Hot Lips' Page's sassy trumpet, Hal Singer's raging tenor sax, Joe Knight's rolling piano, Carl 'Flat Top' Wilson's thumping bass and an insistent, contagious hand-clapping that kept the song rockin'...." Let's not forget Tom Archia's second tenor, Vincent Bair-Bey's alto, and Bobby Donaldson's growling drums.[48]

A mid-tempo boogie (as are Harris' other songs below), "Good Rockin'" opens with the horns riffing on "When the Saints Go Marching In." But each of the first three bars ends with the trumpet's mocking *wah-wah*, and the fourth segues into the sax's groovy intro to Harris' vocal. The opening announces not the good news of gospel but rhythm & blues' secular news of good rockin' and good times rollin'. The lyrics begin in the first person, initially appearing to celebrate the singer's individual sexual satisfaction. But the personal soon becomes communal and the sexual gives way to a scene of broadly democratic social liberation. In subsequent repetitions *I* becomes *you*, then finally *we*—"*everybody's* gonna rock tonight." From two lovers meeting behind a barn, the dreamscape expands into a mythic party on R&B's Mount Olympus. Characters from Black folklore and music convene in a Dionysian romp, stomping and jumping like mad, with churchmen to sanctify the occasion—Elder Brown, Deacon Jones—and a busload of women: Sweet Lorraine, Georgia Brown, Sioux City Sue, and Caldonia. "The record ends," Tony Collins observes, "with Wynonie so caught up in the excitement of the moment that he abandons—or forgets—Roy Brown's lyrics and simply chants 'Hoy, hoy, hoy' as the music fades out." It sounds to me like embrace, not abandonment. The excitement is the point. If the rockin' is good, all will be well.[49]

Two superb songs released the next year show the pros and cons of the gospel according to Mr. Blues. Modeled after Eddie "Cleanhead" Vinson's **"Old Maid Boogie"** (1947), **"Sittin' on It All the Time"** (1949), my second favorite Wynonie opus, riffs on Shakespeare's Seven Ages of Man. In an R&B Eleven Ages of Woman he sings to her about how she wasted her youth refusing to give it up. Now she's old (63) and has decided, too late, to stop sitting on it. The singer perversely complains about her prudery at ages ten and fifteen. For the next nine ages, from twenty-two to sixty-three, he notes the opportunities she passed up. As each verse ends with the band members reminding her in chorus how she kept sittin' on it, Orrington Hall's honking tenor sax ridicules her behavior. Vocally at the top of his game, energetic and confident, Harris romps with the music and hand-clapping. Opening with Bill Martin's trumpet fanfare, the song rocks along with fine sax solos from Hall and LeRoy Harris on alto. The music, lyrics, and vocal performance all make clear that the rockin' can be good even into middle age. But you better get it while you can.

Because not even Mr. Blues has immunity from the ravages of time. Though just thirty-four when he wrote and recorded **"I Feel That Old Age Coming On"** (1949), he already imagines himself old and decrepit. *Carpe diem* leads straight to *memento mori*. The song uses the same upbeat tempo as "Good Rockin'" and "Sittin' on It" but with uncharacteristically downbeat lyrics, vocal, and parts of the orchestration. He looks into his baby's eyes and sees that she doesn't want him anymore. They reflect his image as an aging man. Feeling tapped out, he'll see what the doctor can do. The instrumental break follows with Albert Wallace's upbeat piano and Frank Culley's alto sax offering musical consolation. Then Hal Singer's tenor comes squealing in as if crying "Help!" before modulating into a rockin' transition with the rest of the band, cueing the line where Wynonie optimistically asks his baby to make love to him. But she says no. Finally, when he asks her to marry him, she turns his proposal into an embarrassing joke. Cat Anderson's melancholy trumpet solo follows.

The song ends with Harris repeating the title line as Singer's sax squeals in protest and despair, the last musical gasp of a man who realizes too late that if you live by the body, you'll die by it.

Let's not leave Mr. Blues on the downbeat. Recorded with Todd Rhodes's seven-piece band, **"Lovin' Machine"** (1951), Harris' final *Billboard* hit, sounds like an optimistic sequel to "I Feel That Old Age Coming On." If the rapid onset of aging has made him impotent, he can at least imagine building a machine to do his loving for him, like a male version of Joe Turner's TV Mama. Or maybe it's a bizarre come-on: Come to my house, I'll show you something amazing. Put money in the slot, it kisses and hugs you, makes you scream and shout. It can go all day and night, and leaves you a bottle of Hadacol as a bonus. (Hadacol tonic's twelve percent alcohol content reportedly got you high and horny. Check out Little Willie Littlefield, **"Drinkin' Hadacol"** [1949], Roy Byrd [Professor Longhair] and His Blues Jumpers, **"Hadacol Bounce"** [1950], Nellie's brother Joe Lutcher, **"Give Me My Hadacol"** [1950], and The Treniers, **"Hadacol That's All"** [1952].) The naked ludicrousness of the surrogate fantasy suggests that this guy will say anything to get laid—the name of the rhythm & blues game. King Records always provided Harris with excellent musical accompaniment. Here he's blessed with a fine rhythm section led by Rhodes's boogie woogie piano and a memorable alto sax solo from Holley Dismukes. Harris will have no future with rock 'n' roll around the corner, so let's dance him offstage with the huzzahs he deserves.

Harris' success with "Good Rockin' Tonight" forever connects him to **Roy Brown** (1925–81), whose own recording of his classic song was, ironically, neither good nor rockin'. An imaginative songwriter, Brown charted seventeen times from 1948 to 1957. His influence on singers from B.B. King and Bobby Bland to Jackie Wilson and James Brown remains as important a legacy as the songs he wrote and recorded. Born in New Orleans, he sang in a gospel quartet as an adolescent. Bringing his churchy feel into the secular realm—what John Broven calls "his crying, pleading, swooping gospel-based style"—Brown synthesized it with the shout to create a unique approach to rhythm & blues. "Roy torched the blues with spiritual fire," Lauterbach writes. But his hybrid sound didn't always serve him well. "Brown failed to slot into the contemporaneous trend for shouters because there was just a little too much gospel in his delivery. Naturally, gospel fans found the base, secular strains in his material distasteful."[50]

In "Good Rockin' Tonight," when Brown holds his baby tight she knows he's a mighty man. He expanded that idea in **"Mighty, Mighty Man"** (1948), a 12-bar rocker he recorded for New Jersey's De Luxe label with the otherwise obscure Earl M. Barnes orchestra. You can hear one of the signatures of the shouter style in the way he precedes every line with a loud, drawn-out *WE-E-E-LL* or *YE-E-ES*. Like Muddy Waters in "Hoochie Coochie Man," Brown toots his own horn: he's twenty-five, in his prime, six-feet tall, single, ready to take on and finish any job. He is, indeed, a mighty, mighty man. And he sings mighty, mighty well. The horns roar alongside him, and he gets upbeat solos from Earl Barnes on tenor and Wallace Davenport on trumpet. Although lyrically a series of boasts, the performance comes off as a joyous youthful embrace of the world as possibility. Why not stay single. It's a wonderful life.

By the time Brown cut **"Cadillac Baby"** (1950) for De Luxe in Cincinnati (King Records' Syd Nathan had purchased the label), he had already charted twelve times and called his band the Mighty Mighty Men. Car songs had long been a popular sub-genre of blues, the verb *ride*—as with horse songs—transparently standing for *have sex*. (For the ultimate in this genre, listen to Orville **Fats Noel**'s **"Ride Daddy Ride"** [1951], a frantic rocker complete with Noel's own screaming sax.) The car of choice was the Caddy: classy, elegant, comfortable, top of the line. Another infectious 12-bar rocker written by Brown, "Cadillac Baby" makes *him* the Cadillac in/on which she's crazy about riding all night. In the wittiest line she tells him that if he gets tired of riding, he should park it in her favorite spot. Whoo! The horn-heavy band includes a trumpet, trombone, and two saxophones. Johnny Fontenette takes the solo on tenor. Despite starting each line with that first-word shout, Brown also modulates his voice, hinting at what he could do with a ballad. But he uses the final forty seconds to rock out, repeating eight times that they'll ride all night long.

Midnight seems to have been Brown's favorite time of day. He recorded **"Rockin' at Midnight"** (1948), a fine sequel to "Good Rockin' Tonight"; **"Long about Midnight"** (1948); **"Boogie at Midnight"** (1949); and the only one that didn't chart, an exquisite ballad, **"Trouble at Midnight"** (1954). Unlike compatriot Wynonie Harris, also with King Records at this time, Brown "*cried* the blues," according to Jon Hartley Fox, who catalogues an intense delivery, sense of abandonment, vulnerability, and emotional openness as key elements of Brown's style.[51] All are evident in "Trouble at Midnight." When he comes home and finds his baby gone, he wants to cry. Hard work becomes his antidote to troubled romance. At least it won't kill him or drive him out of his mind. Three horns, a strong rhythm section, and Jimmy Davis' T-Bone-like guitar underline Brown's exceptional vocal passion. This beautiful ballad sits right on the cusp between R&B and rock 'n' roll.

Brown's tenure with King marked a fertile period for him, even if he never commercially matched his earlier work with De Luxe. **"Gal from Kokomo"** (1954) shows that he could still write some of the richest, most fascinating lyrics in rhythm & blues and rock as hard as ever. Returning to New Orleans for this session, he sang with a leaner five-piece version of His Mighty Mighty Men. Lyrically, Brown is audaciously original. The song initially appears to be a standard 12-bar blues about trying to hang onto his Kokomo gal. But it becomes a psychodrama as he struggles with himself and his demons in an almost hallucinatory stream of consciousness. Tired of his drinking, she's leaving on the morning train. He implores her not to go. That morphs into an R&B prayer: Rock me in the cradle and squeeze the whiskey from my soul. Meanwhile, he free-associates arbitrarily violent alternatives to her leaving: shoot the preacher, rob the banker, embalm the undertaker. In a lyrical in-joke, Brown will even sacrifice Ben Bart, his own New York booking agent. Anything but lose his gal! Wild tenor sax and guitar solos from Phillip Scott and Edgar Blanchard respectively and Frank Parker's driving drum beat all join the mad vocal, which devolves into an almost whispered prayer as he desperately begs her not to leave. This guy was a true original.

Jimmy Witherspoon (1923–97) had the best voice of the shouters, and audience reactions on his live recordings testify to his marvelous chops as a performer. Born in rural Arkansas, he sang in a gospel choir as a boy before moving to Los Angeles, where bandleader Jay McShann recruited him in 1944. After a few years as McShann's vocalist, Witherspoon recorded with a variety of backing bands for various labels. "Joe Turner was my idol," he told Arnold Shaw. "He's a blues singer!" But Witherspoon rejected generic labels for himself: "They call me an R&B singer. I'm a singer! I can sing ballads; I can sing church; I can sing Dixieland."[52] In the late 1950s, with rhythm & blues in decline, unable to code-switch to rock 'n' roll, he reinvented himself as a jazz singer and had a notable second career. In fact, he could sing anything jazzy or bluesy, and rock with sanctified joy.

In 1947, accompanied by McShann on piano, Witherspoon recorded for a new Los Angeles label, Supreme, the classic blues ballad made famous by Bessie Smith in 1923 as "'Tain't Nobody's Business If I Do." Witherspoon's **"Ain't Nobody's Business, Parts 1 & 2"** (1948) runs for six minutes on both sides of the record. It hit the *Billboard* R&B chart in 1949 and stayed there for 34 weeks, briefly reaching #1. In its original form as a woman's blues, sung by Smith, Billie Holiday, and others, the song comes off as a declaration of independence: Angela Davis describes it as an "affirmation of women's right as individuals to conduct themselves however they wish—however idiosyncratic their behavior might seem and regardless of the possible consequences." Witherspoon's version tells a more downbeat story, although Jerry Leiber of future Leiber and Stoller fame heard in it something radically liberating.[53]

Witherspoon slows the tempo way down, swinging the lyrics in a melancholy voice reminiscent of Langston Hughes's 1925 poem, "The Weary Blues." Far from an anthem of liberation, this performance smacks of desperation. A seven-piece rhythm & blues band including three horns accompanies the vocal, but McShann's quietly tinkling piano dominates musically, with Louis Speiginer's guitar dipping in midway through Part 1 and the horns barely audible in the background. Part 2 opens with a lovely, downbeat, minute-long tenor sax solo from Charles Thomas. Intensifying the downbeat atmosphere, Witherspoon moans, "Lord, Lord, Lord." Each of the ten verses ends with the statement, "Ain't nobody's business if I do," but the sentiment feels more like "Leave me alone in my misery" than "I'm letting the good times roll and damn the consequences." What's no one's business? He'll go crazy and shoot his baby; jump into the ocean; go to church one day and party the next; stay out all night and spend all his money. Twice he indicates he has nothing to eat—but that's nobody's business either. He ends by stating that he's twenty-one so he can do whatever he wants. But adulthood offers him little profit or joy. The popular success of this achingly beautiful, melancholy ballad suggests that much of the African American audience identified with the dreamer who can't be satisfied, with the dream turned bitter.

Rhythm & blues and jazz were hot commodities in mid-century Los Angeles.

African American promoter Leon Hefflin presented annual Cavalcades of Jazz outdoors in L.A.'s Wrigley Field, and disc jockeys Frank Bull and Gene Norman produced large-scale Blues Jubilee and Just Jazz concerts in Los Angeles and Pasadena. Witherspoon appeared in at least four of the Cavalcades and two of Bull & Norman's extravaganzas. Two songs on Modern Records attest to his electrifying live performances. **"No Rollin' Blues"** (1949), recorded at a Just Jazz affair, spent ten weeks on the charts. Witherspoon would later feature the song in his appearance at the 1959 Monterey Jazz Festival that turned his career around. Accompanied by the Gene Gilbeaux Quartet, he has plenty of leeway for his big voice. The song is a slow 12-bar ballad, a standard lover's complaint, but Witherspoon roars the lyrics and Gilbeaux shouts comments in response. It begins rhetorically. If you've ever loved a woman and caught her fooling around, or if she complains when you come home from work, you might as well pack up and leave. She's obviously rollin' with someone else. Then it gets personal: I went to see her, she said goodbye, no more rollin' for Witherspoon. The exuberant performance and the final verse, in which he expresses his preference for loving in the early morning rain, belie the downbeat lyrics. Witherspoon is clearly enjoying himself, the band is having a ball, and the audience goes crazy. Don Hill's moody alto sax does most of the musical work, Gilbeaux's light-fingered piano keeps a running commentary underneath, and drummer Tucker Green pounds out a strong beat.

Recorded at the same Blues Jubilee as Helen Humes' "Million Dollar Secret," **"New Orleans Woman"** (1950) showcases Witherspoon's facility for jumping the blues. The lyrics matter much less than the rockin' music and vocal performance. Fifteen seconds of Gilbeaux's swinging piano give way to thirty seconds of Hill's screaming sax with Gilbeaux egging him on before Witherspoon comes in wondering what that New Orleans woman is doing to him—another tough woman he can't control. With strong rhythmic drive from the piano and Shifty Henry's bass, he tells a quick story of her trying to hoodoo him, digging a hole and leaving a charm by his door. But he seems less interested in that story than in the wildly energetic break with the sax cutting loose again, the drummer pounding away, and everyone yelling encouragement in an R&B shouter classic.

Balladeers

Arnold Shaw calls them "sepia Sinatras." *Sepia* was a common *Billboard* descriptor for African American singers, Frank Sinatra the young white crooner who defined the late–1940s pop ballad style. By 1952–53, rhythm & blues was shifting away from the shouters and old-style jump blues to younger singers with a smoother sound. The new rhythm & blues fusion, Shaw explains, "mix[ed] elements of country blues, boogie woogie, and jazz in a cauldron fired by the seductive sales of pop balladry." The proponents of this "murmuring, gentle *vibrato* ballad style" included Nat King Cole—the most successful African American pop singer of the day—Cecil Gant, Charles Brown, Ivory Joe Hunter and, in his first incarnation, Ray Charles, along with the artists featured below. Most ended up in Los Angeles. In contrast to the mostly upbeat, up-tempo, celebratory R&B we've heard so far, the balladeers reflected a cloudier assessment of the times. Shaw claims, "the West Coast ballad fusion was marked by frustration, a reflection, perhaps, of the postwar mood of many black people for whom the war to rid the world of racial discrimination was promises, promises—and hollow promises at that." Charlie Gillett concurs:

> While the jump blues served to express whatever confidence people felt on the West Coast during and after the war, the quieter club blues expressed the more dominant mood there, one tinged with despondency.... Living conditions and earnings ... were much better than they had been in Texas, but were still much worse for blacks than for the whites working alongside them.[54]

The focus here was less rhythm and more blues.

The father of soul singer Curtis Mayfield ("People Get Ready," "Super Fly"), Louisiana-born **Percy Mayfield** (1920–84) considered himself a songwriter when he headed to L.A. in 1942. He brought along a song he figured would be perfect for Jimmy Witherspoon, but ended up recording **"Two Years of Torture"** (1949) himself for Supreme. After Specialty Records picked him up, their first Mayfield release, **"Please Send Me Someone to Love"** (1950), charted for 27 weeks, two at #1. The song became an instant classic, covered by numerous singers. Here, writes one critic, Mayfield "stakes his claim as rock's first great poet and its conscience as well." Lyrically unlike anything else in the rhythm & blues canon, it offers a prayer for world peace, understanding, and love. The singer combines his personal anxieties with a general plea for humankind to have a change of heart. He lies awake in misery, pondering the world's troubles—asking not for personal sympathy but heavenly intervention. Mayfield said, "I wrote that as a prayer for peace between the black man and the white man."[55] The United States had begun fighting in Korea a few weeks before, so that likely also factored in. The structure of the lyric suggests that his request for someone to love is an afterthought, subordinated to the more important project of saving the world from hate, strife, and racism. But its repetition and Mayfield's emotional expression of those lines equate the personal and political dreams. Despite the mention of misery and the horns' doleful opening, the song offers a balance of gloom and hope. Mayfield swings his vocal slowly, but with zest. Eddie Beal's piano walks the same fine line as the vocal, while Maxwell Davis offers a melancholy, cerebral tenor solo so brief it barely registers. An outstanding performance of a beautiful, thoughtful song.

We've met Memphis-born John Alexander, aka **Johnny Ace** (1929–54), playing piano in the Beale Streeters band with B.B. King and Bobby Bland. Signed to Memphis' Duke label in 1952, accompanied by the Beale Streeters, Ace aced his first release, **"My Song"** (1952). It quickly climbed to #1 and stayed there for nine weeks. Arnold Shaw describes his singing as plaintive. Ace's biographer, James Salem, calls it a combination of warm, relaxed style and painful, sorrowful mood. Stir in "the Memphis synthesis"—pop sentiment with a blues background—and you have the irresistible sound of "My Song." Essentially doo wop sung solo, it conjures heartbreak, tears, pleading, and eternal togetherness. *Billboard* announced that it initiated a new genre: the *heart ballad*.[56]

The musical minimalism of "My Song," unusual for R&B, showcases Ace's languid vocals with just his piano, Billy Duncan's tenor sax, and Earl Forest's drums. Its trite lyrics represent a dozen ways of saying I love you, please come back. The sensitivity of the male persona echoes the shift to youthful vulnerability in hundreds of doo wop songs of the 1950s, part of the cultural construction of teenage innocence. The emotionally seductive sound of the record dominates the listening experience. Duncan's yearning sax seems to pull the vocals along while piano and drum lay down a slow, pulsing rhythm. Ace's warm voice moves into romantic agony in the highly dramatic bridge. Certain words pop. But the overall mood trumps individual lyrics. Young love painfully grasping for words adequate to the intensity of feeling comes through most clearly. Heart ballad is a good descriptor. "My Song" seems to bypass the brain and come directly from the heart.

Johnny Ace is best remembered today, if remembered at all, for **"Pledging My Love"** (1954), an equally lovely song with less banal lyrics, made infamous by the circumstances surrounding his death at age twenty-five. Christmas Eve 1954, on tour with Big Mama Thornton, Ace was fooling around with a pistol backstage at a Houston club. Either while playing Russian roulette or accidentally—the story varies—he shot himself in the head. His death generated a cult. At least a half-dozen tribute records came out within the year, including "Johnny Has Gone," "Johnny's Still Singing," and "Why, Johnny, Why?" Released on Duke shortly before Ace's death, accompanied by the Johnny Otis Orchestra, "Pledging My Love" rocketed to #1 R&B where it remained for ten weeks, and reached #17 pop.

The song shouldn't have needed tragic publicity to give it momentum. An achingly beautiful heart ballad in which the singer pledges his eternal love, it proceeds at

Johnny Ace at the piano, early 1950s. Album/Alamy Stock Photo.

a slow, stately pace. Otis' vibraphone, the primary instrumental sound along with Ace's plinking piano, tolls like a bell. But the lyrical sentiment, far from funereal, has the singer vouching for the fire in his soul and his intention to make her happy always. The bridge reveals the emotional intensity of the singer's love at its strongest as he insists that his heart is hers to command, and James Von Streeter's sax replicates a lover's hopeful sigh. The singer's absolute commitment, a sentiment frequently heard in harmony group ballads, rarely appears in solo R&B vocals. Ace's voice projects the total sincerity that could make any beloved swoon, accounting for the cultish grief over his death. Even thirty-five years later, James Salem found that Southern Black women retained an extraordinary emotional attachment to Johnny Ace's memory, epitomized in their responses to "Pledging My Love."[57]

His contemporaries considered **Little Willie John** (1937–68) one of the best singers of his time, another ultra-talented young balladeer cut off in his prime. Born in Arkansas, John sang in a gospel quartet as a boy growing up in Detroit. Johnny Otis discovered thirteen-year-old John at a talent show and he had five top-ten hits while still in his teens. Alcohol and drugs cut short his career, and after a conviction for manslaughter John died in penitentiary, just thirty years old. Aretha Franklin sang at his funeral and James Brown recorded a tribute album. Etta James toured with John when they were both teenagers. "He sang with the pain and real-life experience of an adult," she recalls. "He sounded like a Jewish rabbi, wailing with a thousand years of pain." King Records A&R man Henry Glover, who worked with many of the best singers of the era, thought John "the artist of all artists."[58]

Glover produced the New York session for King that yielded **"Need Your Love So Bad"** (1955). Written by John and his brother Mertis, the song spent sixteen weeks on the charts and has since been covered more than fifty times. The power of John's version belies his youth. "Willie infused 'Need Your Love So Bad' with a smoky, late night sadness, as if he'd been loving and losing women for decades," writes his biographer, Susan Whitall.[59] Accompanied by A-list New York session men, John delivers an astonishing vocal performance. The tempo is a little quicker than you might expect, with Mickey Baker's guitar leading the way and pianist Bubber Johnson pounding out triplets. Gator Jackson swoops in gently now and again on tenor sax.

John sings in a high, pained voice wracked with melisma in a style that combines blues with soul. If you didn't know who it was, you might guess early James Brown. Intense in its brevity, the song clocks in at only 2:16 with no instrumental break or chorus. The lyrics reflect the desperation in John's voice without the sentimentality and clichés that mar Ace's "My Song." The title line ends each stanza, but the first two verses detail his plea for *someone's* rather than *your* love. Echoing Mayfield's "Please Send Me Someone to Love," it adds the power and poignancy of prayer to the performance. Along with the standard need of someone to hold and kiss him, John shows his sensitivity in needing to hear a soft voice and asking for someone to let him know when he's lying. Describing John's own voice as "absolutely creaking with agony," Dave Marsh hypothesizes that he was illiterate, based on John's request in the bridge that someone write and read for him. Whatever his reasons, this man needs love *so bad*. "For a mature adult, a performance as dark and knowing as 'Need Your Love So Bad' would have been an achievement worth a lifetime; for a recently turned seventeen-year-old the song is staggering in its depth and sensitivity."[60]

John's biggest hit, **"Fever"** (1956), spent 23 weeks on the R&B chart, five at #1. Though eclipsed by Peggy Lee's great 1958 cover, John's premiere version is in many ways superior. In Marsh's view, "Lee was like an advertisement for sex. Willie John was the thing itself." Ray Felder and Rufus Gore's tenor saxes take the lead in the jazzy, melodramatic arrangement with Edison Gore's snare punctuating the choruses, Bill Jennings playing fills on guitar, and fingers snapping. (Peggy Lee copied Willie John's arrangement "lick for lick," Marsh points out.) Again, John sings as a man who loves—and is loved—*so bad*. He asks for his soul to be blessed, adding a spiritual dimension to their torrid love affair. He burns so hot with love that when she calls his name his eyes blaze, the flames visible in the windows of the soul. *FEVER!* he cries, with "an almost ecstatic lovesickness."[61] The fever of love literally burns the words from his throat at the end, reducing him to a series of murmurs, hums, and moans. A hot, hot record from a singer whose own flame burnt out much too soon.

Mama, He Treats Your Daughters Mean

As softer ballads and more sensitive masculine lyrics gained ground in early-to-mid–1950s rhythm & blues, listeners also showed more interest in female sounds and sensibilities. With some exceptions the male shouters and older-style jump blues artists began losing momentum around the half-century mark. Maybe their familiarity made audiences look for more variety in R&B. Maybe the sounds and beats of rock 'n' roll began overshadowing the older style. Or maybe audiences grew tired of the lyrical emphasis on what Brian Ward describes as "the denigration of women, the aggrandizement of a predatory, irresponsible machismo, and the depiction of preternaturally doomed, exploitative personal relationships" in male rhythm & blues. The songs we've examined have more variety and a deeper humanity than this broad-brush description suggests. And the heart-ballad style certainly represents a shift away from the predatory and denigrating.[62]

We have seen relatively few women in postwar blues. Most fit more comfortably into the rhythm & blues category. But they were outliers even in early postwar R&B when no rhythm & blueswomen other than Dinah Washington, Julia Lee, and Nelly Lutcher consistently hit the *Billboard* charts. This changed in the second half of the decade. Little Esther managed eight *Billboard* top tens from 1950 to 1952. Dinah Washington had twenty more between 1950 and 1955. From 1949–56, Ruth Brown had seventeen top ten R&B hits and her Atlantic labelmate LaVern Baker scored seven in 1955–56 alone. Brian Ward points out that these and other female R&B singers "gave as good as they got in the r&b sex wars ... offer[ing] sharp and witty critiques of black male inadequacies ... and a measure of female assertiveness and genuine eroticism which had no equal in the white pop canon."[63] We have heard these notes sung in much of the female R&B so far. Now let's meet the women who dominated the early-mid-'50s charts.

A white man who lived as if he were Black, Johnny Otis had his fingers in a lot of the tastiest R&B pies of the postwar era as a Los Angeles–based songwriter, bandleader, arranger, musician, and talent scout. He discovered vocalist **Little Esther** Phillips (1935–1984), one of his most successful finds, when she was just thirteen. Born Esther Mae Washington in Texas, she moved with her mother to L.A. as a child, sang in church, then won an amateur talent contest. With a high nasal voice, Esther modeled her vocal style on Dinah Washington. Despite her youth, Otis scooped her up to sing lead for his band, including adult-style teasing duets with male singers, sometimes with harmony-group backing. In 1950, as a 14- and 15-year-old, Esther scored seven R&B top tens with Savoy Records under the supervision of one of the greatest R&B producers, Ralph Bass, including three number one hits. After she left Otis to go solo in the mid–1950s, Esther's career went downhill until she reinvented herself in the 1960s as a pop balladeer with strings. She struggled with alcohol and drugs and died at only 48 years old.

Her first release on Savoy, **"Double Crossing Blues"** (1950), recorded a few weeks before Esther's fourteenth birthday, spent nine weeks at #1, making her the youngest singer to have a #1 R&B hit. The label credits the Johnny Otis Quintette, Vocals by The Robins and Little Esther, but it's definitely Esther's song, establishing her as tough and cocky. The unusual band consists of Otis on vibes plus piano, guitar, bass, and drums—no horns. The Robins quartet harmonizes quietly in the background. Their bass, Bobby Nunn, provides the male vocal in dialogue with Esther. This sultry ballad turns cheeky in the end. The title puns on the two voices, each blaming the other. Esther sings the first two verses, wondering why her guy is cheating and why she can't thrill him. Nunn sings the third verse, blaming her for running around. He's leaving because no matter how hard he tries, he can't satisfy her. The novel fourth verse makes the song. In a non sequitur, Esther tells him he should be in the forest fighting a grizzly bear. Why aren't *you* in the forest, he asks. Because she's a lady, she answers in a line-reading somehow matter-of-fact and coy at the same time. But the woods are full of she-bears, he responds—the

Little Esther Phillips, early promotional photograph, c. 1950. Everett Collection Inc./Alamy Stock Photo.

punchline from an African American vaudeville routine. Bass explained: "*bear* was a jive term for an ugly broad."[64] As Nunn and Little Esther split the final verse, she shrugs off the misogyny and regains the romantic high ground with her final line—she can't use him anymore. This adolescent kid holds her own strategically and emotionally with a mature man. He may have the punchline but she packs a punch.

Another of Little Esther's duets didn't chart but produced my favorite of her songs, **"The Deacon Moves In"** (1951). This time Bass had Billy Ward and His Dominoes backing Esther. Their second tenor, Charlie White, sings in dialogue with her. The song appeared on Federal, the King Records subsidiary that Bass took over, crediting Little Esther with the Dominoes and the Earle Warren Orchestra—actually Otis' orchestra performing under the pseudonym of Warren, his alto sax player, since Otis was still contracted to Savoy.

The superb song and performance may be disturbing. Dawson and Propes call it "one of R&B's most shameless paeans to pedophilia."[65] It dramatizes an attempted seduction or sexual assault, depending on your perspective, as the horny deacon presses himself on his congregant, Sister Pigeon, who resists and resists until she doesn't. We know too much about the sexual histories of various religious authorities to ignore the real-world implications of a song like this. Little Esther was only fifteen when she recorded it—hence the pedophilia accusation. But her *character* in the song gives no indication of being underage. And as in so many other female blues and R&B songs, the female persona retains agency and ultimately controls her own sexual behavior: a significant element of female blues and R&B proto-feminism in the postwar decade. Listen to Esther's **"Cupid's Boogie"** (1950), a delightful duet with Mel Walker and a #1 hit that she recorded at an even younger age. As the two sing about marrying, the would-be man of the house has conditions—until Esther makes clear that she will be the boss.

In "The Deacon Moves In," Sister Pigeon and the deacon trade couplets in the first two verses. He offers her true religion and the spirit; she says she'd better leave. No, he says, sit on my knee. In the bridge he dims the lights and squeezes her hand, though she asks him not to. In the third verse she yells at him to let her go and threatens to stick him with a pin, but again he ignores her. As he and the Dominoes repeat, the deacon is moving in. During the wild instrumental break we hear various male voices cheering him on and confirming his powers of persuasion. In the final verse she goes along, asking him to pour her a gin and kiss her.

The sexual pressure from an authority figure backed by a gang of men could seem ominous, but nothing in the tone of this song does. It has a rich, full jump blues sound with hand-clapping, doo wop background vocals, and an up-tempo beat driven by Pete Lewis' guitar and Devonia Williams' thrilling honkytonk piano.[66] The horns and rhythm section provide groovy fills. White sings the role of the sleazy deacon with just the right sense of privilege and Esther never sounds intimidated, even when the men gang up on her. Though not as overtly irreligious as Hooker's "Burning Hell," "The Deacon Moves In" finds its spirit of true religion where rhythm & blues men and women go to pray, in the bedroom and the bar.

Even when singing solo, Little Esther presents as knowing, experienced, and older than her years (if not wiser). Still barely sixteen, she sings **"Aged and Mellow"**

(1952) on Federal with the kind of worldly languor associated with Billie Holiday or Esther's idol, Dinah Washington. A beautiful, smoky late-night ballad with the Otis orchestra in top form, the performance features Williams' mellow doodling on keyboards and a gorgeous, boozy sax break from tenor great Ben Webster. Esther explains her philosophy: she prefers her men, like her liquor, aged and mellow. Young men just don't do it for her; she'll take grandpa any day. Unlike Helen Humes' "Million Dollar Secret," Esther isn't in it for the money. Older daddies just have more experience. Her vocal makes clear her pleasure in well-aged whiskey and mature lovers. Before each of five repetitions of the title phrase in the refrain, she expressively *mmm*'s, *oooh*'s and *hah*'s in a contained but unequivocal confirmation of her young-womanly satisfaction.

Ruth Brown (1928–2006), America's best-selling Black female recording artist of the early 1950s, helped make New York's Atlantic Records the number one R&B label. In 1955, Brown sold her five millionth record for Atlantic, which came to be known as "The House That Ruth Built" (the same phrase that linked Babe Ruth and Yankee Stadium). Born Ruth Weston in Virginia, she sang in her father's church choir before following her dream to be a secular singer, winning an Amateur Night competition at the Apollo with a Bing Crosby song. After a stint with the Lucky Millinder band, Ruth married trumpeter Jimmy Brown and signed with Atlantic. She would go on to be called the first female rock 'n' roll singer, and would later have an acting career in TV, film, and on Broadway, where she won a Tony Award. She would also wage a high-profile battle with Atlantic over unpaid royalties. In 1988, she founded the Rhythm and Blues Foundation to help indigent R&B artists. But before all that Ruth Brown, nicknamed Miss Rhythm, simply sang great rhythm & blues.[67]

Her first Atlantic recording, the fine blues ballad **"Rain Is a Bringdown"** (1949), went unreleased until the 1960s. The spare orchestration with Amos Milburn on piano nicely sets up Brown's vocals. But she approaches the song conservatively, seemingly content to let her slow, downbeat performance echo the gloomy lyrics. The first of her records released, **"So Long"** (1949), suffers from orchestral overproduction but features a sensational vocal performance. Eddie Condon's NBC Television Orchestra backed the torchy ballad. Atlantic's Ahmet Ertegun felt privileged to get this prestigious group. Ed Ward agrees: "What a pickup band it was!" But I agree with another critic, who describes Condon's band as "stuck in the past … its pop-centric arrangement complete with trumpets and light-fingered piano accompaniment designed to keep every song's emotions at arm's length."[68] The horns especially overstay their welcome. Brown's performance triumphs despite her accompaniment.

The lyrics tell of loss and resilience. He has left her sad and lonely. The opening horns sound despondent, but the first verse emphasizes her hope: they will meet again. In the end she will keep him in her heart and never say goodbye, just so long. Brown's emotional and vocal control reflects her strength as she varies the volume and plays with the phrasing. She begins high and dips way down low, putting a tear in one phrase then scraping the bottom with another, as if making fun of her own sorrow. The subtext: "I can do and feel whatever I choose. I choose to regret his loss but I won't grovel because I *know* I can get him back." A remarkable debut.

Over the next few years Brown became a hit machine. But her biggest hits reflected the pop direction in which Atlantic steered her. Ertegun himself admitted, "The blues we made with Ruth Brown came out like urbanized, watered-down versions of real blues."[69] **"Teardrops from My Eyes"** (1950), **"5–10–15 Hours"** (1952), and **"(Mama) He Treats Your Daughter Mean"** (1953)—not to mention the inane "Mambo Baby" (1954)—are bouncy, mid-tempo numbers that sound like pop songs written and arranged for broad commercial appeal with little regard for Brown's vocal artistry or the strong female persona that makes "So Long" so powerful. All spent multiple weeks at #1. But today they sound dated. Not great R&B, not quite rock 'n' roll.

My Ruth Brown choices were less successful commercially but much better artistically. **"Wild Wild Young Men"** (1953), written by Ertegun, reached #3 R&B. Though still watered-down, it rocks harder than any of her previous records. The song presents Brown as a good-time girl who prefers her men wild and knows how to keep them in line. The wild young men all want to be hers. Anticipating the girl group era, she has girlfriends who want to know how she does it. She explains in 1950s terms, teasing without entirely pleasing: winking and whispering, heaving and sighing, rolling her hips—leaving the boys unsatisfied. The typically tight Atlantic house band includes Piano Man Walls and drummer Connie Kay, but Haywood Henry's scorching baritone sax solo stars, screaming and hollering like her wild young boyfriends when they thrill her soul and lose their minds.

Nothing else in Brown's discography resembles **"Hello Little Boy"** (1954), 2:36 of insane rock 'n' roll. Wild young men have nothing on this young woman. Just before Christmas 1953, Brown and her band recorded the song "at the end of a long night in the studio, 3 or 4 a.m.," she recalled. "We were all dead tired and more than a little crazy. We were watching the clock and didn't want to run into overtime. I never sang like that before, or since!"[70] Unconstrained by her Atlantic overseers, Brown storms through the song, a 12-bar blues she wrote about her relationship with a ragged, ordinary-looking guy who makes her scream when he loves her. Lyrically and vocally, we again hear a woman in control. The man is her little boy. He's no one's dream but she wants him anyway because of the very good sex—*ooooh wee!* She wants him until she doesn't anymore. When she feels he has done her wrong, she hops a train and leaves him crying the blues.

"Hello Little Boy" scores ten out of ten on the sheer exuberance scale. Speeding right out of the gate, Brown and the musicians push each other hard until the repetition of the final twelve bars when the band roars along even faster, as if daring her to keep up. Everyone is having a helluva time, especially Brown herself, egging on gonzo saxmen Sam "The Man" Taylor and Paul "Hucklebuck" Williams, who honk and wail as if playing for their lives. "I feel so unnecessary," she laughs during the second break. Brown and her boys (John Lewis piano, Mickey Baker guitar, Lloyd Trotman bass, Joe Marshall drums), in perfect sync, are coloring outside the lines, way ahead of their time. That's my only explanation for why this astonishing record failed to chart. "Hello Little Boy" also graphically illustrates why we should distrust online lyrical transcriptions. One of the websites on Google announcing lyrics for the song claims that the first line of the second verse reads, "Well I met you bay, it was right near by the mall." Mmm … don't think so.

Despite initially being saddled with a bizarre stage name, Dolores **LaVern Baker** (1929–97) (also spelled Lavern, La Vern, or LaVerne) built a stellar career as a rhythm & blues star in the mid–1950s and a rock 'n' roll star over the next decade. Born in Chicago, she sang in church, but inspired by her blues singer relatives Memphis Minnie and Merline Johnson, quickly embraced secular music. In imitation of a popular singer called Little Miss Cornshucks, Baker first appeared on stage billed as Little Miss Sharecropper. She recorded under that name for RCA-Victor and National Records, 1949–51, as Bea Baker for Columbia and Okeh, then as LaVern Baker/Miss Sharecropper for King, but without much success. In 1953, she joined Ruth Brown at Atlantic and her career took off.

Her first Atlantic release was one of her best. In his memoir, producer Jerry Wexler offers Baker backhanded compliments, praising her uncompromising, "undiluted" bluesy delivery while dismissing the songs he co-wrote for her as "formula ditties matched with lyrics not likely to rival Cole Porter's." Subsequently, like Brown, Baker recorded mostly commercial pop tunes for Atlantic, unworthy of her R&B talents—especially her breakout hit, "Tweedlee Dee" (1955). But **"Soul on Fire"** (1953) is terrific, "a wonderfully bluesy record," Marv Goldberg writes, "and a perfect showcase for her voice."[71] Baker sings as if she were testifying in church. Despite Wexler's claim of co-authorship, writing credits on the label go to Baker and Jernet, one of Ertegun's pen names, and the lyrics are more original than the usual bluesy love ballad. She played the game with other guys but now she knows better. No need to play around when her true love sets her soul on fire and shows her how to *really* have fun. Baker caresses key words with her deep, warm voice, growls the title line in stop time, and uses her higher range and melisma to great effect. Gene Redd's band sits back and lets Baker do her thing, with pianist Hank Jones's triplets dominant alongside Baker's rich, soulful vocal.

Baker sang with deep soul but she could also rock. **"Jim Dandy"** (1956), her only record to make #1 R&B, also hit the Pop chart. An infectious rocker with screaming tenor sax from Sam "The Man" Taylor, the song was accompanied by The Gliders, Atlantic's four-man in-house backup group that sang behind Baker, Ruth Brown, and Big Joe Turner under different names. Baker growls the lyrics celebrating mythic hero Jim Dandy, who comes to the rescue of various damsels in distress: a woman on a mountaintop, a crying little girl, a mermaid stuck on a fish hook. Brian Ward hears in the song "a portent of the idealized black hero eulogized by the girl groups of the black pop era." We shouldn't underestimate the subversive nature of Jim Dandy's idealized heroism. African American songwriter Lincoln Chase likely adapted the character from a nineteenth-century slave song, "Dandy Jim from Caroline." Dandy Jim's "ole massa" tells him he's "de best lookin N____ in de county," and in the degrading comic tone and dialect of minstrelsy Jim chronicles his potency in siring at least nine little Dandy Jims.[72] Chase re-appropriates the character, reverses his name so it echoes the iconic John Henry, and turns him into a Black superhero. At that crucial historical juncture in the battle for civil rights, Jim Dandy led a posse of powerful Black pop icons that would include Lloyd Price's badman "Stagger Lee" (1958) and the western cartoon hero in the Coasters' "Along Came Jones" (1959). Invoking Jim Dandy's name over and over, Baker cheers him on with R&B urgency.

Laissez les bons temps rouler

Rhythm & blues arrived a little late in New Orleans. "In the 1940s, it was all jazz," said Ralph Bass. But once its musicians caught on to what was happening in Los Angeles, Chicago, New York, Houston, and Cincinnati, New Orleans embraced its own unique good-time R&B sound. Only record labels De Luxe and Ace made their home in the city, but Los Angeles labels Imperial, Aladdin, and Specialty all struck gold with New Orleans music, recording prolifically in Cosimo Matassa's J&M studio, from which the distinctive New Orleans R&B sound came to be known as "Cosimo's sound."[73] It might also have been called "Dave's sound," given trumpeter/bandleader Dave Bartholomew's pervasive influence in producing Crescent City hits. Jive DJs Poppa Stoppa and Dr. Daddy-O promoted rhythm & blues on local radio station WJMR. Roy Brown recorded his best records in his native city. Influential pianist Professor Longhair made his mark there. Smiley Lewis, Lloyd Price, Guitar Slim, and Shirley & Lee had R&B hits. Little Richard's **"Tutti Frutti"** (1955) would explode out of Cosimo's studio. But first came Fats Domino.

Cherub-faced New Orleans-born local club sensation Antoine **Fats Domino** (1928–2017) stood five-feet-five and weighed in at 225. Domino liked the *nom de plume* "Fats" because it associated him with great jazz pianist Fats Waller. When Imperial Records' Lew Chudd saw Domino pounding the piano and singing a rockin' version of "Junker's Blues," a popular tune about drug addiction, Chudd had Dave Bartholomew record him. Domino and Bartholomew rewrote the downbeat lyrics and retitled the song **"The Fat Man"** (1950). *Spontaneous Lunacy* calls it "arguably the single greatest debut record in the entire history of rock 'n' roll." A #2 R&B hit, it was the first of Domino's 25 R&B top tens from 1950 to 1956. Seven of his records rose to #1 R&B in 1955–56, including **"Ain't That a Shame," "I'm in Love Again," "Blueberry Hill,"** and **"Blue Monday,"** which all reached *Billboard*'s Pop top ten as well, making Domino a certified rock 'n' roll star. James Miller suggests that his "cuddly" looks and "warm Creole accent" helped him cross over. Charlie Gillett adds that Domino's plaintive vocals "did not seem so adult and alien as did the tone of most of his contemporary rhythm and blues singers."[74]

Complex synergies go into producing any great record. In the case of "The Fat Man" a mistake proved productive. "Fats played loud at the piano," Bartholomew recalled. "We made a mistake and sent the record out." Bartholomew embraced it for good reason. "[Fats] played the best boogie woogie on earth," he'd later say. The record opens with thirty seconds of Domino's distinctive boogie. Despite three saxophones and Bartholomew's trumpet, Domino gets both back-to-back breaks. In the first, Fats vocalizes *wah wah wah*—the sound of a sax or blues harp—and immediately follows with a lengthy, infectious piano solo while Earl Palmer, who became one of the great rock 'n' roll drummers, provides the backbeat. The *wah wah* vocalizing is head-shakingly compelling. Watch any YouTube video of Domino's later live performances of the song where a horn does the *wah wah* to see and hear how unique the original is. In the brief lyrics (only forty-five seconds of the record's 2:43), Domino introduces himself as the fat man, an accomplished lover, standing on the corner of Rampart and Canal streets, watching the Creole girls. "Rampart and Canal were the major black and white thoroughfares in New Orleans," Rick Coleman observes, "so Domino was metaphorically already suggesting the social intersection of black and white worlds through music, which would be his greatest achievement." The mixed-race girls represent another racial crossroads, symbolizing how this rollicking fat man would help bridge Black rhythm & blues and racially integrated rock 'n' roll. A great, sociologically astute piece of music.[75]

Domino's plaintive Creole vocal sound remained constant from his earliest records through his rock stardom. But he presents a lot tougher persona in the early R&B songs than in the later records. Consider the lyrics of **"Ain't That a Shame"** (1955), the long-running #1 R&B hit that pushed him across the threshold into top-ten Pop. He sings the part of the sensitive, broken-hearted lover who cries when she says goodbye, repeated four times in the refrain. The confident, quietly boastful fat man of his first record would never cry. Nor would the singer in **"Don't You Lie to Me"** (1951), another great early rocker, one of Domino's few records that didn't chart. A Tampa Red song from 1940, its blues lyrics emphasize the singer's anger with his lying woman. The title line doesn't request, it warns. Four times he says her lies make him angry—and anger makes him evil. Tampa Red performs it at mid-tempo with his guitar and Blind John Davis' piano. Domino retains Red's blues lyrics but he and Bartholomew transform the song into rocketing rhythm & blues. They up the tempo, bury the guitar sound under a couple of saxophones, and make Fats' piano louder and more dominant. His rolling boogie woogie pattern emphasizes the bass notes, deepening and darkening the music. His warm vocal tone and delivery mitigate some of the lyrical threat. You never feel that Fats will really get evil. Still, this self-presentation feels far different from what young white record buyers would hear from the Fats Domino who found his thrill a few years later on Blueberry Hill.

New Orleans-born **Lloyd Price** (1933–2021) became a huge hitmaker in the late 1950s when his "Stagger Lee" (1958), "Personality" (1959), and "I'm Gonna Get Married" (1959) all spent weeks at #1 R&B and top-three Pop. But he scored his biggest R&B hit with his first record, **"Lawdy Miss Clawdy"** (1952), which charted for 26 weeks, seven at #1. Specialty's Art Rupe, on a scouting trip to New Orleans, held auditions in Cosimo's studio with Bartholomew's band. Teenage Price brought along the self-penned song, and in a lucky accident Fats Domino happened to drop by and sat in on piano. Domino's rolling triplets open the record and Fats also gets one of the solos with Herb Hardesty blowing tenor sax in the other. Earl Palmer's pounding drum is the third driving force. Price sings to Miss Clawdy about how fine she is, but how miserable she makes him. Along with the catchy title and its internal rhyme, the cry in Price's voice got to Rupe ("it was very emotional"). That vocal and the band's distinctive sound made "Lawdy Miss Clawdy" not just a terrific record but an important prototype. Coleman calls it "the forerunner of the primary rock 'n' roll sound, a powerful combination of Roy Brown–style fiery wails and New Orleans rhythms anchored by the father of the backbeat, Earl Palmer." Plus, it introduced the layered rhythms of "*The New Orleans Sound* that became the signature of Domino and Bartholomew … [and] the forerunner of Phil Spector's 'wall of sound' a decade later." Elvis, Little Richard, and the Beatles would all record the song, but Price's howling version remains definitive.[76]

Local teens Shirley Goodman (1936–2005) and Leonard Lee (1936–1976) became **Shirley & Lee** when they first recorded in Cosimo's studio in 1952. They hit it big with their initial release and had three more top-three R&B hits for Aladdin in 1955–56. As their records traced a fictional romance between the two, they became known as "The Sweethearts of the Blues." In his book on New Orleans rhythm & blues, John Broven dismisses Shirley's "theatrical, shrill, childlike voice" in contrast to Lee's "remarkable blues voice."[77] To me Shirley's voice resembles Little Esther's: not purely instrumental but full of expressive youthful energy, curiosity, and possibility. Like Esther, Shirley & Lee don't harmonize but engage in musical dialogues. Unlike Esther's ironic adult-oriented duets, Shirley & Lee's duets skew towards teen innocence (with one key exception) but maintain an edgy dynamism.

Like the other successful New Orleans R&B acts, Shirley & Lee benefited from Dave Bartholomew's production and the talented musicians in his band, including tenor great Lee Allen. Bartholomew wrote and plays trumpet on their debut single, **"I'm Gone"** (1952). The rhythm section (Frank Fields bass, Palmer drums) lays down a slow 2/4 beat while piano, guitar, and horns quietly roll out the simple, repetitious tune. The effect is almost hypnotic. Lee and Shirley alternate the four verses. Sleepless and out of his mind, he begs her to come back. She toys with him a little, coos, wonders why he lied, but will give him another chance. They exit singing together, repeating the line that reiterates their love. The title provides a nice twist. Lee doesn't sing "*You're* gone," the conventional statement in these circumstances. Instead, his grief drives him out of his mind: *he's* gone somewhere out of himself since she has gone. He's a real gone guy in a different sense than Nellie Lutcher's. Then Shirley's childlike, theatrical voice works its magic and he's gone again in another way entirely.

By the mid–1950s, Shirley & Lee had been absorbed into rock 'n' roll. All three of their later hits crossed over onto the Pop chart. The biggest was **"Let the Good Times Roll"** (1956), #1 R&B, #20 Pop, a different song than Louis Jordan's 1946 hit. Shirley & Lee based it on the popular Cajun reference to Mardi Gras, *Laissez les bons temps rouler*. Now twenty-year-olds, they put their teenage innocence behind them in a provocative call-and-response to a private Mardi Gras orgy, unusual for 1956.

A Black R&B act crossing over would normally tone down the adult language and behavior the way Fats Domino did. The energetic vocals and music take some of the erotic sting out of the lyrics. In the first two verses Lee politely invites her not just to let him thrill her soul but to roll with him all night. Shirley's response echoes his and raises the stakes. It feels so good, let's rock some more. Here we have *rock* and *roll* in their primal usage. Musically, the song employs the rhythm method, a two-note mid-tempo riff: *bomp-BOM, bomp-BOM*. It re-introduces the instrumental break missing from "I'm Gone," but never mind that undistinguished sax solo. We want to hear those voices, the Sweethearts enjoying one of the sweetest perks of adulthood.

Rock the Joint

So much of the critical literature insistently values postwar rhythm & blues only insofar as it presumably precedes, predicts, or *is* rock 'n' roll. That annoys me, and helped prompt me to write this book. For example, citing Roy Brown, Wynonie Harris, Amos Milburn, and Wild Bill Moore, *Spontaneous Lunacy*'s Sampson writes, "*These* artists—*this* music ... is rock 'n' roll. Not 'pre-rock,' not 'roots of rock,' not 'early influences ON rock,' but full-fledged *rock 'n' fuckin' roll*." I myself have used the term *rockin'* to describe many of the songs and singers I've talked about. Clearly, rhythm & blues in the postwar decade and especially in the early-mid-1950s overlapped with rock 'n' roll. Wynonie Harris recorded "Good Rockin' Tonight" and Wild Bill Moore "We're Gonna Rock" as early as 1947, and Nick Tosches lists eight more R&B records released in 1948 with *Rock* or *Rockin'* in their titles. Pioneering disc jockey Alan Freed used the phrases "rock 'n' roll" and "blues and rhythm" synonymously in his ground-breaking early-1950s radio show.[78] Continuing to argue for the autonomy of African American rhythm & blues as a discrete category with its own aesthetics, politics, and musical value, I end this chapter with some of my favorite rockers who emerged from the rhythm & blues community at mid-century. Their music articulates the postwar African American dream of possibility at high tempo and high volume: the freedom to go wild, the freedom to rock.

Texas-born tenor saxophonist **Wild Bill Moore** (1918–83) played on Helen Humes' "Be-Baba-Leba" as well as records by Big Maybelle and Big Joe Turner before moving to Detroit, where he recorded **"We're Gonna Rock"** (1948) for Savoy, essentially an instrumental. The label subsequently retitled the record "We're Gonna Rock, We're Gonna Roll"—its only lyrics, chanted by a chorus of male voices, besides Moore's shout-out to boogie woogie pianist T.J. Fowler to play all night long. Then Moore blasts his tenor solo with Paul Williams' deep-down baritone sax honking back at him alongside the hard-driving rhythm of Herman Hopkins' thumping bass. Jim Dawson calls this "the first honking hit record," although it was at best a minor hit: one week at #14 R&B.[79] It brings together the two primary sounds of rhythm & blues—boogie woogie piano and tenor sax—in a musical workout about the intense pleasure of making music that rocks as hard as it can, all night long.

If "We're Gonna Rock" set the bar, **"Rock the Joint"** (1949) vaulted right over it. Alto saxman Danny Turner, a member of the Count Basie orchestra for a quarter-century, starred on two versions of the screamingest rocker of 1949. The recording by **Jimmy Preston** (1913–84) and His Prestonians on New York's Gotham Records reached #6 on *Billboard* a few months before **Chris Powell** and the Five Blue Flames recorded their uncharted take for Columbia. Three years later, Bill Haley would record the best-known version, a pale imitation of these two. Philadelphians Turner, alto saxophonist Preston, and drummer Powell make this tune sound like the party of all parties. Dawson & Propes describe Preston's track as "a raucous, hand-clappin', sax-screamin', rockin' piece of excitement." In a detailed musical analysis of Preston's record, Graeme Boone notes how the chanted vocal riff is sung entirely on offbeats, "as if by rocking the beat so strongly they could shake the pillars of your body and soul, if not the dance hall." The band members shout, laugh, scream, and banter behind Preston's vocal and over his and Danny Turner's wailing saxes. Turner "blew his brains out on his solos, he squealed and shrieked behind the Prestonians' chanting vocal refrain … turning 'Rock the Joint' into one of the most exciting, chaotic recordings ever made."[80]

Powell and the Blue Flames' "Rock the Joint" goes Preston's raucous shuffle one better, accelerating the already speedy tempo. Although it features less vocal chaos, this record is red hot. Turner honks and squeals more wildly on this track, where his is the only sax. *Spontaneous Lunacy*'s Sampson says Turner blows "with a force that few, if any, sax stars in rock have displayed," and guitarist Eddie Lambert plays "as if the strings were on fire."[81] The same lyrics grace both versions and the title chant echoes the chant on Moore's record. But Preston and Powell also sing about drinking and dancing until the floor gets torn up, the walls and ceiling collapse, and the cops arrive. This is the Saturday night fish fry with a vengeance, rockin' the joint 'til the joint comes tumbling down.

While those guys were tearing up Philadelphia, Goree Carter & His Hepcats were throwing down their gauntlet in Houston. Freedom Records, looking for the next T-Bone Walker, brought local guitarist **Goree Carter** (1930–90) into the studio where he scribbled the perfunctory lyrics to a tune his band recorded later that day, **"Rock Awhile"** (1949). Though Carter has fallen into deep obscurity, some critics see this song as a prime candidate for the impossible-to-define first rock 'n' roll record with a direct line to Chuck Berry.[82] Carter plays in the single-string T-Bone style, but hard, fast, and loud, straining his amp to the max. He shares the breaks with alto saxman Conrad O. Johnson, whose solo, including a phrase from "Jingle Bells," is more playful than screaming, and with Lonnie Lyons' boogie woogie piano. A strong singer with relentlessly upbeat lyrics, Carter, unlike Preston and Powell, won't be hung over. He rocks not as an expression of Dionysian frenzy but of sheer pleasure. He wakes up feeling good—no blues for Goree. His desire to rock awhile speaks to a whole array of activities, not just sex. This man has the world at his feet.

The qualifier *awhile* suggests restraint in contrast to *all night long*. By comparison with his peers, Carter and His Hepcats sound almost wholesome in their fierce commitment to rock.

The stage name of Robert **H-Bomb Ferguson** (1929–2006) incorporated the notion of R&B that rocked so hard it exploded.[83] A singer and sometime pianist from South Carolina, he moved to New York and modelled himself on Wynonie Harris, developing a shouting style that appears at its best in his anthemic **"Rock H-Bomb Rock"** (1951) for Atlas Records with the Charlie Singleton Orchestra. In a call-and-response with the musicians who chant the title, H-Bomb sings about rockin' with his baby. He references Lollipop Mama and Fanny Brown from fellow shouters Harris and Roy Brown. Tenor saxman Singleton's smokin' solo constitutes the instrumental highlight. And how about this for the prophetic nature of Black R&B: H-Bomb got his stage name and cut this record a year *before* the first U.S. hydrogen bomb test in 1952.

H-Bomb toured and sang with **Joe Liggins** and His Honeydrippers before recording on his own. Liggins' "The Honeydripper" spent eighteen weeks at #1 in 1945, and he had another long-running R&B hit with **"Pink Champagne"** (1950). Both Joe and less successful younger brother **Jimmy Liggins** (1918–83) came from Oklahoma, landed in L.A., and recorded for Specialty. Though a below-average singer and only a minor hitmaker, guitarist Jimmy rocked much harder than his brother. Jimmy Liggins and His Drops of Joy made "one monumental record [that] encapsulated the optimistic mood of the young and ambitious post-war black American culture": **"Cadillac Boogie"** (1948). Car songs had been part of the blues repertoire as far back as the 1920s.[84] Freedom of movement and the status of ownership made cars a potent symbol. In early blues the car of choice was the T-Model Ford, "the poor man's friend." Robert Johnson's "Terraplane Blues" (1937) celebrated a more obscure model Hudson and sexualized the car as metaphor. As cars became ubiquitous symbols of mid-century American modernity and prosperity, African Americans striving to partake in the dream of postwar possibility chose, as its ultimate symbol, the glamorous, pricey Cadillac, the postwar blues and R&B stars' bling. Muddy Waters and B.B. King each drove one. Chuck Berry races Maybellene's Coupe de Ville. Remember Roy Brown's "Cadillac Baby" from 1950.

Liggins' ode to the Caddy, recorded in 1947, foresaw all that. This hip anthem celebrates the long black Cadillac V-8 with its modern streamlined design—and its long Black driver. The lyrics metaphorically compress man and vehicle: the purring Cat-ty and the hep cat behind the wheel. Car and driver roll along together in the fabulous NOW, pickin' up chicks in style. This hard-driving boogie, fueled by four horns and Jonathan Bagsby's bass, leaves Liggins' guitar and the piano inaudible. Three tasty sax solos punctuate the song. Harold Land (tenor) and James Dedmon (alto) salute the sportin'est car in America, then go boogying off all reet, squealing in absolute joy.

"Cadillac Boogie" inspired Jackie Brenston & His Delta Cats' **"Rocket '88'"** (1951), the best-known R&B rocker and primary candidate for that elusive first rock 'n' roll record. Nick Tosches describes the performance: "The overcharged amplification of Willie Kizart's electric guitar, the careening glissandi and manic triplets issuing from Ike Turner's piano … Raymond Hill's post-melodic saxophone shriekings, Willie Sim's trash-can drumming, and the raw, heartfelt degeneracy of Jackie Brenston's singing, shouting, and yelping…." "Rocket '88'" is a spectacular record, another thoroughly contemporary dream of movement, affluence, and control. It borrows its melody, boogie rhythm, and car theme from Liggins' song, Brenston admitted, but sounds and feels very different. Five young men from the Mississippi Delta, Brenston & His Delta Cats, aka Ike Turner's Rhythm Kings, recorded in Sam Phillips' Memphis Studio. Saxman **Jackie Brenston** (c. 1930–79)—on vocals here—and pianist/bandleader Turner, an important rhythm & blues figure before he got together with Tina, were both Clarksdale-born. Their big small-band Delta sound had to differ from the L.A. stylings of Liggins and his eight musicians. The car also reflected their differences. Brenston replaced Liggins' Caddy with a super-hot, ultra-modern Oldsmobile 88 convertible. With its powerful Rocket 88 engine and lightweight body, the high-performance model dominated the NASCAR circuit from 1949 to 1952. Another symbol of high-energy modernity, *rocket* contains the word *rock*. The almost mythic tale of the record's creation—how Kizart's guitar amp fell off their car on the way to the studio, how Phillips used its damaged sound to great effect on the record, how the song ended up as Chess Records' first #1 hit and got credited to Brenston instead of Turner—all that has been retold many times.[85]

"Rocket '88'" shares some of the language and tone of "Cadillac Boogie": pride in the powerful V-8 engine and modern design, the joy and excitement of driving around in style. It rockets to a start with Turner's crackling boogie woogie, Kizart's fuzzy guitar providing the bass line. Brenston's singing is mixed down as if his voice were just another instrument. In the first break the sax plays one riff over and over while Turner pounds the piano, the garage-band sound fantastically unpolished. After the brief second verse, describing the joy of cruising around town, Brenston shouts for Raymond Hill to blow *his* horn. The teenage tenor (who fathered Tina Turner's first child) honks, squeaks, and squeals in a manic 56-second solo with the adrenaline-powered exultation of a kid speeding along in his new wheels, top down and radio blasting. Plenty of rhythm, not much blues, rocketing rock 'n' roll. Jackie Brenston and His Delta Cats' follow-up, **"In My Real Gone Rocket"** (1951), rocked just as hard. And listen to the Jimmy Cotton Blues Quartet do "Rocket 88" (1965) with Cotton's vocal, his harp replacing Hill's sax, and Otis Spann on piano.

By the early 1950s, it would seem, the big band sound had been completely superseded by what would become the standard rock band configuration plus a horn or two. But one of the hottest R&B rockers of the decade declared otherwise. Ohio-born, Chicago-raised, short-lived vocalist Willis **Sonny Parker** (1925–57)

fronted Lionel Hampton's legendary orchestra from 1949 to 1952. Going solo, backed by nine of Hampton's musicians whom the Peacock label calls Gladys Hampton Blues Boys (Gladys was Lionel's wife and business manager), Parker recorded his own scorching 12-bar boogie, **"She Sets My Soul on Fire"** (1953). As Parker drinks wine in the Bronze Peacock, Don Robey's Houston nightclub that gave the record label its name, he spots a woman across the floor. The rest is shouting, screaming, honking R&B heaven with little more to the lyric than the title. But Parker is a terrific shouter, and the band—initially sounding a little old-fashioned with three saxes, trumpet, and trombone—rocks out in the long central break: Billy Nackel's guitar sandwiched between alto and tenor solos by Bobby Plater and Johnny Board, and Milt Buckner's piano showing the way. Those flames of jive burned bright.

Let's end with a name, like so many in this chapter, that has lapsed into obscurity. The fame of **The Treniers**, a group that rocked and clowned its way across racial borders in the transition from R&B to rock 'n' roll, rested not on record sales or charted hits but on their wildly entertaining stage act. Among the first Black performers to appear on the early network TV variety shows of Red Skelton, Ed Sullivan, Jackie Gleason, and Martin & Lewis, they were regularly playing Las Vegas by the late 1950s. Their **"Rockin' Is Our Bizness"** (1953), on OKeh Records, encapsulates how Black R&B could be commodified and re-packaged as commercially lucrative rock 'n' roll.

Identical twins Claude and Cliff Trenier, born in Alabama in 1919, sang with Louis Jordan, Jimmie Lunceford's swing orchestra, Wynonie Harris, and Johnny Otis before putting together their own act in Los Angeles with college friends Gene Gilbeaux on piano and Don Hill on alto sax—the same Gilbeaux Quartet that backed Jimmy Witherspoon on his live recordings. When brothers Buddy and Milt Trenier joined the act in the early 1950s, the Trenier Twins became The Treniers. The "frantic synchronization" of their manic performance style included their *bug dance*, a staccato freak-out, as if their bodies crawled with bugs that band members could transfer to one another.[86] Watch the Treniers perform "Rockin' Is Our Bizness" on *The Colgate Comedy Hour* in 1954, joined by a very game Dean Martin and Jerry Lewis, the latter doing an astonishing bug dance solo (https://www.youtube.com/watch?v=UOrjlAy5M1Y). The band performs a toned-down version without Martin & Lewis in the 1956 rock musical, *The Girl Can't Help It*.

A Treniers truism: their records could never capture the dynamism and sheer fun of their live jivin' performances. But even without the visuals—the twins riffing off one another, the bug dance and acrobatics, Gilbeaux playing piano with his legs in the air—"Rockin' Is Our Bizness" remains a rockin' treat. The unequivocal star of the OKeh recording, Don Hill delivers one of the all-time great ear-splitting, brain-blowing, super-squealing alto workouts. Claude's cool introduction of the band members prefigures Sly Stone's introduction of the Family Stone on his "Dance to the Music" (1968). Along with the invitation for everyone to rock, the song proudly, unashamedly, advertises the band's availability. If you hire a hall and want it to rock, just call them. It's their business. Rockin' into the future, the postwar economic dream could come true on the rhythm & blues stage.

Chapter Three

Gospel
Too Close to Heaven

"Freedom might account for it. The freedom of a different location, change of venue and some money in the pocket might account for the release, the liberation into being freer and shouting, and some of that shout is jubilation."

—Maya Angelou

"Gospel was therapy for the stress and pressure of being Black in America."

—Rev. Al Sharpton

"Gospel was my favorite type of music, not for religious reasons but because of the feeling and the soul and the honesty of it."

—Art Rupe, Specialty Records

"The sweet stuff is the brain stuff but the hard is heart and emotion."
—Ira Tucker, The Dixie Hummingbirds[1]

Of all the music in this book, Black gospel is the least well known outside the African American community. Emerging from the Black church and nourished in its congregations, gospel became commercialized during the postwar decade. It flourished along the Gospel Highway, a network of halls, churches, storefronts, and theaters in African American neighborhoods across the country—the Christian chitlin' circuit. Gospel singers and quartets toured extensively and did musical battle with one another for enthusiastic audiences that got worship and entertainment for one price. A handful of gospel artists crossed over into general celebrity, most notably Mahalia Jackson. Sam Cooke and others left sacred music for the more lucrative fields of pop and rock 'n' roll. Artists like Aretha Franklin mated their gospel with blues and rhythm & blues to birth soul music. The sonic vocabulary of gospel—falsetto whoops, screams, shouts—became trademarks of Little Richard, Ray Charles, James Brown, Wilson Pickett, the Isley Brothers. Gospel also became part of the repertoire of freedom songs in the civil rights era. But most of the great gospel performances of the postwar decade, "the first ten years of the Golden Age of Gospel,"[2] never reached beyond the African American audience to which it almost exclusively played. This astonishing cache of musical genius remains today, for most of us outside that community, a well-kept secret.

African American sacred music has its deep roots in Africa, its American roots in eighteenth-century Protestant hymns and the spirituals and shouts created during slavery and Jim Crow. The first public performances of the music occurred when the classically trained Fisk Jubilee Singers, from Nashville's all–Black Fisk University, went on the road in 1871 with formal concerts of tightly harmonized spirituals. In the early twentieth century the demonstrative worship of the rapidly growing African American Pentecostal and Holiness (Church of God in Christ or COGIC) congregations was reflected in their passionate, semi-improvised singing with instrumental accompaniment, hand-clapping, and foot-stomping. Gayle Wald explains, "COGIC admitted into its musical repertory elements of blues, work songs, and ragtime, cross-fertilizing these in a glorious hybrid with slave spirituals and traditional hymns. Like speaking in tongues, exuberant singing and 'holy dancing' affirmed the body, in its instinctive response to rhythm, as an instrument of God." In the 1920s, with the publication of *Gospel Pearls*, a Black Baptist collection of sacred songs reflecting the new style of music, plus the proliferation of *a cappella* quartets and instrument-accompanied Pentecostal/Holiness song, the record companies got on board.[3]

The primary catalyst for the transition to the gospel blues style that we hear in postwar song was converted blues singer and pianist Thomas A. Dorsey. The Georgia-born son of a Baptist preacher, Dorsey played and wrote urban blues in Chicago through the 1920s. He accompanied the great Ma Rainey, then christened himself Georgia Tom and teamed up with guitarist Tampa Red to form the most successful *hokum* act of the era, writing and singing double entendre honkytonk blues. In the midst of all this, Dorsey underwent a religious conversion and began writing sacred music as well, incorporating the style and feeling of blues. He would later explain the logic of that synthesis:

> What we call low-down in blues doesn't mean that it's dirty or bad or something like that. It gets down into the individual to set him on fire.... If they're in the church, they say, "Amen." If they're in the blues, they say, "Sing it now" ... but it's the same feeling, a grasping of the heart.

In 1932, Dorsey became choir director at Chicago's Pilgrim Baptist church and trained his chorus in the expansive blues performance style. Comparing another church choir to his own, he observed, "See, they didn't shout the gospel like we did. See, they was kind of a reserved group. They sang. They gave [a] message. But they didn't jump up and shout, run, and holler 'Amen' and all the stuff we put in it." That same year Dorsey's wife and newborn child suddenly died. In response he wrote "Take My Hand, Precious Lord," the song most often cited as launching modern gospel. "Dorsey," notes his biographer, "had finally given his gospel blues music a truly complementary blues text."[4]

Through a combination of religious passion, musical genius, and the marketing skills of fellow Chicago gospel singer Sallie Martin, Dorsey spread gospel blues across Black America over the next decade. In 1937, Mahalia Jackson began to travel with him, singing Dorsey's songs, wrecking church after Black church, converting worshippers to gospel music. Many in the urban congregations of the North, whose Europeanized services had become decorous and tame, welcomed its exuberant emotion. Rural Black Southerners flooding into Northern cities brought to their storefront churches the shouting and moaning, clapping and foot-stomping, call-and-response worship they had practiced down home. Gospel spoke a sanctified musical language of jubilation they understood.

The elements of that music and performance style are central to the great gospel soloists and quartets of the postwar decade. The mid–1940s transition from jubilee quartet to gospel quartet, as described by Opal Louis Nations, illustrates the performative difference between the old and new styles:

> Crooning and the one-mike huddle of standing on a dime, the performance mode of jubilee singing, was being replaced by the jazzier, booming basso, call and response, alternating pitch, falsetto flight, swing lead face-off, microphone throwing, knee drops, thigh slaps, lavish vocal ornamentation, devilish shrieking, dramatic creeps among the assembled and fainting members of the audience "falling out."

Male gospel performers aimed to make female congregants scream, pull up their skirts, faint. Female quartets went house-wrecking, too. This was *hard gospel*, heartfelt and emotional, "characterized by straining the voice during periods of spiritual ecstasy for spiritual and dramatic expression, singing at the extremes of the range." Its intention: to "wreak emotional havoc."[5]

The sonic vocabulary of hard gospel, according to Nations, includes "whoops, moans, screams, yells, grunts, shrieks and wails," articulating the intense emotional experience of Black Christianity's promise of redemption. These techniques derived directly from the demonstrative worship of African Americans in the rural South. In his seminal 1903 volume, *The Souls of Black Folk*, W.E.B. Du Bois describes "the frenzy of shouting" when parishioners felt infused with the Holy Spirit. "It varied in expression from the silent rapt countenance or the low murmur and moan to the mad abandon of physical fervor—the stamping, shrieking, and shouting, the rushing to and fro and wild waving of arms, the weeping and laughing, the vision and the trance." Jerry Zolten details some of the similar sources of the Dixie Hummingbirds' evolving "hard soul gospel" style in the 1940s: "the shouted sermons of emotive preachers, the cross-rhythmic hand-clapping of church congregations, the flatfoot dancing of Carolina and Georgia sea island Gullah ring shouts, the 'catch-on-fire' style of Alabama quartets and the jubilant prayer services in the 'Birds' own Holiness Church."[6]

The Blind Boys of Alabama's **"Power of the Lord"** (1951) illustrates and celebrates many of the vocalisms Du Bois, Nations, and Zolten catalog. Besides interpolating the first verse of "Amazing Grace," its up-tempo lyrics consist only of encouragement to sing, pray, moan, and shout until the power of the Lord comes down. The Blind Boys sing, shout, cry, and moan their jubilation. They also give us a taste of the male falsetto and *high who*, an extended high note delivered as the sound "whoooo." Introduced by Marion Williams of the Ward Singers in the late 1940s, it was rapidly adopted across the gospel spectrum and imported into rock 'n' roll by Little Richard. The *pumping bass*, a vocalism developed by jubilee quartets to replicate the sound of the stand-up bass, also appears in gospel quartets. The bass singer pumps out a deep percussive sound under the lead or within the choral harmonies.

Chicago's Soul Stirrers introduced another important innovation in postwar quartet performance, the *switch lead* or *swing lead*: a second lead singer steps in mid-song for the original lead who sometimes switches back in later. Listen to Blind Boys' tenor the Rev. Paul Exkano and the great baritone Clarence Fountain switch leads on "Power of the Lord" as they compete to drive the emotion higher. The popularity of switch leading led to the expansion of quartets to five or six members. When the second lead emerges from the chorus of a five-member quartet, the first lead steps back into it, keeping the four-part harmony intact. Anthony Heilbut calls this possibly the most revolutionary move in the history of quartet performance. It plays an important role in many of the songs we'll discuss.[7]

My taste in gospel leans towards the drama of the hard quartet sound. Great groups like the Blind Boys of Alabama strategically built intensification into their songs through *elevation*: raising the pitch, propelling the tempo, layering rhythms, and switching leads. An important elevating device is *the drive*: "a carefully arranged song section that stalls melodic progress while freeing the lead to improvise" over the *repeat* or *riff* or *vamp*, Glenn Hinson explains. While the chorus repeats a single phrase over and over, the lead builds a dramatic, semi-improvised testimony, often about movement toward salvation, but sometimes as simply as in "Power of the Lord," where Fountain riffs on the phrase "let's shout" while the chorus vamps "let's shout" behind him. Hinson lists some of its effects:

> The quick turnaround of the drive phrase forces the lead to shorten the lead lines and voice them quickly. The percussive loudness of the overlapping backup pressures the lead to utter the lines at a heightened volume. And the elevated pitch plateau from which many drives begin compels the lead to forcibly project each phrase, giving them a particularly explosive quality.

The combination of extraordinary voices, complex arrangements, explosive builds, and profound religious feeling gives the best gospel quartets unequalled affective power. The major rhythm & blues labels saw the commercial attraction of that sound, and in the 1950s, according to Zolten, they "sought a fresh brand of soul-rending gospel that played up the male group sound, intense angst-driven leads with equally intense call and response backup, forays into shouting and startling falsetto, and an instrumentation—drums, bass, electric guitar, piano—that sounded more barrelhouse than praise house." Though sharing elements of rhythm & blues, Zolten adds, "this new-style gospel ... burned with a passion simply not heard in R&B."[8]

Not all the gospel discussed in this chapter is hard; some is *sweet*, some builds from sweet to hard. But it all burns with passion, and an assurance that the dream of life eternal will be guaranteed through the power of faith and the promise of salvation. Among the commonest phrases in postwar gospel song, *by and by* represents the certainty that sooner or later, in God's own time, striving for the right will get you to the promised land. The same faith infused the civil rights movement. Sometimes that certainty is tested, that passion for transcendence and salvation accompanied by a tug back toward the seductive mortal world where the singer may feel 'buked and scorned but also feels the power of the body and its temptations warring with the power of the Lord. The tension gives those songs additional dimension.

Although quartets comprise most of the chapter, we begin with solo artists. They often sang in duets, with backup groups, or entire congregations, so *solo* isn't entirely accurate. We then move from the sweetest to the hardest quartets. As usual, men make up the majority but the great women of postwar gospel are well represented. Most of the artists in this chapter would appear on any list of major figures of gospel's Golden Age. But their music, if not their names, will likely sound as unfamiliar to most readers as the more obscure choices. Shamefully, these marvelous voices remain little known today. You'll hear vocalists the caliber of James Brown, Otis Redding, Jackie Wilson, Aretha Franklin, Etta James, Patti LaBelle. Put the religion aside if you choose. The music will make its own converts.

Mahalia Jackson and the Big Bang

Let's start with **Mahalia Jackson** (1911–72), gospel's greatest superstar. "All by herself," writes Anthony Heilbut, "Mahalia was the vocal, physical, spiritual symbol of gospel music." She had the first multi-million-selling gospel record and her own TV show on CBS. She sang at Carnegie Hall, in London and Paris, on *Ed Sullivan*, at John F. Kennedy's inauguration, alongside Martin Luther King, Jr., at the March on Washington, and at Dr. King's funeral. African American audiences venerated other gospel stars but none as passionately as Mahalia. And for audiences outside the Black community Mahalia Jackson *was* Black gospel, especially after 1954, when she signed with Columbia Records and expanded her repertoire to include what her most recent biographer calls "religious pop." Her earlier recordings for New York's Apollo Records (1947–53) represent for many critics the apogee of Black gospel performance. *The Gospel Music Encyclopedia* goes so far as to describe them as "the *definitive* recordings that demonstrate how *authentic* gospel music *should* be sung" (my italics).[9]

Portrait of Mahalia Jackson by Carl Van Vechten, 1962. Library of Congress, Prints & Photographs Division, Carl Van Vechten Collection, [reproduction number, e.g., LC-USZ62-54231] (163).

Definitive or not, Mahalia's vocal performances sound a little too stately and contained for my taste. Given her status and importance, we at least need to listen to her first hit record. Born in New Orleans, she grew up on jazz and blues, sang with a Baptist congregation, and heard the wilder sounds coming from the Holiness church next door. Moving to Chicago in 1927, she quickly became a star on the Baptist circuit with what Horace Clarence Boyer calls "her big, dark, liquid, burnished contralto." Jackson's association and travels with Dorsey gave her reputation wider circulation, though her first recordings had little impact. But all the elements of her mature vocal style came together when she signed with Apollo in 1947. Boyer lists them:

> from Bessie Smith and Ma Rainey she borrowed a deep and dark resonance that complemented her own timbre; from the Baptist church she inherited the moaning and bending of final notes in phrases ... and from the sanctified church she adopted a full-throated tone, delivered with a holy beat and the body rhythm to accent that beat.

Jackson often acknowledged the influence of Bessie Smith and the Holiness churches that encouraged her to put a "bounce" in her music and move: "The Lord don't like us to act dead. If you feel it, tap your feet a little—dance to the glory of the Lord!"[10] Some Baptist churches even condemned her for moving her hips, lifting her skirt, singing too physically.

"Move on Up a Little Higher, Pt. 1 & 2" (1947) did more than just launch Jackson into the gospel stratosphere. Its popular and commercial success encouraged other gospel singers to overcome their reluctance to record. Jackson said it showed "you could take religious songs and sing them just like you sing in the church, put them on records, and people would buy them." Someone has called it gospel's Big Bang. Written by popular gospel composer the Rev. William Brewster, the song richly elaborates on the genre's most common theme: moving on up from this world to the next. But Brewster was also encouraging postwar African American resistance and uplift. Written during the fight for civil rights in Memphis, the song not only concerned "a Christian climbing the ladder to heaven," Brewster said, "it was an exaltation of Black people to keep moving." Accompanied by James Lee on piano and organist James "Blind" Francis, Jackson opens the song with her best Bessie Smith blues moan. Singing over a slow musical vamp, she shouts the lyric to Part One, her intention to live forever with God. Much of Part Two consists of a solo call-and-response, alternating repetition of the title line with lines about her meeting various biblical figures, her loving mother, and manifestations of Christ. Robert Darden writes of how Jackson's "improvised moans, trills, whoops, glissandos and rhythmic risk-taking" fuel the song's propulsive power.[11] If this solid gospel performance moves you, listen to any of the other sixty songs collected on *Mahalia Jackson: The Original Apollo Sessions* album.

Madame, Sister, Mother, Professor, Reverend

"Just as Mahalia was the biggest female soloist for the white audience, Madame was the biggest star for the black world." **Madame Edna Gallmon Cooke** (1917–67) may not have been quite as big a star as fellow singer J. Lowe claimed, but she had a wonderful voice and a substantial following on the gospel highway. Opal Nations calls "her mournful mezzo soprano ... exquisitely delicate and fragile." Bil Carpenter in *The Gospel Music Encyclopedia* says she could "moan and bend a note beyond recognition."[12] Nevertheless, her star has now almost completely faded. Born in South Carolina where her father was a Baptist preacher, she grew up in D.C., attended Temple University, and joined the Holiness church in the 1940s. She did most of her recording in Nashville.

Listen to what Cooke could do with country-style gospel tunes. **"Build Me a Cabin"** (1953) is her version of Alabaman Curtis Stewart's "Lord Build Me a Cabin in Glory," recorded by Hank Williams, Bill Monroe, Roy Acuff, and Charlie Pride among others. On Nashville's Republic Records, accompanied by just a quiet piano, Cooke at first discards Stewart's loping country rhythms for an achingly slow but bluesy, prayerful appeal for a modest home in glory. She cares nothing for the world's riches or mansions in the sky. Evoking the sharecroppers' shotgun shacks that so many of her listeners once called home, she just wants a little cabin where she can get personal with her savior and have him hold her like a child. She explodes with excitement when singing about the corner in glory where she imagines her Lord building her cabin. When she calls out to God about two-thirds through the song, the piano transitions into a bright, almost vaudevillian gallop that Cooke rides to the end, reiterating her less-is-more rejection of material wealth. And listen to her gorgeous vocal workout on another Southern gospel favorite, **"Somebody Touched Me"** (1953). Backed by her Republic labelmates the Radio Four, whom we'll meet shortly, she celebrates the redemptive power of her Lord's touch. Falling somewhere between Mahalia Jackson's stateliness and Sister Rosetta Tharpe's romps, Cooke's intense, joyous gospel richly repays close listening.

Before Mahalia and Madame Cooke, the most popular voice in gospel belonged to **Sister Rosetta Tharpe** (1915–73). She was one of a kind. Raised in the Holiness church, she sang and played on the margins between sacred and secular, blurring genres and blazing a trail of self-promotion decades ahead of her time. Whereas Jackson militantly stuck to her gospel guns, Sister Rosetta crossed back and forth between secular music and gospel, between churches and venues like Harlem's Cotton Club. She accompanied herself on guitar, "a big, solid-body Gibson like T-Bone Walker's, plucking the notes as cleanly and forcefully as T-Bone as well. Her voice escaped her short, plump frame with Devil-crushing urgency," Preston Lauterbach writes. The facility and ferocity of her playing and singing won her a following among future rock stars. Little Richard opened for her in his first stage appearance and called her his favorite singer. Johnny Cash, Jerry Lee Lewis, and Elvis Presley were acolytes. Later, traveling through the UK, she influenced many of Britain's future guitar gods. In 1951, she staged her third wedding in Washington's Griffith Stadium, charging her fans for the religious music and spectacle. Over 20,000 paid to attend. Then she released a live album of the proceedings. Inducting her in 2018, the Rock & Roll Hall of Fame calls Sister Rosetta "the first guitar heroine of rock & roll." Robert Darden compares her to Madonna ("fearlessly challenging roles and costumes and social mores"), Dolly Parton ("irrepressible, unfazed by criticism, a sexy girl from the country"), and Queen Latifah ("larger than life, lavishly talented, able to move between seemingly irreconcilable worlds with consummate ease").[13]

Born in rural Arkansas, Rosetta moved to Chicago with her mother, **Katie Bell Nubin**, in 1920. A child prodigy, she sang and played guitar, proselytizing for the Church of God in Christ alongside Mother Bell, as Nubin was called. In 1934, Rosetta married and took her husband's name, Tharpe, but divorced him a few years later. She and her mother moved to New York where she sang with Cab Calloway and made her first recordings in 1938, alternating religious and secular songs. Rosetta appeared with Count Basie, was the first gospel soloist to play the Apollo, and performed in John Hammond's *From Spirituals to Swing*. She sang for a couple of years with Lucky Millinder's orchestra, then went solo and took on the Holiness moniker Sister. Her first hit record, "Strange Things Happening Every Day" (1944), climbed to #2 on the Race chart. Recognizing her unique musical hybridity, her Decca label assigned the jazzy Sam Price Trio to accompany her vocals and guitar. Price plays boogie woogie piano on all three recordings discussed below with a different bassist and drummer on each. At her best Tharpe played and sang up-tempo gospel odes to joy. Heilbut writes, "She could pick blues guitar like a Memphis Minnie. Her song style was filled with blues inversions, and a resonating vibrato…. She bent her notes like a horn player, and syncopated in swing band manner." Like a jazz singer, Gayle Wald adds, "Rosetta tended to sing around the beat rather than on top of it, allowing for rhythmic complexity and improvisation."[14]

You can hear all these techniques on **"Cain't No Grave Hold My Body Down"** (1947). Written by Pentecostal preacher Claude Ely, the song begins with Christ's resurrection. From it the singer extrapolates that when Gabriel's trumpet sounds, her own body will rise from the grave. Piano and guitar jauntily open the song and Tharpe's vocals sustain that tone right to the end. The Dance of Death has rarely swung so hard. Like "Move on Up a Little Higher," the song begins with an evocation of early morning, an almost sure sign in blues that things won't turn out well. But gospel mornings represent an annunciation, a promise of miracles to come. Ely's lyrics suit her attitude. Tharpe immediately shows her pleasure at the notion of resurrection, telling Gabriel not to blow his trumpet until *she* says so. After a modest guitar solo with subtle support from the trio, she repeats the opening verse even more playfully. For Mahalia Jackson and most of the other premier gospel singers, salvation is serious business. For Sister Rosetta it sounds like great fun.

In 1946, she teamed up with another Holiness singer, **Madame Marie Knight**. They performed together for five years. Knight's controlled contralto in call-and-response with Tharpe's playful soprano produced some excellent recordings, including **"Up Above My Head"** (1948), another joyous, up-tempo celebration of this world and the next seen through believers' eyes. Tharpe could carve out beautiful gospel ballads like **"Beams of Heaven"** (1948), but listen to her rock out here with what Gayle Wald calls "an ear-popping display of vocal fireworks." The traditional lyrics reiterate that they hear music and see trouble up above their heads. But they believe strongly in heaven. Only that line do they sing together. Otherwise, they echo each other. Knight sings her lines straight while Tharpe swoops, swirls, and embroiders. Price plays a pulsating boogie and Sister Rosetta showcases her instrumental skills, especially in the break. An early 1960s solo performance of the song vividly illustrates Tharpe's electric guitar virtuosity (https://www.youtube.com/watch?v=JeaBNAXfHfQ). This great record has what Wald calls "an undeniable energy that paralleled the collective optimism of black people in the postwar years"—an optimism fueled by faith.[15]

Tharpe began her career as a child singing alongside her mother. Thirty years later, the two still made a joyful noise together. Like "Up Above My Head," Sister Rosetta's free-for-all version of Dorothy Love Coates's **"99½ Won't Do"** (1951) strips the lyrics down to a single basic verse, repeated multiple times with slight variations. Wilson Pickett would funkify this same title and tune with completely different lyrics in 1966. Tharpe and Nubin assure the Lord they're praying and living right, trying for a hundred percent, because 99½ won't do for God. Christian perfection may be the goal but the singers have a great time en route. Daughter and mother sing the same lines out of sync with each other by just a couple of beats until coming together on the title line while Price pounds out the rhythm.

When Coates and the Gospel Harmonettes record their version a few years later, they slow the tempo and moan their way along the difficult journey toward spiritual worthiness. Mother Bell and Sister Rosetta have no such anxiety. Nor does trying to make a hundred mean suspending their affectionate intergenerational one-upmanship as they engage in switch-leading duet-style. Nubin "had a flat, moaning delivery that imbued her singing with spiritual authenticity," but unlike Marie Knight, she won't let Sister have all the fun. She embellishes as much as Rosetta does. Tharpe takes two breaks from mama with strong guitar solos but seems impatient to get back to their singing. Stubbornly striving toward the finish line and refusing to give up until winning the race makes for potent spiritual enjoyment. The song was adapted as a civil rights anthem during the

Sister Rosetta (left) and Marie Knight, promotional photograph during their time as a duo, about 1949. Pictorial Press Ltd./Alamy Stock Photo.

Birmingham Campaign in 1963, and again by Mavis Staples for her 2007 album, *We'll Never Turn Back*.[16] Much of Sister Rosetta's spirited repertoire has hardly dated at all.

The hopeful, forward-looking strain of postwar gospel bound by faith easily translated into civil rights uplift. Recorded by **Sister Jessie Mae Renfro** (1921–96), another fine female soloist with little contemporary visibility, the traditional **"No Room in the Hotel"** (1952) doubled as an incisive protest song. The Chosen Gospel Singers also waxed it, and under the title "No Room at the Inn" so did the Fairfield Four and Mahalia Jackson. Texas-born Renfro lived in Oklahoma with her COGIC preacher husband and recorded for Houston's Peacock label. She had a "powerful, bluesy soprano," Carpenter writes, that could explode with "volcanic eruptions of passion."[17] On this record, accompanied by pianist Eloise Hayes, she sings the entire lyric with passion, shouting the words, sometimes at the top of her range, in a combination of jubilation—after all, the Savior will soon be born—and protest at the blatant injustice of the Bethlehem hotel's sending pregnant Mary away to wander in the night. With multiple repetitions the lyric emphasizes the active discrimination inherent in the lame, familiar excuse. It wasn't that there *was* no room; rather, the hotel *made* no room for her. In the key verse the implicitly African American staff—bellboy, porter, maid, and cook—will testify at the final judgment that they overheard the manager lie to evict Mary. What goes around will come around. The dream of social justice made for a powerful gospel imperative in the postwar era.

Along with the great women soloists of gospel a couple of men stand out. Dave Marsh calls **Alex Bradford** (1927–78) "the most influential male artist of gospel's post–World War II Golden Age."[18] Born in rural Alabama, Bradford began performing as a young boy and joined the Holiness church. He moved to Chicago in 1947 and toured with Mahalia Jackson before launching his solo career. Nicknamed Professor and The Singing Rage of the Gospel Age, he put together the Bradford Specials quintet to perform with him, and signed with Specialty Records. At his first Specialty session Bradford recorded his own composition, **"Too Close to Heaven"** (1953). One of the most powerful gospel songs of the era, it sold a million records and became an instant standard, especially for quartets. The Davis Sisters, Meditation Singers, Christland Singers, and Blind Boys of Alabama all recorded outstanding versions of the song, along with **Bessie Griffin**'s electrifying live solo performance, **"Too Close"** (1954).

Critics cite Bradford's "effervescent ... kinetic stage presence and falsetto leaps" and the flamboyant performance of the Bradford Specials, Bradford's "rough and energetic vocal style" and his "aerobicized workout" of the song.[19] Yet his dramatically contained rendition seems less flamboyant than any of the quartet covers, with only a single falsetto leap, no aerobics to speak of, and minimal harmonic assistance. He sings slowly with little embellishment in his rich, husky, impassioned voice. Twice he quietly interpolates *hallelujah*, and once he lets go a falsetto high who. The

Specials join him only for the two choruses. Bradford's piano underscores his vocal along with a churchy organ. A vibraphone suggests a softly tolling bell, and a drumbeat paces some of the strongest lyrics in gospel. The singer is too close to heaven to turn around. He has almost arrived, his soul is almost saved, he can almost see God's face, his mother, his friends. But his anxiety at being so close tempers his palpable excitement at being so close. Ninety-nine-and-a-half just won't do. Not quite there yet, he feels the sinful world calling, tempting him to turn back. The tension that gives the song its power makes it paradigmatic of much gospel in which salvation's promise lives alongside the terror of its elusiveness. He *can't* turn around, he repeats in the chorus, but the terrible paradox of Judeo-Christian free will makes him know he can. We hear and feel Bradford's struggle with his own nature, drawn by both the magnetic attraction of heaven and the seductive pull of this life.

The charismatic preachers of the Black Baptist and Pentecostal tradition make powerful music even when they don't sing. The cadences of Martin Luther King's speeches are as familiar as the rhythms of Motown. Such preachers have played an important role in the development of gospel from the beginning, and record companies wasted no time seeing their commercial potential. The recorded sermons of the Rev. J.M Coates and the Rev. A.W. Nix were big sellers in the 1920s, and Dorsey invoked them both in proselytizing for the new music. The hellfire approach of Coates's "Death's Black Train Is Coming" and Nix's "Black Diamond Express to Hell" lost favor by the 1940s when the more modern sound of preachers like Detroit's the Rev. C.L. Franklin, Aretha's father, dominated gospel radio.

The most extraordinary singing, sermonizing voice in postwar gospel music belonged to D.C.'s the **Rev. Samuel Kelsey** (1897–1993). Georgia-born like Dorsey and the Reverend Coates, Kelsey grew up in the Pentecostal church and moved to Washington where he established his own congregation, the Temple Church of God in Christ. In 1941, he began broadcasting his sermons on radio, and in 1951 he made a series of records for Decca, which had recorded Sister Rosetta's wedding with the now Bishop Kelsey presiding. Recording live in his own church, Kelsey would begin by citing a biblical verse, elaborate on its meaning, then lead his congregation in a rollicking call-and-response on the biblical theme, accompanied by clapping hands, piano, and trombone.

We have three Kelsey songs on our playlist: **"Little Boy"** (1947), **"I'm a Soldier"** (1947), and **"I'm a Royal Child"** (1951). One of the most successful religious records of the period, "Little Boy" briefly appeared on the *Billboard* R&B chart. Boyer calls it "a gospelized spiritual."[20] Kelsey spends the first minute of the record growling out the biblical story of Jesus preaching in the temple, exchanges Amen's with the congregation, then launches into a series of roars and responses. Kelsey can rock with the best of them, and the congregation sings with obvious joy. In "I'm a Soldier" Kelsey compares his experience in the U.S. Army to becoming a soldier in the army of the Lord, stripping away his civilian clothes to assume a new uniform and identity. All three songs have identical structure, high volume and tempo. "I'm a Royal Child" rocks even harder than the others. Kelsey's theme: since the Lord has saved us, we've been adopted into the royal family. He couldn't sing the title line any louder, especially the word *ROYAL*, underlining the aristocracy of the sanctified. Listen to these songs to experience the power and jubilation of the African American church and its music with congregants and charismatic clergy in perfect sync.

Jubilee to Gospel: How Sweet the Quartet Sound

The transition from jubilee to gospel was never absolute. In many cases postwar gospel quartets incorporated the sweet, intricate harmonies of jubilee into their bluesier, more demonstratively emotional sound. The most successful jubilee group, **the Golden Gate Quartet**, had a huge influence on the sweet gospel sounds of the postwar decade. Formed by Virginia high school students in the late 1920s as the Golden Gate Jubilee Quartet, they sang spirituals with tight harmonies and a jazzy beat, what one member called "vocal percussion." By the early 1940s, they had dropped Jubilee from their name and become hugely popular, singing at *From Spirituals to Swing*, on their own national radio show, and at Franklin D. Roosevelt's inauguration. Like Sister Rosetta, they also performed and recorded secular music. One 1946 session for Columbia illustrates their typical repertoire: "Joshua Fit de Battle of Jericho," "Shadrach," "Swing Down, Chariot," "Wade in the Water," and "Atom and Evil," about the dangers of nuclear war.[21]

Listen to their gorgeous **"Wade in the Water"** (1946), a traditional spiritual that the Fisk Jubilee Singers had performed, evoking the Israelites' escape from Egypt, immersion in the Jordan's waters of salvation, and the slaves' flight to freedom via the underground railroad. Only a single verse features the beautiful lead voice of tenor William Langford. Choral singing makes up most of the song, with stirring cross-harmonies. A guitar provides the rhythmic bass line. Though more constrained than subsequent gospel, the Golden Gates' impassioned vocal chemistry and elegant arrangements encouraged a similar sound in numerous quartets of the postwar period.

One of the most similar, Baltimore's **Trumpeteers**, later called the C.B.S. Trumpeteers, formed in 1946. Boyer describes the Trumpeteers, led by Joseph Johnson, who had sung with the Golden Gates, as "the personification of the jubilee quartet: tight and sweet harmony, tenor voice lead, and attacks and releases that were perfectly coordinated." Their exquisite recording of **"Milky White Way"** (1947) on Aladdin's Score subsidiary was one of the biggest gospel hits of the decade. It spent three weeks on the R&B chart. Elvis, Sister Rosetta, Little Richard, and others covered it. The simple arrangement showcases Johnson's sweet tenor as he anticipates walking the Milky Way, greeting his loving mother, and sitting for a chat with God. The second tenor and baritone hum the background along with James Keels' subtle pumping bass while a guitar provides an almost metronomic second lead. The music and vocal presentation project the idea of a Christian death with absolute comfort and a reassuring lack of drama. "Like the lead singer[s] of other jubilee quartets who were making the transition to gospel," Boyer comments, "Johnson sings with equal amounts of vigor and restraint, permitting the beauty of his voice and singing style to carry the message of the song."[22]

The Bells of Joy, from Austin, Texas, were also transitioning from jubilee to gospel. Originally called the Starlight Singers, they signed with Peacock in 1951, later touring with labelmate Sister Jessie Mae Renfro. The five vocalists plus guitarist recorded a series of terrific up-tempo songs with A.C. Littlefield and Clem J. Reed switching tenor leads. A guitar and drums "heightened a distinctive, rhythmic call and response counterpoint."[23] Their sweet, jubilee-inflected gospel provides plenty of drama in their presentation of the transition from life to death. The utterly addictive **"Leak in This Old Building"** (1951) and **"Fare Ye Well"** (1952) both concern that movement across the great divide.

The traditional "Leak in This Old Building" uses the same metaphor as another popular gospel tune, **"Working on the Building"** (listen to the Highway QCs' 1955 version). *This* building—this body, this worldly home—is corrupt. You can work at building a relationship with God or, in the case of the leak, move on to another home, a better one. The emphatic instrumental rhythm grounds a call-and-response between lead and background as they repeat the two-line refrain over and over, broken only by the bridge where the singer meets his savior. As Littlefield and Reed switch leads, they add exclamations and tease with brief reaches into falsetto. The excitement of the *moo-hoo-hoo-hoove* at the end of the song expresses the anticipation of attaining a better home.

More dramatic still, "Fare Ye Well" says goodbye, I'm going home. I may never see you again, but I'll meet you on that other shore. In addition to the instruments pounding away and the call-and-response between lead and background, a distinctive pumping bass joins in every few bars. Along with a greater contrast between the two lead voices and many more falsetto swoops and trills, the whole group works the elevation. The drive picks up intensity as the background repeats *never-never, never-never* and the two leads enter into a call-and-response, growling and shouting *bye-bye*. What a splendid farewell. But you can hear the ambivalence that comes with leaving mother, father, and this oh so attractive mortal life, leaks and all, for that better place.

Another group that could sing straightforward, up-tempo sweet gospel or build harder, more elaborate harmonic call-and-response structures, Nashville's **Radio Four** consisted of five Babb brothers with Morgan Babb on lead vocal and guitar. We met them earlier singing backup for Madame Edna Cooke, but they also recorded their own potent body of songs for Republic Records. From rural Kentucky, the group began as a family jug band. Nations says they "stuck pretty much to their countryside roots, tending to carry over their former jug-band timbres into four- and five-part harmony," with Morgan's "soulful persuasion and preacher-like testimony" out front.[24]

Remarkable for its insistent lyric minimalism, **"Blood Done Signed My Name"** (1952) repeats the title line twenty-five times, echoed by background harmonies. The almost hypnotic repetition drives home the message of Christian salvation. The intensification comes entirely from switching leads, building from bass to baritone to tenor. The Radio Four's extraordinary apocalyptic **"What'cha Gonna Do"** (1953) also relies on the repetition of the title line for much of its effect. What'cha gonna do when the world's on fire, sinner? The question gets asked of mother and father, too—although they appear to be crossing the River Jordan to glory—and possibly the singer himself as the song ends with a request that we pray for him. It's hard to know the exact sentiment because the lyrics are obscured by the syncopated voices shouting and growling over one another, the amplified din of strong accents, extremely quick tempo, strumming guitar, and fuzzy recording quality. The song elevates very quickly as the two lead voices engage in a call-and-response duel over the vamping background. The increasingly hoarse cries announce the arrival of a harder sound and one of the most exciting records in the gospel canon.

For some, in 1953, the world *was* on fire. Tens of thousands of Americans had died in the Korean War, raging since 1950. Detroit's **The Violinaires**, the first iteration of a group that later included Wilson Pickett before he went secular, commemorated those deaths in one of the great gospel ballads, **"Another Soldier Gone"** (1953). It appeared on Detroit's tiny Drummond label credited to the misspelled Voilinaires, backed with another dynamite song, **"Joy in the Beulah Land."** Pickett's biographer describes how the record "balanced a delicately crooning A-side against a surprisingly rhythmic vocal assault on the flip."[25] *Delicately crooning* perfectly describes how Isaiah Jones exquisitely voices the lyric about a soldier who kept the faith, fought until he fell, and now stands on the heavenly throne while we mourn. A bluesy acoustic guitar and doo wop style background—literally chanting *doo wop* along with blow harmonies and a quietly *boom-boom-boo*ming bass—provide the canvas on which Jones paints the tale in his sweet high tenor, modulating into beautiful falsetto. The song both mourns and celebrates the sacrificial warrior who died for both his country and his God. "Joy in the Beulah Land" might be sung by that dead soldier. He finds nothing but joy—the most often repeated word, an article of faith—in the promised land. Hoarse shouting replaces sweet falsetto, and the record builds with a pumping bass and dynamic drive as the Violinaires shift towards a hard gospel celebration of that good place.

Often described as a farm team for the Soul Stirrers, whom we'll meet shortly, Chicago's **Highway QCs** did send some heavy hitters to the majors. Sam Cooke, Lou Rawls, and Johnnie Taylor all sang lead for the QCs before moving on to more significant gospel groups and then to substantial secular music careers. Formed in 1945 by Cook (who would later add an *e* to his name) and a group of fellow high schoolers, the Highway QCs took their name from a combination of Highway Baptist Church and Quincy College High School. Cooke left in 1951 to join the Soul Stirrers. Rawls succeeded him, then joined the Chosen Gospel Singers in 1955. We'll meet them eventually, too. The Highway QCs songs below were recorded near the end of our postwar decade, featuring the sweet tenor of **Johnnie Taylor** (1934–2000) on lead, sounding remarkably like Sam Cooke.

Taylor joined the QCs with a song he wrote that became the group's first release on Vee-Jay Records, **"Somewhere to Lay My Head"** (1955). The Sensational Nightingales (we'll meet them, too) simultaneously recorded it in a version that "offered a more driving, apocalyptic sound," Peter Guralnick observes, while the QCs' was "slower, more plaintive, with Johnnie Taylor's voice virtually indistinguishable from Sam's." Over background harmonies repeating the title phrase, Taylor's ethereal voice floats in, singing of his tribulations. He has been 'buked and scorned, and is looking for somewhere to rest his weary head. "Taylor yodeled and juggled bent notes just like Cook to the quartet's close harmonies."[26] A quiet organ and pumping bass vocal provide the bottom and Taylor adds Cooke's signature flourishes: *Whoa-a-whoa-a-whoa-whoa*. Its few calls to the Lord and hallelujahs mark this as one of the least explicitly religious of the great gospel songs—and one of the most beautiful.

Taylor's up-tempo composition **"I Dreamed Heaven Was Like This"** (1956) imagines that place where he will one day lay his head. His dream of heaven includes a vision of a smiling God showing him a bright celestial city where he will see his parents again and escape this world's misunderstandings and complaints. A strong bass vocal and percussion help drive the tempo, along with a vamping background and a second lead that swings in briefly. Taylor's beautiful tenor closes on three repetitions of *I believe*, soaring into spine-tingling falsetto. From his excellent gospel writing to his distinctive sweet vocals, Taylor proved himself much more than just a Sam Cooke clone.

We heard the Babb brothers earlier as the Radio Four. Another gospel family, **The Staple Singers**, was launching their extraordinary career at the end of our postwar decade. The Staples would go on to become the nation's best-selling gospel quartet and an eloquent voice in the civil rights movement. They would later cross over into secular music with great success but never lose their connection with faith and freedom songs. **Roebuck "Pops" Staples** (1914–2000), born in the Mississippi Delta, grew up on the Dockery plantation and learned blues guitar alongside legends Charlie Patton and Howlin' Wolf. He also sang in church choirs. When he moved his family to Chicago in 1936, he decided they should sing church music. He put together a quartet with son Pervis and daughters Cleotha, his eldest child, and Mavis, his youngest. **Mavis Staples** (1939–) initially sang bass, but soon Pops and Mavis alternated leads. They first recorded in 1953 but their success came a few years later with Vee-Jay Records. The group's unique sound resulted from Mavis' "smoky, gut-bucket, sometimes basso, sometimes contralto, vocal stylings" and more:

> When the Staples harmonized, their blend was high and keening, with Pops singing falsetto alongside his daughter Cleotha, a soprano, and Pervis, a high tenor.... [T]he electric guitar playing of Pops ... [featured] finger-picked arpeggios, amplified in a wash of reverb and tremolo, anchoring the bottom of the sound.[27]

Their first Vee-Jay session provides a wonderful introduction to Pops' shimmering guitar, the Staples' harmonies, and teenage Mavis' soulful voice and stylings. A killer record, **"Calling Me"** (1955) didn't initially make much of an impression. Written by Dorothy Love Coates and recorded by Coates and the Gospel Harmonettes earlier that year, the song joyfully embraces Jesus' call to eternal life. Pops slows the tempo slightly and Mavis avoids the ecstatic leaps that Coates brought to all her performances. (We'll meet Coates and the Harmonettes soon, too.) Mavis doesn't need to shout. Listen to the passion cracking her voice in the opening lines, illustrating Pete Welding's comment that "Her performances are less interpretations than they are effusions of her own deep-seated conviction and religiosity."[28] After a catalog of biblical figures the drive focuses on the singer's personal response as the background vamps on the title phrase. An irresistible record.

Their next session, in September 1956, marked the group's breakthrough. Mavis' lead on **"Uncloudy Day"** (1956) put them on the map. Their slow, quietly impassioned arrangement of a nineteenth-century hymn has just a single repeated verse: They tell me of a home with no clouds at all, an unclouded day. The group's harmonies and what Staples biographer Greg Kot calls "the heavy drapery of Pops' guitar" take up the first minute and a half before "the dark gravity of Mavis' voice" takes over. You can't be sure whether it's a man or a woman singing in her deepest basso. "[T]he song enters like a mirage or a hallucination, evoking a cotton field on a summer afternoon … a glimpse from a dream."[29] The success of "Uncloudy Day" gave the Staple Singers national recognition. It's an impressive record, but I prefer the group with more tempo and swing.

Perhaps their producer did, too. At the same session they recorded **"Swing Down, Chariot"** (1956), a traditional spiritual popularized by the Golden Gate Quartet. Pops' ringing guitar gets a fifteen second intro, then the rest of the record rocks along to the group's harmonies with the exception of a brief drive where Mavis takes the lead. The imagery-rich lyrics begin with a request to ride that sweet chariot and be rocked by the Lord. They pick up urgency as the singer tries to get to heaven before the doors close: wake and shake me so I can swing on the golden gate and grab the starry crown. The Staples made the sweet, joyful jubilee sound of the 1940s modern and fresh.

A Little Bit Harder Now

These next selections belong to quartets that brought a little more grit, growl, and church-wrecking demolition to their gospel. In subtitling this section I jumped to the Isley Brothers' "Shout" (1959), my favorite rockin' song as an early teen. Like me, the Isleys moved from Cincinnati to New York, and their song was THE fast house-wrecking dance tune for my circle of high school friends. Not surprisingly, the Isleys had originally sung gospel. "Shout" came directly out of the church onto the dance floor. The best section was the elevation. After singing progressively softer, Ronnie Isley's voice dropping with each repetition to almost a whisper, he begins building a little louder until he repeatedly shouts while the background overlaps with "Shout!" and high whos. Though secularized, this first intense experience of the ecstasy generated by the little bit harder gospel sound marked me for life.

In the following songs you can hear the emotional complexity, ambivalence, and even desperation that sometimes bumps up against the faith of these artists in harder gospel performances. The aesthetic composition of their songs may convey something other than what a listener might expect. Allan F. Moore refers to a *friction* between "the expectations listeners may bring to a track, on the basis of normative assumptions, and a track's frequent refusal to conform to those assumptions." Anthony Heilbut, gospel's foremost scholar, writes, "One of gospel's great appeals to this nonbeliever has been the vast emotional territory it claims for itself."[30] The intricate arts of gospel encompass an enormous range of personal, emotional, philosophical, and theological positions. This marvelous music grants us the pleasures of exploring its entire vast territory, frictions and all, especially in the context of changing times: the new dream world unfolding outside the church doors.

Just as the 1942 Petrillo strike hastened the evolution of rhythm & blues recording, a 1948 musicians' strike led by union head James C. Petrillo (listen to Dinah Washington's **"Record Ban Blues"** [1948]) gave impetus to *a cappella* gospel quartets, which could record because they used no musicians. Formed in Houston in 1936, **The Pilgrim Travelers** moved to Los Angeles and signed with Specialty in 1947. Known for their athletic choreography, they sang *a cappella* and tapped their feet for percussion—on mic'd plywood when recording—a device called *walking rhythm*. Their two leads, cousins Kylo Turner and Keith Barber, embodied the sweet jubilee and hard gospel sounds respectively: Turner's falsetto crooning and Barber's harsh growls and screams.[31] In the Pilgrim Travelers' relatively unimaginative arrangements the harmonizing background simply repeats a single phrase. But the contrasting leads crossing over each other create beautiful sonic drama.

"Mother Bowed" (1948), the group's first hit record, begins quietly with a slow, steady walking rhythm and the background harmonizing *ooh ooh* while Turner sweetly sings about sitting on his mother's knee, listening to her teaching from the bible and bowing to pray for him to be saved. Things heat up in the second verse as Turner intensifies his vocal, crying and howling at the memories of his mother's prayerful lessons while the background repeats that she prayed for him, and Barber moans in counterpoint. More of the same in verse three: in a beautiful burst of falsetto, the singer recalls hearing his mother's whispered midnight prayers and *see-ee-ee-ing* her on her knees. The song resolves in sweet harmony once again.

The intensity and what sounds like anguish in the vocal operate in tension with the straightforward virtues of mother's piety, her teaching, and prayers on his behalf. Does the memory of his beloved mother who may no longer be alive prompt the cries, howls, and moans, as happens in the Pilgrim Travelers' excellent **"Good News"** (1948), where both leads shift into a pained cry when singing the equivocal good news that mother lay down in this world and made it home to see her savior? Or does his own sense of unworthiness, a failure to live up to mother's values and sacrifices, torment the singer? This underlying element of doubt, regret, or fear turns what might otherwise sound like doctrinaire pieties into powerful drama. Even the choral repetition of mother's praying suggests something more than acknowledgment or gratitude. A mother prays to show her son the way. But the repetition drains the matter-of-factness from the phrase. Yes, she prayed for him; yes, she did. Why did she need to pray for him so much, so hard, at midnight, whispering in the dark? Is there an implied *but* at the end of the phrase? Could even the life eternal be a dream for some, notwithstanding mother's prayers?

As a complement, listen to the beautiful, solemn **"My Road's So Rough and Rocky"** (1950). It begins with a verse expressing the title notion. The singer has been saved from his tough life and God is calling him home. While the background harmonies repeat the title phrase under the first verse, they shift to the negative for the second and third verses—no more rough rocky road—as Turner's lead swings over to Barber. His path will be smoother as he keeps on working for the Lord, who promises him his just reward. Barber's vocal and Turner's moaning counterpoint approach the intensity of "Mother Bowed" at moments, but pull back, never suggesting the same anxiety. The less personally detailed first-person confessional dilutes the tension.

In **"Jesus Hits Like the Atom Bomb"** (1950) the Pilgrim Travelers move even further from the personal and pained. Despite the apocalyptic subject—nuclear holocaust and the second coming—the song's tone and texture remain unruffled. The lyrics express an irony: everyone worries about the atomic bomb when they should worry about the coming of the Lord. The bomb becomes a metaphor for the explosiveness of Revelation: the fire next time. Covered by several gospel groups in 1950,[32] shortly after Russia's first A-bomb test and only five years after Hiroshima and Nagasaki, the song would seem a natural for the kind of vocal anxiety we hear in "Mother Bowed." But the opposite proves to be the case: no howls or cries, almost no elevating devices at all but for a gentle *hey, hey, hey*. The calm lead and lovely harmonies express total faith in the impersonal lyrical message: Don't worry, God's on it.

Here's a mystery. Specialty's Art Rupe had an ear for great music and soon would have the most impressive stable of gospel singers and quartets in the nation. Among his first gospel signings, **The Golden Echoes** got only one recording session and a single release on Specialty before Rupe let them go. The group had some of the best singers in the business: leads **Paul Foster** (1920–95) and **Wilmer "Little Axe" Broadnax** (1916–92), and bass James Ricks. Foster, one of the greatest of all time, would soon join the Soul Stirrers. Broadnax (revealed after death as transgender) moved over to the Spirit of Memphis.[33] The Golden Echoes' *a cappella* rendition of the classic **"When the Saints Go Marching In"** (1949) absolutely kills.

Foster opens the song almost mournfully, his downbeat baritone echoed by a bassy background chanting the title phrase. By the end of the second verse he begins to lift the refrain—maybe he really does *want to be* in that holy number. Then the leads switch, Broadnax's passionate tenor takes over, the background elevates its pitch to match, and the tempo picks up incrementally. The vocal enthusiasm is contagious. When Foster resumes the lead with his own voice pitched higher, the saints are not just marching but running in, accompanied by a high *whoo*. In the drive he repeats, "Yeah, let me be," and invokes his mother and father as the background completes the sentence, "in the holy number." By the end, with the saints virtually sprinting in, Foster is shouting his desire to join them. In the passion of the moment his voice coarsens to a near-growl, but what we hear sounds nothing like the drama of ambivalence. If he had any doubt about celebrating the end of days at the start, he has none by the finish.

Little Axe's arrival gave **The Spirit of Memphis Quartet** a triumvirate of great lead voices. The group originally came together in the 1920s, taking its name from Charles Lindbergh's trans–Atlantic *Spirit of St. Louis*. They really took flight during their tenure with King Records, 1949–52. Opal Nations describes their lineup during that period: Broadnax "possessed a clear, peerless, almost operatic tenor which he used with boisterous effect"; tenor Jet Bledsoe "caressed his listeners in a smooth, soulful, rarely unrestrained singing style"; Silas Steele, Jr., "shook the rafters of the church with his bellowing, thunderous baritone." Baritone James Darling and bass Earl D. Malone sang in support. Viv Broughton points out that even with thunderous Silas Steele in the mix, "Their trademark was their subdued emotional intensity," and many of their best records featured jubilee-style *a cappella* arrangements.[34]

Insistent repetition, varied by changes in pitch and pace, and lead switches provide the key to Spirit of Memphis songs. You hear all these elements in the traditional spiritual, **"Every Time I Feel the Spirit"** (1951), arranged by Earl Malone. The song consists essentially of a single line: Every time he feels the spirit in his heart, he will pray. Along with a quickening tempo and heavy percussion, the dynamism comes from the three different voices that take the lead, beginning with Bledsoe's measured pacing, followed by Steele's elevation of the tempo and intensity. After that boost, Little Axe takes off with it.

Their most exciting performance is another spiritual, **"Toll the Bell Easy"** (1952), an up-tempo celebration of Christian death. Bledsoe and Steele share the leads, insisting that when they die no one should cry or moan. Just toll the bell easy and Jesus will take care of the rest. Ironically, background crying and moaning in counterpoint with Bledsoe's passionate howling inform the group's most complex, energetic arrangement. But the moaning definitely does not represent mourning. Steele settles things down in the verses, matter-of-factly preparing to meet Jesus as Malone pumps the bass. No one is reconciled to taking things easy. The preparation to pass over calls for nothing less than ecstatic song.

When Bishop Samuel Kelsey presided over Sister Rosetta Tharpe's marriage vows in front of twenty thousand gospel fans in 1951, the **Harmonizing Four** helped provide the entertainment. Another group dating back to the 1920s, they got together in their Richmond elementary school and adopted the Virginia jubilee style, Opal Nations reports: "a smooth, polished, tight hymn-singing approach to quartet … sweet, lilting backgrounds behind a tenor's sweeping dramatic lead."

While recording for a variety of labels in the 1940s, they developed a dynamic performance style that made them a formidable entry in the increasingly popular battles of the gospel groups, in which the audience chose the victor. "Can the famous Harmonizing 4 of Richmond, VA stop the Sensational 5 Blind Boys of Jackson, Miss.?" reads a 1947 ad.[35] With Gotham Records, 1951–55, they produced a sound rooted in jubilee but sporting a wildly passionate, battling gospel heart.

Tommy Johnson, who had been with the group since 1932, sings the sweeping dramatic lead on **"Say a Word"** (1952). Nations describes it as "a song from the call-and-response catalog [that] heightens with vigor as Johnson piles on the emotive fuel."[36] I call it one of the most joyous songs in the gospel canon. Second tenor Lonnie Smith on guitar and the background's tight echoing harmonies and jolly *doot-doo-doo*'s accompany this up-tempo tribute to the power of prayer. Johnson's impassioned high tenor highlights the record, testifying that despite a world full of trouble and a rocky personal road, the family altar provides the fuel for salvation. His modest request to include him in your evening prayer compels him, in a series of verses, to think about going home: getting to the other side of the deep, wide, cold Jordan River without chilling his soul. From the domestic warmth of the family altar, the song takes him to a celebration in heaven. Johnson does all the elevating himself, embroidering his narrative with melisma and a brief drive. Great voice, great song.

In 1953, tenor James Walker briefly joined the group before moving on to the Dixie Hummingbirds. "A jewel of a performer," Jerry Zolten calls him, he took the lead on the marvelous, emotionally exhausting **"Working for the Lord"** (1953), and does he ever work it.[37] His much rougher voice than Johnson's pushes this song towards hard gospel. It has a completely different sound than "Say a Word," with an organ, drums, and hands clapping. Once more we hear a call-and-response between lead and background, but without the prominent bass of "Say a Word," and the background harmonizes in a much higher range. The song begins melodically but Walker starts his elevation very quickly. He's working, singing, and shouting for his Jesus. His working days will soon be over and he's going home to be rewarded. But the way doesn't seem easy. His Lord is a hard taskmaster and he still has much work to do. Walker's highly emotional vocalizing lacks joy but feels determined. Beginning at 1:05, the drive lasts to the end of the song while the background riffs "going on home" almost in falsetto. In the words of another spiritual, you got to move. He's driving hard to the finish line. Going home in his dying hour to meet his sister and brother, growling and howling, he has just a little farther to go, and he's *gonna MOO-OO-OOVE*. He made it over, he repeats at the end. And he earned it.

Many of the female quartets on my playlist skew towards hard gospel, with lead voices like wrecking balls. The **Angelic Gospel Singers** reside just on the edge of that sound. Four women from South Carolina who moved to Philadelphia, the Angelics formed in 1944, led by **Margaret Allison** (1921–2008), whose Pentecostal/COGIC upbringing can be heard in her rollicking singing and piano-playing. They continued performing for over sixty years, right up to Allison's death. Critics consider the

Angelics "a simple, down-homey act" who practiced "the old-fashioned southern style of church music." Whether a result of their downhome style or belief system, they sang about death with unabashed joy. Nations calls **"Back to the Dust"** (1950) "a jumping foot tapper in the Wards' vein" (we'll meet the Ward Singers down the road apiece).[38] The song riffs on the notion from Ecclesiastes 3:20 that we come from dust and to dust we return. It's the return they celebrate.

This song rocks from its opening bars with Allison on piano, organist Doc Bagby (who co-wrote "Rock the Joint"), and a drummer banging away. Different from other quartets, Allison's lead voice is buried amid what would normally be the background (Lucille Shird, Ella Mae Norris, and Josephine McDowell, Allison's sister). They sing the verses, too, in four-part harmony—no lead. In the Angelics, Nations writes, "all were equal. Solo primadonnaing was not a concern."[39] Allison can really wail, and her voice gives the song its dramatic intensity. In an utterly positive and unequivocal tone the song says that God made your body but *loves* your soul. Going back to the dust means entering God's love. For the Angelics dying is cause for joy.

They recorded "Back to the Dust" for Philadelphia's Gotham Records. Because of their democratic group-centric sound, or to promote two of its acts at once, Gotham arranged for the Angelics to tour and record with another of its groups, one of the greatest gospel quartets, the Dixie Hummingbirds. This unusual coupling—women and men, nine singers on one song, ten on the other—led to terrific joint releases: "In the Morning" and, for Columbia's OKeh subsidiary, "One Day." **The Dixie Hummingbirds**, like the Angelics, began singing in South Carolina Holiness churches before moving to Philadelphia in the 1940s. One of their original members from the 1920s, James Davis, stayed with the group for sixty years. Along the way they picked up

The Dixie Hummingbirds, Peacock Records publicity still, 1950s. Front, from left: Ira Tucker, Willie Bobo; middle: James Walker; back, from left: Howard Carroll, Beachy Thompson, James Davis. Pictorial Press Ltd./Alamy Stock Photo.

tenors Ernest James and Beachey Thompson, great bass Willie Bobo, and lead tenor **Ira Tucker** (1925–2008), one of gospel's most venerated singers. The Dixie Hummingbirds' joint efforts with the Angelics required both groups to trade leads and sacrifice precise background harmonies for overlapping multiple voices. The Hummingbirds usually sang *a cappella*, but here they had to accommodate the Angelics' instrumentation.[40]

The groups meld nicely on the traditional **"In the Morning"** (1950), where two Angelics (Allison and Norris) and four Hummingbirds (baritones Tucker and Davis, tenors James and Thompson) take turns improvising verse lines about shouting, singing, and wearing starry crowns while the background responds "in the morning" and the ensemble completes the line, "when the dark clouds roll away." The up-tempo and celebratory mood has the singers growling, shouting, and vocally embroidering both the lead lines and background, and everyone clapping hands. The occasion calls for jubilation. Morning represents the dawning of Revelation.[41]

An even better Dorsey song, adapted as a showcase for joint harmonies, **"One Day"** (1951) has three wonderful lead voices begin each line with "One day," while the chorus completes it with a range of references to salvation. Zolten describes the performance "rid[ing] along on Allison's rocking piano and the rousing exchange between male and female units." Ira Tucker, tenor Paul Owens (who replaced Ernest James after coming over from the Sensational Nightingales and would later find fame with the Swan Silvertones), and Bernice Cole, who joined the Angelics for this session, trade leads and shouts. They save their best for the final thirty seconds "with Tucker and Owens shifting into overdrive, pumping rapid-fire like alternating pistons on the single word, 'one.'" Tucker called their vocal synergy *trickeration*, explaining that he and Owens "knew the range of each other so good until I could always depend on him to pick a note up where I left it off. A split second before I finished, he got it."[42] Cole got it, too. Her banshee wail over top of the sanctified exchange between Tucker and Owens takes this remarkable record to another dimension.

What Then: Hard Gospel Voices of Salvation and Doubt

The categories of *sweet* and *hard* gospel, and everything in between, are fluid and open to interpretation.[43] We've seen in the previous sections how the sweet sounds of the Radio Four and the Violinaires could turn hard. The Pilgrim Travelers could go sweet and hard within the same song. The Dixie Hummingbirds' "I'll Be Satisfied," examined in our opening chapter, expresses unequivocal faith and satisfaction in the notion of a Christian afterlife with not a howl, growl, or moan from Ira Tucker or the background. Yet parts of the Hummingbirds' other songs operate in a realm of super-intensity bordering on anguish.

An epigraph from Tucker begins this chapter. Hard gospel, he insists, is "heart and emotion." What more could one want from musical expressions of faith than the sincerity, directness, centrality, and power of heart and emotion. The songs that follow, with their elements of hard gospel, speak directly to the emotions. The lead voices in these quartets are vortices of power. Their dialogues with the background, arranged for maximum effect, further intensify the message. But in some cases the messages seem mixed. Tucker says the sweet stuff is the brain stuff. But the hard is brain stuff, too, in a different way. Great art complicates, generating feeling *and* thought. Life *could* be a dream for African Americans in the postwar decade. We've seen in blues and rhythm & blues how the great music of the era could reflect and be inflected by social, sexual, economic, and political circumstances. The same holds true for gospel. Life in the hereafter could be a dream. Amid the faith and grace in the music that follows echo notes of doubt, fear, and wishful thinking. Nothing could be more deeply human.

Listen to the Dixie Hummingbirds perform Dorsey's **"What Then"** (1950). The Hummingbirds' recording exists online in three forms. A version titled "Oh Lord, What Then" (3:34) is found in the album *Look Down Upon Me, Lord: The Dixie Hummingbirds* on iTunes and the anthology *1950s Southern Gospel* (iTunes and Spotify). "What Then" (3:07) in *Golden Gospel Classics: The Dixie Hummingbirds* (iTunes and Spotify) abruptly abbreviates the 3:34 version. Finally, the Dixie Hummingbirds' "What Then" on YouTube showcases a 3:41 recording from an album called *Gospel Nostalgia*. The two equally powerful longer versions were likely recorded at one session with the same personnel.

Ernest James and Ira Tucker share the lead on this mid-tempo *a cappella* masterpiece, a meditation on the end of days. The title expresses the rhetorical question asked throughout the song: after the apocalypse, what then? The series of vivid scenarios that cumulatively describe the end never make explicit the nature of God's judgment. The lyrics indicate nothing like fire and brimstone or flocks of angels. Just absence. A closed bible on an altar before empty pews. No more choirs singing or preachers praying, bugles blowing or flags flying. But when the great book opens, each of us will face the record of our life.

On the comparatively rougher 3:41 performance James takes the lead for the first half, his singing emotional and melismatic. The 3:34 version, "Oh Lord, What Then," has a cleaner sound, a slightly quicker tempo, and one additional verse when Tucker switches in, asking what happens after the actors have played their last drama and the audience has vanished. In both, the background begins with a quiet series of *ooh*s and *mmm*s, then chants "oh, what then" as the leads elevate the intensity, shouting and howling over each other. The apocalyptic cacophony of the final minute, especially in the 3:41 version, offers something closest to the title question's answer: confusion, chaos, terror. In contrast to the welcome certainty of joy in "One Day" or "In the Morning," "What Then" embraces the possibility of latter-day doom.

The Dixie Hummingbirds inaugurated their move to the Peacock label with a Tucker composition, **"Wading Through Blood and Water"** (1952). It came out in April 1952: the Korean War had been raging for almost two years and the U.S. had already lost the majority of the more than 33,000 lives that war would cost the country. Tucker begins the song as a sweet dirge, keening in his falsetto against quiet background harmonies, setting the battlefield scene with the song's titular refrain: the soldiers wading through blood and water are trying to make it home. In the only other verse he addresses a mother praying to end the war. Though burdens seem hard to bear, he assures her that Jesus will answer her prayer. The background begins chanting the word *wading* behind those lyrics, which also sounds like *waiting*: for prayers to be answered, the war to end, to get home. Then in a brief drive Tucker takes up the word himself, repeating it nine times, echoed by the background, before the song concludes in a beautiful harmonic resolve, a patented Hummingbirds ending.

Zolten describes the song building with "underlying urgency" from its somber opening to the "anguish coming through in Tucker's growling moans and cries."[44] The anguish no doubt refers to the soldiers' physical suffering, their struggle to survive, and the terrible burdens borne by their families at home. But along with the repeated growls as he drives the word *wading*, Tucker cries out when invoking his certainty that Jesus will respond to prayer. Since making it home has a double meaning in the context of gospel, where the journey home always signifies the passage to death, the anguish in Tucker's performance may involve not just combat and the home front but also his own faith and the ultimate fate of those who won't survive the war. It never quite reaches the intensity of "What Then," and the ten seconds of lovely harmony at the end offer a reassuring salve. But the song's turn from sweet to hard opens a schism. There may be no atheists in foxholes, but can faith alone make sense of the carnage?

The second Hummingbirds' single on Peacock could almost be a response to "Wading Through Blood and Water." **"Trouble in My Way"** (1952) re-examines the relationship of life's travails to Christian faith and finds no cause for lamentation, only excitement. The previous song's concrete war imagery gives way to generalized troubles and an acknowledgment that tears and moans are inevitable, but so is salvation. Singing the first two verses in his clear tenor, Beachey Thompson pins down the theme with his certainty that Jesus will take him by and by. Zolten cites "the sheer energy of the performance" as it gallops along on the guitar work of the group's newest member, Howard Carroll, plus Willie Bobo's pumping bass and a drummer. When the lead switches just past the one-minute mark, Ira Tucker invokes both the Old and New Testaments in a lengthy drive: "Coming on like a Southern preacher, Tucker growls, 'Hey Father, Father of Abraham,' repeats the phrase, then throws it to the Birds, who chant it fervently while he interpolates a new set of couplets...."[45] The most powerful line is Tucker's personal testimonial: *But I, but I, I-I-I-I-I-I call him Jesus*. Thompson knows that Jesus will take him but Tucker addresses Jesus directly, confident of an answer by and by. The phrase *by and by*, a gospel commonplace, suggests the inevitability of grace. No need for urgency, no notes of doubt here or howls of anguish; just growls and shouts of enthusiasm at the joyful certainty of a divine response to the human call.

Call-and-response is the bread-and-butter of the gospel group sound, and at mid-century none did it better than **The Ward Singers**, aka The Famous Ward

Singers or The Clara Ward Singers. Their story begins in 1931 in the gospel hotbed of Philadelphia where Gertrude Ward formed a trio with her young daughters Willa and Clara. In 1947, Henrietta Waddy and Floridian **Marion Williams** (1927–94) joined the group. **Clara Ward** (1924–73) arranged their songs, played piano, and alternated leads with Williams. Famous for their showmanship, the group sported elaborate dresses and increasingly outrageous wigs. But the spectacle paled in the face of Clara's dynamic arrangements and the group's vocal prowess. "At her peak, Clara's voice was an exceptionally beautiful alto, a clearer and firmer version of Aretha's," according to Heilbut, who calls her Aretha Franklin's "musical mother." The Wards' primary singing star, however, was Marion Williams, one of gospel's greatest vocalists. Robert Santelli describes how "Williams could hit the highest notes and then suddenly drop two octaves or intonate with strains of deep blues or turn her voice into a wildly improvisational instrument the way Louis Armstrong did with his trumpet...."[46]

The Wards' recording of Brewster's **"Surely God Is Able"** (1949), released on both Savoy (as Ward Singers) and Gotham (as The Famous Ward Singers of Philadelphia), sold a million records and made them the most famous female gospel group of the era. What a brilliant record. "The arrangement was unique and completely new to gospel," Boyer claims. In stately piano waltz rhythm, the song opens with an echoing call-and-response chorus. Clara and the background repeat the word *Surely* eight times, emphasizing God's ability "to carry you through." All five women harmonize the verse in a high key, followed by an echoing refrain. Then Clara sings five lines about God's Old Testament miracles, the background affirming each with a testifying exclamation. Clara and the background repeat the echo-effect chorus until Williams comes in blasting a high *who* and singing the refrain, which she ends with a scream. That takes her into a second testimonial to God's abilities. In nine lines, divided by the background's affirmations, she sings of the friendship, hope, support, and salvation God brings us. Intermittently growling and howling, Williams ends with a chorus of *surely*'s that Heilbut describes as "the most terrifying blast out of gospel in the fifties."[47] This hard gospel approaches sheer ecstasy.

Williams takes a back seat on another Brewster composition, **"The Old Landmark"** (1951) on Savoy, with the same personnel plus an organ. Clara Ward's lead features few hard edges and less vociferous shouting, but the outcome is no less joyous. The lyrics call for a revival of the old ways of worship to serve the Lord, who will answer by saving the world from sin. The verses alternate with a rapid-fire call-and-response marked by very short lines and abundant rhymes. The piano vamps on a two-note musical phrase as Ward begins each line and the background completes it. Boyer calls this Brewster-style vamp a *cumulative song*: "the words begin to pile on one another and the element of repetition becomes the strength of the performance."[48] The number of lines increases each time the device repeats, amplifying and elevating the excitement: twelve lines, then sixteen, then twenty-four. The Wards influenced two spectacular later recordings of the song that take the tempo and temperature even higher: Aretha Franklin's earthshaking live performance on her *Amazing Grace* album (1972) and James Brown's fiery the Reverend Kelsey–like tribute in the *Blues Brothers* movie (1980). Backed by James

Cleveland's large choir, both performances are set in church. Aretha's real church has Clara Ward in the audience; JB's movie set has dancers in the aisles.

The Wards' second biggest hit, recorded in December 1956 but not released until 1958, proves they could rock their faith as hard as anyone. Written by Brewster, arranged by Clara, with Williams singing lead and a background fortified by two additional singers plus piano, organ, and drums, **"Packin' Up"** (1956) comes closer than anything else in gospel to Little Richard's powerhouse rock 'n' roll. Marion is packin' up, excited, getting ready to go to the New Jerusalem. She has her sword, shield, and ticket. For much of the song she riffs on the Lord while the background vamps the title phrase. Unable to contain her enthusiasm, she lets loose a series of high who's. The background singers match her energy in perfect synergy.

But professional unhappiness nearly undid the spiritual joy. Objecting to their pay and treatment by Gertrude Ward, Williams and three others packed themselves up and left the group in 1958 to form Marion Williams and the Stars of Faith. Hear how thrilling "Packin' Up" can be when the charismatic Williams and her new group perform it on the TV show *Hootenanny* in 1963 (https://www.youtube.com/watch?v=1QlDUmX_3yA), and when Aretha, Little Richard, and Billy Preston go house-wrecking with the song and a hundred-member choir at the Kennedy Center Honors for Williams in 1993, preceded (at 2:30) by Aretha's glorious rendition of "Surely God Is Able" (https://www.youtube.com/watch?v=gvhQ5ZPHMwI).

The Wards laid down a marker for mid-century female gospel groups to try to match or exceed. **The Soul Stirrers** did the same for male quartets. Heilbut calls them "the real creators of the modern gospel sound." They date from 1926, when baritone S.R. Crain formed a quartet in East Texas. In 1937, fellow Texan **R.H. Harris** (1916–2000) joined as lead tenor. The intense emotional pitch to which Harris brought their songs and his influential innovation of the swing lead made the Soul Stirrers the most important gospel quartet of the early postwar years. "Almost all the trademarks of the modern quartet style are traceable to Harris," Viv Broughton writes. Moving to Chicago in the mid-1940s, picking up hard-singing tenor Paul Foster from the Golden Echoes and signing with Specialty, the Soul Stirrers cemented their reputation. In 1950, *Ebony* magazine named them the top gospel group in the country.[49] That year Harris participated in only two Specialty sessions before abruptly leaving the Soul Stirrers, but they resulted in several *a cappella* gems. From 1951–56, the group featured the most popular lead in gospel, Sam Cooke.

Peter Guralnick describes Harris as a *hard* singer: "for all of his precise articulation, the controlled drama of his delivery, and the soaring sweep of his falsetto flights, [he] bore down relentlessly in his vocal attack...." Yet Harris' tone retains an intrinsic sweetness that Foster's harder, harsher, darker notes perfectly complement, just as they would Cooke's silky vocals. The Harris-Foster combination shows to great advantage on the magnificent **"By and By, Parts 1 & 2"** (1950), the Soul Stirrers' first Specialty release and my single favorite gospel recording. A Tindley composition from 1905, "By and By" is one of those "old hymns," Harris told Heilbut, that were "my meat, a sad slow minor song." It starts slowly but never really gets sad, despite

Heilbut's assertion that Harris' vocal "has the heavy impact of a farmer broadcasting bad news about crop failure or drought." The refrain, repeated many times, explains that we'll arrive at a better understanding of God's plan by and by, specifically on that morning when the saints gather to come home. One of the most positive lines in gospel, "We'll tell the story of how *we've* overcome," looks ahead to a satisfying look back at victory. The Soul Stirrers change Tindley's line slightly but significantly, first shifting the tense from past to future, singing of how *we'll* overcome—anticipating the next decade's civil rights anthem, "We Shall Overcome"—then to the present tense, how *we* overcome.⁵⁰

The Soul Stirrers, Specialty Records publicity photograph, c. 1950. Front, from left: S.R. Crain, R.B. Robinson; back, from left: Paul Foster, J.J. Farley, Thomas L. Bruster (?), R.H. Harris. Pictorial Press Ltd./Alamy Stock Photo.

Part one opens jubilee-style with the entire six-man group singing the refrain in harmony, very slowly, punctuated by Jesse Farley's basso *hallelujah*. The tempo and vocal energy gradually ramp up as Foster repeats the refrain, then switches over to Harris, whose beautiful performance of the verse begins by citing dark trials in abundance. A heavy darkness weighs on his voice, mitigated by his melismatic embroidery of phrases like *promised la-a-and*. Foster swings back in with a more passionate refrain and his own embroidery: *a-a-a-a-all the saints*. This kicks off "By and By, Part 2," often found independently on playlists and YouTube. The lead now swings back over to Harris, who sings a gorgeous, moving second verse emphasizing God's mysterious ways: how the *wo-o-onders* He performs are so *ha-a-a-ard* to understand. Foster switches back in for the final minute. Echoed by the background's chants, he shouts the refrain at his most intensely guttural and powers to the finish. Gospel at its most supremely, affirmatively transcendent *and* this-worldly tells God's story and overcomes the darkest trials. A great, great performance.

Two more fine songs from the same February 1950 session showcase Harris' vocals and illustrate the Soul Stirrers' clean rhythmic sound. **"Feel Like My Time Ain't Long"** (1950) seems like it ought to be grim. But Harris' vocal and the group's echoing harmonies turn it into an anthem of equanimity and acceptance. Foster opens with the refrain that makes up the entire song: his mother, father, and brother have gone, making him feel like his own time is nearly up. The lead then switches to Harris, who repeats Foster's lines. Heartache and pain make him feel the same, and the hearse keeps rolling. Although the song lacks any reference to God, Jesus, heaven, or redemption, the lilting rhythm, quick tempo, and Harris' high, sweet tenor keep the mood surprisingly positive.

Why should we have no fear of death? Equally up-tempo and more upbeat, **"I Have a Right to the Tree of Life"** (1950) provides an answer: Jesus died for us. After Foster introduces the argument, Harris elaborates on it. The performance doesn't protest or demand that he *should* have the right. This right seems absolute and pre-ordained. With Farley's bass bubbling along underneath the background harmonies, Harris leaps into falsetto, performs a few of the yodels (*whoa-oh-oh*) that would become Sam Cooke's trademark, and throws in a high who. An even better song from the second Specialty session joyfully reiterates the certainty of salvation: **"I'm Gonna Move in the Room with the Lord"** (1950). Foster establishes the theme, then Harris develops it with every lovely trick in his extensive musical book. What a voice! He especially savors the word *moo-oo-oove*, the dynamic that will bring him to heaven where he'll sing and shout in celebration—as he's doing here. A few months later in 1950, the Five Blind Boys of Mississippi released harder, grittier, equally marvelous recordings of both songs, retitled **"I've Got a Right"** and **"Move in the Room with the Lord."**

Two other releases from the Soul Stirrers' second 1950 session show how effectively Harris could take on the harder sound. James Medlock, whom Foster had replaced as second lead, briefly returned to the Soul Stirrers for that session and sang lead on **"Faith and Grace"** (1950) and his own composition, **"How Long"** (1950). Farley's emphatic bass marks both gospel ballads. Medlock opens "How Long," another Korean War-inspired tune, by wondering how long Jesus suffered, the suffering evident in his vocal. The lead then switches to Harris. Against the background's chanting, his tortured testimony introduces the apocalyptic theme. With the sweetness utterly gone from his voice, Harris asks whether all this wartime destruction and death will result in the end of the world. No resolution or salvation appears, no *by and by* when all will be revealed, no crossing over to that better place.

"Faith and Grace" offers a tentatively positive response. The reassuring lyrics promise that when burdens get hard to bear, you need only call on Jesus. Faith will get you the grace to see you through. But the vocals make clear how hard it may be. Medlock *KNO-O-OWs* Jesus will hear him. But Harris reaches and strains when he switches in. He insists that when he can't see the way, he just needs a little more faith and grace—but his scream between the two lines plus his emphases suggest the difficulty of attaining that *little more*. Medlock ends by insisting that God will give you what you need if you just believe, but the vocal harshness of the line reiterates the arduousness of attaining grace *just* by having faith.

When Harris and Medlock left the Soul Stirrers at the end of 1950 to form the Christland Singers, Crain recruited **Sam Cooke** (1931–64) from the Highway QCs to be the Soul Stirrers' new lead singer. Cooke had emigrated to Chicago from his birthplace in Clarksdale, Mississippi, but he had a radically different sound than Clarksdale's other musical sons who came north. Critics talk about Cooke's "light lyrical tenor voice," his "supple sensuality and flowing melisma," his "wondrous rhythmic and melodic invention," his gracefully soaring phrasing.[51] And everyone mentions his sex appeal. After first trying to emulate Harris, Cooke quickly developed his own unique sound and style. Soon he was also writing and arranging Soul Stirrers' songs. Within a year or two of joining the group, Sam Cooke had become gospel's Golden Boy. He would later be the first gospel-convert-to-pop superstar, start his own record label, write and record the great soul anthem "A Change Is Gonna Come," and die a sordid death in a Los Angeles motel, just 33 years old.

Cooke's lilting, lyrical tenor worked best when set off by a harsher, darker voice, usually Paul Foster's. But listen first to two beautiful celebratory songs, at the beginning and end of his time with the Soul Stirrers, in which Cooke carried the lead alone. He recorded Lucie E. Campbell's **"Jesus Gave Me Water"** (1951) at his first session with the group. From the opening note he establishes his graceful, soaring vocal over the background's chanting and Farley's pumping bass, telling of a woman who experienced Jesus' life-giving presence at a well. "The brisk, almost dancing vocal arrangement gives free rein to the most flexible and *playful* elements of Sam's voice," Guralnick writes, "elongating the pronunciation of the central element of the story until it becomes a kind of patented ululation ('wa-a-a-a-ter')...."[52]

That ululation is even more evident in Cooke's **"Touch the Hem of His Garment"** (1956). Accompanied by a piano, organ, drums, and Bob King's guitar (King joined the group in 1953), this song has a thicker sound. Cooke's voice has a more guttural quality, as if without Foster's hard gospel edge he had to provide it himself. The sick woman who meets Jesus knows that if she just touches the hem of His garment, she'll be made whole. The most prominent element is Cooke's patented yodel, that *whoa-a-oh-a-oh* many of us first heard on his initial pop hit, "You Send Me" (1957). More than an embellishment here, he builds it into the song structure as the cry of the woman in her suffering and, as the divine touch cures her, her ecstasy. The background harmony echoes it. That vocalism became an important element of the Soul Stirrers' musical vocabulary.

Sam Cooke, 1958. Everett Collection Inc./ Alamy Stock Photo.

Though the group's star, Cooke didn't seem to mind sharing the spotlight. On many of his best songs the second lead gets at least equal time with him. Listen to the Soul Stirrers' exquisite arrangement of Dorsey's **"Peace in the Valley"** (1951), recorded *a cappella* at Cooke's first session. With the background joining his lead in harmony, Cooke opens with the chorus, promising his transformation from sorrow and trouble to peace in the valley someday. Foster briefly takes over before Cooke returns for the only verse. If he never sang another line of religious music, these forty seconds would guarantee his gospel immortality. For each enumeration of the animals in this valley paradise, he gives special treatment to one word, elevating his pitch or introducing the melisma for which he became famous: the gentle *bear*, the *tame* wolf, the *li-i-i-ion* that lies down with the lamb. And when the little child leads them out of the wild, he knows he'll be changed "from this creature that *I–I–I–I–I–I–I* am." More Cooke might only spoil the perfection of that verse. So Foster switches in for the final 1:20, shouting and screaming the chorus—a powerfully dramatic conclusion to a knockout song but oddly discordant, given Cooke's gloriously serene tone and the theme of peace about which they both sing.

The mid-tempo **"Just Another Day"** (1952), a lovely Cooke composition, derives some of its power from a steady drumbeat. Here Cooke and Foster get equal time, two verses each with little vocal contrast. Laboring in God's vineyard, Foster pronounces the word *layb'in'*, as if almost too worn out to get his tongue around every consonant and syllable. The more privileged Cooke, literally welcomed by God with open arms, sits beside His throne, absorbing peace and joy. Foster, however, has the last words as God invites him to sit down and rest. Those final words resolve on a sweet harmonic associated more with Cooke's style than Foster's. Behind it all, the background chants the title phrase, suggesting how routine these miracles are in the realm of God's grace.

Cooke put together an almost relentlessly positive gospel repertoire. In **"Come and Go to That Land"** (1953) Foster again tones down the harshness with which he could torque a lyric and simply adds vocal muscle to Cooke's lively message of good news and joy, recorded with Hawaiian steel guitar and drums. The theme: let's all go to that land where God makes everything good. Foster sings verses about burdens lightening and trials ending. Cooke sings the refrain, rallying us to find peace and especially joy, a word he repeats eighteen times in the last 55 seconds, shouting it, not in the hard gospel style but in what Guralnick calls his "new, almost scatting style ... his syllable-lengthening yodel...." One *joy* has nine syllables. This song may be the quintessence of what Robert Palmer calls Cooke's inspirational power: "His music was so spiritually resonant and nurturing, it preached so eloquently and prayed for a better day with such contagious fervor, that it could penetrate the deepest despair, find a glimmer of hope even in the heart of darkness."[53]

Paul Foster took the role of the Soul Stirrers' light-heavyweight, recruited for the hard sound the group needed to compete with quartets like the Blind Boys of Mississippi, the Blind Boys of Alabama, and the Sensational Nightingales—we'll meet them all shortly—with their hard-singing heavyweights: Archie Brownlee, Clarence Fountain, and Julius "June" Cheeks. They were the true shouters and screamers, the earth quakers, the church wreckers. In 1953, Cheeks briefly left the

Nightingales and joined the Soul Stirrers for a single recording session. He epitomized "the hard gospel shouter," according to Heilbut, his "gorgeous baritone splintered into hoarseness." His session with the Stirrers produced one great record, "All Right Now," and changed the way Cooke sang. "Sam used to stand real pretty on stage," Cheeks recalled. "I was the one caused Sam Cooke to sing hard."[54] He showed Cooke how stage movement could fell an audience, and modelled a different kind of vocalism. Cooke adopted some of Cheeks' dynamism and intensity, the guttural edge we hear in "Touch the Hem of His Garment," and the hoarse shouting Cooke added to his vocal mix in the live performances we'll hear next.

Guralnick defines **"All Right Now"** (1954) as "the kind of incantatory extemporization that was commonplace for Cheeks but not for the Stirrers." The mid-tempo number opens in familiar Soul Stirrers fashion. Foster sings the chorus and refrain: he's all right since he fixed things with Jesus. The lead switches to Cooke who tells of being burdened by sin until Jesus saved him. When Cheeks comes roaring in, getting all right with Jesus turns into an entirely different experience. Elevating the intensity in his verse, Cheeks sings about being in trouble—and you believe this man was in *trouble*—until Jesus came to lead him to the promised land. The background chant of the title phrase increases in power. Then Cheeks launches into a drive, which the Soul Stirrers rarely used, riffing on the traditional verse about baptism chilling his body but not his soul, concluding with the chorus. He growls, shouts, or screams every keyword. Guralnick describes "June unleashing his full-throated scream and chuffing like a preacher, his expelled breath rasping both to punctuate the sermon and raise it to higher, more ecstatic ground"—different ecstatic ground than Cooke's beautiful lyricism usually attained.[55]

Early in 1955, the Soul Stirrers recorded two relatively ordinary songs which became transcendent when the group performed them live at the First Annual Mid-Summer Festival of Gospel Music at Los Angeles' Shrine Auditorium in July 1955, showcasing the sounds of contemporary gospel with many of the best voices in the business. The sixteen combined minutes of these two Soul Stirrers masterpieces, "Be with Me Jesus" and "Nearer to Thee," make up the highlights of the album, *The Great 1955 Shrine Concert*.

On Cooke's **"Be with Me Jesus"** (1955), an extended call-and-response, Cooke and Foster trade leads for the first 2:30. Cooke sings the chorus and refrain—asking the Lord to stay with him in his dying hour—and Foster elaborates in a series of short lines. Cooke echoes or responds to each one as the background chants the title phrase and claps hands. For the next 4:45 Foster takes the lead, improvising increasingly desperate requests for God not to leave him when his way gets dark. Foster punctuates his urgent pleas with guttural shouts and Cooke's responses are nearly as hoarse. Guralnick describes the next section:

> Paul embarks upon a fervent recitation of the Twenty-third Psalm, with the calming words delivered in a way that both intensifies and crumbles meaning, as Paul enters into a state where he is practically speaking in tongues. "Oh, oh, oh, oh, surely, surely, surely, oh oh oh oh oh."

As if signifying on Clara Ward and Marion Williams' famous chorus of *Surely*'s, Foster repeats the word a dozen times, the last four screamed, each one echoed by Cooke. In the final seconds Cooke takes back the lead, "resolving the tension," Guralnick claims.[56] But the exhaustion and desperation in Cooke's voice when he begs the Lord to stay with him suggest otherwise. Think of the lines in "A Change Is Gonna Come" about being afraid to die, not knowing what's up there in the sky.

This tremendous, tremendously lacerating song was just the appetizer for **"Nearer to Thee"** (1955), Cooke's eight-and-a-half-minute version of the hymn, "Nearer My God to Thee." Singing along with King's guitar, clapping hands, and an increasingly enthusiastic audience, Cooke has the lead to himself until the final minute. This song tells of the consolations singing "Nearer My God to Thee" brings. But singing isn't enough. The singer wants to *be* near to God, wants desperately to feel those consolations. We require God's presence, the song implies, to make life bearable in this fraught world. Cooke informs his vocal with intensity and urgency—"the phlegmy gargle of the preacher himself," in Guralnick's juicy phrase. He opens with a scream and the tension only builds from there. Usually satin to Foster's sandpaper, Cooke sounds here as if he has taken the sandpaper to his own vocal chords. At the end of the second verse he absolutely growls, his usual yodel sounding more like a roar. No video of this concert exists but you can hear the audience's responses grow each time Cooke elevates and the background completes the refrain: "(I wanna be) nearer my God to thee." At the end of the next verse about trials and trouble, the audience gets louder, encouraging Cooke as he does them. At about 4:00, Foster comes in with some sanctified screaming behind Cooke's *Nea-rer my God*, seconding his emotion, leading to an even gruffer, hoarser *Whoa-a-wo-a-oh-whoa-oh*, and the room explodes. Cooke bears down on the next verse about how song and prayer can console him, then moves in for the wrecking. When he sings that bad company can make a child go wrong but the mother will always say the child is hers, the crowd goes berserk and Foster leaps in with a banshee yell. Cooke calms things down for the final verse about his own mother's songs and prayers when he was a child. He and Foster trade shouts to put an exclamation mark on things before Foster takes the song out. The performance stunned producer Bumps Blackwell, who would soon spirit Cooke off to record his first secular tunes: "It was awesome, phenomenal: [Sam] was like a black Billy Graham."[57] He flatters Graham by the comparison.

The hard gospel sound has irresistible affective power. Among the women who sang gospel, none could channel that power better than **Dorothy Love Coates** (1928–2002) and **The Original Gospel Harmonettes**. A terrific songwriter and brilliant lead, Coates had a voice, writes Heilbut, that was "not great. A shabby contralto, frayed at the edges...." Yet he compares her to Billie Holliday. Another critic calls her "a lead singer with a husky, ragged voice that popped, snapped, and crackled as she relived every song as if it were her personal testimony." She appeared to embody what she sang, and her passion was contagious. "[T]he supreme hard gospel singer, Coates could 'take a house' and have everybody standing up, swaying, shouting, crying or fainting...." The Harmonettes who backed her had their own dynamism. In their call-and-response dialogues with Coates they didn't just chant song titles. Coates's sparkling arrangements gave the background equal ownership of the message on a number of great gospel tunes, creating superb gospel chemistry. Coates and the Harmonettes, Boyer concludes, "brought a new intensity to gospel that could only be matched by the frenzy of a joyful sanctified shout."[58]

The Harmonettes hailed from Birmingham, Alabama. Pianist Evelyn Starks and mezzo-soprano Mildred Miller, who sang lead until Coates joined, brought them together in 1940. Born Dorothy McGriff, Coates married gospel singer Willie Love of the Fairfield Four, and called herself Dorothy Love for much of her time with the Harmonettes. Divorcing him, she married the Sensational Nightingales' Carl Coates and took his name. The group signed with Specialty in 1951 and Dorothy Love Coates stayed with the Harmonettes until they broke up in 1970, having meanwhile become a stalwart of the civil rights movement.

How often have we seen a singer or group hit pay dirt in their first session? The Harmonettes did it with Coates's impassioned lead on "**I'm Sealed**" (1951). "From the first note," says Boyer, "it was apparent that this soloist was extraordinary: a singer with a sanctified timbre and a preacher's delivery."[59] Coates shouts the slow, stately song with remarkable fervor. In contrast to most of the gospel we've heard so far, the Harmonettes sang with a piano, organ, guitar, and drums, with the background harmonies prominent in the mix. Coates's deep, powerful contralto perfectly fits the dark world of sin of which she sings, being bound and alone on life's stormy seas. But then she soars, testifying that she's saved—*sealed*—for redemption, certain that Jesus will take her to live in glory. She swoops and shouts with excitement (*Aaaaahhh, O-o-o-o-o-ohh, Ye-e-e-s!!!*) and with the ecstatic thrill of *knowing* Jesus will come for her. When she thanks God that she has been sealed, no one could doubt her conviction. The Harmonettes don't lay back either, meeting her call with their assertive response: they are surely sealed.

Dorothy Love Coates and the Original Gospel Harmonettes, about 1952. Dorothy is at the top. Pictorial Press Ltd./Alamy Stock Photo.

They all stretch out on Dorsey's "**Every Day Will Be Sunday**" (1952) with a strong bass line and drums driving almost a dance beat. Whereas "I'm Sealed" suggests the difficult costs of the miraculous transformation from this life's imprisoning darkness to the bright light of glory, "Every Day Will Be Sunday" celebrates the miracle with only dips into the fallen state. Accentuating the positive, the Harmonettes drop Dorsey's line about pain and sickness. By and by, every day will be Sunday in that land beyond the sky. Like Tindley's "By & By," this song assumes the inevitability of paradise. But instead of Tindley's understanding, Dorsey's singers find an eternal weekend. The organ's jaunty opening notes create a mood of pure delight. Coates sings with a smile in her voice, and the Harmonettes echo her lines with joyous enthusiasm. In the verse Coates imagines arriving at that fair city, meeting her friends, and changing into her party dress—actually a white robe, but the occasion feels like a party. In the bridge the Harmonettes mark the days and Coates sings of what she will do daily. On Saturday they will sing together, turning Dorsey's obscure line about biblical figures into jazzy, syncopated fun.

Coates's arrangement of **"Where Shall I Be?"** (1953) applies a similar treatment to the resurrection, rocking Charles Price Jones's 1899 hymn. Where will I be when the first trumpet blows to wake the dead? It seems like a rhetorical question. Coates sounds completely confident that she will be in the right place, in the right frame of spirit, and the Harmonettes in the background shout the question in triumph. When Coates sings a traditional verse about God, Noah, and the rainbow sign, she growls the line about what comes next, as if to say, "I *know* what's going on." She howls the chorus and refrain, almost as if mimicking the trumpet "that's gonna *SOU-OUND* so loud" on *that GREAT, whoo, morning* of the resurrection, when she'll gladly say farewell.

Dorothy and the Harmonettes generally sang about death and its aftermath as if they were the best things ever, with romping music and positive vocals. Not so their version of the traditional **"No Hiding Place"** (1954), a scare-fest describing the fate of the damned, those who fear death and the end of days. The slightly slower tempo here still feels relatively jaunty. A piano and organ accompany the vocals. Coates shifts the point of view back and forth from first-person to third. In the verses, as the background sings "Save my soul!" she references the sinners, the gamblers, the liars who will be running when the world catches fire: *They'll* be trying to find a hiding place. In the chorus and refrain she puts herself in the sinners' shoes, singing how *she* goes to the rock to hide *her* face. But no one can hide down there. Coates uses her hoarsest, most guttural voice to underline the agonizing hopelessness of trying to avoid judgment: even the rock will cry out *NO NO NO*. Another powerful moment comes at the end of the line about the time to *DIE*. The Harmonettes' great soprano, Vera Colb, turns the last word into an extended high C, a cry of fearsome despair.

None of their upbeat embraces of the sweet hereafter has more up-tempo energy and drive than Coates's sensational growling, whooping version of the traditional **"I Wouldn't Mind Dying"** (1956). Still, the lyrics and performance suggest that something has shaken her confidence: maybe imagining herself in the sinner's situation in "No Hiding Place." The refrain—"I wouldn't mind dying if dying was all"—puts a condition on her embrace of death. Dying *is not* all; she would have to face judgment and whatever comes after that, and she seems unsure of the outcome. She stresses and growls most the word *mi-i-ind*. Hamlet-like, perhaps she thinks too much about death. Amid grim imagery of the grave and her decaying body, she knows she must go and knows she'll be all right, *if*. God sees all, and His judgment, though just, is harsh. Tears won't get you in or excuses. Near the conclusion she stutters, *I-I-I-I got to go by myself*, then repeats it, stutter included, and adds that there's no one to defend her. As she reprises the title phrase at the end, Colb accompanies her with a series of howling, agonized-sounding high who's. One of the finest performances of this formidable group.

I think of the final Harmonettes songs on our playlist as Coates's responses to the cracks in her spiritual armor that the previous two songs reveal. Shortly after the release of "No Hiding Place" came **"You Must Be Born Again"** (1954), perhaps Coates's finest composition, suggests Boyer, and certainly one of the group's most powerful performances. She sings the first verse alone against a background of *ooh*s, explaining how she had heard about Jesus' love but never felt it. So she asked her mother how she might know it. Mother told her, "You must be born again." The next verse becomes a sanctified march. Coates and the background, together and apart, sing what her mother presumably explained to her: you must have the fire of the Holy Ghost inside you, the kind of religion that makes you move and shout. As Coates improvises in the solo, the group attacks the lines in short staccato bursts, driving her into a vocal frenzy of growls, shrieks, and grunts.[60] Nothing else in the Harmonettes' canon matches the intensity of feeling in these sections. Coates and the group are laying down the law, preaching a gospel of absolute, radical faith. You *must* be born again. Both preacher and congregant, Coates aims the message outward and back at herself.

Shortly after recording "I Wouldn't Mind Dying," the Harmonettes released **"Ninety-Nine and a Half Won't Do"** (1956). Remember Sister Rosetta Tharpe's version back in 1949? Why did Coates only now record one of her own best compositions? Maybe after singing about the anxiety of attaining salvation in "I Wouldn't Mind Dying," she felt the need to re-commit to born-again absolutism. Like "You Must Be Born Again," the tempo slows here as she lays out her methodical argument. It begins with her running uphill. The journey to get to a hundred—to be sealed, certain of salvation—is hard but necessary. *Almost* will not be good enough: 99½ won't do it. To show us what a hundred looks like she sings a verse about how John the Baptist maintained his faith and looked death in the eye even with his head on a platter. The rest of the song simply reiterates the need to get to a hundred. Anything less WON'T do; it won't DO (a high who); NINETY-NINE AND A HALF won't do. Against the background's doo-wop-like chant, *doo-doo* (or *do-do!*), Coates counts down: Seventy and eighty, no good. Ninety, close. Ninety-nine, almost. It's a hundred or nothing for the Gospel Harmonettes. And no group in gospel comes as close to perfection.

Like the Harmonettes, **The Blind Boys of Alabama** hailed from the Birmingham area. In 1938, a group of nine-to-twelve-year-olds at Alabama's Talladega

Institute for the Negro Deaf and Blind formed The Happy Land Jubilee Singers. They left the school in 1944 and began touring professionally. When a New Jersey promoter billed a concert featuring the Happy Lands and a blind quartet from Mississippi called the Jackson Harmoneers as a battle of the Blind Boys of Alabama vs. the Blind Boys of Mississippi, both groups changed their names accordingly. After the Alabamans signed with Specialty in 1952, their record labels read, "The Happyland Singers also known as Original Five Blind Boys of Alabama."

The Blind Boys of Alabama have remained among the most popular quartets in gospel and continue to tour and record today. For over seventy years "the savagely commanding voice" of lead baritone **Clarence Fountain** (1929–2018), "a screamer of epic proportions," provided the group's signature sound. An obituary describes how, with his "inimitable and bloodcurdling shout, ... Fountain sang with all the fire and fury of a Pentecostal preacher, crouching low into a rasping growl before leaping into a shrieking falsetto."[61] Check out one of the best of all gospel videos, a 1958 performance of Fountain and the Blind Boys singing Alex Bradford's "Too Close to Heaven" (https://www.youtube.com/watch?v=Ms4LbE18P3U).

Unfortunately, iTunes and YouTube make the Alabama Blind Boys' initial release for Coleman Records, **"I Can See Everybody's Mother but Mine"** (1948), accessible only as their heavily instrumented 1963 re-recording for Vee-Jay. Though a wonderful record with a bravura lead from Fountain, it doesn't fall within our time frame. Let's begin instead with a great song from their first Specialty session with the same slow, steady pace and highly dramatic tone, **"Without the Help of Jesus"** (1952), with George Scott's guitar accompaniment. The sighted the Rev. Samuel K. Lewis, a sanctified screamer in his own right, and Fountain take the primary leads. A couple of other voices briefly sing solo at the beginning. I'm guessing Scott and the Rev. Paul Exkano. The group's CD *The Sermon* lists Lewis, Scott, and Exkano as "tenor and second lead."[62]

The chorus, sung twice, the second time by Lewis, makes the song's straightforward theme clear: *Without the help of Jesus we are lost.* Fountain switches in for the final minute with a verse about walking down a road, hearing a heavenly voice offering to lift his heavy load, filling his heart with love. Both Lewis and Fountain scream and shout, Lewis in his hoarse, agonized squall even more than Fountain. Fountain's verse affirms the heavenly intercession that Lewis' chorus desperately desires. Yet the song's dominant voice may be the background's chant, *We are lost*, repeated about fifty times. The song ends on its final two repetitions. Being lost seems like the default. The cry for Jesus' help comes from a deep, dark place along the hard, heavy road to salvation.

The Alabama Blind Boys' **"This May Be the Last Time"** (1953) concerns the *musical* road towards death, one not so hard nor heavy. It exists in at least two takes, both impassioned and dynamic, neither released until much later. The group's 1993 Specialty collection, *The Sermon*, lists the song as "Take 1—alternate." The other version appeared on the Blind Boys' 1970 Specialty album, *Oh Lord–Stand by Me*, then later as a single. Both high-tempo arrangements of this traditional song use the same melody, Scott's guitar accompaniment, and the same basic lyrics: *This may be the last time we sing/play/moan/shout together.* Fountain sings lead throughout *The Sermon's* alternate take. For the drive he improvises the Lord's Prayer over the intensifying background chant of the title. The other version elevates more dramatically, beginning with Lewis and another lead before Fountain switches in for the drive, singing about the crucifixion. The livelier but harsher, hoarser three-lead version includes Fountain's scream as he riffs on *last time*. Both versions urge that we be spiritually prepared for death and the final judgment, which may come at any time. But their most compelling message: If this performance does turn out to be our final time together, let's make it as exciting a tribute to our musical chemistry as possible. And they do.

They recorded an especially exciting example of their chemistry, **"Sit Down Servant"** (1953), at the same session. Fountain and Exkano don't just switch leads, they share them and provide background exclamations, celebratory hoots and shrieks, while the rest of the group interjects with more vocal variety than on any of their other songs. Ironically, the song proposes that when you pass over, Jesus will ask you to sit down and take a little rest. No one rests at all on this lively tune.

There was no one way to go church-wrecking. Or to sing about dying. Fountain and the Blind Boys could raise the roof with their up-tempo shouting or bring down the house grinding out a ballad like **"You Got to Move"** (1953). The Rolling Stones made this traditional spiritual widely popular, basing their 1971 version on Mississippi Fred McDowell's great 1965 slide guitar performance. The Blind Boys of Alabama did two powerful hard gospel blues takes with George Scott's guitar prominent. Again, both went unreleased in the 1950s but can be found on the albums *The Sermon* and *Oh Lord—Stand by Me*. Ignore the 3:35 YouTube recording that sounds like a country hoedown. *The Sermon*'s version, "Take 3—alternate," features Fountain's solo lead and limited lyrics. You may be high, low, rich, or poor, but when the Lord gets ready, you got to move. The phrase *when the Lord gets ready* elicits three mighty screams. Death is fearsome and the Lord awesome. The more dramatic swing-lead take on *Oh Lord—Stand by Me* features three voices and more elaborate lyrics. Each lead gets a verse. The liar and gambler need to know you got to move. Mother told me this journey would be hard to run, but you got to move. Both first two leads, Lewis and probably Scott, interpolate freely and work the elevation. Fountain switches in last with his high, low, rich, poor verse and the most piercing scream we've heard from him. The knowledge that death entails God's intervention moves them all profoundly.

Found everywhere in gospel, dead mother songs put an emotional premium on mother's absence and the singer's anticipated reunion with her in the afterlife, especially when sung by men. Fountain leans into his own composition, **"Alone and Motherless"** (1954), with extra feeling. A slow 12-bar blues in three verses, the song features a strong second voice in Scott's guitar. But Fountain has the lyrics to himself. No swing leads, and only wordless background harmonies. He sings about being alone and motherless since childhood. While mother lived, he could take things easily. But with her resting in glory, he feels he has to please the world. His poignant final verse wonders if he treated his mother right, recalling how she prayed for him morning and night. Fountain's signature screams feel rich in emotional nuance: pain, as he recalls her goodness and remembers her absence; gratitude, that she rests in glory; guilt, that maybe he didn't treat her right; relief, that all will be over for himself soon enough.

References to the Blind Boys can be confusing. The two groups had similar origins, a somewhat similar sound, and a variety of similar-sounding names. **The Five Blind Boys of Mississippi** formed during the Depression as the Cotton Blossom Singers in the Piney Woods School for the Blind near Jackson. In 1937, Alan Lomax recorded them for the Library of Congress. Turning professional, they changed their name to the Jackson Harmoneers, then renamed themselves the Five Blind Boys of Mississippi and first recorded in 1947. They moved to Houston in 1950 and became Peacock Records' first gospel signing. Their Peacock labels never mention Mississippi, billing them as the Five Blind Boys or Original Five Blind Boys, with "Jackson Harmoneers" in smaller print along with the names of the leads.

One of those leads, a founding member of the group, was always **Archie Brownlee** (1925–60), another tragically short-lived musical genius, generally considered "the trendsetter when it came to soul gospel shouting" and "the hardest quartet singer of all time." With his high tenor, Brownlee developed a shouting, screaming style shaped by R.H. Harris, and he in turn influenced Clarence Fountain. Fountain frequently went up against Brownlee in quartet battles between the two groups of Blind Boys and gave his fellow screamer the ultimate compliment: "Archie, he could sing you to death." Heilbut describes him "demolish[ing] huge auditoriums ... interrupt[ing] his songs with an unresolved falsetto shriek that conjured up images of witchcraft or bedlam."[63] Under Brownlee's influence the Blind Boys of Mississippi tapped into the *deep gospel* equivalent of Mississippi deep blues and established themselves as the hardest of all gospel quartets.

The Original Five Blind Boys of Mississippi, onstage, c. 1955. From left: Lloyd Woodard, Archie Brownlee, Rev. Percell Perkins (top), Lawrence Abrams, J.T. Clinkscales. Hooks Bros photographers, Memphis. Pictorial Press Ltd./Alamy Stock Photo.

An early example of Brownlee's powerfully affecting vocal quality and the excitement these Blind Boys could generate can be heard on Thomas Dorsey's **"Never Turn Back"** (1948), recorded *a cappella* for Coleman, a song in the same vein as "Too Close to Heaven" and "99½ Won't Do." Although he uses his piercing scream only twice, Brownlee shouts almost the whole song, often hoarsely at the top of his range, singing about how he started for heaven some time ago but the world of temptation held him back. Now he has hit the road again, intending to reach that other shore, and he'll never turn back. The background echoes Brownlee's lyrics and harmonizes with him. Joseph Ford's spare bass provides effective punctuation. A great record despite terrible sound quality.

One of the early Peacock sessions produced the Mississippi Blind Boys' best-seller. Their version of the Lord's Prayer, **"Our Father"** (1950), spent two weeks on *Billboard*'s R&B charts. For Zolten, it established their signature sound: "heavy drum back beat, group in harmony, Brownlee pleading over top, his sweepingly emotive voice leaping into sudden shrieks and moans." Sung at a very slow pace, the song owes its effectiveness almost entirely to Brownlee's dramatic, emotional presentation, although Peacock's Don Robey took credit for putting "the beat [in this case the drum] into religious records."[64] Brownlee holds back until his startling first scream at 1:30. The second follows his line, "When my voice cannot be heard." No way we're not hearing that voice. The third scream accompanies the final line: "Thine is the kingdom (*AAAAHHH*), power and the glory...." Prayer has rarely sounded so compelling.

When the second lead, baritone the Rev. Percell Perkins, temporarily left for the Swan Silvertones in 1950, tenor Vance Powell took his place. Powell and Brownlee share leads on the traditional **"He's My Rock"** (1950), sung at a funereal pace with a heavy drumbeat. The background provides a percussive *ba-oom-wop* sound. Nations writes, "Both Powell and Brownlee possessed spirit-killing voices that when added to tough-minded personalities created friction...."[65] Powell wouldn't last long with the group, but his competition with Brownlee made for a terrific record. Powell opens with a sensational rendition of the lines that begin every version of this old-time hymn: "*OHHHH HEEEE*'s my rock, sword and *shie-e-e-ld*." He ends his half of the song down on his knees, waiting for Jesus, with another well-worn line that he might have directed at Brownlee: "Makes no difference what you say." Brownlee restrains himself, declining to blow Powell away with his mighty shrieks and howls. He throws in one falsetto note as a reminder that he could, but lets the lyrics and his extraordinary phrasing elevate his half of the song and one-up Powell's second lead. In the *ea-ea-ea-rly* morning or *la-a-a-ate* night he'll reach that city where the saints gather to crown the Lord. Waiting for Jesus, *he* won't have to kneel like Powell: Sit down and rest, he'll be told. He's a royal child.

Nothing feels weary about the magnificent up-tempo performance of **"Jesus Is a Rock in a Weary Land"** (1953), Brownlee's adaptation of a nineteenth-century praise song with traditional lyrics. Accompanied by a guitar and drums, it sounds more modern than the group's earlier records, though the sentiment is similar to "He's My Rock." Perkins, back with the group, trades leads with Brownlee for the first minute. His voice has a beautiful tone and he can growl in Archie's league, but Brownlee takes over for the final 1:45, driving the song to the end with J.T. Clinkscales' bass underneath. This is the first drive we've heard on a Mississippi Blind Boys record, another effective weapon in Brownlee's substantial armory.

The group uses similar elements in **"All Aboard"** (1954), a terrific variation of the train-carrying-me-to-glory song, composed by Perkins. It starts achingly slowly, then accelerates after the first verse. Drums and piano give it a full sound, the leads switch, the bass bubbles, and it ends with a drive. Brownlee puts on a gospel clinic. Over ominous background *boom boom boom*s, he's getting dressed, putting on his traveling shoes, starting from home to face God. The train in the yard just waits for the conductor to cry, "All aboard!" Brownlee fills his rich vocal with anticipation and anxiety, punctuating it with a falsetto *Ooooh*, a screaming *Aaaahhh*, and a couple of shouts. Like a train gaining speed, the pace picks up when Perkins swings in, singing how the train carries all the righteous. In the minute-long drive Perkins references the end of the war in Korea and his relationship with the savior. In his dying hour he's going home. Nothing fancy, just powerful gospel testimony.

Despite its title, **"In the Wilderness"** (1954) turns out to be the most upbeat, quickest paced, sweetest of Brownlee and company's hard gospel nuggets, and my personal favorite. This Brownlee composition expresses, musically and vocally, the ecstatic joy of feeling God on your side in the wilderness of this world. The lead switches back and forth, Perkins enumerating all the things he'll be and do in the wilderness with the Lord. Brownlee swings in each time with a scream, coming in over the word *Lord* with an *AAAAHHHH!!!* On his second entrance, he sings self-referentially in triumph that he'll *shout* in the wilderness till he dies. The song ends with his beautiful seven-second-long falsetto *Oooh-oo-oo-oooh-ooooh*. Gospel genius personified.

Just as Archie Brownlee and the Five Blind Boys of Mississippi epitomized the hard gospel sound of male quartets, **The Famous Davis Sisters** topped the female side. Lead **Ruth "Baby Sis" Davis** (1928–70) wore the moniker, "the hardest female belter in gospel." Raised in the Mount Zion Fire Baptized Holiness Church and performing in choir robes, the four sisters from Philadelphia infused their music with their intense Pentecostal faith. Baby Sis, ironically the oldest of the four, "thundered forth with consummate ease, her lustrous contralto as hard as nails."[66] Thelma and Audrey sang soprano and Alfreda second contralto. The group formed in 1945. Joined by male cousin Curtis Dublin on piano and occasional vocals, and alto Imogene Greene as second lead, they began recording for Gotham Records alongside Clara Ward, the Angelics, and the Harmonizing Four.

"When He Spoke" (1951) exemplifies Ruth's power and the Davis Sisters' fervor. The very slow tempo allows Ruth to work every line. The background loudly echoes the title phrase with the sopranos at the top of their range, forcing Ruth to meet their volume with an extended shout at the start of each verse. Dublin's piano and an organ play quietly underneath. The lyrics simply enumerate a succession of things that occurred when the man from Galilee spoke: my heart rejoiced, everything obeyed His will, Lazarus rose from the dead. Listen to the passion in Ruth's vocal and you'll understand why R.H. Harris called her "the most spiritual singer I have ever heard."[67]

The phrase "by and by" appears in countless gospel songs, signifying the radical optimism of African American faith, the inevitability of a future so much better than the present. YouTube features a rockin' black-and-white video of the Davis Sisters performing Tindley's "By and By" sometime post–1955, with Jackie Verdell, who replaced Imogene Greene, and Ruth Davis switching leads (https://www.youtube.com/watch?v=PI1wVzJ6CZk). This is the same song the Soul Stirrers did so brilliantly. Earlier, though, the Davis Sisters made their mark with a different song that, confusedly, shares Tindley's and the Soul Stirrers' title. Gotham even released it as a two-sided single: **"By and By, Pt 1 & Pt. 2"** (1952) by the Davis Sisters and Curtis Dublin. This version promises not a future understanding of God's mysterious ways but simply the glory, grace, and reward of heaven. The Davis Sisters later re-did it as "Bye and Bye" for Savoy with Verdell and Ruth again sharing leads.

Accompanied by piano, organ, bass, and drums, Imogene Greene takes the lead on the very slow first part, singing two beautifully restrained verses about her old soul preparing to live with God. She sings quietly, almost carefully, as if trying to avoid any hubris that might jinx her journey home. She looks forward to her troubles being over, her battles being won. What a day that will be, by and by! The background is virtually inaudible except for a gentle *oo-oo-ooh* between verses, until near the end of her section Greene begins to crescendo and the background interjects affirmations. At the 2:30 mark, Ruth switches in for the "up-tempo, scream and shout, pew-jumping" Part 2.[68] The tempo gets very quick, clapping starts, and the background jumps in, echoing Ruth's shouting. In these final two minutes, among the most joyous in gospel, Ruth confirms that the day will surely come, she'll meet her savior, and sing a new song early in that morning of peace and happiness, good times, and *JO-OYYY* by and by.

The Davis Sisters' **"Too Close to Heaven"** (1953) provides further evidence that Ruth Davis had gospel's hardest belting female voice. The controlled anxiety we hear in Alex Bradford's voice, as he contemplates attaining heaven and fears losing it, Ruth translates into excruciating urgency. She sounds literally tormented. Dublin's prominent piano along with a quieter organ and doo wop style background provide dramatic accompaniment as Ruth sees the finish line in the near distance and pushes herself harder to make it. She wastes no time establishing the dilemma. In her first line she sings of being too close to heaven, *to-oo* her journey's end, agonizing over the preposition that both connects her to and separates her from her goal. She can't imagine turning around but can't help imagining it. Just after she tells the Lord she wants *e-eternal* life, the background comes in with the prompt, *too-oo-oo-oo close,* and Ruth lets out a scream, a kind of pleading: don't let me lose this, Lord. This wonderful recording embodies for me the quintessence of great gospel, the certainty and doubt, agony and ecstasy, glory and terror.

The quartet sound is an ensemble sound, but every gospel quartet featured an extraordinary lead singer or two. Always included in discussions of the greatest quartets, the **Swan Silvertones** showcased the beautiful tenor and masterful falsetto of **Claude Jeter** (1914–2009) in combination with a succession of heavy-duty screamers—particularly the Rev. **Robert Crenshaw** (1923–2018). Born in Alabama, Jeter worked as a coal miner in West Virginia where he formed the Four Harmony Kings. They changed their name to the Silvertone Singers, and when the Swan Bakery began sponsoring their Knoxville, Tennessee, radio show, to the Swan Silvertones. The group had three productive recording periods: with King, 1946–51; Specialty, where they developed a harder sound, 1951–55; and Vee-Jay, 1955–64. Jeter became an ordained Holiness minister in the 1960s and quit the group. We'll focus on several hard *a cappella* masterpieces from the Swans' Specialty period, but their Vee-Jay recording of "Oh Mary Don't You Weep" (1959) might be the best sweet gospel song of all.[69]

A Swan Silvertones double album re-release, *Love Lifted Me/My Rock* (1991), collects the Specialty recordings. Reviewing it, Robert Christgau writes, "The center is always Claude Jeter, direct forebear of Al Green and a more crucial gospel falsetto than Rebert Harris himself. But at Specialty Jeter is in a sense the straight man ... the star holding steady as hard-shouting Solomon Womack and Robert Crenshaw wild out." Tenors Womack and Crenshaw, and Paul Owens, who came over from the Dixie Hummingbirds in 1952, shared the leads with Jeter and did the wilding. Broughton refers to "the amazing Robert Crenshaw who screamed ecstatically all over their early Specialty recordings."[70] Listen to **"Love Lifted Me"** (1952), written by the group's baritone, John Myles, the title and chorus taken from James Rowe's turn-of-the-century hymn. A vehicle for Jeter's gorgeous falsetto, which he uses sparely and judiciously here, the mid-tempo song with its rich harmonic background shocks with Crenshaw's power and intensity when he takes the lead halfway through. The sentiment: when nothing else could help, God's love lifted me. Jeter seems buoyed by it, Crenshaw shattered. God speaks to Crenshaw, offers him healing and salvation, so that must be ecstasy ripping away at his throat as he croaks the lyrics with Jeter's falsetto in counterpoint. What a record!

Many of the Swans' best recordings of this era operate similarly. One of their most exciting, **"My Rock"** (1952), is a different song than the Mississippi Blind Boys' "He's My Rock." A driving, up-tempo number arranged by Paul Owens around traditional Christian metaphors, it opens with Jeter singing, moaning, humming, shouting how Jesus is his rock, always beside him, always satisfying. A heavy drumbeat, strong background vocal support, and Henry Bossard's prominent pumping bass create a full sound and propulsive momentum leading to Crenshaw switching in for a ninety-second-long screaming, howling drive, growling how he'll sing and shout when he gets to heaven. Along with a string of *Lord Lord Lord*s, Crenshaw runs together no fewer than twelve *I*'s, a vocal expression of personal salvation and subjectivity that will find its apotheosis in James Brown. **"He Won't Deny Me"** (1953) and **"Trouble in My Way"** (1953) are other superb Jeter-Crenshaw combinations in this same vein. Listen to the latter alongside the Dixie Hummingbirds' **"Trouble in My Way"** (1952) for a double trouble treat.

We've already met the great screamer **Julius "June" Cheeks** (1929–81) singing with Sam Cooke and the Soul Stirrers on "All Right Now" in 1954. At the heart of his career Cheeks, "the rawest of gospel's baritones," the only man Archie Brownlee refused to follow on live programs, sang lead for the **Sensational Nightingales**, one of the hardest *and* most lyrical quartets. After the war Cheeks, from Spartanburg, South Carolina (also the birthplace of Ira Tucker), joined Philadelphia's Nightingales, formed by Paul Owens. By 1952, the Nightingales had become the Sensational Nightingales and signed with Peacock Records. Owens moved over to the Dixie Hummingbirds in exchange for the Hummingbirds' second lead tenor, Ernest James. "Cheeks' anguished squalling pitted against James' high tenor screams turned the Sensational Nightingales into a force to be reckoned with," Nations writes.[71] Cheeks became a COGIC reverend in 1954, his sanctified shouting, howling, and growling turned to preaching.

An excellent rocker with shared leads James and Cheeks showing restraint in the scream department, **"Will He Welcome Me There"** (1952) kicked off the Nightingales' tenure with Peacock. "Cheeks jousts with James," Nations observes, "but keeps reasonably fixed at the boundaries of being in control."[72] Tenor Jo Jo Wallace leads the way on guitar, and bass John Jefferson pumps hard to keep up. The lyrics emphasize the singer's need to know if God will welcome him to that city bright and fair. Both music and vocals suggest that the motivating force is curiosity rather than desperation. Cheeks lets out just one shrieking *YEAH*, doubting not what amazing grace will deliver.

In the 1960s, I heard Leon Bibb sing "Sinner Man" in a Washington, D.C., club. When I moved to Vancouver, Canada, I was thrilled to learn that Bibb had moved here, too, and was performing with a local theater company. "Sinner Man" has always held a special place in my musical pantheon. Like the Gospel Harmonettes' "No Hiding Place," the Sensational Nightingales' **"On the Judgement Day"** (1955) is a spectacular version of the song. "Cheeks and James tried to out-sing each other on this mid-tempo burner that finds Cheeks at the peak of his saved and sanctified powers," Nations writes. Heilbut adds, "When James leads 'Sinner Man,' it recalls the folkloric efforts of 1930s South Carolina quartets. But when Cheeks bursts in, so impassioned that he can barely contain himself, we've abandoned jubilee for rock-and-roll; Wilson Pickett was never so delirious."[73] The song asks the sinner man where he'll run on judgment day. James's lyrical first-half lead predicts that the sinner will try to hide behind a rock or under the sea, but nature will reject him. In response to James's high tenor the background's chant, *Where you gonna run to*, shifts into falsetto, contrasting dramatically with Cheeks' baritone growl on his entrance. He repeats the verse in which the sinner runs to rock and sea to hide, but transforms James's lyricism into ominous Old Testament prophesy. Driving to the finish of this harshly beautiful performance, Cheeks envisions an apocalyptic world on fire, where this *sinner man, lying man, dying man* will have nowhere to hide and no escape from judgment.

Cheeks' profoundly dark vision of sin and its consequences underlies his approach to **"Somewhere to Lay My Head"** (1955) in contrast to Johnnie Taylor and the Highway QCs' treatment. While Taylor's ethereal vocal expresses his weariness with life and longing for a place where he can get a good rest, Cheeks uses his ravaged voice—with James gone from the Nightingales by this time, Cheeks has the lead to himself—to sketch a vivid world of suffering and evil, where flesh falls from bones and the devil is afoot. The song's tempo, much quicker than the QCs' version, as if he can't get to that somewhere fast enough, reflects his quest for sanctuary, less desperate than the sinner man's but nearly as urgent; so too his repeated appeal, *Lord Lord Lord oh Lord*, as the background sings *Hallelujah*. A wonderful live performance of the song by the Sensational Nightingales from the late 1950s or early '60s features Carl Coates, Dorothy Love Coates's husband, singing bass: https://www.youtube.com/watch?v=L77wwwxvuKQ. Before a live audience and camera, Cheeks' showmanship tones down the anxieties that the record foregrounds.

Let's bid adieu to the Nightingales with the gorgeous **"Burying Ground"** (1956). Nations calls it "one of the finest moments in recorded quartet history...." Heilbut describes Cheeks' baritone as "resonant and exceptionally beautiful." One of those rare gospel songs that barely mentions divinity, except for a parenthetical "Lord help me now," this is a secular meditation on mortality. Like a *memento mori* skull in a Renaissance painting, it operates by implication: "I wonder," he sings, if you can hear the church bells tolling and see the hearse rolling. *Way over yonder* it may be, but that *new* burying ground is awaiting those of us listening. Heilbut gets the song right: "It's chilling and satisfying and almost consoling."[74]

Some of the best pop and soul singers of the 1960s and '70s emerged from among the Golden Age of Gospel's many extraordinary voices. One of the founding members of Detroit's **Meditation Singers**, formed in 1947, Delloreese Early left the group in 1954 for fame as Della Reese. Replacing her, teenage Laura Lee Rundless later had a solid career as soul diva Laura Lee. But the heart of the group, one of the great female voices in gospel, never went secular. Laura Lee's mother, **Earnestine Rundless** (1914–2007), sounding a lot like Dorothy Love Coates, growled and roared while the background generated some of the most exciting sounds the Motor City produced before the Motown era. Check out any of the Meditations' performances on YouTube. Their best work, in the early-mid–1950s on Specialty, included **"I'm Determined to Run This Race"** (1954). Rundless sings with fierce determination while the background encourages her with doo wop-ish *too-OOHs*. Composer James Cleveland accompanies on piano along with a bass drum. She's *determined* to run her race and make it in. She won't be turned around, oh no.

One of the biggest post-gospel success stories, Chicago's **Lou Rawls** (1933–2006) sold forty million records as a star of R&B and soul. Rawls replaced Sam Cooke in the Highway QCs and ended his gospel career with the Pilgrim Travelers. In between, he sang lead for a couple of years for the **Chosen Gospel Singers**, formed in Houston in 1950. Listen to the stirring **"I'm Going Back with Him"** (1954) with its poly-rhythmic bass drum, tambourine, and hand-clapping accompaniment. Consisting of little more than the line, "I'm going back with Him when He comes," the song features hard leads from Rawls with his "velvet baritone," and tenor J.T. Ratley, "who possessed an unusual, rapidly fluttering vibrato."⁷⁵ Their call-and-response in the drive conjures echoes of Cooke and Paul Foster on "Be with Me Jesus."

Their one-two punch on **"Watch Ye Therefore"** (1954) was even better. This dynamite record, unissued at the time, appeared on the Chosen Gospel Singers' 1992 Specialty CD, *The Lifeboat*. Based on Mark 13:35 and credited to the group's bassman, J.B. Randall, it opens with Rawls singing a warning: Watch out, because you know not the day when the Lord will come for you. Strive for the right if you want to reach that city in glory and live in the heavenly light. Ratley switches in for the final 1:40, seemingly confirming the good news: If you strive for righteousness, you'll get to wear a starry crown. The background echoes him, while a deeper voice—Randall or baritone Sam Thomas—provides counterpoint *He-e-y*s and *Whoa-oa*s. A funereal bass drumbeat accompanies it all. But making the song unique, love it or hate it, Ratley virtually screams his way through the entire second half. If you're a fan of hard gospel screaming, as I am, you'll love it. But what does the performance say? You can attain glory if you're ready and willing to work for it. But it isn't inevitable and doesn't come easily. *Striving for the right* also has clear civil rights implications in 1954. Watch ye, because God doesn't knock before he arrives. Neither does the sheriff or the mob. And if you're not ready, sinner man, you may be screaming, too. Gospel doesn't get more intense than this.

So much great gospel remains in the shadows of that long-ago decade. Let's end with two obscure quartets that connect back to blues and ahead to doo wop. **The Jackson Gospel Singers** (aka The Jackson Singers) took their name not from Mississippi's capital but from the Jackson family members who came together in 1936 and still comprised much of the all-female group when they recorded in the early 1950s for Atlantic's Gospel Series.⁷⁶ They hailed from New Orleans but appear to have been unrelated to the Crescent City's most famous gospel Jackson, Mahalia. Rocking along to a honkytonk piano, **"I Can't Walk This Highway"** (1954) uses the same trope as the Big Road/Dark Road blues songs to praise the virtues of Jesus as a traveling companion. The Jacksons' dynamic gospel sound includes a couple of lead switches, a drive, witty lyrics, and Jesus himself providing comfort and advice. The song opens with the first lead confessing that she can't walk life's highway by herself and wants Jesus to walk with her. After the second lead switch, during the drive, the power of God gets inside her head. Jesus speaks to her directly, promising that if she follows Him, she will surely arrive on high. The singer then confidently asserts that she'll look up David, God, and the Son when she gets to heaven, telling them about the world she just came from. I hope she and her sisters got rewarded for their chutzpah and high-powered infectious vocals.

Our final gospel entry takes us to another crucible of African American music, Kansas City. Listening to the **Kansas City Soul Revivers**, you have to wonder why, as Nations does, "they lacked what it took to put their music over commercially on a nationwide basis." Starting out in the 1920s as the Gaston Brothers, they changed their name to the Kansas City Gospel Singers, and in 1964 to the Los Angeles Soul

Revivers. As the Kansas City Soul Revivers, they cut a series of singles for L.A.'s Dootone Records, including **"I Don't Need No One Else"** (1956). *Billboard* said of it, "The lead singer is terrific with his emotional chanting. A thoroly (sic) satisfying side, with the group displaying fervor and technical excellence." Nations describes "a beautiful wailing song with sweeping Sensational Nightingale–like refrains and tough-sounding lead vocals."[77] Lead tenor Willie Gilmore sings with high emotion about how he can make it just by holding Jesus' hand. He doesn't need money or anyone else. Accompanied by guitar, drum, and Stacy Gaston's pumping bass, the background chants and Gilmore elevates towards the end, adding screams to his affirmations of love. Subtract the screams, change *Jesus* to *Venus* or *Denise,* and you'd have a doo wop classic. Shows of affection (holding hands), exclusivity (don't need no one else), and intense emotional commitment are formulas for doo wop success, as we'll see in the next chapter.

Chapter Four

Doo Wop
The Glory of Love

"I did used to listen to quite a few of the groups, spiritual groups, like the Dixie Hummingbirds, the Five Blind Boys, the Swan Silvertones, and Sam Cooke and the Soul Stirrers. ... That was the mother music."
—Earl Carroll, The Cadillacs

"And your buddies, the guys who did it with you, they were your *heart*. You could get so in tune it seemed you all had but one heart between you. Man, you knew when all the other guys were gonna *breathe*."
—Ben E. King, The Drifters

"We wanted to sing. So that's what we did. We sang, day after day."
—Herman Denby, The Swallows[1]

Doo wop, the music of postwar secular harmony groups, is the youngest and most precocious of our four genres, the love child of blues, rhythm & blues, and gospel. The R&B harmony group sound first appeared around 1946. By September 1951, a column in *Billboard* announced, "Vocal groups have taken command in the R&B field ... away from the small instrumental groups and intimate solo blues singers which held sway for some time." The Dominoes, Five Keys, and Clovers had the top three best-selling records on the rhythm & blues chart that week. The prevalence of vocal group records in the *Billboard* R&B top ten increased exponentially through the early 1950s. In 1953, fifteen songs by eight different groups made the lists. By 1956, 29 songs by sixteen groups charted top ten. With the success of the Orioles' "Crying in the Chapel" (1953), the Crows' "Gee" (1954), the Spaniels' "Goodnite Sweetheart, Goodnite" (1954), the Chords' "Sh-Boom" (1954), and the Penguins' "Earth Angel" (1954), secular vocal group records—retroactively dubbed *doo wop*—led the march of Black R&B across to the pop charts, helping fuel the rock 'n' roll revolution.[2] The mid–1950s represented the height of doo wop artistry. In the early '60s, the beginning of the "oldies" phenomenon brought doo wop back as nostalgia. My personal guru, disc jockey Murray Kaufman on New York's WINS, had this signature riff: "This is Murray the K and his Swingin' Soiree with a *blast* from the *past*...."

Secular harmony group lyrics are sometimes bluesy, bemoaning lost or frustrated love; sometimes celebratory and up-tempo in the rhythm & blues mode; and often worshipful like gospel. Doo wop celebrates interpersonal love in a harmony quartet format drawn in large part from gospel. The purveyors of doo wop were almost always young, often teens. Their music and lyrics yearn; even the most lovelorn, melancholy, heartbroken ballads have a dreamy innocence that implies the promise of a better world. "Even when ballads ... did introduce classic blues themes of personal loss, loneliness and pain into the idyllic world of teenage romance," Brian Ward observes, "the sheer inescapable youthfulness of the vocals implied a transient, finite quality to the suffering." Nelson George calls doo wop "a form of innovative innocence.... [B]y and large doo wop projected the warmth and optimism of its young singers."[3]

Though some gospel groups from the South transitioned to doo wop, it arose mostly in northern cities, with New York its epicenter. Young African Americans sang in harmony, without instruments, on street corners or in schoolyards, gyms or school bathrooms, inspired by the successful Black harmony groups that first formed in the 1930s. The Mills Brothers and Ink Spots became radio and TV stars, gained international status, and sold millions of records. Both groups sang in barbershop quartet style with a silky, crooning lead, smooth harmonies, and a wholesome pop sound acceptable to white audiences. Listen to the Ink Spots' "The Gypsy," a #1 hit on both Race and Pop charts in 1946.

The postwar groups added blues along with the emotion and techniques of gospel to the harmonic mix. The group of four or five singers only rarely included an instrumentalist, usually a guitarist. Most often they just sang, backed by a studio band when recording or a pick-up band when performing live, with a saxophone solo frequently filling the instrumental breaks, significantly shorter than those in R&B songs. The standard vocal format has a tenor singing lead, backed by another tenor or two, a baritone, and bass. The second tenor and baritone harmonize; the bass provides rhythmic counterpoint. The background consists of *blow harmonies*, a sound resembling air blowing out of the singers' mouths: *oooh aaah*. Or vocables, nonsense syllables free of semantic content, like *doo wop doo wop*. Or, as in gospel, the background singers vocalize lyrics in a call-and-response with the lead. The tenor lead sometimes switches with the second tenor, baritone, or bass. Sometimes—as in the Ravens' "Ol' Man River" or the Dominoes' "Sixty Minute Man"—the bass sings lead. More rarely, groups like the Channels ("The Closer You Are") and Harptones ("My Memories of You") use harmonizing leads; the background and lead harmonize on the same lyric for a verse or line. The lead sometimes ascends into falsetto, in small dramatic doses (Solitaires, "I Don't Stand a Ghost of a Chance") or for an entire song (Blue Jays, "White Cliffs of Dover"). Falsetto more often appears in the background, the second tenor framing the lead in counterpoint with the bass. One soars above it, the other rumbles below.

Doo woppers were rarely trained singers, so the music usually lacked complexity. Examining 365 vocal group songs from two Best Of lists, John Michael Runowicz found that seventy per cent utilized the standard doo wop ballad chord changes: I-vi-IV-V (C major, A minor, F major, G major), aka *the ice cream changes, the Blue Moon changes* or *the '50s progression*. Despite the relatively uncomplicated music, the recording sessions for smaller labels could be haphazard. Atlantic producer Jerry

Wexler claimed, "As a rule, vocal groups were not rehearsed. Most of the doo wop producers ... lined up their groups in droves and pushed them in front of the mike to do their songs in one take. There were no arrangements and the band ... hadn't even heard the tune and certainly not the key." But as Ed Ward points out in *The Rolling Stone History of Rock & Roll*, "Wexler considered the style unsophisticated and crude, which is just what appealed to the teens who bought it...." In fact, the best vocal group performances have complex, careful arrangements, and multiple takes appear to have been commonplace. But complexity or its lack, professionalism, or technical sophistication hardly mattered to the kids buying and listening to the records. They danced to the fast jump tunes. Slow ballads about love desired, frustrated, found or lost were also for dancing, and making out, and dreaming about love and sex. To Ward, the doo wop chord progression "seemed to cry out for emotive tenor work and the sort of slow dancing where you and your partner just draped yourselves across each other and shuffled."[4]

An important element of doo wop song structure, the *bridge* or *channel* follows the first two verses. The mood, tempo, melody, or vocal texture might change dramatically in this section. Another verse generally follows. Often, a second bridge or channel follows that third verse. In it the bass or another lead voice might take over, the background voices might sing the lyrics in harmony, or the lyrics might be spoken rather than sung. The song usually ends with a reprise of the verse, making the standard song structure VVBV or VVBVBV, where V = verse and B = bridge. The bridge or channel "sounded the emotional heartbeat of many songs," Brian Ward asserts. "It was also communally acknowledged as the moment when a group showcased its talents. Tiny nuances and manipulations of harmony, timbre and rhythm, often undetected by outsiders, carried great import for black cognoscenti."[5]

If the recorded songs lacked polish, groups compensated with emotional authenticity. The matrix was the neighborhood. Doo wop scholars stress the importance of togetherness—the solidarity of the group, "the sensibility of guys 'backing' each other"—to help explain the power of the music. "The notion of 'group' and togetherness as a musical unit was very important to singers, and it reflected values that obtained at home and in the neighborhood," Stuart Goosman found in his study of Baltimore harmony groups. No one said *got your back* yet, but interdependence and trust were keys to relationships within the group and the quality of the sounds they produced. As an expression of community in the postwar era, the group ethos also had sociocultural ramifications: "These singers working together were the musical prophets of the coming civil rights and black power movements," Runowicz argues. "Their music making provided a model of ideal behavior where sonic harmony and social harmony are part of the same equation, a glimpse of utopian communal cooperation and aspiration."[6] In its structures, vocal group harmony embodied the idealized postwar dream of egalitarianism.

As noted earlier, the term *doo wop* came into use in the 1960s, applied retroactively to the harmony group songs of the postwar decade. The nonsense syllables that generated the term carried some historical weight. In their *Complete Book of Doo Wop*, Anthony Gribin and Matthew Schiff find the origins of those vocalizations in West African chants, scat singing, vocal mimicry of instruments by groups like the

Mills Brothers, and the need for street corner harmonizers, lacking instruments, to vocalize instrumental sounds. Runowicz hears socio-political significance in some contentless sounds, like the syllable *woo*: "a simulation of weeping or moaning," it became "a recognizable expression of a distinctive type of communal sorrow."[7]

Of the four genres in this book, the secular harmony group sound will likely be the most familiar. Repackaged and anthologized as Oldies but Goodies, replayed on oldies radio, recycled in films and TV—*American Graffiti, Grease, Happy Days, Goodfellas*, PBS fundraisers—doo wop has developed a canon, and many of the songs featured in this chapter are among the best-known classics of the genre. Doo wop has also become a pop culture cliché, easily parodied, perceived as empty of significance, symbolic of white baby boomer nostalgia. But at its best it remains beautiful, powerful music, a showcase for great voices and marvelous arrangements, the psychic soundtrack for a generation coming of age just before rock 'n' roll got serious. Many of those great voices have been forgotten, like so much African American music of this era. They deserve twenty-first-century homage, revaluation, and resurrection.

Recent music scholarship has reclaimed the seriousness and weight of secular harmony group music for the African American audiences who listened to it and valued it as rhythm & blues before white audiences appropriated it as doo wop. Critics have offered compelling ideas about the music's socio-political significance for Black audiences in the postwar decade. Brian Ward argues that the gentle romanticism and sensitive masculinity of doo wop ballads helped Black R&B cross over into the broader pop/rock 'n' roll market by representing "an idealized vision of relations between the sexes which increasingly eclipsed the lusty adventurism, misogyny and fatalism" of the blues. He suggests that the popularity of doo wop among Black audiences may have reflected their own changing attitudes.[8] If postwar African American music embodies the dream of a new way of living, doo wop romance might be one manifestation.

Harmony group lyrics can be banal and trite, sometimes inane. "For the most part, both the words and melodies of the doo wop genre touch the emotions while leaving the intellect unscathed," Gribin and Schiff assert. I would emphasize *for the most part*, because doo wop lyrics, like those of the other genres, often repay careful listening, especially in the socio-political contexts of postwar African America. Glenn Altschuler finds coded racial references in the subtexts of African American popular music like the Platters' **"The Great Pretender"** (1956), its lyrics thematically analogous, he argues, to Ralph Ellison's *Invisible Man*: "In the white world, they implied, blacks wore masks." Though the group's white manager, Buck Ram, wrote the song, Altschuler cites Du Bois' notion of African American double consciousness to propose that Black listeners may have heard it "as the story of the double lives of African Americans."[9] We can easily undervalue doo wop by assuming the absence of significant lyrical content. The very term *doo wop* emphasizes sound over sense. I follow Altschuler in looking for the sense within and behind the sound.

Singers make their own interpretive statement when performing or recording a song, even if they did not write it themselves. Brian Ward cites what he calls the Ravens' and Drifters' "radical deconstruction" of the classic "White Christmas," both versions utilizing slow tempo, vocal slurs, and a "slightly menacing bass vocal line which ruptured rather than underpinned the well-known melody." The result: "a black satire on all things white." Ann Powers characterizes the young Black men who sang doo wop as "the children of the Great Migration, awash in hormones and hope and a stubborn insistence on liberty, pushing against the bonds of Jim Crow."[10] Doo wop as protest music is an idea worth seriously pondering.

Gribin & Schiff's *Complete Book of Doo-Wop* divides the music into chronological sub-categories such as The Birth of Doo-Wop, Paleo Doo-Wop (1948–1954), and Classical Doo-Wop (1955–59); separate sections on women in doo wop and schoolboy doo-wop; and doo wop geography in Baltimore/D.C., New York, Chicago, Los Angeles, and Philadelphia. Wikipedia's very good Doo-Wop entry also contains individual sections on those cities plus Detroit. My organization of this chapter partly follows the chronological model, partly the geographic, and partly the generic: doo wop groups that began in gospel, women and schoolboy doo woppers. We end with a series of anomalous groups, all represented here by one great song.

Birds Take Flight

The pioneering groups that started the doo wop rage and set the stage for the great secular harmony music to come in the postwar era, the Ravens and Orioles, laid down their markers in the late 1940s. The songs of all the other groups here date from the early- to mid–1950s, doo wop's Golden Age. Around forty percent of the songs in this chapter were recorded or released in 1955–56. The success of the Ravens and Orioles also jump-started the *bird group* phenomenon. Birds sing, ravens are black, the Orioles were from Baltimore. Except for the Crows, similar logic isn't evident in the names of the bird groups that followed, including the Swallows, Larks, Cardinals, Flamingos, Penguins, Blue Jays, Meadowlarks, and Robins.

Probably the most influential vocal group of the postwar period, **The Ravens**, organized in Harlem in 1945, established templates for the groups that followed: a bass lead in the great **Jimmy Ricks** (1924–74) with his reputed three-octave range, who set the standard for all subsequent doo wop bass singers; a falsetto lead in tenor Maithe Marshall; and a rhythmic, bluesy group sound that hadn't been heard before. "The Mills Brothers and Ink Spots may have hinted at melodic blues inflections, jazz bass lines, and gospel call-and-response forms, but the Ravens moved these characteristically black elements front and centre," Runowicz writes.[11] Harlemites who grew up in Florida, Ricks and Marshall combined Southern blues sensibility with an urbane postwar sound.

The Ravens had nine top ten R&B hits with New York's National Records, 1947–50, most notably **"Ol' Man River"** (1947). Ricks sang lead as bass Paul Robeson had in Hammerstein and Kern's 1927 musical, *Show Boat*. "What made the group special was Ricks," say Gribin & Schiff, "doing things better and lower and different than any bass before him." Ricks' approach and the Ravens' arrangement transform Robeson's somewhat doleful interpretation into something much more upbeat. *Billboard*'s reviewer noted "The deep bass voice carrying the lead all the way, with a flair for the rhythmic in his phrasings, the Ravens impart plenty of bounce to the old ballad...."[12] A tinkling piano and background *doot doots* accompany Ricks' jazzy lead that stresses the river's rolling rather than the singer's weariness and fear of dying. The background takes the lead on parts of the bridge, their bouncy harmonies mitigating the sweat and strain in those lyrics. The second time the bridge comes around, Ricks finishes the lyric about getting thrown in jail. Listen to how very low he goes on the word *jail*, a reminder of the historical reality underlying the vocal fun. Besides showing what a great bass lead could do, this first genuine doo wop hit established that R&B vocal groups could successfully cover show tunes and Tin Pan Alley classics.

On their other classic cover, **"White Christmas"** (1948), Ricks swings the lead through two verses, then hands it over to Marshall, whose distinctive high tenor is absent from "Ol' Man River." He repeats the verses, adding a few falsetto notes. Near the end, the group samples lines from "Jingle Bells," led by Marshall in falsetto. Despite the novel approach, Marshall's crooning-style tenor and campy-sounding "Jingle Bells" falsetto riff date the recording.

My number one Ravens song is the beautiful ballad **"Count Every Star"** (1950), written by bandleader Ray Anthony. Mellifluous baritone Louis Heyward sings lead as the superb arrangement utilizes all the group's best tools. Ricks opens with a series of earthquakingly deep *doo-doo-doo doo-doo-doo*s, the background harmonizes chime-like *bong*s, and Marshall's falsetto floats over top. After Heyward completes the two verses, the background repeats the first part in harmony until Ricks' bass takes the lead. The singer offers his lover a catalog of things to count, from the stars in the sky to the leaves on the trees and the waves in the sea. That's how much he misses her and how often he cries for her. The hyperbole and tearful masculinity of the grieving lover will prove typical of doo wop ballads. Subtle guitar, piano, and drums give the song a fully modern sound without distracting from the fine voices.

As important as the Ravens in establishing the new R&B-influenced secular harmony group sound, **The Orioles**, Marv Goldberg claims, "literally inspired an entire generation of black singers." Formed in Baltimore in 1948 as The Vibra-Naires, but soon changing their name to the Orioles, the group revolved around lead tenor Earlington Tilghman, aka **Sonny Til** (1925–81). Baritone George Nelson sang second lead, tenor Tommy Gaither played guitar, and Johnny Reed played stand-up bass and sang the bass parts. The Orioles' sound incorporated both rhythm & blues and gospel influences without the former's raucous aggression or the latter's overt emotion. "The group held in their emotion," Goosman argues, "it was close-coiled, and yet there was something slightly dissolute about the vocal lead, in a charming sort of way." Til was doo wop's first sex symbol. Women screamed and fainted at his performances and tore at his clothes. "Sonny's voice was full of heartbreak," says Arnold Shaw, "and a palpably horny sound."[13]

The Orioles broke through with their first recording, a rendition of local songwriter Deborah Chessler's **"It's Too Soon to Know"** (1948) on the short-lived It's a Natural label, which soon became Jubilee Records. It spent seventeen weeks on

The Orioles promotional photograph about 1950. Bottom, from left: **Sonny Til, George Nelson, Johnny Reed, Tommy Gaither**; top: **Alexander Sharp**. Pictorial Press Ltd./Alamy Stock Photo.

Billboard's R&B chart, a week at #1, and made it to #13 Pop. Sonny Til was one of the best of many gorgeous tenor lead voices to grace doo wop, as his stellar performance on this song attests: a tentative, quietly tormented soul in doubt about his lover's commitment. Guitar, bass, and piano gently accompany his emotional journey, which may end in tears. Does she love me? Can I believe her, or is she acting? Til wants desperately to be the fire but wonders if maybe he's just another flame. "Sonny Til's keening tenor moved so slowly, with such caution, desire, and dread," Greil Marcus observes. "Alexander Sharp and Johnny Reed moaned wordlessly, humming like ghosts in the background." Another critic says, "It came off sounding like a personal revelation delivered from singers in not much different circumstances than the ones who bought the record."[14] That intimate, personal language of desire would speak to the hearts of young people of all races over the next decade in yearning doo wop ballads inspired by this one.

Managed by Chessler, the Orioles had eight other top tens on Jubilee between 1948 and 1953, seven of them ballads. They released **"I Miss You So"** (1951) shortly after Tommy Gaither died in a car crash. The record had been cut before his death, yet it must have felt like a warm goodbye. The group had all their royalties from the record paid to Gaither's family.[15] Another song with strong lyrics, it was written and first recorded in 1940 by proto-harmony group The Cats and the Fiddle at a jaunty tempo accompanied by a ukulele. Its many subsequent covers included one by Sonny

Til's idol, Nat King Cole. A bluesy, late-night-sounding piano provides the melody for the Orioles' slow version, and soft bass, guitar, and drums the rhythm. Sharp's background falsetto reinforces the yearning and vulnerability in Til's elastic, marvelously dreamy voice. Til addresses his estranged lover in absolutes, cataloguing their past together, the things he misses so much and can't stop remembering—her voice, her touch. Incarnating the newly emergent sensitive masculinity of doo wop, Til professes that everything with which she once filled his heart has been replaced by his tears. When George Nelson takes the second bridge, the tears are gone.

By the time the Orioles recorded their biggest hit, **"Crying in the Chapel"** (1953), Nelson had left the group, replaced by Gregory Carroll, with Ralph Williams on guitar. A country-and-western song by Artie Glenn first recorded in 1953 by his son Darrell, it was covered that year by everyone from Ella Fitzgerald to Sister Rosetta Tharpe. The Orioles' doo wop cover spent eighteen weeks on *Billboard's* R&B chart, five at #1, and climbed to #11 on the Pop chart. Elvis Presley's 1960 version trumped them all, but that's another story. Minus the piano, with chiming church-like bells, the Orioles' arrangement basically replicates "It's Too Soon to Know" and "I Miss You So": slow tempo, subtle music, blow harmonies, and Sharp's falsetto floating above Til's quietly intense vocal. Til cries tears of joy here as he prays contentedly in the chapel, having found the peace of mind he had sought in vain—as though the doubt and heartbreak of the previous songs made him renounce earthly love for the divine. Given the tone, mood, and Til's vocal quality, a few changes in the lyrics could turn it back into a secular love song, so permeable was the line between gospel and doo wop. Peter Guralnick calls the Orioles' record a direct precursor of soul music: "they muddled the distinctions—stylistic, harmonic, and lyrical—between gospel and r&b."[16] The Orioles, however, did not begin as a gospel group. The overlap of secular and sacred in this record suggests how deeply the gospel feeling infused African American song at the time.

Gospel Goes Doo Wop

Unlike the Ravens and Orioles, other harmony groups that would shape rhythm & blues in the 1950s had deep roots in the South and its church music. Two of those groups, the Dominoes and Drifters, were led for a time by **Clyde McPhatter** (1932–72), the finest singer of the doo wop era. McPhatter grew up in North Carolina, son of a Baptist preacher, singing in the choir. After his family moved to New York, teenage Clyde formed a gospel group, the Mount Lebanon Singers. After he won amateur night at the Apollo, vocal coach, pianist, arranger, and former choirboy Billy Ward recruited him in 1950 to sing lead tenor in a new secular quartet, **The Dominoes** (soon called Billy Ward and His Dominoes). In 1953, chafing under Ward's strict paternalism, McPhatter left the Dominoes and formed The Drifters. After a stint in the Army he went solo and had a series of hits including two wonderful ballads in the last year of our era, **"Treasure of Love"** (1956) and **"Without Love (There Is Nothing)"** (1956). Sadly, he died before his fortieth birthday.

With Ward and talent agent partner Rose Marks writing most of their songs, the

Dominoes recorded for King Records' Federal subsidiary, produced by Ralph Bass. They scored nine R&B top tens between 1951 and 1953, including their first release, the ballad **"Do Something for Me"** (1950), a showcase for McPhatter's "dramatic tenor style, filled with effortlessly soaring glides, fluttering sobs, cascading melismas, and great rhythmic invention." Gerri Hirshey describes his vocal approach as "a house-wrecking style that set off traditional major-chord group harmonies with the unpredictable minor-note pyrotechnics of the gospel shout."[17] With minimal musical backing (guitar, bass, drum), and background blow harmonies, McPhatter lets loose on this seductive musical proposition, soaring, swooping, and worrying the lyrics, pleading with her to do that special something for him. For a taste of McPhatter's gorgeous tenor balladry without embroidery, listen to his treatment of the 1935 standard, **"These Foolish Things Remind Me of You"** (1953). Ward's piano joins the mix and McPhatter provides a spoken intro and bridge, soon-to-be frequent doo wop devices. Bassman Bill Brown adds basso *OHH*s to the background and second tenor Charlie White counters with falsetto *ooooohs*. The result is particularly beautiful.

The Dominoes' mega-hit, **"Sixty-Minute Man"** (1951), relegated McPhatter to the background while Brown sang bass lead in the style of Raven Jimmy Ricks. Its success owed something to Brown's good-natured delivery but its blatantly suggestive lyrics really sold the song. The biggest R&B hit of 1951 and one of the biggest of the decade, it spent thirty weeks on the chart, fourteen at #1, and crossed over to #17 Pop. Lovin' Dan delivers the goods: fifteen minutes of kissing (she begs him not to stop), fifteen minutes each of squeezing and teasing, concluding with fifteen minutes of *blowing his top*. He rocks and rolls 'em all night. Dawson & Propes argue that "Sixty-Minute Man" succeeded with white audiences because "the song was a novelty, a throwback to minstrel songs...."[18] Still, imagine the anti-*leer-ic* hysteria as the song crossed over into the white pop market. This *was* the thin edge of the wedge.

But McPhatter's voice ultimately defined his tenure with the Dominoes. In addition to his gorgeous balladry he could rock, and his gospel training infused his rocking with soul. In a study of New York's R&B harmony groups, Philip Groia cites **"That's What You're Doing to Me"** (1952) and **"Have Mercy Baby"** (1952) as keys to the Dominoes' "creation of the gospel-blues oriented Rock 'n' Roll jump tune." Classic up-tempo rhythm & blues with hand-clapping and shouts of "Go! Go!" during the squalling sax break, "That's What You're Doing to Me" has some nice falsetto touches and background harmonies, but the song lives on McPhatter's growling lead. The craziness she causes him makes him want to laugh and cry, leave and stay, fight and play, and most importantly, rock and roll. It spent five weeks on the R&B chart. Then the rockin' "Have Mercy Baby" superseded it with ten weeks at #1. Ed Ward describes its sound as "the urgency of the church coupled with the urgency of awakening sexual need."[19] Musically almost a clone of "That's What You're Doing to Me," but with more bass (David McNeil replaced Bill Brown) and less falsetto (Charlie White had moved to the Clovers), the song finds McPhatter confessing his bad behavior and begging his baby not to slam the door. Unlike other doo wop ballads of repentance, his plea for forgiveness seems strictly tongue-in-cheek. Listen to McPhatter sob as the song fades out. Bawling on a larger scale would appear in and ruin coulda-been doo wop classics like the Dominoes' **"The Bells"** (1952) and Jackie and the Starlites' "Valerie" (1960).

Originally from Durham, North Carolina, like McPhatter, the Dominoes' new bass man, David McNeil, came over from **The Larks**, a doo wop group with deep gospel roots in that state. Formed in the 1930s in Brooklyn by Thermon Ruth as the Selah Jubilee Singers, the Larks recorded extensively in the 1940s, re-settling in Raleigh during the war. Ruth recruited several North Carolinians, including lead tenor **Eugene Mumford** (1925–77), who had spent the previous few years on a chain gang before being pardoned for a trumped-up rape conviction. They moved back to New York in 1950. In a single day, they recorded gospel and secular tunes for four different labels under four different names: Selah Singers, Jubilators, Four Barons, and Southern Harmonaires. Listen to the Harmonaires' terrific version of **"Honey in the Rock"** (1950; released 1958) on Apollo with baritone Hadie Rowe singing lead. Signed by Apollo, they changed their name to the Larks and devoted themselves to secular harmony.[20]

In his *American Singing Groups*, Jay Warner calls the song for which the Larks are best remembered, **"My Reverie"** (1951), "the most beautifully performed rhythm and blues ballad ever." Todd Baptista adds, the "spare instrumentation showcased Mumford's golden tenor and the group's exquisite spiritual harmony, right down to David McNeil's round bass notes."[21] Written in 1938, based on a Debussy piano piece and performed at a very slow tempo, this genuinely gorgeous song profits from Mumford's beautiful almost falsetto pleading lead. McNeil's *boom boom-boom* punctuation lends a note of foreboding to the dreamy lyrics. The singer worries that his reverie of love could prove a cruel disappointment, and he implores his lover to transform his dream into reality. I can't help hearing the romance theme as a surrogate for the more momentous postwar dream. Its failure would be cruel but the possibility of its reality well worth the risk. Will the doo wop lover have the courage to invest in the dream?

Mumford's time in prison left an impression on a couple of the Larks' other best songs. While still in jail, he wrote **"When I Leave These Prison Walls"** (1951), a behind-bars reverie set against a soft piano, guitar, and Ravens-like *doot doot* harmonies. Mumford fantasizes about freedom: waking and sleeping when he wants, catching a train, picking up women. He's gonna ball on the other side of the wall. A lovelier song, **"In My Lonely Room"** (1952) offers the flip side of that fantasy: no balling and no exit. Haunting refrains and McNeil's quietly booming *doo doo doo* provide the soundtrack to the singer's impotence. Tormented by broken dreams, imprisoned in his room by his memories of her, he asks: What can I do? Nothing left but to cry.

Another North Carolina gospel quartet transformed themselves into a topnotch doo wop group. **The "5" Royales** began life as the Royal Sons Quintet, organized by bass Lowman Pauling, who also played guitar and wrote many of their songs. Like the Larks, they headed to New York in the early 1950s, signed with Apollo, switched from sacred to secular, and changed their name. Initially dubbed the Royals, they changed again to the "5" Royales, with those odd quotation marks, to avoid confusion with a Detroit R&B group called the Royals (who eventually became the Midnighters). Though little-known today, the gospel-rooted "5" Royales directly influenced James Brown and His Famous Flames, and in Lowman Pauling they had what Robert Palmer calls one of "the music's greatest songwriters and most influential electric guitarists."[22] Pauling's great guitar work doesn't appear on their records until after our era but his excellent songwriting does.

Pauling wrote two fine #1 hits for the Royales on Apollo, backed by saxman Charlie Ferguson and his Orchestra, and led by tenor Johnny Tanner, who "had a vocal tone similar to McPhatter's, slightly more hesitant and less melodic, more mature and with a harder drive at fast tempos."[23] The harder drive stands out on those early hits, **"Baby Don't Do It"** (1952) and **"Help Me Somebody"** (1953). Both feature a repentant, pleading lover, but the vocal and musical attack counters the pathos in Pauling's lyrics, making Tanner's poor suffering heart (crying in one song, aching in the other) seem almost ironic. In "Baby Don't Do It" he pleads with his lover to change her mind before rejecting him. The title phrase, repeated eight times consecutively in each of the two channels, sounds more manic demand than plea. In the slower "Help Me Somebody" broken-hearted, depressed Tanner admits his faults, confesses his wrongs, and asks help from *somebody*, anybody, to get him back in her good graces as the background howls and moans in sympathy. The tempo picks up in the bridge where a second voice tells him he did wrong, manically laughing as if he were talking to himself. His request for help near the end repeats five times in succession, another strong vocal moment that makes this tender-hearted lover sound both desperate and tough.

In 1954, the "5" Royales moved to King Records and made maybe their best record, which went nowhere. Tanner never sounded so impassioned as on **"One Mistake"** (1954), another of Pauling's superb requests to a wronged lover that she forgive and forget. The singer explains in the refrain that he doesn't want to spend the rest of his life paying for a single mistake. With horns providing the fills and a tinkling piano, he tries to argue rationally: I can do nothing now about what I've done previously except convince you that I know I did wrong and love you exceptionally well. He finds several ways to tell her how much she means to him, often crying out at the top of his range. The group harmonizes on the first bridge, multiple voices taking up his argument. On the second, another lead voice explains to her how boys will be boys. Finally, he pleads with her to love him and not leave him *for goodness sake*, less an expression of exasperation than a literal appeal to her goodness. Few doo wop strategies have been so compelling.

The Atlantic seaboard was a hotbed for gospel groups that converted to doo wop. **The Five Keys** came together in 1945 as the Sentimental Four, two sets of brothers singing gospel in Newport News, Virginia. By 1950, they had changed their name and personnel, started singing secular, and traveled to New York for amateur night at the Apollo, where they took first place and signed with Aladdin. Jay Warner ascribes to them three of "the most talented lead singers any group ever had. [Baritone] Dickie Smith was a soulful lead, [second tenor] Maryland Pierce had a fantastic blues sound, and [first tenor] Rudy West possessed a smooth, polished, clear-as-a-bell tenor." A 1992 survey of "doo wop cognoscenti" ranked the Five Keys #1 all-time among harmony groups, ahead of the Orioles (#3), Dominoes (7), Ravens (8), and Larks (14).[24]

The Five Keys' **"The Glory of Love"** (1951) ranks high on any list of most beautiful doo wop ballads. Originally recorded by Benny Goodman's orchestra in 1936, the song gave the Keys their only #1 hit. Rudy West sings lead in his velvety high tenor and Dickie Smith takes the second bridge, although its first eight bars are oddly omitted, likely cut because the record exceeded three minutes. The blow harmonies are relatively forward in the mix, along with a subtle falsetto. Minimal instrumental accompaniment by pianist Joe Jones and a guitar or bass provides a solid rhythmic bottom. A sublime performance complements the song's meaty existential lyrics. The story and glory of love involves giving and taking, laughing and crying, winning and losing, and suffering heartbreak. The bridge offers its own philosophical consolation: the two of us have the world; when it's through with us we'll have each other. A glorious record in every regard.

In 1954, the Five Keys became the first rhythm & blues group to sign with a major label, leaving Aladdin for Capitol Records' advanced audio techniques and equipment. With their new crystal-clear sound, the Keys produced the exquisite ballad **"Close Your Eyes"** (1954). Phil Groia calls it "the greatest high tenor echo record ever made."[25] Written by R&B performer Chuck Willis, it features stop-time elements and a double lead, Rudy West echoing Maryland Pierce's lyrics. West sings at the top of his range, and the background harmonies caress both lead vocals. Sometimes West plays the part of Pierce's lover, responding to his requests to take a deep breath and whisper sweet endearments. Primarily, West's vocal reinforces Pierce, who implores his lover to hold him and tell him she loves him—even if she's only pretending. Like "The Glory of Love," this is doo wop for adults.

When Clyde McPhatter left Billy Ward's Dominoes in 1953, wanting more control over his career, more money, and more respect (he had sometimes been billed as Clyde Ward), Atlantic's Ahmet Ertegun grabbed him, offering McPhatter, whom he considered "a singer from heaven with the most lyrical voice," the opportunity to build a new group around himself.[26] It would be called **The Drifters**. McPhatter spent only a year as a Drifter. He entered the U.S. Army in 1954 and came out a solo act. But even his short-lived Drifters involved two completely different groups of singers. Subsequently, the Drifters would change personnel at a mind-boggling rate. Their Wikipedia entry lists 39 different lineups with 66 different members between 1953 and 1972. In nearly every manifestation the Drifters were a hit machine, especially with McPhatter and later Ben E. King singing lead.

McPhatter made it clear that gospel remained at the heart of his approach to song by stocking his new group with guys from his Mount Lebanon gospel quartet.

Those Drifters had only one recording session and released only a single record before Atlantic decided they didn't have the right sound and asked McPhatter to form yet another group. But what a record! McPhatter's **"Lucille"** (1953) presents Clyde at his most soulful. In this 12-bar blues ballad, remarkable for its sheer emotive power, he complains about her behavior but confesses that he did her wrong. Stunned by Lucille's leaving, he stares speechlessly into space. When he finds the words, he beseeches her to come home, crying out her name in that high, plangent, heartbreaking tenor, dragging it out, *Lu-u-u-u-u-u-cille,* as if to hang onto her as long as possible. A piano and drums bang out triplets while the background wails along with him, echoing her name in high harmony with a falsetto thrown in. Ertegun apparently felt there wasn't enough contrast in the voices. But this masterpiece has a more genuine gospel feel than any of the other great records the Drifters subsequently made. Is it a coincidence that B.B. King named his guitar Lucille and Albert King his Lucy?

When McPhatter put together his second rendition of the Drifters in 1953, he again drafted veteran gospelers: Alabaman brothers Gerhart and Andrew Thrasher, and South Carolina native Bill Pinkney. In their brief time together they recorded many excellent songs, credited to Clyde McPhatter and the Drifters, or The Drifters featuring Clyde McPhatter. Clyde's superb versatility in every mood, the new Drifters' rich sound, Jesse Stone's consistently first-rate arrangements, and Atlantic's A-list musicians made for marvelous chemistry and great music. The group succeeded commercially most often with mid- and up-tempo numbers. Their first release, the romping **"Money Honey"** (1953), spent eleven weeks at #1. Stone wrote it, one of the best rhythm & blues songs about the power of cash, with Mickey Baker on guitar and Sam "The Man" Taylor blowing tenor sax. The clever, cynical lyrics follow a money trail from the singer's landlord to the

Second incarnation of The Drifters, 1953. Bottom, from left: Clyde McPhatter, Andrew Thrasher; top, from left: Gerhart Thrasher, Bill Pinkney. Glasshouse Images/Alamy Stock Photo.

singer's girlfriend to the girlfriend's other man, ending with the singer vowing that any woman he loves will have to pay for him. Clyde's voice, Stone's lyrics, and Taylor's sax solo highlight this catchy tune.

The A-side of "Lucille," **"Such a Night"** (1954), climbed to #2, and **"Honey Love"** (1954) to #1 for eight weeks. Set to Latin beats and showing Clyde's lascivious side, they led to censorship and radio bans. "Such a Night" leaves something to the imagination as McPhatter sings about his night of love with a sprinkling of *oohs* and the background riffing *da dooby dooby doo*. McPhatter and Jerry Wexler wrote the superior, more explicit "Honey Love," a horny man's anthem. Against a background of bongos and innocent *lendy lendy lendy lendy lows*, Clyde details in how many ways, how much, and how often (pretty much all the time) he wants it, needs it, and is gonna get it. The group helps out when Clyde vocalizes the *squeeze oooh* that represents the honey love he's after. An exceptional record.

Number one on my personal Drifters' hit parade is the sublime rocker **"What'cha Gonna Do"** (1955). *The Drifters* author Bill Millar considers it their finest recording of gospel-inspired material and their best up-tempo performance. Ertegun wrote it under his backwards pseudonym, Nugetre. It celebrates what Albert Murray called the Saturday Night Function: rockin' and reelin', dancing and drinking, and having a ball, with another fine sax solo and Clyde in his best rock 'n' roll voice.[27] If I had a radio show, this would be its theme song. The background pulls him along like a locomotive—*doo doo doo doo WHOA-OH*—and the call-and-response between Clyde, background, and band drives the high tempo. Clyde builds a dream date with this pretty, struttin', black-haired woman. At eight-thirty he'll hold her hand, then they'll rock and never stop. He's so hot the sax solo has to be kept short. And when the place is on fire? They'll climb even higher, until at four a.m. they're flying and she's hollering, *please, more!*

One of Clyde and the Drifters' best known songs, **"White Christmas"** (1954), a much-improved copy of the Ravens' ground-breaking 1948 version, peaked at #2. Bass Bill Pinkney takes the comfortably swinging lead. The background duplicates the Ravens' *doot doot doots* but with richer texture and superior sound. A prominent snare marks the rhythm. When McPhatter switches in at about the one-minute mark, the song soars. Pinkney returns at two minutes, and the group ends with a brief harmonic homage to the Ravens' near-fatal interpolation of "Jingle Bells." *Timeless* may be a cliché, but seventy years on, you can play this song at any Christmas party without embarrassment.

The Drifters also recorded a series of beautiful ballads that failed to chart, including **"The Way I Feel"** (1953) and **"Warm Your Heart"** (1953). The B-side of "White Christmas," **"The Bells of St. Mary's"** (1954), and the only other song on which McPhatter and Pinkney shared the leads, **"Someday You'll Want Me to Want You"** (1954), showcase Clyde's dramatic tenor. The pseudo-gospel, pseudo–Christmas song "The Bells of St. Mary's," composed in 1917, tells of bells ringing out for true young lovers. A sound like church bells gives the song a religious flavor, and McPhatter and the group sing it with reverence. Clyde exercises his melisma, as he does on "Someday You'll Want Me to Want You," a country song from 1945. The only country in the Drifters' version might be Central Park. With piano triplets pounding,

Clyde and the Drifters sing an uptown, impassioned ode to wishful regret. The title says it all. Pinkney speaks a verse in the song's third minute, an effect that works only to make you better appreciate Clyde's voice.

Another great ballad, **"Everyone's Laughing"** (1954), came out after McPhatter began his solo career. It was credited to him alone, even though he recorded it with the Drifters before leaving them. The drummer lays down a hard beat, a piano tinkles, and the blow harmonies echo Clyde's regret as he sings about his fair-weather friends laughing at him ever since she left. The combination of heartbreak and embarrassment provides an emotional complexity worthy of McPhatter's substantial ability to wrench meaning from even banal lyrics.

These Drifters made some fine records after McPhatter's departure. Clyde-sound-alike tenor Johnny Moore sang lead on "**Adorable**" (1955), a cover of the Colts' love song that reached #1 for the Drifters. Listen to the bridge where Moore sings about her having come from *hea-ea-ea-ven*. His voice is lower than McPhatter's with a pleasant texture that melds nicely with the Drifters' harmonies. Dave Marsh singles out the beautifully nuanced arrangement "with grunting sax, restless drums, and staccato piano."[28] On the other notable Drifters song of the immediate post–Clyde era, "**Your Promise to Be Mine**" (1956), a moody, romantic composition by Drifters' guitarist Jimmy Oliver, baritone Gerhart Thrasher sings lead. A sexy late-night saxophone sets the tone as Moore's falsetto and Pinkney's bass frame Thrasher's expressive vocal. The great Drifters tradition continued with wonderful singers like these and, of course, Ben E. King. But there would never be another Clyde McPhatter.

Where Were You in '52?

Gribin & Schiff observe that the years 1952–53 saw a concentration of harmony groups in New York, Los Angeles, and Chicago where so many independent labels recording doo wop were located. We've seen how the gospel quartets that turned secular often moved from their homes in the South to New York. But other centers of doo wop power competed, especially the Baltimore-D.C. area that produced the Orioles. Though this region lacked major record labels, Washington's Howard Theater and Baltimore's Royal—its versions of New York's Apollo—were important stops on the chitlin' circuit and crucial venues for showcasing local and regional talent, along with Chicago's Regal, Detroit's Paradise, and Philadelphia's Uptown Theater.[29] This section will focus on the great songs of groups that shaped the years when doo wop exploded across the United States, 1951–53.

When Ahmet Ertegun visited Baltimore while talent-scouting through the South in 1951, a neighborhood group called the Mellotones auditioned for him. He immediately signed them to Atlantic and changed their name to **The Cardinals**. Jesse Stone arranged the first song they recorded, **"Shouldn't I Know"** (1951), written by the group's second tenor, Prince Brothers, with echoes of the Orioles' "It's Too

Soon to Know." Lead singer Ernest Warren "had a solid, graceful tenor voice," Stuart Goosman writes. "Yet, he had a matter-of-fact delivery, almost detached…."[30] I find Warren's voice engaged and expressive. If this pretty ballad feels detached, it comes from the slightly off-kilter lyrics. In doubt about his lover's feelings, the singer never asks her directly if she still cares for him. He only asks, rhetorically, Shouldn't I know whether you love me? He spends his lonely nights crying, the sensitive doo wop male too afraid *really* to know. Mickey Baker's lyrical guitar dominates instrumentally. Jack Johnson and bass Leon Hardy briefly take the lead on the two bridges with Warren singing falsetto behind Johnson's baritone and soaring into falsetto again on the song's final *know*, that fearful signifier of certainty.

The Cardinals' tenure at Atlantic overlapped with the McPhatter/Drifters era. Its influence shows in the Cardinals' beautiful rendition of the Chuck Willis–penned **"The Door Is Still Open"** (1955). Ernest Warren sounds a lot like Clyde as Leon Hardy's rolling bass counterpoint, mellow backing from Jesse Stone on piano, and a typically rich tenor sax solo from Sam "The Man" Taylor provide the musical atmosphere.[31] The singer confesses that he cries from loneliness. He feels no shame because it's better than repressing his sorrow. Besides gently showing off his sensitivity and psychological acuity, he woos his reluctant lover with clever analogies. Instead of pleading he plays hard-to-get. He leaves the door of his heart open; she'll have the next move.

A third strong Baltimore group also came together in the late 1940s, calling themselves the Oakaleers, influenced by the neighboring Vibra-Naires before that group became the Orioles. With the Orioles' success the Oakaleers changed their name to **The Swallows**, and lead tenor Eddie Rich developed a singing style like Sonny Til's. When they signed with King Records, A&R man Henry Glover made them change their style to avoid sounding like an Orioles clone. With Glover's help they changed their harmony and eventually their lead singer.[32]

Baritone Herman "Junior" Denby wrote **"Dearest"** (1951), the Swallows' first release on King, but only its flip side, **"Will You Be Mine,"** charted. Like the Orioles' ballads, the background harmonies and instrumentation on "Dearest" (prominent bass and Sonny Thompson's piano) are relatively muted. Eddie Rich's lead vocal has a slightly affected, coy, intoxicating (if not intoxicated) drawl. Bassman Norris "Bunky" Mack gets to lead for a couple of lines but Rich's voice dominates. He praises her beauty—people on the street stop and stare—but wonders about the folly of his affection if she doesn't care for him. In any event his heart tells him she's his dearest, and he talks himself into sticking around despite the rumors.

In autumn 1951, with the Dominoes' "Sixty-Minute Man" topping the charts for King's sister label, Federal, Glover wrote and arranged **"It Ain't the Meat"** (1951) for the Swallows. In "Sixty-Minute Man" mode, Mack's bass takes the lead with piano swinging, hands clapping, and the group providing animated harmonies. The song straightforwardly explains that the meat, not the motion, makes daddy wanna do it. With skinny or fat women, big or small, movement counts, not size. Glover even copped a line from "Sixty-Minute Man" about the guy blowing his top. Along with a guitar solo the song features a stand-up bass solo, extremely unusual for doo wop. Despite failing to chart, it indicates the further infiltration of R&B sexuality into the mainstream. Maria Muldaur's 1974 cover reversed the gender argument.

Junior Denby sings lead on his own composition, **"Beside You"** (1952), the Swallows' most beautiful song. His mellow baritone duets with Thompson's moody piano against the background's quiet blow harmonies. The song begins conventionally. He needs her, wants to be with her forever, asks her to make his dreams come true. The interesting twist in doo wop courtship psychology comes towards the end. Before she has even rejected him, he sings pre-emptively: If I bore you, you'll leave me for someone else. I'll wish you happiness. But if you tire of him, know I'm still here for you, beside you always. Smooth, Junior.

A near-neighbor of the Baltimore bird groups, Washington, D.C.'s **The Clovers** landed nineteen songs on *Billboard*'s R&B top ten from 1951 to 1956, establishing them as America's most popular vocal quartet. When Ertegun first heard them in 1950, they were singing pop standards Ink Spots–style. He wanted a more bluesy, more Southern sound. Under Jesse Stone's coaching and arranging, with Stone and Ertegun co-writing their songs, the Clovers developed a rougher performance style. They became the first traditional vocal group, in Nick Tosches' inimitable metaphor, "to make the leap across the Jordan to the chicken shack that transcends all knowing."[33]

The Clovers' first Atlantic sessions produced a #1 hit, **"Fool, Fool, Fool"** (1951), with all the hallmarks of their new R&B orientation. They sound rough and unpolished, with Buddy Bailey's bluesy lead lamenting his folly in falling in love with her while bass Harold Winley riffs *doo doo doo*.[34] Ertegun's otherwise uninspired lyrics include one memorable line: in the

The Clovers, c. 1955. From left: Bill Harris, Harold Winley, Billy Mitchell, Buddy Bailey, Matthew McQuater. Pictorial Press Ltd./Alamy Stock Photo.

stop-time bridge the singer calls her his meat. No wonder she ditched you, fool! Funky sax from Sam the Man and Harry Van Walls' piano round out the classic Clovers sound.

Over the next few years the group recorded hit after catchy hit in a similar mode: bluesy, mid-tempo, rough-edged, with nonsense syllables from the bass and background and a distinctive Clovers groove. It didn't matter who sang lead. When Buddy Bailey joined the army, Charlie White came over from the Dominoes and took the lead on **"Good Lovin'"** (1953) and **"Lovey Dovey"** (1954). Both climbed to #2. After White left the group, Billy Mitchell sang lead on **"Your Cash Ain't Nothin' But Trash"** (1954), written by Jesse Stone under his pen name, Charles Calhoun. Stone's witty lyrics challenge the Dominoes' "Money Honey": with a honkytonk piano and wailing sax, a series of scenarios throws doubt on the value of that lean green—until the ironic ending.

When Bailey came out of the army, he rejoined the Clovers to sing lead on two gorgeous ballads, **"Blue Velvet"** (1955), originally recorded by Tony Bennett, and **"Devil or Angel"** (1956). Both are better known by their pop covers, the one by Bobby Vinton (ugh), the other by Bobby Vee (not bad). But the Clovers produced the definitive doo wop versions. Taylor's ultra-mellow, super-sexy tenor sax accompanies Bailey's beautiful vocal on "Blue Velvet," the singer's lament for a lost love whose eyes match the color and texture of her clothing and the night. He sings it in retrospect through his tears with the background reduced to blow harmonies and Winley's bass taking the lead for a couple of bars. "Devil or Angel," with the singer caught in the classic doo wop not-knowing position, has more tempo, driven by piano triplets and a bell-like sound. The *doo doo doo doo* bassline returns with the background more fully engaged. "Devil or Angel" yearns with more energy than the sexier, moodier "Blue Velvet." Both love songs are superb.

The cultural capital of Black America, Harlem was ground zero for the emergence of doo wop with its Apollo Theater, on 125th Street, the make-it-or-break-it center of the universe for groups wanting the cachet of Black audiences' approval. Along with the Ravens, Dominoes, and original Drifters, more harmony groups came out of upper Manhattan than any other region in the country. One four-block stretch of 115th Street produced more successful groups than some entire cities: the Willows, Harptones, and Channels all originated there. Before them came **The Five Crowns**, who made some terrific records for labels so rare they have become collectors' items. How oddball was the group? All their original members sang tenor. The Orioles' valet managed them. In 1958, the Drifters' then-manager fired his entire group and hired the Crowns to be the new Drifters. By then, they had added tenor Benjamin Nelson, who soon changed his name to Ben E. King.[35]

Built around three Clark brothers, the Crowns first recorded **"You're My Inspiration"** (1952), a pretty ballad on the tiny Rainbow label with James "Papa" Clark singing lead. It became a minor regional hit, as popular a record as the group ever achieved. Changing labels to Old Town, they produced a double-sided jewel: the ballad **"You Could Be My Love"** b/w the rocker **"Good Luck Darlin'"** (1953). Wilbur

"Yonkie" Paul sings lead on both. I have trouble making sense of their lyrics, but doo wop's sound and feeling frequently trump words and logic. What does the singer mean by the title of the ballad? "You *could* be my love"—*if you wanted to* seems to be the sentiment. But in one verse he sings that she could be his love *if she'd only try harder*. She walked in and then out of his life. So maybe *he* should have tried harder. Nice harmonies, a subtle sax, and Paul's passionate styling override the somewhat nonsensical lyrics. Ditto for "Good Luck Darlin'." Driven by a hot boogie woogie piano and *doot doot dootin'* harmonies, she's on her way and he wishes her luck. He loves her and hopes she loves him. But in another verse *he's* going away after she took all his money. The sax roars through the break while the background goes *bop bop bop bop bop be-da*. Simply fine rock 'n' roll.

Some other young men, singing on the same 115th Street corners in 1951, eventually became **The Harptones**. The key members were lead tenor **Willie Winfield** (1929–2021), a native Virginian and cousin of the Five Keys' Dickie Smith; second lead Nicky Clark, one of the Five Crowns' Clark brothers; and bass Billy Brown. Pianist/arranger Raoul Cita sometimes sang with them. Their exquisite sound and Winfield's divine lead made them the "most beloved" New York R&B group of the 1950s. The Harptones recorded three of the most profoundly beautiful doo wop ballads

The Harptones, 1954. From left: William Dempsy, Billy Brown, Nicky Clark, Dicey Galloway, Willie Winfield, Raoul Cita. Pictorial Press Ltd./Alamy Stock Photo.

ever. Yet despite being heroes in New York and a few other east coast cities with the help and promotion of Alan Freed, they never scored a single record on the *Billboard* charts, victimized by poor distribution from their small independent labels.[36]

After an amateur night win at the Apollo in 1953, the Harptones signed with local Bruce Records, whose first release was their **"A Sunday Kind of Love"** (1953). Co-written by Louis Prima in 1946, the ballad became one of the top doo wop group favorites (along with "Over the Rainbow" and "Gloria"). The Harptones' version got less than high-end recording along with lousy distribution. Critics cite its crude sound quality. One claims that during the "corny organ" intro, "a bottle can clearly be heard shattering on the studio floor." I can't hear that bottle, and I like the churchy dimension the organ gives Sunday love. I stand with Jay Warner: "From the eerie organ intro to the group's deep harmony to Willie's velvety vocalizing, 'A Sunday Kind of Love' was a classic."[37]

Al Caiola's guitar and a bass dominate the quiet instrumental accompaniment—none of the usual piano or sax, and the organ soon fades away. Raoul Cita wrote the introductory quatrain, sung by bass Billy Brown with background harmonies, indicating that the singer is on the rebound, wondering if his new lover could be you. That complicates the song's meaning. Its original meditative lyrics do not address *you* but suggest a person thinking aloud, systematically defining his ideal love. Winfield slowly sings the opening line *a cappella*, as if in the silence of his room or his mind. He goes on in hushed tones, backed with beautiful harmonies. The entire group sings the bridge. Brown intones the final words in his deepest bass, connoting an earthy quality to this sublime musical fantasy—a Saturday night *and* Sunday kind of love.

A Cita composition as divine as "Sunday Kind of Love," graced with intelligent lyrics and a simple, gentle melody, **"My Memories of You"** (1954) re-uses the organ and single-string guitar style to accompany the distressed lover's plea. He wonders what he did to lose her, consoles himself with memories, pleads with her, and admits to himself that maybe he let his heart rule his head. Following Winfield's *a cappella* intro, the song proceeds in five-part harmony, each verse sung in chorus with Winfield's silky voice out front. He takes the refrains solo. The final thirty seconds reprise his intro followed by a gorgeous harmonic outro. Doo wop magic.

Cita also wrote the Harptones' third classic, **"Life Is But a Dream"** (1955). By this time they had left Bruce Records for Old Town, which released the song on its Paradise label. The group should have learned from the Five Crowns' experience that Old Town's distribution wouldn't get them national exposure. That none of these three superb ballads even dented the R&B charts seems astonishing. "Life Is But a Dream" has a fuller sound than their previous work, accompanied by Sam Kimble blowing sexy sax and Ram Ramirez on organ. "The song has since become a street-corner classic," Warner notes, "and the solo singer's opening line … has become a measuring stick for group leads."[38] It got a second life when featured on the *Goodfellas* soundtrack. The song utilizes the fully harmonized lead sparingly but effectively, and Winfield is in brilliant voice. Listen to that intro and the way he ends the outro on a lengthy falsetto note. Though primarily a love song, it speaks to many of the themes that underlie African American music of the postwar era:

resilience, resolution, and a fundamental, openhearted optimism. You can live the dream. Make of it whatever you will. Give it a try. But releasing the record just two months before the brutal murder of Emmett Till gave the lyrics a chilling irony that may have dampened the song's popularity.

The Five Willows formed in the same Harlem neighborhood in 1952. Twins Ralph and Joe Martin sang second tenor and baritone. Original member Bobby Robinson owned Bobby's Record Shop on 125th Street. It became an audition center for local artists, especially after Robinson founded R&B and doo wop labels Red Robin in 1952, Whirlin' Disc and Fury in 1956. The Five Willows released several records in 1953–54 that went nowhere. But after switching to the obscure Melba label and changing their name to **The Willows**, they scored with the joyful rocker **"Church Bells May Ring"** (1956), written by lead tenor Tony Middleton and the group. The record reached #11 R&B and crossed over to #62 Pop until a cover by the Diamonds (#14) overwhelmed it. Wedding and chapel bells show up frequently in doo wop songs, and this is one of the best. It offers just the tantalizing *possibility* of a wedding—church bells *may* ring—against a background of vocalized bells: *ling a-ling a-ling ding dong*. The record, Groia writes, "had all the ingredients of a fifties smash: the five-part harmony, the surging beat, the talking bass break, the fade-away ending and Tony's rough and ready lead." The song opens in harmony until Middleton's rousing lead takes over. The group's regular bass missed the session so Richard Simon, a neighbor, performed the talking bass part in the second bridge. A young Neil Sedaka played the chimes.[39]

The east coast had no monopoly on early-'50s harmony groups. Hailing from Gary, Indiana, **The Spaniels** delivered one of the best and most enduring late-night doo wop anthems. The first group to sign with Gary DJ Vivian Carter's new Vee-Jay Records, which soon relocated to Chicago, they got together in high school in 1952, led by tenor James **"Pookie" Hudson** (1934–2007). The Spaniels' initial release, Hudson's composition **"Baby It's You"** (1953), reached #10 R&B so Vee-Jay licensed it to Chance Records to get wider distribution. A pretty ballad with conventional lyrics, the record features a bassy piano riff (borrowed from Shirley & Lee's "I'm Gone") with bass Gerald Gregory's *doo doo doos* alongside it in the bridge, a soaring falsetto background from tenors Ernest Warren and Willie C. Jackson, and Hudson's high, quavering lead. "Gregory was outstanding because his bass singing actually sounded like an instrument, and Pookie had that great quiver in his voice," Vivian Carter observed. "And the Spaniels were the first group I remember who had two falsetto voices on top."[40]

Hudson also wrote the Spaniels' most memorable song. **"Goodnite Sweetheart, Goodnite"** (1954) made it only to #5 R&B but crossed over to #24 Pop, was played near the end of every dance and party in the 1950s and early '60s, and later featured in *American Graffiti*. It's time to go and parting is such sweet sorrow. Gregory's booming bass riff gives the song gravitas. Hudson's keening vocal manages to encompass both the trepidation of the teenage boy fearing his girlfriend's parents' anger if he gets her home too late, and the aching lover who just wants to devour her and be devoured in return. Listen to that first bridge: at three in the morning, likely way past her curfew already, he *hates* to leave her, it's really messing him up. This beautiful song captured accurately, for one of the first times in popular music, the emotional turmoil of 1950s adolescence and pre-sexual-revolution early adulthood.

With only Hudson and Gregory remaining from the original group the Spaniels' best song never charted. But as Robert Pruter notes, **"You Gave Me Peace of Mind"** (1956) "was a superb exhibit of the vocal talents of the new group of background singers," as well as Hudson's "heartfelt lead."[41] It has the Spaniels' best lyrics, too. The title refers not to the singer's relief from the jealousy or suspicion that so often taints R&B relationships. Rather, the second verse explains, the singer prays to God to end our evils ways (crime? racial violence? segregation?), and he gains relief in his lover's embrace. The solemnity of Hudson's vocal as well as the references to prayer, God, and a wandering light in the sky give the song a religious tone. The very slow tempo, an emphatic drumbeat, and the almost ecstatic *aahh aahh* background reinforce it. This love is blessed. The moody sax break reminds us that we remain in rhythm & bluesland, but the harmonics that close the song offer the vocal equivalent of *Amen*.

Exquisite harmonies characterize a Chicago group that shared the Chance label with the Spaniels for a while. Two of its members, originally from Baltimore, had been Sonny Til's neighbors. Jay Warner considers **The Flamingos** the best vocal group in history. Their unique harmonies stemmed from the core of the group. Cousins John Carter (first tenor) and Paul Wilson (baritone) and cousins Zeke Carey (second tenor) and Jake Carey (bass) were so-called Black Jews. They sang together in Chicago's Church of God and Saints of Christ. Their hybrid worship combined elements of Pentecostalism, Black nationalism, and Judaism. As lead Nate Nelson explained, "Our harmonies were different because we dealt with a lot of minor chords, which is how Jewish music is written."[42]

The group formed in 1952, singing on street corners, then clubs, and signed with Chance. Sollie McElroy, who preceded Nate Nelson, sang lead on both the ballad **"Golden Teardrops"** (1953) and the up-tempo **"Jump Children"** (1954). Doo wop critics often cite "Golden Teardrops" as a masterpiece: "Carter's surreal high falsetto hovered over McElroy's forlorn low tenor to achieve one of the most haunting sounds in the annals of black harmony." I'm not a big fan of the record—nor was Zeke Carey, who thought the vocals completely drowned out the music. The melody seems awkward, and McElroy sometimes strains to stay on key. Of all McElroy's leads I prefer the dance tune "Jump Children" with its blasting horns and riffing *voit-voit voy baba doobee* background. It has some nice falsetto accents, a judicious use of the bass, and an entire bridge of McElroy's scatting plus a screaming sax break. His baby has left him crying but he'll send her off with a great party. Her loss. For years, the group made it their closing number at live performances with wild choreography by Paul Wilson. It appears in Alan Freed's 1959 movie *Go Johnny Go!* with Nate Nelson singing lead, incredible dancing, and a chorus of *rock, rock and roll*: https://www.youtube.com/watch?v=SUEunq3jihE.⁴³

Nate Nelson (1932–84) replaced McElroy in 1954 as the group cycled through record labels, leaving Chance for Parrot, then moving to Checker, which released **"I'll Be Home"** (1955), the Nelson-led Flamingos' first great ballad. It reached #5 R&B, the group's biggest hit until their iconic "I Only Have Eyes for You" (1959). For Todd Baptista, Nelson's "echo-drenched lead, reportedly captured inadvertently through a triple feedback process, brimmed with an ideal blend of romanticism, skill, and raw emotion."⁴⁴ In the song, framed as a letter home from a soldier or sailor, the singer asks his lover to wait for him. The echo-effect suggests he's rehearsing the sentiments aloud. Quiet four-part harmonies and a spoken bridge by Paul Wilson accompany Nelson's passionate appeal. The even better **"A Kiss from Your Lips"** (1956) has clearer sound, piano triplets, and extremely beautiful high harmonies. Nelson celebrates the precious kiss that changed his life. He can't help the hyperbole: the million years he has loved and the thousands of lips he has kissed meant nothing until he kissed her. *Gee*, he sings, acknowledging how blessed he feels, invoking teen innocence along with the religious sense of blessedness. Young love and gospel faith continually proved a winning combination in doo wop ballads.

The most assertive of these ballads, **"The Vow"** (1956), finds Nelson in his best voice with piano triplets leading the way again and enthusiastic background harmonies. The song employs half a spoken bridge with a second voice echoing each of Nelson's sung lines. The lyrics continue the Flamingos' fervent, idealized approach to romance. The singer believes in the immortality of love and the incomparability of theirs. He vows to love her alone, always. Nelson's compelling vocals keep the sentiment from feeling corny. To the teenage brain this sounded like gospel truth.

We end this section with a gorgeous ballad from an obscure group that made only one record, personnel unknown. At least three **Blue Jays** groups recorded doo wop in the 1950s and '60s. The best known, from Los Angeles, cut their first and finest record, "Lover's Island," in 1961. Our Blue Jays hailed from Chicago. Their sole release on Checker, **"White Cliffs of Dover"** (1953), covered Vera Lynn's Second World War classic, a doo wop favorite. Fifteen different groups recorded it.⁴⁵ Here, accompanied by Gene Ammons' beautifully muted sax and an organ, the lead sings entirely in falsetto with the background offering quiet *bah bah doo wah* harmonies. Lynn's 1942 original helped rally Britons during the dark days of the Battle of Britain. The song promises that bluebirds will again fly over those cliffs where, at the time, the Luftwaffe flew. It looks forward to a bright tomorrow of love, laughter, innocence, and peace. These Blue Jays do justice to those bluebirds. The transposition of the song to 1953 America makes good sense as the U.S. transitioned out of the Korean War. I like to imagine a broader meaning for its African American performers and audience: that the dream of full citizenship and equality could have a radically ideal awakening, a happy, victorious ending. Listen to another great 1953 version, a swinging up-tempo jump arrangement by the Checkers with bass Bill Brown, originally of the Dominoes, singing lead and Red Prysock on tenor sax.

1954: *The Revolution Will Not (Yet) Be Televised*

Billboard's lead article on April 24, 1954, read,

> Rhythm and blues records, once limited in sales appeal to the relatively small Negro market, has blossomed into one of the fastest growing areas of the entire record business. ... The growing popularity of this music is further reflected in its wide use by disk jockeys and juke box operators. ... Teen-agers have spearheaded the current swing to r&b, and are largely responsible for keeping its sales mounting.

In other words, white kids were buying Black records and listening to Black music on juke boxes and the more than 700 radio shows nationwide that, *Billboard* reported, "devote their air time exclusively to rhythm and blues recordings." Doo wop would play a big part in this revolution that would create rock 'n' roll and put the fear of rebellion, miscegenation, and colorblindness into parents and racists of all kinds. It was, at first, almost entirely an aural revolution. The Chords sang "Sh-Boom" on TV's Colgate Comedy Hour that summer, but television wouldn't begin regularly featuring R&B or rock 'n' roll acts for another year or two.

As more and more live performances became integrated, doo wop led the crossover. In 1953–54, Alan Freed produced a series of Rhythm & Blues Shows, primarily in Cleveland, that included the Clovers, Dominoes, Drifters, Harptones, Moonglows, Five Keys, and Spaniels. White kids made up an estimated twenty percent of his audiences. Without question, the breakthroughs of 1954 transcended doo wop. On May 17, the United States Supreme Court's *Brown v. Board of Education* decision ruled "separate but equal" schools for Black children unconstitutional. In June, a *Life* magazine article called "The Luckiest Generation" referenced the 16–20 age group, the same demographic the *Billboard* article featured. *Life*'s luckiest generation appeared not to include any people of color.[46] Nevertheless, the walls of segregation in education, music, and perhaps luck were coming down. Over the next few months, along with the Spaniels' "Goodnite Sweetheart, Goodnite" and the Drifters' "Honey Love," six more doo wop hits crossed over, prying open the door between R&B and Pop, scoring on both charts. Let's have a look at the other groups that proved most popular on both sides of music's dissolving racial border in 1954.

Harlem's **The Crows** scored with **"Gee"** (1954), a catchy jump tune that made history as "the first 'reverse crossover' rhythm and blues hit," rising on the Pop chart to #14 *before* charting R&B (#2). Winners of a competition at the Apollo, the Crows signed with George Goldner's new Rama label. Goldner produced great doo wop on multiple New York labels including Rama, Gee, Gone, and End. Reportedly written in less than ten minutes by Crows' baritone Bill Davis, "Gee" was the B-side of their first Rama release, **"I Love You So,"** a pretty ballad despite its banal lyrics, with Sonny Norton singing lead. Goldner's far superior girl group, the Chantels, would later have a minor hit with "I Love You So." Besides bass Gerald Hamilton's flat lead in the bridge, its *doo-it doo-ee-oo* and *boom boom boom* background stands out on the Crows' version. The heart and soul of "Gee," nonsense syllables would prove a popular component of most doo wop crossover hits from 1954 on. As Norton repeats the innocent teen expletive *gee*, the chorus "adds steroids to its message about the pleasures of hugging and squeezing and kissing with some aggressive *doot-doot-doots*...."⁴⁷ No secret teenage code for sex, the background riffs complement Norton's transformation of ordinary words into their component syllables. Sexually inexplicit but infectious and energizing, the song sparks joy and you could dance to it. A definite winner.

One-hit wonders from the Bronx, **The Chords**, like the Crows, had a B-side as their one hit. But what a hit. Led by tenor Carl Feaster, the Chords had their own pianist, Rupert Branker, who would later play with the Platters. The group auditioned for Atlantic Records with the "strange, jazzy, swingin' concoction" they had jointly written, full of tight harmonies, a variety of nonsense syllables, and an optimistic key line that proposes the possibility of a dream life, counterpointed by an exclamation resembling the sound of a detonating bomb: *Sh-boom!* Because white Southern teenagers called R&B *cat music*, Atlantic had created a new label, Cat, and signed the Chords to it. The b-side of their first record, an R&B cover of Patti Page's pop hit "Cross Over the Bridge," took off. Arranged by Jesse Stone, **"Sh-Boom"** (1954) charted for fifteen weeks R&B, reaching #3. More significantly, it peaked at #9 Pop, the first R&B or doo wop record to break into the pop top ten in the 1950s.⁴⁸

The bouncy, upbeat rhythm, playful innocence, and sunny '50s optimism of "Sh-Boom" made its crossover, like that of "Gee," less threatening than the more sexually oriented R&B tunes. The intro showcases its complex harmonies, and Feaster's joyful lead is seductive. Dawson & Propes argue that when bass Ricky Edwards sings the bridge, he "skips the nonsense and gets to the nitty gritty." He looks at her and gets something on his mind; if she does what he wants, all will be fine. But for me the song's real nitty gritty resides in its romantic, non-sexual proposition, the 1950s American Dream of spiritually blessed, monogamous true love: Tell me I'm your only love and I'll spend my life with you.

But as I have been arguing, African American popular songs of the era take a complicated, multivalent approach to the notion that life could be a dream. Here, the song's breezy romantic optimism comes up against a repeated onomatopoeic exclamation that might have derived from Cold War paranoia: the fear of nuclear nightmare in the context of Russian and American H-bomb tests. According to Marv Goldberg, Chords first tenor Jimmy Keyes claimed that the group developed the "sound like a bomb: 'shhhhhh-BOOM'" from *boom*, a slang term that all the local kids were using—the contemporary anxieties of the American psyche replicated in a doo wop anthem.⁴⁹

The Chords' "Sh-Boom" had many things going for it, including first-class orchestration with Mickey Baker on guitar and Sam "The Man" Taylor's dynamite tenor solo. Commercially, though, a white Canadian group, the Crew-Cuts, robbed them with a cover that spent nine weeks at #1 pop. This was not the first or last such theft. Remember Georgia Gibbs's cover of Etta James's "The Wallflower." Pat Boone bumped the Flamingos' "I'll Be Home" from the charts. But the Crew-Cuts' transformation of "Sh-Boom" was particularly egregious to James Miller, who hears a tympani, "sounding like a giant trampoline making an elephant airborne. Combined with the group's glee-club harmonies, the arrangement took the off-hand whimsy of the original and turned it into a piece of surreal kitsch."[50]

Covering records most often meant a white pop or country & western copy of a Black rhythm & blues release: another way the world ripped off the talents of African American musical artists. Often short-changed by their usually white label owners, Black R&B artists got screwed by nearly everyone, Black-owned Duke/Peacock and Vee-Jay Records just as notoriously. And covering worked in more than one direction. Black artists would replicate white hits—the Chords covering Patti Page, for example—though the resources and reach of the R&B labels and the restricted radio play of Black music in the 1950s made it hard for them to compete. As well, R&B groups would frequently cover one another's hot songs. Take the case of **"Hearts of Stone"** (1954). **The Jewels** wrote and originally recorded the song on L.A.'s tiny R&B label. Cincinnati's **The Charms** redid it almost identically on King's DeLuxe affiliate and released it a week later. With much wider distribution, the Charms version spent nine weeks at #1 R&B and climbed to #15 Pop—until a cover by the white Fontane Sisters went to #1 Pop, knocking the Charms off that chart. The Jewels version never charted anywhere.[51]

The Charms' "Hearts of Stone" almost exactly replicates the Jewels'. They have identical lyrics. Identical—*dooda wadda dooda wadda doo*—backgrounds. Virtually note-for-note sax breaks in each. Both versions sing the same one-syllable words as two syllables. The Charms' record boasts better sound quality, and Charms lead singer Otis Williams has a marginally stronger voice than songwriter Rudy Jackson, the Jewels' lead. But both terrific records rock. The impersonal lyrics differ from the usual doo wop love lament. The singer complains not about his particular lover but about hearts of stone. They take and take and give you pain but never break. Ask them for a little vulnerability and they answer *no*: fourteen times. That repetition in the channel gives the song its uniqueness. I favor Jackson's articulation as he pronounces it something like *naw*. In either case you can hear a precursor of James Brown's technique of sheer over-repetition that could drive an audience crazy and raise a word or idea to another level.

If "Gee" and "Sh-Boom" represented doo wop innocence, **"Work with Me Annie"** (1954) was the dreaded bogeyman of illicit sex, leaving the ghetto to stalk the streets and pollute the youth of white America with its *leer-ics*. Blame Detroit's **The Royals**. All its members worked on the assembly lines at Ford and Chrysler until Johnny Otis recruited them for King Records' Federal label. Their first session premiered Otis' beautiful composition, **"Every Beat of My Heart"** (1952), later sung to perfection by Gladys Knight and the Pips (1961). Baritone Charles Sutton's Ink Spots–style crooning lead makes the Royals' otherwise sweet pressing sound old-fashioned.

Nothing was old-fashioned about the new lead singer the group soon picked up. He sang gospel while growing up in Alabama, loved up-tempo blues, idolized Clyde McPhatter and Gene Autry, and was willing, in Dawson & Propes' words, to "sing dirty." **Hank Ballard** (1936–2003) changed the direction of the Royals with both his writing and singing style. With Federal's A&R man, Ralph Bass, he wrote "Work with Me Annie"—"a pretty unambiguous tune," says Ed Ward, "with lyrics that did not seem to indicate that Ballard needed help around the office." It spent 26 weeks on the R&B chart, seven at #1, and reached #22 Pop. Ballard's follow-up, his "lust-filled" **"Sexy Ways"** (1954), charted for another 17 weeks and peaked at #2 R&B. "Work with Me Annie" launched no fewer than 21 sequels and response songs. In the midst of all the excitement around its success, the Royals got into a legal tangle because of confusion with the "5" Royales and changed their name to **The Midnighters**. Federal released "Work with Me, Annie" in March by the Royals, then again in April by the Midnighters.[52]

For Marv Goldberg, "Work with Me Annie" "probably had more to do with introducing white teenagers to R&B than any other song: It had a simple, primitive, driving gospel-blues beat. It was 'dirty.' It was fun. It was raw, earthy R&B." After the guitar intro, Ballard opens with a squeal: *Oooh!* Like "Gee," it talks about hugging and squeezing, but this song needs no nudging or winking for the audience to get it. (**"Get It"** [1953], the first song Ballard wrote and sang with the group, had nine weeks in the Top Ten.) The title phrase, repeated multiple times, highlights the transparent euphemism of *work*, especially when Ballard implores Annie to give him her meat. The background reinforces the message, riffing *ahh-oom*, which sounds a lot like *mmmm*. "Work with Me, Annie" along with "Sexy Ways" set off a firestorm of protest and censorship. "The problem was that white kids were listening to these things for the first time," Ralph Bass explained. "It was all right as long as [only] blacks were listening." The Annie phenomenon would die down within a year. But Ballard and the Royals/Midnighters' recording portended more than its notoriety, according to Dawson & Propes:

> With Arthur Porter's driving electric guitar (predating Chuck Berry by a year), Alonza Tucker's throbbing electrified bass (one of its first appearances on a recording), Sonny Thompson's boogie piano and the group's vocal "ahh-oom" riffs pushing Hank Ballard's excited squeals through the seduction, "Work with Me, Annie" defined the coming rock 'n' roll sound.[53]

Alan Freed played a major role in defining the coming rock 'n' roll sound in 1954, and helped make **The Moonglows** one of the era's dominant doo wop groups. Tenor **Bobby Lester** (1930–80) and baritone **Harvey Fuqua** (1929–2010) began singing together in Louisville in 1949. After moving to Cleveland, Fuqua recruited the rest of the group and local DJ Freed became their manager. They first recorded on Freed's Champagne label, then signed with Chicago's Chance. Freed gave the group exposure through his Rhythm & Blues and Rock 'n' Roll shows, and his 1956 movie *Rock, Rock, Rock* (also featuring the Flamingos), and he took co-writing credits on most of their songs. Even before the hits began appearing, you can hear the elements that make Moonglows records model doo wop.

Listen to their cover of the Doris Day ballad **"Secret Love"** b/w Fuqua's jump tune **"Real Gone Mama"** (1954). "Secret Love" had been a #1 pop hit for Day in 1953, and both the Orioles and Moonglows rushed to cover its dramatic lyrics. Sublime doo wop, the Moonglow's version spotlights a passionate lead by Lester and an exquisite arrangement. It opens with bass Prentiss Barnes' *doh doh doh* followed by the group's harmonized intro, dominated by a beautiful falsetto, segueing into Lester's lead. Each time Lester sings the title phrase in the verse, Barnes responds with a basso *yeah*. Singing "Real Gone Mama," Fuqua shows some vocal chops of his own. A rollicking ode to a series of different-colored mamas who really know the score, it features Fuqua's squealing, a *wop bah doo* background, jazzy drums, and Red Holloway's tenor sax that honks and squawks through the lengthy instrumental break accompanied by general raucousness.[54]

As both Freed and the Moonglows rose in prominence, the group left Chance for Chess in late 1954. Their first Chess release, Fuqua's **"Sincerely"** (1955), proved their biggest hit. It spent twenty weeks on the R&B chart, two at #1, and reached #20 Pop—until the McGuire Sisters' lame #1 Pop cover annihilated it. The spectacular arrangement begins with a thirty second intro: "the warbling of Barnes' classic bass riff, 'bah, bah, bah-doh,' followed after a few bars with a layered-on separate riff sung by tenor [Pete] Graves and baritone Fuqua." The subtly ringing guitar of Billy Johnson, who joined the Moonglows when they joined Chess, adds another sweet musical voice to the mix. The group came to be known as masters of blow harmony. Listen to the background's hypnotic *ooh ooh-bee-ooh vooit vooit*.[55] Lester sings of how sincerely he loves her. He desperately pleads with her to be his. In the highly dramatic bridge he invokes God. Then he insists with a tear in his voice that he won't let her go, *ever*, even though she doesn't want him. Sincere or not, the passionate lover's compulsive possessiveness can be slightly creepy.

"Most of All" (1955), another beautiful doo wop ballad written by Fuqua and led by Lester, reached #5 R&B. "Barnes opens the song with a descending bass that introduces Lester's emotional lead, which gets fantastic support with stop-time falsetto-edged chorusing by the group."[56] In Lester's most passionate vocal he sings of how he dreams of her and misses her caresses and kisses. Despite these conventional doo wop sentiments, Fuqua put the lyrics together with restraint and Lester avoids self-pity, frustration, and sentimentality. Most of all he needs her. Each verse opens with the Moonglows' now-classic bass intro (*doh doh doh*) and the song ends on their classic *ooh-wah* harmony. Not just falsetto-*edged*, the choruses are dominated by Pete Graves's soaring falsetto. The beautiful blow harmonies behind the verses sound like *wha ha ha hoo*. Piano triplets ramp up the drama in the bridge, both bass and falsetto echo the lyrics, and the background harmonizes on the syllables *doo wop*, almost as if to say, This is *the* classic doo wop ballad.

The Moonglows would hit the pop charts again with up-tempo **"See Saw"** (1956) and Harvey & the Moonglows' "Ten Commandments of Love" (1958). But their exquisite **"In My Diary"** (1955) never charted. The group changed the formula for this ballad. They dropped the bass intro and *ooh-wah* outro and increased the tempo. Lester and Graves trade leads in this strangely oblique love song with a superb arrangement and harmonies and intelligent, off-kilter lyrics. The singer tells his lover that he'll write in his diary about the moon, the night, and—almost an afterthought—her charms. He says he'll write about her so he won't forget. Is she so forgettable that he wouldn't otherwise remember her? He wants to make the world understand. But the privacy of a diary, not for publication, seems a strange way to let the world know how he feels about her. In any case the Moonglows paint a gorgeous picture with sounds as well as words. Lester is in fine voice, as always, and Graves launches the title line into falsetto each time he takes over. The background caresses the leads with beautiful harmonies, and Barnes subtly uses his descending *doh doh doh doh*, reinforcing the excellent rhythm section while a tinkling piano adds jazzy sophistication to the whole affair. Doo wop at its finest from the Moonglows.

One of the most familiar doo wops appeared at the end of musically momentous 1954. L.A.'s Dootone label, known at the time for its raunchy Redd Foxx comedy records, released **"Earth Angel"** (1954) by **The Penguins**, four Los Angeles high school grads. The Penguins' strange, sad story involves squabbles, mismanagement, lawsuits, and personal bankruptcy, despite their record reaching #1 R&B and #8 Pop (even after the Crew-Cuts covered it), and eventually selling over ten million copies. Written by the group's baritone/bass, Curtis Williams, literally recorded in a garage and unfinished—the released record was intended as a demo—"Earth Angel" and its A-side, **"Hey Senorita,"** remain fresh, tuneful representations of the doo wop explosion that popular music was experiencing.[57]

Like "Gee" and "Sh-Boom," "Earth Angel" was originally a B-side. Indie label owners and producers didn't always have their fingers on the pulse of the record-buying public. But remember the volatile nature of this cultural moment with musical tastes changing rapidly across racial and demographic lines. And in this case the terrifically upbeat "Hey Senorita" occupied the A-side, a jumpin' dance tune with a Latin beat. Songwriter Williams plays piano and sings lead. Accompanied by bongos and hand-claps, Williams asks his little senorita to let him take her home. By the end she seems willing.

But the people wanted to hear "Earth Angel." Cleve Duncan sings lead in his sweet high tenor, passing it over to Dexter Tisby for the second bridge. Williams adds bass *doo doo doo doos*, and Duncan throws in some tasty, subtle falsetto behind Tisby's lead. Pianist Williams plays those familiar ice cream changes alongside a heavy bass and drumbeat. The background helps keep the temperature up, regularly adding a melancholy wail to their blow harmonies: *ooh ooh-ooh ooh WAH-oh-oh ooh ooh-ooh ooh*. The lyrics present the singer as an absolute fool for love, a mere mortal pursuing and consumed by divinity. He adores her forever, this vision. He prays that she'll reciprocate but wonders if she will. Greil Marcus hears in "Earth Angel" "an awareness of how perfect life could be and an awareness that as soon as you formed the image of perfection it would disappear. The only way to make it last was to turn it into a song."[58] This is another way of saying that life *could* be a dream. Even if it can't be realized on this fallen earth, we can glimpse the angelic, the ideal, for two or three lyrical minutes in a great song.

More from '54

These next four groups didn't cross over in 1954. But they produced high-quality doo wop alongside the big sellers. **The Cadillacs**, a Harlem street corner group featuring tenor lead **Earl Carroll** (1937–2012), proved as classy as their name with a single as worshipful and transcendent as "Earth Angel." Their manager, Esther Navarro, wrote their best songs and sent the group to Cholly Atkins, who would gain fame as Motown's choreographer-in-chief. Atkins developed and polished the Cadillacs' elaborate stage presentation, helping make them the mid-'50s' top live doo wop act.

Although it never charted, the magnificent **"Gloria"** (1954), their first recording for New York's Josie Records, became "the measure by which every East Coast would-be doo wop group for the next 30 years would judge their harmonizing abilities."[59] With a tinkling piano the only audible instrument, the song has an *a cappella* quality, underlined by Carroll's solo opening. Bobby Phillips' bass *doh doh doh*'s and the background's rich blow harmonies add texture to Carroll's highly emotional vocal, sung with more vibrato than any other doo wop I know. The very slow tempo, slight echo effect, and prayerful cry give the song a religious feeling, as if it were part of a church service. Latin for glory, *gloria* appears in much of the Christian liturgy. Another signal characteristic is Carroll's soaring falsetto when he names the women who are not his beloved. The simple lyrics place the singer in the position of the classically longing, unrequited doo wop lover. Certain in the verse that Gloria does not love him, he thinks in the bridge that she *may*. But how would he ever know? He embodies the '50s male teenager in all his vulnerable, self-deprecating romantic confusion.

Carroll changed personas for the Cadillacs' most commercially successful song, the exhilarating up-tempo **"Speedoo"** (1955), which climbed to #3 R&B and #17 Pop early in 1956. "This recording had everything," Groia declares, "the bass beginning, followed by the vocal background, followed by the lead singer in a vocal pattern which was very similar to the African chant where vocal syncopation overlapped a leading melody or voice."[60] With the background's *bop ba doo-did-it* chugging along, Carroll sings about his nickname, Speedoo. He never goes slow. Just listen to Jesse Powell's zippy sax solo. A fast mover when it comes to pretty women, Speedoo has a specialty: taking other folkses' girls. *Mmm hmm*, he hums with self-satisfaction, although the overall tone of the song avoids boastfulness. He appears matter-of-fact about everything, including his repeated insistence that his real name is Mr. Earl. Not Earl but *Mr.* Earl. Recorded in the fall of 1955, between Emmett Till's funeral and the Montgomery, Alabama, bus boycott, "Speedoo" is a reminder that, up in Harlem, too, Black people were demanding their R-E-S-P-E-C-T.

Another Harlem quartet, **The Solitaires,** teens who had all formerly played with other groups, recorded for Old Town Records. In 1954, their second session birthed a beautiful ballad, **"I Don't Stand a Ghost of a Chance"** (1954). Old Town's Sam Weiss said of the Solitaires, "Fans used to talk of them as a solid New York group. That was high praise. It had something to do with a feeling they seemed to communicate of being lonely and down-hearted in a big city like New York...." Second tenor Bobby Williams arranged, sang lead, and played piano on what had been a Five Keys song, while tenor Herman Dunham (aka Herman Curtis) provided "the ghostly falsetto."[61] The song has a haunted, lonesome quality. Listen to Dunham's fifteen-second intro of the title line in his stratospheric falsetto. Williams' lead follows in a similar vein, backed by blow harmonies. Another of those vulnerable, self-deprecating doo wop boys, the singer confesses in the verse that he doesn't stand a chance with her. Then, in the even slower stop-time channel, he changes tactics, offering himself as her ideal lover if she would just try a couple of kisses. But returning to the verse, the harmonizing background insists that he must be dreaming. Dunham reprises the opening line in a twenty-second falsetto outro.

Like nearly all the great doo wop groups, the Solitaires could sing slow or fast songs. Recorded at the tail end of 1956, their **"Walking Along"** was another New York hit that never cracked the national charts. The group's personnel had changed to feature a new lead, Milton Love, and a new bass, Freddy Barksdale. Propelled by the percussion of stamping feet and Barksdale's bass *boom ba boom boom*, Love sounds like he's marching or skipping along rather than walking. Feeling merry, he joyfully sings about this happy day, *whoa whoa whoa whoa*, because the one he loves loves him back. The screaming tenor sax solo (likely Sam "The Man" Taylor) makes you want to *move*. If life were a dream, this could be its anthem.

In *The Heart of Rock & Soul: The 1001 Greatest Singles Ever Made*, rock critic Dave Marsh doesn't give a lot of love to doo wop songs pre–1957. In fact, only one makes his top 100: **"The Wind"** (1954) by Detroit's **Nolan Strong and the Diablos**. Written jointly by the group, the song appeared on Detroit's Fortune label. A local hit, it never charted, likely due to the label's lack of distributive muscle. "The Wind" has the same slow, stately, ethereal quality as "I Don't Stand a Ghost of a Chance." With the background chanting, Strong sings in a high tenor of the wind bringing memories and dreams of his lost love back to him. Born in Alabama, he had "one of the most sensitive and beautiful falsetto voices ever," according to Jay Warner, who calls "The Wind" "the eeriest of '50s vocal group records...." Heavily influenced by Clyde McPhatter, Strong himself influenced Smokey Robinson. And in the spoken bridge he sounds remarkably like Michael Jackson. Marsh has a funny way of complimenting a song. With "the bass chanting 'Wind, wind' underneath the corniest recitation you've ever heard Strong speaks in a surreally wimpy voice that nevertheless possesses a certain kind of power."[62] Spoken bridges sound corny most of the time. Here it's just a curiosity. The record's otherworldly quality saves the day. Laura Nyro and Labelle recorded a beautiful cover version on Nyro's 1971 album, *Gonna Take a Miracle*.

Let's dance out of the very good year 1954 with an obscure, rip-roarin', fast and witty doo wop, written and produced by Jerry Leiber and Mike Stoller for their short-lived L.A. label, Spark. Hailing from the Bay area, the **Honey Bears** recorded the high-tempo 12-bar blues **"One Bad Stud"** (1954), one of the earliest of what Leiber and Stoller called their *playlets*: "a kind of three-minute audio drama with music."[63] Against the background's propulsive *doot doo wha, doot doot doo wha*, the lead singer describes the big bad stud who moved into his 'hood and hangs out on the corner, fat and barefoot. He loves good whiskey and looks like a bear. And if he likes your baby, he will have her. Uh oh, guess whose baby posted his bail when he got thrown in jail. The singer expresses his obsession with this problem guy in the chorus, repeating the title phrase over and over as the background echoes it. He can't get Mr. Bad Stud out of his head. Not even the sax man's rockin' solo can exorcise him.

A Rare Species: Women in Doo Wop

I'm almost embarrassed to include this as a sub-category, but as noted earlier, female doo wop before 1957 was scarce. "Women in groups," Gribin & Schiff shrug, "virtually disappear from the Rhythm & Blues charts for just about six years," 1948–54. None of the earlier women in groups they reference sang doo wop, and most were white (Savannah Churchill, the Andrews Sisters). Women singing lead with male groups made the R&B chart three times during that period, Ella Fitzgerald twice and Little Esther with the Robins ("Double Crossing Blues"). It would be a stretch to call even the latter song doo wop. But never mind the charts. Women in African American secular harmony groups, 1946–56, were simply the rarest of breeds. Why? Gribin & Schiff offer several hypotheses. First, "Guys hung out; girls didn't, weren't allowed to. ... When girl groups formed, they usually did so in their school, under the tutelage of some choral teacher who liked real music. Now, if you're not allowed to hang out on the streets after school and in the evening, how are you going to sing doo-wops?" Second, they posit "a belief on the part of record company executives that groups made up exclusively of women wouldn't sell." Finally, they argue, female groups had too much uniformity in their voices. In her scholarly study of '60s girl groups, Jacqueline Warwick counters Gribin & Schiff's third point, elaborating the different vocal ranges, singing styles, and harmonies in girl group songs. She does agree with their initial point: "while upwardly mobile African American city boys in the 1950s were able to form doo wop groups and roam the streets in search of adventure, their sisters were more likely to sing in the school choir and to harmonize behind closed doors at home."[64]

All these arguments seem logical. Gender roles asserted powerful influence in 1950s culture. The containment and policing of young women's behaviors no doubt factored into the much easier path to musical success for young Black women in gospel groups than in R&B. Music executives' prejudices and audience tastes might also have deterred the development of female doo wop. But none of these explanations accounts for why, relatively suddenly, female doo wop took off in 1957–58. The Bobbettes' "Mr. Lee" (1957) spent four weeks at #1 R&B and reached #6 Pop, while "Maybe," the first of the Chantels' three great 1958 hits, reached #2 R&B and #15 Pop. Those successes broke the ice for the female harmony groups to come.

Back in 1954, some mellifluous female doo-woppers emerged from their own primordial ooze. Something was stirring in the musical universe—a "general demand for offbeat stuff," *Variety* called it in a February 1955 article on the increased popularity of R&B. Among the newly attractive offbeat, "Femme vocal groups, which used to be a drug on the market only a few months ago, are now hitting big." The article specifically mentions only white sister groups—the McGuire Sisters, Fontane Sisters, De John Sisters—but the new vogue for *femme vocal groups* seems to have been broader. Enter L.A.'s **Shirley Gunter and the Queens**, the first all-female R&B group according to Gribin & Schiff.[65] Their **"Oop Shoop"** (1954) on the Flair label, written by lead singer Shirley Gunter, sister of the Coasters' Cornell Gunter, briefly crept into *Billboard's* R&B top ten—and its cover by the Crew-Cuts rose to #13 Pop. In this good-natured up-tempo romp, Gunter tells her baby how much she needs his love. The *oop shoop bedoop bedoobie doobie* background consumes almost as much of the record's 2:17 as the lyric, and Maxwell Davis blows a brief tenor solo. The Queens were history by 1955.

Another girl group came together on the east coast. **The Hearts**, a quartet of 12–15-year-olds from the Bronx, recorded **"Lonely Nights"** (1955) on New York's tiny Baton label. Written by their manager, Zell Sanders, it spent fifteen weeks on the R&B chart. Gribin & Schiff claim that purists consider it the best female R&B recording ever. Not the best in my book, but definitely fine doo wop. Accompanied by a moaning saxophone, piano triplets, pounding drum, and echoing harmonies that sometimes revert to *hoo hoo hoo hoo hoo*, Joyce James (aka Joyce West) howls her regrets about those lonely nights and how much she misses her lover. The group sings with real passion but little variety except for its spoken bridge where bass Louise Harris Murray implores her big ol' sugarman to come home. The Hearts continued recording through the early 1960s with many changes of personnel, but never replicated the magic of "Lonely Nights."[66]

The Bronx was a relative hotbed of female doo wop in the mid–1950s with the Hearts, Chantels, and a male group called the Mellows that utilized a female lead. For Gribin & Schiff, "**Lillian Leach and the Mellows** may qualify as the most talented group to ever record and yet never chart." They cut a number of songs for Jay-Dee records including the beautiful ballad, **"Smoke from Your Cigarette"** (1954), written by second tenor Harold Johnson. The deluxe band featured Mickey Baker on guitar, Sam "The Man" Taylor's moody tenor sax, Milt Hinton bass, and Howard Biggs's sensitive piano. Lillian Leach sings plaintively to her lover: she remembers when she was the only one, those days are gone, he has found someone else. The cigarette smoke, both a sensual memory and metaphor for their relationship, now turned to smoke, clouds her eyes. A "wistful ballad," Baptista calls it. "'Smoke' was perfectly suited to Leach. As a 17-year old, she was able to bring credible tenderness and longing to Johnson's well-crafted lament."[67] Lillian Leach left a respectable doo wop legacy.

Californian Shirley Haven, on the other hand, left few traces. She struggled as an actress before taking up an equally rocky R&B singing career. On her three recorded songs she fronted the male Four Jacks quartet on Federal Records. Their best work: **"Sure Cure for the Blues"** (1952) by **Shirley Haven and the Four Jacks**, a swinging mid-tempo number with Haven and bass Ellison White switching leads. The label apparently had such little faith in Haven that they used a different female singer, Cora Williams, to lead the Jacks on the record's flip side.[68] But "Sure Cure" is a sure winner, reminiscent of Little Esther's musical dialogues with a more fully formed doo wop background. Haven happily describes various love-sicknesses while White offers himself as the doctor with the sure cure. Along with clapping hands and jolly *de doop de doop* harmonies, a bizarre falsetto soaring over the choruses and a tasty guitar solo, the song features the fascinating, mysterious female vocalist whose brief foray into doo wop yielded this gem.

Rolling on the R&B Tide

The February 23, 1955, front-page *Variety* article marveling at the renewed popularity of femme vocal groups is titled, "Top Names Singing the Blues as Newcomers Roll on R&B Tide." It focuses on "the current rhythm & blues phase of the music biz," which sees smaller labels challenging the Big Four record companies and their established vocalists with "new combos and singers," including the Charms, Five Keys, Moonglows, Lavern Baker, and Fats Domino.

> The kids not only are going for the tunes and the beat, but they seem to be going for the original interpretations as well. Several covers of r&b tunes by pop names have not been able to gain ground because they lacked that authentic low-down quality accented on the indie labels.

Oddly, illustrating how even white cover artists were having trouble, the article cites the Penguins, "clicking with their original r&b interpretation of 'Earth Angel,' *although the Crew-Cuts are outpacing them in sales*" (my italics).[69] By 1955, the current rhythm & blues phase, with or without its "authentic low-down quality," was erasing some of the boundaries between Black and white, between R&B and rock 'n' roll. *The kids*—white as well as Black—embraced R&B, including the harmony groups that so powerfully articulated the romantic dreams of adolescence. The years 1955–56 represent the apogee of doo wop. The groups and songs in this section, even those that didn't fully cross over at the time, became avatars of the dream of life transformed.

By far the most successful of all doo wop groups, **The Platters** reached #1 R&B and #1 Pop four times between 1955 and 1958. Led by the extraordinary operatic tenor of **Tony Williams** (1928–92) and shaped by their songwriter/manager Buck Ram, the Platters flipped the script, selling more records than the white artists who covered them. They embodied R&B's breakthrough into broadly popular music. But there's the rub. Their crossover success, abandoning that *low-down quality*, turned them, for some, into a mere pop group, "crooning 'whitened' ballads like 'Only You' and 'Twilight Time' that resembled pop hits from the 1930s...." Could a Black group in 1955–56 remain *authentic*, whatever that meant, yet also appeal to white disc jockeys and promoters, white kids, and even their parents? Were the Platters merely the second coming of the Ink Spots? Listen to the faint praise with which Charlie Gillett describes them and their beautiful, moving ballads (my italics):

> The back-up singers in the Platters never sounded as *interesting* as most of the other groups of the day, and in many ways the group's records could have been billed by Tony Williams. He had a *genuinely good* voice, obviously influenced by gospel, and he *threw in a kind of hiccup* on the high notes which became his trademark.[70]

Williams' voice, much more than just good, informs a vocal technique far more adept than hiccupping. The group's minimalist background harmonies serve to foreground the strength of the ensemble.

Federal Records' Ralph Bass brought Tony Williams together with a Los Angeles group in 1952. Buck Ram was managing Williams' sister, R&B singer Linda Hayes, and agreed to manage the group called the Platters. Ram added a female voice to the male quartet: Zola Taylor of Shirley Gunter and the Queens. After a few unproductive sessions with Federal, Ram took them to Mercury Records where he polished the Platters' sound and image. The sound was paramount but their image also proved crucial in breaking out of the R&B ghetto. "The Platters with their neat tuxedos and pretty girl singer ... seemed reassuringly safe," Brian Ward points out, "when contrasted with Hank Ballard and the Midnighters and their odes to 'Annie' and her sexual adventures."[71]

The Platters, 1955. From left: Herb Reed, Tony Williams, Zola Taylor, Paul Robi, Dave Lynch. Pictorial Press Ltd./Alamy Stock Photo.

At their first Mercury session, Ram re-arranged and played piano on an unreleased song of his that the Platters had recorded on Federal: "Only You," retitled **"Only You (and You Alone)"** (1955). It spent thirty weeks on the R&B chart, seven at #1, and reached #5 Pop. The Mercury recording is sublime. Ram's piano triplets, a guitar, string bass, and blow harmonies provide the backdrop for Williams' ode to idealized, exclusive love. He embellishes his passionate vocal, breaking up key words as though his feelings were too strong to contain them—*oh-oh-only you-hoo-hoo*—and pushing them to the highest edge of his tenor, towards the falsetto *you* that ends the song. But consciously or not, Williams subverts the seamless vocal perfection with a seductive imperfection. His consistently odd mispronunciation, "Only you *cand* make"—especially notable because of his crisp, perfect diction elsewhere—may be the *authentic low-down* residue beneath the surface of this lovely confection, the grain of sand that produces the pearl. The Platters lip-sync the song in Alan Freed's 1956 movie, *Rock Around the Clock*: https://www.youtube.com/watch?v=3FygIKsnkCw. Note the sophisticated white tuxes, evening gown, gently swaying choreography, and all-white supper club audience.

Their next single, Ram's **"The Great Pretender"** (1955), stayed at #1 R&B for eleven weeks and made it to #1 Pop. With triplets banging away and the background assertively *ahh ooh ooh*-ing, Williams' relatively unadorned vocal lets the rich lyrics speak. The abandoned lover, pretending not to be lonely, adrift in a world of artifice, *conceals* the *real* that he *feels*. The neat internal rhyming accompanies surprising imagery. Instead of a mask hiding the laughing clown's true feelings, this royal clown crowns himself with his own heart: Pretender the Great. Whether or not the song contains subliminal messages for Black audiences, as suggested earlier, it raises doo wop lyricism to another level.

With **"My Prayer"** (1956) the Platters fully crossed over. "Not only did it reach #1 on both the R&B *and* Pop charts," Marv Goldberg points out, "it spent *longer* on Pop (23 weeks, as opposed to 17) and remained #1 longer (5 weeks, as opposed to 2)." A top ten hit for both Glenn Miller's orchestra and the Ink Spots in 1939, the song's classical quality matched the Platters' sophisticated new image as upscale balladeers. And its theological vocabulary—*prayer, rapture, divine*—satisfied the audience's expectations for doo wop celebrations of transcendent love. He prays for a love so ideal it lives only as a dream in his heart. Even nature is absent: no twilight, no songbirds. The lovers exist in an eternal present where nothing changes. She'll *always* be there. Instead of hitting impossibly high notes, Williams launches vocal crescendos. But in the call-and-response between Williams and the background, does their *aaahhh* sound like an ironic, half-mocking *aaawww*? If life can *only be* a dream, the real gets refined out of existence. Even so beautiful a performance, one might argue, needs at least a modicum of that authentic low-down quality to ground it in the here and now. But let me defer to Bob Dylan, who hears "My Prayer" differently: "The Platters don't need back-alley blues full of flatted notes and double entendres, they carry their soul with a cooler-than-thou looseness, offhand and urbane, exuding hipness the way James Dean exhaled cigarette smoke…."[72]

The Platters' doo wop ballads and those of other harmony groups made great make-out music. But the kids buying R&B records and plugging the jukeboxes also wanted songs they could dance to, hard and fast as well as slow and sensual. The Dionysian, lose-yourself-in-the-music quality of rock 'n' roll spawned by R&B created a culture of dance centered in Philadelphia, home of the original *Bandstand*, a radio and TV show begun in 1952, where kids danced to records and to the performers who lip-synched them. The show morphed into TV's popular, influential *American Bandstand*, which continued broadcasting from Philadelphia until 1964. Appropriately, the hottest disc to come out of Philly in the mid–1950s was **"When You Dance"** (1955) by **The Turbans**. Formed in 1953, they wore turbans as a gimmick. "When You Dance," the B-side of their first release on New York's Herald Records, quickly reached #3 R&B. It also stayed on the Pop chart for five months. An advice song for guys, it stresses the sensual side of dance: hold her tight, squeeze her, feel her warmth. Its irresistible Latin beat marked a flavor becoming increasingly popular in American music and dance. The song mentions the rhumba, tango, and mambo. Tenor Al Banks delivers a wonderful lead vocal, launching into sweet falsetto when he describes the thrill of dancing close to her. The arrangement makes judicious use of Chet Jones's bass, the background's *doo wop be doobie doobie*, and the sax solo, now *de rigeur* on all fast doo wop. An exhilarating song.[73]

From a South Side Chicago high school whose custodian became their manager, **The El Dorados** specialized in fast songs. Signing with Vee-Jay in 1954, they made little noise with their early releases, though I'm a big fan of **"Little Miss Love"** (1954). It couldn't be more lightweight, but Pirkle Lee Moses, who sings lead on all their tunes, had the perfect voice and style to bop along, telling little Miss Love in a half-dozen ways that he loves her. The background chants the title, while in the break a sax honks alongside clapping hands and cries of "Hey hey!" and "Blow, blow!" A classic case of making much out of little.[74]

Given more to work with, the group had its biggest success with **"At My Front Door"** (1955). Spending 18 weeks on the R&B chart, it hit #1 R&B and #17 Pop, although Pat Boone's cover vaulted over it to #7. Moses creates a saga about the crazy little mama who keeps showing up at his front door, knock knock knocking to be let in. If you want to hang onto *your* little mama, better keep her off his street. The song gets plenty of instrumental action, the background has fun with a *womp womp doodly womp, womp womp* riff, and Moses throws in some falsetto.[75] **"Bim Bam Boom"** (1956), the group's rockin' sequel, had another little mama banging on his back door. In its novelty lyrics the bass man contradicts Moses' portrayal of this pretty woman, describing instead a grotesque escapee from a zoo.

If "Bim Bam Boom" suggests doo wop decadence, its flip side, **"There in the Night"** (1956), shows the El Dorados capable of shaping a fine dramatic love ballad. Moses exercises his falsetto, and the group provides rich harmonic support. But the El Dorados' strong suit was jump. Seeing the writing on the zeitgeist wall, they put out a lame record called "Rock 'n' Roll's for Me" (1956). And it was. The contagious rocker **"I'll Be Forever Loving You"** (1956) got them onto the charts for the final time. Trying to assess his lover's commitment, Moses asks if she feels tipsy with love when they're together like he does. The sax solo sizzles along with the doodling doo wop background—*doop a bop bop*. Doo wop's nonsense syllable signature would mark the best harmony group efforts of 1956.

One of the best known, most distinctive, best-selling doo wop ballads of all time begins with a riff that every fan will recognize: *shoo dootin shoobie doo*. New Haven's **The Five Satins** formed in 1954, led by tenor/songwriter **Fred Parris** (1936–2022). A couple of local teens convinced the Satins to record two of Parris' songs on their new Standord label. The recording took place in a church basement, secured for the group by a kid named Vinny Mazzetta. In exchange, the Satins let Vinny blow sax on their record. The Five Satins were only four that night: Parris, tenor Al Denby, baritone Ed Martin, and bass Jim Freeman. As prominent as Parris on the record's B-side, **"In the Still of the Nite"** (1956), they voice the opening riff, carry it under the verses, and chant it in the bridge. The minimal lyrics create an image of that quiet starlit May night when he holds her, promises never to let her go, and prays for their precious love. The passionate promise and prayer evoke an atmosphere of intense young romance. *Shoo dootin shoobie doo* somehow makes it feel profound. Released on the Ember label, the song reached #3 R&B and #24 Pop, nothing record-breaking, but has since sold millions of copies. Greil Marcus finds "In the Still of the Nite" transcendent. He describes Mazzetta's sax solo as "the sound of someone completely lost in a song, in a nowhere Parris has not yet found, a utopia where there are no dreams to realize, no debts to pay, where there is only reverie, where for a few seconds every dream is fulfilled and every debt forgiven…."[76]

The long forgotten original A-side, **"The Jones Girl"** (1956), is a terrific rocker. On Fred Parris' ode to Ms. Jones the whole group chants the refrain: everyone is talking about her. When Parris saw her on the street, he knew she was his. Freeman's bassy *dah-oom* prefaces each repeat of "Jones girl," and Mazzetta rocks out on an extended solo. Just to show that "In the Still of the Nite" was no fluke, the group produced another gorgeous ballad that year, **"Wonderful Girl"** (1956). Parris does nearly all the work with the background reduced to blow harmonies. Piano triplets create the dramatic atmosphere. He sings of how much he loves his girl, how she makes him lose his mind. A wonderful song from a wonderful group.

Another of the most distinctive sounds of mid-'50s doo wop came from a group of Air Force men stationed in Pittsburgh: *dum dum dum dum dum, dum de doobie dum, wah wah wah wa-ah*. **The Dell-Vikings** (aka Del-Vikings, Del Vikings and Dell Vikings), four African Americans and a white guy, became the first integrated group to have a top ten hit when **"Come Go with Me"** (1956) charted as high as #2 R&B and #4 Pop. Bass Clarence Quick, who has plenty to do in the arrangement, wrote the song, led by baritone Norman Wright. Like "In the Still of the Nite," the Dell-Vikings recorded "Come Go with Me" in a basement and released it on a tiny, obscure label (Fee Bee) before Dot re-released it for national distribution.[77] The dynamic musical drive and lyrical theme strike a strong note of optimism. I love you, come with me and tell me you'll never leave. "Go, go, go!" the group shouts during George Upshaw's stuttering sax solo. The snappy bridge ends with Quick's bass raising doubts and a falsetto cry, the kind of self-mocking fun that underlies many of the best doo wops. And of course, you may hear the song's addictive riff as "dumb dumb dumb dumb dumb." Still, it hasn't lost an ounce of buoyant energy over the decades.

Here's another nonsense riff, less well known today, but anyone who listened to doo wop in 1956 would have recognized it: *diddle liddle liddle liddle lit, yeah* from the **Cleftones**' **"Little Girl of Mine"** (1956), a moderate R&B and Pop hit on George Goldner's Gee label. Baritone Herb Cox sang lead for the Cleftones, high school students from Queens, and wrote their up-tempo songs. Cox sings in praise of his girl, for whom all his guy friends envy him. He's obsessed with having her, maybe a little too possessively. Fifties doo wop romance could be a gendered prison for young women. Still, as they would say on *Bandstand*, you could dance to it, and the riff wormed its way into your brain along with the background's *dit dit dit dit*. Jimmy Wright's wild honking sax solo is a bonus. The group cut another rockin' dance record that year, **"Can't We Be Sweethearts"** (1956). This time the formula foregrounds bass Warren Corbin's *bow bow bow bow bow*. Cox less possessively *asks* her if they can be sweethearts. With the help of choreographer Cholly Atkins, the Cleftones became a hot live act in Alan Freed's rock 'n' roll shows and at the Apollo, where they appeared twelve times one year.[78]

Like most doo wop groups coming up, the Cleftones competed with neighborhood rivals. One of their primary Queens competitors, a male quartet called the Hearts, changed their name to **The Heartbeats** when the female Hearts broke out with "Lonely Nights." Specializing in ballads written by lead tenor **James "Shep" Sheppard** (1935–70), the group began recording in 1955 for tiny Hull Records and quickly became New York favorites with dreamy love songs like **"Crazy for You"** (1955). Groia describes their distinctive characteristics: Sheppard's silky lead, their closed-mouth harmony and use of the celesta, Wally Roker's mellow bass, and the technique of second tenor Robbie Tatum and baritone Vernon Sievers, "derived from African call and response vocal patterns, putting various sounds to harmony, i.e., 'chop-chop-chop,' 'rat-tat-tat-too'...." When their early successes led to performances at the Apollo and rock 'n' roll shows, the Heartbeats' manager decided they needed a more up-tempo style to compete with groups like the Cadillacs. So they recorded **"Oh Baby Don't"** (1956), a rocker with Roker's bass lead asking his baby not to leave, Sheppard singing the bridge in falsetto at a slower tempo, and the background chanting the title at top speed. But the Heartbeats' substantial fan base demanded that local DJs flip the record over and play the ballad side, a Sheppard song called **"A Thousand Miles Away"** (1956).[79]

Like many other best-selling doo wops, "A Thousand Miles Away" proved too successful for its original small label. Hull licensed it to Goldner's Rama, whose distribution enabled the song to reach #5 R&B and #53 Pop. Re-issued in 1960, "A Thousand Miles Away" again made *Billboard*'s top 100. Its inclusion on the 1973 *American Graffiti* soundtrack extended its life once more. By any measure the song is a doo wop masterpiece. Sheppard's impassioned vocal promises his lover that he will pray to preserve their long-distance love and soon he'll come home. The lover's vague promises are accompanied by semi-specific details. When will he come? Maybe on a Sunday morning or a Tuesday afternoon. His passion detonates his diction. The word *darling* can't contain what he feels for his *dar-har-har-ling* when he implores her to dry her eyes. The bell-like celesta and pounding drumbeat combine delicacy of feeling and powerful insistence. And the arrangement brings the background's *rat-a-tat-tat* and almost falsetto-high harmonies together with Roker's bassy echo of Sheppard's lyrics in perfect synergy. Altogether one of the best doo wop performances ever.

Sheppard wrote and sang a terrific sequel, "Daddy's Home" (1961), with a new group, Shep and the Limelites. Dave Marsh claims that fifteen songs written by Sheppard and recorded by the Heartbeats or Shep's Limelites constitute "part of the same yarn, an ongoing saga of a boy, a girl, and the physical and emotional distance between them," beginning with "Crazy for You," including "A Thousand Miles Away" and "Daddy's Home," and ending with "I'm All Alone" (1962). Like so many postwar greats, Shep's genius had much too short a time to flourish. He was murdered at age 35.[80]

A group from suburban Chicago made another of the best mid-'50s ballads. The El Rays had one 1954 recording session for Checker. Renamed the **Dells**, they moved over to Chicago's other R&B label, Vee-Jay. The group would record and perform for almost sixty years with nearly all the same personnel, continually reinventing themselves as soul, disco, and rhythm & blues artists. Though they charted only once in the 1950s, they hit the R&B chart over forty times and the Pop chart more than twenty after 1965. Their one early hit (#4 R&B) was a keeper. The group's two leads, tenor Johnny Funches and baritone Marvin Junior, co-wrote **"Oh What a Nite"** (1956), a vibrant ballad with rich harmonies and beautiful call-and-response vocals. Technically, Funches sings lead, but only the title phrase. The entire group harmonizes on the phrases that complete each statement. Logically, the lyrics make little sense. It's a beautiful night to love you; that's why I love you. Here's another case where doo wop sentiment trumps sense. Emotionally, we know exactly what they mean. Junior relayed a telling anecdote. The group was rehearsing the song "but it just wasn't coming off right. [Vee-Jay founder] Vivian Carter ... suggested that we express ourselves more on the 'oh,' bring out the 'oh.' And that's the one thing that made the song!" But not the only thing. Piano triplets and a sexy tenor sax solo underscore the emotions. And the bass's subtle *doo doo doo* provides a strong bottom. Regular bassman Chuck Barksdale couldn't make the session so Vee-Jay's A&R man, Vivian's brother Calvin Carter, sang the bass part. The Dells re-did the song as a soul anthem in 1969, correcting the spelling and punctuation. "Oh, What a Night" reached #1.[81]

Like the Harptones, Harlem's **The Channels** created phenomenal doo wop, starred along the east coast, yet, unbelievably, never charted nationally. Formed in 1955, the group gelled the following year when joined by bass Clifton Wright and lead tenor **Earl Lewis** (1939–), who wrote their best songs. Bobby Robinson signed the Channels to his newest label, Whirlin' Disc. While still in high school they released their first record, the all-time great ballad **"The Closer You Are"** (1956), an exquisite love song of yearning and adoration. Lewis wrote it when he was just fourteen. Its innovative sound derives from its harmony lead—tenors Larry Hampden and Billy Morris along with baritone Edward Doulphin—framed by Lewis' spectacular falsetto and Wright's bass. Lewis takes over in the channel, his lyric punctuated by Wright's distinctive *bong bong*. When the harmony re-takes the lead to tell her that his love increases every day, Lewis literally howls in falsetto ecstasy. The beautiful, compelling vocals make it almost credible that the stars in the sky and fire in his heart actually grow brighter each time she comes near. And that they will *always* be lovers.[82] The Channels inspired a terrific fast version, "The Closer You Are" (1961) by the Magnificent Four.

The B-side, Lewis' **"Now You Know"** (1956), a great rocker with similar sentiments, has a more conventional vocal structure. Lewis sings lead throughout, the harmony stays in the background chanting *badda chadda oowee doo*, and Wright provides strong bass counterpoint. A pianist hits a couple of the highest keys and the great King Curtis blows a dynamite tenor solo. But the Channels were primarily balladeers. On their second release, Lewis' **"The Gleam in Your Eyes"** (1956), as brilliant as their first, Larry Hampden sings falsetto behind Lewis' lead. Sam "The Man" Taylor's moody tenor sax accompanies the tinkling piano and rich harmonies in another exquisite arrangement. Lewis' lyrics re-commit to his love with absolute fidelity. He can't resist her or forget her, and vows to keep her in his heart until death do them part. The sincerity and credibility of a teenage lover's commitment would prove a paradigm for the schoolboy groups that emerged in the mid–1950s.

Teenagers in Love: Schoolboy Doo Wop

As *Billboard* and *Variety* pointed out, "the kids" consuming the new music were reshaping the mid-'50s music business. The cult of the teenager appeared in full force at this historical moment. As popular styles shifted towards teenage tastes and consumption, kids also *created* much of the new music. Most doo wop groups formed while their members were in high school or even earlier, and first recorded while they were still teens. This young people's music lyrically mimicked the traditional experiences of adult romantic balladry (true love and heartbreak), and reflected the romantic idealism of aspirational adolescents. Brian Ward notes that the more cynical, sexual approach of blues and earlier R&B rarely occurred to the doo woppers who "largely ignored 'adult' material and concentrated almost exclusively on evoking a juvenile world of specifically teen trauma and romantic delight."

For Ann Powers, doo wop infused "romance with a sense of wonder … recasting R&B's grown-up leer as a winning smile."[83]

The 1950s invented the very notion of the teenager with a distinctive identity tied to his/her own habits, desires, values, behaviors, and musical tastes. As the decade progressed, the image of *the teenager in love* came to the fore in popular music, including doo wop and rock 'n' roll. Dion and the Belmonts' "A Teenager in Love" (1959) was one of the formative songs of my adolescence. Pop, rock, and even some rhythm & blues settled on sixteen as the key age for teenage girls to love and be loved. But what about the fifteen- and fourteen- and thirteen-year-olds? And the boys? Mid-fifties doo wop got consistently younger, exploding with early-teen groups, what Gribin & Schiff call Schoolboy Doo-Wop. Frankie Lymon and the Teenagers, Lewis Lymon and the Teenchords, and The Schoolboys all emerged in 1955–56, and The Students in 1957, their names foregrounding their adolescence. The groups included junior high schoolers, thirteen- and fourteen-year-olds. Possessing "unstable voices that reflected their unstable identities," Powers argues, these boys "inevitably communicated a different kind of bravado—one grounded in inexperience and hormonal flux." James Miller describes the voice of Frankie Lymon, the thirteen-year-old schoolboy doo wopper par excellence, as "a girlish soprano [that] tended to crack and break…. Before his voice changed, he used his wavering vibrato to deliver his lyrics with an uncertain pitch and yaw that promised romantic shipwreck."[84] These kids put their unique stamp on the doo wop brand.

Although doo wop's youth movement emerged later in the decade, the pioneer schoolboy group appeared in Harlem around 1950. Its name suggests the style to which these boys aspired. **The Mello-Moods** sang songs aimed at grown-ups, even though their ages, when they recorded their only minor hit, ranged from about thirteen to sixteen. Accompanied by the Schubert Swanston Trio (piano, sax, and drums), the Mello-Moods' first release on the Red Robin label, **"Where Are You (Now That I Need You)"** (1951), managed one week at #7 R&B. Musical theater tunesmith Frank Loesser (*Guys & Dolls*) wrote it, Betty Hutton first sang it in the 1949 movie *Red, Hot and Blue*, and Doris Day covered the song the same year. Jay Warner observes of the Mello-Moods' version, "The soft ballad, with [Buddy Wooten's] mellow tenor lead, became the first teen group national R&B charter, but unlike later teen groups' singles it offered nary a hint of the group's age thanks to their mature sound." The recording may sound mature overall, but Wooten's high schoolboy tenor gives him away. He sounds very young as he sings about how much he took her for granted. Now the roles are reversed and he wonders where she has gone. Bass James Bethea quietly *doo doo doo*s and a barely audible falsetto wails in the background while Swanston's piano adds sophistication to the sound. By 1953, three of the Mello-Moods had joined the Solitaires and the group was history.[85]

Another group from Harlem, appropriately called **The Schoolboys**, were attending junior high in 1955 when they won first prize on *Ted Mack's Original Amateur*

Hour, got a contract with OKeh Records, and cut one of the most beautiful doo wop ballads of the decade, **"Please Say You Want Me"** b/w **"Shirley"** (1956), a fine doo wop rocker. Groia calls this "the first nationally successful adolescent tenor record," but it had middling national success at best. "Shirley" reached #91 Pop and "Please Say You Want Me" peaked at #13 R&B for a week. "Please Say You Want Me" nevertheless remains a deeply gorgeous experience. Marsh describes it as "the most melancholy disc ever cut by an actual teenager ... swamped in echo and accompanied by a stately arrangement." The group may have been schoolkids but the lead vocal of boy soprano Leslie Martin, with its "almost operatic intensity," projects passion and neediness in powerfully moving ways. This teenager pleads to have his romantic feelings taken seriously. Even amid the sax-led rocking of "Shirley," Martin earnestly assures his girl that he tries his best to love her. In "Please Say You Want Me" his assertion that the tears he has shed for her have almost killed him reinforces how traditional rhythm & blues masculinity—reduced here to Renaldo Gamble's bass—has fully transformed into the vulnerability of sensitive young males unafraid to show their emotions. The background completes each of the lead singer's sentences in the verses, as if it takes all five boys to make one credible romantic adult.[86]

Marv Goldberg compares **Frankie Lymon** (1942–68) to Clyde McPhatter and Sonny Til. Add to them twelve-year-old musical phenoms Stevie Wonder and Michael Jackson. **Frankie Lymon and the Teenagers** became a boy band sensation and the immediate predecessor of Motown's Jackson Five. Lymon's voice and his explosive success directly influenced Arlene Smith of the Chantels, Ronnie Spector of the Ronettes, the Supremes' Diana Ross, the Imperials' Little Anthony, and Michael Jackson himself. Formed in upper Manhattan's Washington Heights (the setting for Lin-Manuel Miranda's *In the Heights*), the group of three African Americans and two Puerto Ricans signed with Goldner's Gee Records. They brought along a song they wrote called "Why Do Birds Sing So Gay." In the studio Goldner changed the title to **"Why Do Fools Fall in Love"** (1955) and decided that Lymon should sing lead. Frankie had just turned thirteen. First tenor Herman Santiago was fifteen; second tenor Jimmy Merchant, baritone Joe Negroni, and bass Sherman Garnes sixteen. Within a few months the record reached #1 R&B and #6 Pop in the United States and #1 in England. The Teenagers had four other U.S. top tens in 1956.[87]

A great rocker that never gets stale, "Why Do Fools Fall in Love" opens with a brief bass riff from Garnes, a device that would begin all the Teenagers' up-tempo songs and grow more elaborate with each one. Although Lymon sings in the first-person—*his* heart skips a beat; *he's* the fool in love—the song poses questions about love more metaphysical than personal, as does another of the group's best rockers, **"Who Can Explain"** (1956). The contrast between Lymon's adolescent voice and his mature persona gives these songs a fascinating ironic resonance. Albin Zak finds additional creative tension in the way "[Jimmy] Wright's hard-swinging, bluesy tenor saxophone solo and Lymon's angelic voice [create] a contrast between an impression of naïve wonder ... and grown-up sexiness."[88] The quality of Lymon's voice would be a key selling point on all his records. His *ooh wah, ooh wah* opening

Frankie Lymon and the Teenagers publicity photograph, 1956. From left: Joe Negroni, Herman Santiago, Jimmy Merchant, Frankie Lymon, Sherman Garnes. Pictorial Press Ltd./ Alamy Stock Photo.

and seven-second-long high *why-y-y-y-y-y* near the end of "Why Do Fools Fall in Love," shaky pitch and all, anticipate the sonic elements that showcase his vocals in the Teenagers' subsequent songs.

With Wright's hard-driving five-piece band and screaming sax solos backing them, the Teenagers rolled out the rockin' hits. On **"I Want You to Be My Girl"** (1956) (#3 R&B/13 Pop) Frankie can't decide if he wants his *gi-irl* to consider him a *kid* or her grown-up *lover man*. He adds some adventurous stylization to his vocal against the background's *bum dooby doo wop*, more prominent than before. Notably, Frankie gets two full choruses just to howl: *uh oh, oh oh, uh oh*. **"I Promise to Remember"** (1956) (#10 R&B/57 Pop) similarly features a series of *oh oh oh oh*s sounding less like orgasmic expressions of sexual pleasure than bellows of youthful enthusiasm. As he promises to be true, his self-deprecating denial of wisdom calls attention to his youthfulness. Frankie really stretches out here, turning one-syllable words into two (*do-oo, throu-ough*), two-syllables into three (*rom-a-ance*), and three into ten (*re-al-i-i-i-i-i-i-ize*). The song is also memorable for what Dave Marsh calls "Sherman Garnes' brilliantly straight-faced rendition of the opening line: 'Hooly bop a cow, bop a cow, bop a cow cow.'" Marsh's verdict: "Everything squares hate about doo-wop is in those syllables, and everything worth loving about it's there, too."

Marsh also favors **"The ABCs of Love"** (1956) (#8 R&B/77 Pop), one of the best doo wop list-songs (along with the Students' "Every Day of the Week" and Harvey and the Moonglows' "The Ten Commandments of Love"). "Nobody's ever made 'J, K, L, M, N-O-P, Q' sound so sexy or so fully of the moment," Marsh concludes. Both lyrics and performance manage to call attention again to both Frankie's supposed sophistication—he's going to *teach* her the ABCs of love—and the wholesomeness that made Lymon and the Teenagers so attractive to white audiences.[89] "Gosh knows I love you," Frankie sings, pronouncing the first word *garsh*, as if shying away from even that ultra-mild expletive.

The beautiful ballad **"I'm Not a Know It All"** (1956) expands the modesty of Lymon's self-presentation. Lyrically, Frankie walks back the adult sophistication he showed on the metaphysical tunes. Here, he admits to being virtually a know-nothing, unwise when it comes to anything except what involves her. Grooming Lymon as a solo act, Goldner arranged the background, including Garnes' bass, to sound almost incidental, and made Frankie even more harmlessly wholesome. Singing the title line, he twice seems unable to refer to himself without stuttering: "I–I–I–I–I–I'm not a know-it-all." But as is so often the case with R&B, extreme repetition has a kind of power, conjuring the self that these latter songs attempt to grind down, insisting on the "I" that the lyrics want to make disappear into modesty and wholesomeness. This insistence may be an act of self-preservation.

The year 1956 ended with the Teenagers appearing in Alan Freed's film *Rock, Rock, Rock* alongside the Moonglows, Flamingos, Chuck Berry, and LaVern Baker. Frankie had just turned fourteen. Already veterans of live stage shows and TV, their act choreographed by Cholly Atkins, with Lymon able to kibbitz like a show biz pro, the group was slick. But management continued to shape their image as All-American good boys, dressing them in preppy white crewneck sweaters emblazoned with the letter "T" for the movie where they sang their latest recording, **"I'm Not a Juvenile Delinquent"** (1956). Watch the video: https://www.youtube.com/watch?v=PCj1zy-ehPs&list=PLkEXWrMwCdPufnN2Co3UffR5JAz7Zm4p5&index=12.

Freed and Goldner had the Teenagers model a reassuring gospel of clean-cut Black teen behavior for their white audience in an era dominated by the cult of the teenager and obsessed by its dark side, an exaggerated epidemic of youthful criminality: "From the late 1940s, both the American Justice Department and the Senate became almost as active in rooting out juvenile delinquents as they were in chasing Communists," while Hollywood "portrayed youth as alternately alienated and depraved, or both."[90] The manufactured fear of Black urban youth crime compounded the paranoia about juvenile delinquency. Using their own Hollywood movie as a jazzed-up public service announcement, the Teenagers offer a response in "I'm Not a Juvenile Delinquent": Look at us. We're Black, we rock & roll, and we just say no. Addressing his Black brothers and sisters, Frankie appears to offer yet another version of the postwar African American dream. Life will be so nice, even paradisal, if you stay on the right side of the law, avoid the criminal behavior America expects of young Black men and women, and dress and act like a respectable white kid. "*This is my story*," he sings, using himself as a case study. Being good is easy, he claims. Just keep out of trouble.

But Frankie never found trouble easy to avoid. He grew up too fast to ever really be a kid. "No, no, no, I'm *not a juvenile*," he sings near the end. As he told *Ebony* magazine in 1967, "In the neighborhood where I lived, there was no time to be a child. ... When I was 10, I made a good living hustling prostitutes for the white men who would come up to Harlem looking for Negro girls." The article focused on Frankie's attempt to break his heroin habit. "I had been smoking marijuana when I was in grade school. But I didn't start using the real stuff [heroin] until I got into show business"—when he was thirteen.[91] What about the fruits of his show business success, the wealth and fame? Frankie Lymon and the Teenagers flamed out as quickly as they had burst onto the scene. Frankie left the group in 1957 for a solo career, a fifteen-year-old addict whose voice had changed. His career soon crashed. Frankie Lymon died penniless a year after the *Ebony* article, overdosing on heroin at just twenty-five, the saddest of this book's many sad stories of ultra-talented young Black men and women crushed by sudden fame, racism, and a cruel, cut-throat business.

At the close of "I'm Not a Juvenile Delinquent" Frankie sings at least 22 repetitions of the word NO as the song fades out. To what is he saying no? No, he's not a juvenile delinquent? No, he's not a juvenile? Note at that point in the *Rock, Rock, Rock* performance the ironic expression on his face, the ironic gesture of prayer, and the group's ironic bow. I hear: "No no no, don't believe any of the above. No no no, it was all crap: the collegiate sweaters, the clean-cut white-boy look, the moralizing about staying out of trouble. Like hell it's easy. No no no no no, life is not *at all* like this in 1956 for Black kids from the ghetto, even stars like us. No no no, nothing has really changed."

If a thirteen-year-old Lymon could create a sensation, why not a twelve-year-old? At the height of the Teenagers' fame in 1956, Frankie's younger brother Lewis got some friends together to form **Lewis Lymon and the Teenchords**. Frankie sound-alike Lewis sang lead. Bobby Robinson signed the group to his new Fury label and wrote a song that captured their exuberance and fed into the same image Goldner was creating for big brother Frankie. **"I'm So Happy"** (1956) opens with bass David Little doing his best Sherman Garnes imitation, riffing on the phrase *tra la la*, announcing the song's youthful innocence. It ends with Lewis chorusing *whoa whoa whoa*, echoing the *oh oh oh* big brother Frankie vocalized in his early songs. Lewis—who sounds his age—sounds so happy because the girl he loves loves him back. The song became a regional hit, but after a couple of years of limited success the Teenchords were no more.[92]

Signed to Old Town Records, Harlemite **Ruth McFadden** (1938–) recorded with local groups the Supremes and Royaltones in the mid–1950s, and would go on to sing soul on the Gamble & Huff label in the 1960s and '70s. In 1956, backed by her Old Town labelmates the Harptones, eighteen-year-old Ruth recorded **"Schoolboy"** (1956) by **Ruth McFadden and the Harptones**, a brief, beautiful doo wop ode to a schoolgirl romance. Though her voice is a little deeper than his, McFadden sounds remarkably like Frankie Lymon.

The Best of the Rest

Let's end this chapter with a sprinkling of marvelous doo wops that don't easily fit any of the previous categories. So many mid–1950s groups produced just a single memorable record. These five songs stand in for the many others that we might include if we had but world enough and time.

Like the Five Satins, **The Nutmegs** hailed from Connecticut, the Nutmeg State. Tenor Leroy Griffin wrote and sang lead on their first and best record, the beautiful ballad **"Story Untold"** (1955) for Herald Records. Against a background of *ooh wha wha* harmonies and Leroy McNeil's mournful bass, Griffin's tearful voice gives credence to the claim that he hasn't had a single day of happiness since his girl left him. The untold love story remains in his heart. He prays that she'll come back. But just in case, he reminds her in the bridge how she broke his heart. The apotheosis of the wounded, abandoned doo wop lover, the Nutmegs' "Story Untold" reached #2 R&B but a cover by the Crew-Cuts kept it from charting Pop.[93]

Both the Meadowlarks and Jaguars formed in L.A.'s Fremont High School around the same time as Fremont grads the Penguins were burning up the charts with "Earth Angel." Among the first groups to integrate, both had one white member. The Meadowlarks recorded the lovely ballad **"Heaven and Paradise"** (1955) on the Penguins' label, Dootone, under the name **Don Julian and the Meadowlarks**. **The Jaguars** made a few records in 1955 before getting everything right on the Dorothy Fields/Jerome Kern standard, **"The Way You Look Tonight"** (1956). Lead singer Julian wrote the Meadowlarks' lyrically banal and redundant "Heaven and Paradise" (he wants them to be in heaven *and* paradise, which he pronounces par*o*dise). But Julian has a terrific voice, and the strange musical alchemy of doo wop somehow transforms the lyrically ordinary into the emotionally extraordinary by his simply adding an *oh oh oh* each time he sings the title phrase and the background responds *wha ooh*. Jaguars lead Sonny Chaney had an even better voice, and the superb lyrics of "The Way You Look Tonight" combined with an elegant arrangement make it one of the classiest doo wop ballads. A piano accompanies Chaney's lead and the background's blow harmonies with the melody of "Moonlight Sonata," switching to triplets for the dramatic bridge. The Jaguars' performance reflects the theme of her loveliness: doo wop loveliness personified.[94]

In the late 1950s, I couldn't stop singing my favorite ballad, a little-known record by an obscure New York group called **The Wheels** on the New Jersey label Premium. The group's manager and arranger, guitarist Allen Bunn, wrote their first release, **"My Heart's Desire"** (1956). Bunn had sung gospel with the Selah Jubilee Singers and doo wop with the Larks, and would later reinvent himself as bluesman Tarheel Slim. "My Heart's Desire" is the ultimate teenage romantic ballad: intense, extreme, divine. Lead Rudy Anderson sings with what still sounds to me like profound conviction. The *Billboard* reviewer wrote, "The lead singer shows a wild, enthusiastic style on the impressive topside r.&b. ballad," though this ballad seems anything but *wild*.[95] Bunn's superb arrangement gets a lot of action from bass Lorenzo Cook and the background's *doo wop*s. Anderson addresses his heart's desire with absolute adoration—listen to the way he sings the word *adore*—and his love for her infuses him with superpowers. He climbs mountains, swims oceans, leaps over buildings, and walks across deserts just to get that erotic thrill when she *whis*-(gasp)-*pers* in his ear that she remains his. I still love this song.

The Chips got together in 1956 in Brooklyn's Bedford-Stuyvesant, recording one of the most unusual and politically powerful doo wops of the era. Lead Charles Johnson had spent time in the New York State Training School for Boys upstate in Warwick, where he wrote **"Rubber Biscuit"** (1956), released on Josie Records. Unusually, Gribin & Schiff utterly dismiss the song: "the lyric has no meaning and little redeeming value. It is consistently vacuous and puerile from beginning to end." They quote:

> Gow gow lubba 'n' a-blubba lubba,
> Ow rown hibb'n 'n' a-hibba-lu

And so on. Groia thinks Johnson may have conceived the song "as a rhythmic alternative to the military cadence of 'hey, ho, one, two … sound off'" while marching around the juvenile facility. One can easily imagine the boys mocking the paramilitary discipline of their school/prison. The wonderfully bizarre novelty syllables sound like a doo wop parody: straight nonsense framed by a *ba bom bom* bass and falsetto.

But listen to the four surreal spoken stanzas. Johnson talks about a certain kind of sandwich that you *wish* had some meat to go between slices of bread. He references what might have been a sadistic game they played at Warwick: a biscuit has to ricochet off the wall into your mouth. If it misses, you get nothing to eat. Rubber biscuit indeed. He did eat a pseudo-sandwich, a *cool-water* melon slice, along with a bun he might have gnawed on the way to Sunday chapel. Not much protein. But hey, he rhetorically shrugs, what do you want? Johnson sounds like he's singing with a goofy smile—except when he prefaces each spoken verse with a descending *hmmm mmm mmm*, somewhere between an ironic laugh and sob. A more overt laugh-sob occurs just before the line "you go hungry." Despite the generally upbeat tone, the song calls attention to conditions at the school and likely elsewhere. More than a few teenage boys went hungry in Bed-Stuy in 1956. "We wear the mask that grins and lies," poet Paul Laurence Dunbar wrote sixty years earlier.[96] Remember "The Great Pretender" example.

Martin Scorsese revived "Rubber Biscuit" in 1973 for his *Mean Streets* soundtrack, and in 1978 the best known Blues Brothers' version cracked *Billboard*'s top 100. That accounts for much of the song's reputation as a goof. But even as novelty the Chips' version rocks pretty hard. Wikipedia lists a world-class band including Mickey Baker on guitar, Panama Francis drums, and King Curtis tenor sax. Some producer knew that this song was worthy of talented musicians who would have been wasted on something merely "vacuous and puerile." The moral: *listen* to this remarkable song, and to what all the great music in this book has to say.

Chapter Five

Roots of a Revolution

> "Later on they'd call it soul music. But the names don't matter. It's the same mixture of gospel and blues with maybe a sweet melody thrown in for good measure."
>
> —Ray Charles[1]

The generation of postwar African American musical artists who made the decade 1946–56 so memorable led the late-1950s transition into rock 'n' roll and soul. Some of the biggest stars of the next decade debuted before 1957: we've met Etta James and Bobby "Blue" Bland, Fats Domino, Lloyd Price, and LaVern Baker, Sam Cooke, the Drifters, and the Platters. Bluesmen like Muddy Waters, B.B. King, and John Lee Hooker also got adopted by rock fans, and they adapted to the new music without losing their blues authenticity. Muddy would sing, "The Blues Had a Baby and They Named It Rock 'n' Roll" (1977). The rock 'n' roll baby and its half-sibling, soul, had many progenitors.

This final chapter focuses on four giants whose first recordings fall within our decade: Aretha Franklin, Ray Charles, Little Richard, and James Brown. Each of them carved out a definitive, influential body of work, a distinctive domain in rock and/or soul that had its roots in the rhythm & blues of the early/mid-1950s. All four were steeped in the African American gospel tradition, and their music fused the influences of the church with blues, rhythm & blues, and even doo wop. A collection of James Brown's early recordings (1956-64) called *Roots of a Revolution* inspired the title for this chapter. I want to call attention to these artists' roots and early shoots and buds, the music they were making that would blossom into the better-known, more popular material they would create later. I omit Chuck Berry and Elias McDaniel, aka Bo Diddley, on the grounds that their 1955–56 recordings were already rock 'n' roll.

The Blues Had a Baby

A quick word first about **Aretha Franklin** (1942–2018), the Queen of Soul. Born in Memphis, she grew up in Detroit and began her career singing gospel in her famous father the Rev. C.L. Franklin's New Bethel Baptist Church, where she recorded a live album on Checker in 1956 called *Songs of Faith*. Accompanying herself on piano, Aretha sings nine songs including a double-sided version of Dorsey's **"Precious Lord"** (1956). Anthony Heilbut claims that she sings them exactly as her idol, Clara Ward, would have, "complete with moans and ad-libbed 'Good Lords.'"[2] Derivative or not, the artistry of the fourteen-year-old is extraordinary. Listen to anything on the album and marvel at the quality of her voice and what she could do with it. These recordings announce the single most special talent of the era in American music and anticipate her later mastery of gospel and the gospel-infused soul she would practically patent. In its stateliness and formality, this early work of Aretha's reminds me of Mahalia Jackson's gospel more than Clara Ward's. Unsurprisingly, Aretha also sang "Precious Lord" at Jackson's funeral. For a more mature, more masterful, more varied series of live gospel performances, listen to Aretha's *Amazing Grace* album (1972). Add her 1998 *Greatest Hits* compilation of soul and rock 'n' roll, and you can hear with absolute clarity a singer for the ages.

Viv Broughton writes, "For many people, **Ray Charles** [1930–2004] is the greatest gospel singer who never was." A musical polymath, Charles immersed himself in blues and rhythm & blues, jazz, big band, pop, and country & western, straining them all through a gospel sensibility: "breaking down the division between pulpit and bandstand, recharging blues concerns with transcendental fervor, unashamedly linking the spiritual and the sexual," and engendering what would be called *soul*. Charles himself acknowledged his gospel education. In his memoir he mentions listening to and sometimes jamming on the road with "the best singers I ever heard in my life"—Ira Tucker, Archie Brownlee, Claude Jeter, the Pilgrim Travelers. But he also insisted on *rhythm & blues* as still the best description of his pioneering hybrid of gospel and blues.[3]

Ray Charles came by his blues honestly, considering the obstacles he faced. The Oscar-winning feature film *Ray* (2004), starring Jamie Foxx, traces the general outline of Charles's remarkable life. Born in Georgia, Ray Charles Robinson moved to Florida with his family when he was a baby. He gradually lost his sight until he was blind by age seven and was sent to live at the state school for the deaf and blind in St. Augustine. His only brother drowned when Ray was a child, and his mother and father were dead by the time he was sixteen. Though poor, Black, blind, orphaned, and alone in the Jim Crow South, young Ray did not lack resources. At school he had sung in the choir, learned to play piano and clarinet, and taught himself to arrange and score for big band and orchestra. A musical sponge with great faith in himself and his abilities, even at fifteen he knew he could play almost any kind of music anyone wanted: "I wasn't about to get a tin cup, a cane and find myself a street corner." He quit school in 1945 and for the next few years kicked around Florida picking up gigs. In 1948, he played with an otherwise all-white country & western group, the Florida Playboys.[4]

Ambitious and restless, he soon hopped a Greyhound and moved across the country to Seattle, where he formed the McSon Trio (aka Maxin Trio, aka Ray Charles Trio), playing piano and singing in the mellow, laid back, west coast "blues-and-cocktail" style of Nat King Cole and Charles Brown with a guitar and bass for company. He cut his first records with the trio for the Downbeat (soon to be Swing Time) label, whose major artist at the time was bluesman Lowell Fulson. Charles hit the R&B charts in the Cole-Brown mode with self-penned tunes **"Confession Blues"** (1949) and **"Baby Let Me Hold Your Hand"** (1951). At first, having his work confused with Cole's and Brown's delighted him. But after a while, "I thought it'd be nice if people began to recognize *me*, if they'd tell me I sounded like Ray Charles. So I started experimenting with a different voice. Strangely enough, that voice turned out to be *mine*." Listening to him being himself on **"Kissa Me Baby"** (1952), an exciting rave-up credited to Ray Charles and Orchestra, David Ritz hears in Charles's "coarse and harsh voice ... the very antithesis of Cole's, a terribly lonely, ecstatically happy sensual voice which seems to contain the whole of black suffering and celebration." Traveling to Los Angeles to record the song, Charles left behind the intimate trio sound for the backing of Lowell Fulson's jazzy seven-piece blues band, including great tenor saxman Stanley Turrentine. Charles would later go on tour with Fulson's band, an experience he said changed everything for him. Here, he shouts along with them, plays and sings with a little stop-time, and gives himself a swinging piano solo before letting the horns bring it home. "Charles," writes Bill Dahl, "wailed 'Kissa Me Baby' with house-rocking abandon."[5] You can hear just how free he must have felt.

Signing with Atlantic Records in 1952, Charles clicked with Ahmet Ertegun and Jerry Wexler from the start. But still without his own band, he sounds tentative on his first Atlantic recordings, using Jesse Stone's arrangements with the label's session musicians, including guitarist Mickey Baker and Connie Kay on drums. "The resulting sides were good journeyman r&b," Wexler admitted, "but Ray was still under wraps...." His second Atlantic session did produce a couple of gems. **"Sinner's Prayer"** (1953), a slow blues written and first recorded by Fulson, features Charles's anguished vocal and bluesy piano in a small combo setting without horns. Charles would record it again a half-century later with B.B. King. Even better was **"Mess Around"** (1953), written by Nuggy, an Ertegun pen name, based on boogie woogie piano pieces from 1928 by bluesmen Cow Cow Davenport and Pinetop Smith. Charles's rockin' piano leads the way on this exultant party tune. With everyone juiced, the jumping band at the barbecue pit has them dancing the mess around to the boogie woogie sound. Charles sings with expressive zest. Ertegun's biographer suggests that Charles himself came up with the soon-classic R&B trope, the girl with the diamond ring shakin' her thing.[6] Listen to Ray Charles busting loose. "Now, lemme have it there, boy!" he shouts, leading into his piano solo before giving it over to tenor Freddie Mitchell for a torrid sax workout.

That same year, Charles produced, arranged, and played piano on Guitar Slim's "The Things That I Used to Do" in New Orleans, where he also recorded his own work and began gathering his own band. He had definite ideas about what he wanted: tenor, baritone, and alto saxes, and two trumpets. "Each of my horn players had to be able to stretch out on jazz tunes, play a lot of complicated figures and also have that basic, bluesy, down-home sound." Charles played alto himself when needed, with David "Fathead" Newman on baritone sax and Amos Milburn alumnus Don Wilkerson blowing tenor, anchored by piano, bass, and drums. In November 1954, Charles invited Atlantic's execs to Atlanta to record his new sound.[7]

With his own band Charles felt creatively liberated, turning gospel into secular song. "I'd been singing spirituals since I was three, and I'd been hearing the blues for just as long. ... So what could be more natural than to combine them?" Taking a gospel tune that he and bandleader Renald Richard had heard on the road, Charles turned it into "**I've Got a Woman**" (1954), his first #1 R&B hit. Though it never made the pop charts, Peter Guralnick thinks "it probably exerted as profound an influence on the course of American popular music as any single record before or since." Why? "For the first time in the history of popular music, an artist had blended the blues and gospel into a single song," with "a vocal that bounced between the bedroom and the blessed."[8] Soul music had its template.

Almost seventy years on, its joyful, rhythmic enthusiasm hasn't waned, but the song doesn't feel quite so revolutionary. Wilkerson's tenor solo is nothing special. And the singer's celebration of his woman retains a strong dose of the reactionary gender perspective typical of so much traditional rhythm & blues. She gives him her money and loving on demand, never complains or runs around. Even though she lives far across town, she knows her place: at home. The verse sung in stop-time for emphasis contains nearly all those elements. Genuinely exceptional, however, synthesizing gospel and up-tempo blues, Charles's vocal underlines his baby's virtues with a sound not at all like the characteristic rhythm & blues intensifier of a Roy Brown or Wynonie Harris but like the ecstatic affirmation of the gospelers. The gospel-derived "low moans and falsetto shrieks" that Gerry Hirshey hears in the song Charles parcels out sparingly, letting his voice break into falsetto when she gives him *monEY*, when she saves her *lovIN'* for him, when *SHE* loves him so tenderly that he can't contain the strength of his feelings for her. Guralnick describes that gospel-infused moment as "a tribute to Archie Brownlee's all-out attack...."[9] The low moans come at the end when Charles repeats how *all right* she is.

Even if this record wasn't entirely revolutionary, many African Americans considered it and his subsequent gospel-based hits sacrilege. Charles got serious blowback. But he claimed that those reactions never bothered him. "I'd always thought that the blues and spirituals were close—close musically, close emotionally—and I was happy to hook 'em up." And soon the tide turned. Guralnick asserts that Ray Charles "became a hero to the black community in a mythic sense that no other popular entertainer, with the possible exception of Louis Armstrong, has ever approached." Robert Palmer argues that at this crucial juncture in music history, when Black rhythm & blues was morphing into rock 'n' roll, "Charles refused to compromise his music with the simpler beat, more adolescent lyrics, and smoother singing that white rock & roll fans seemed to favor." Let the records show: between 1949 and 1956, fifteen Ray Charles releases made *Billboard*'s R&B top ten but not one crossed over into the Pop 100. Only after "What'd I Say" (1959) would he break into the Pop top ten eleven times in seven years. "[M]id-fifties Charles landmarks," Palmer writes, "recorded during rock & roll's breakthrough period from late 1954 to late 1955, were more soulfully incendiary, churchy, and rootsy—more 'black,' if you will—than many of his earlier discs." And his later ones.[10]

Released in 1957, *Ray Charles*, Atlantic's first Ray Charles album (later retitled *Hallelujah, I Love Her So*), covered that mid-fifties period. Ironically, "Rock & Roll" is printed over his photo on the front cover. The mid-fifties songs he transposed most directly from gospel rocked the hardest: "I've Got a Woman," **"This Little Girl of Mine"** (1955), **"Hallelujah I Love Her So"** (1956). Yet Charles never considered himself a rock 'n' roller: "[S]o much of my music was sad or down. A tune like Little Richard's 'Tutti Frutti' was fun. Less serious. And kids could identify with it a lot easier than my 'A Fool for You' or 'Drown in My Own Tears.'"[11]

Ray Charles at his piano, 1950s. Album/Alamy Stock Photo.

His songs that he mentions here lean more toward gospel-infused blues or rhythm & blues. Incendiary, churchy, rootsy, sad, serious—all those terms apply. **"A Fool for You"** (1955), his bluest, funkiest, most gospel-drenched record to date, became Charles's second #1 R&B hit. "His aching moans of devotion and two-fisted piano sprang directly from the front pew," Bill Dahl writes, "even as his horns responded in blues-bathed sympathy."[12] Against a strong beat from the rhythm section Charles moans and howls his frustrated love. Pining for this woman since she was five years old, he's confused about why he remains a fool for her even though she emphatically rejects him. Ray the arranger works well with Ray the writer, using the modified stop-time bridge to register how he misses her so badly that his crying gives his neighbor the blues. Ray the singer delivers a sublime performance. Listen to the way he builds the refrain around "I'm a fool for you," lamenting his condition, his obsession, as if he can't believe it himself, gasping *oh nahhh*, as if he can hardly bear the pain of reminding himself yet again of his sublimely excruciating constancy. A guttural shriek acknowledges that she has a man way across town, echoing "I've Got a Woman" with the aching irony that this man ain't him. His agonized final line, "*AAAHH-ahh-ahh oh Lord yeah*," emulates the gospel screamers he carefully studied. Ray Charles had come into his power.

Uncharacteristically, Charles didn't compose his third #1, **"Drown in My Own Tears"** (1956). King Records A&R man Henry Glover wrote **"I'll Drown in My Tears"** (1952) for pianist Sonny Thompson and singer Lula Reed. On their excellent version Reed swings the ballad in her high vocal. With a nearly identical melody, Charles slows it down to the same tempo as "A Fool for You." Panama Francis' metronome-like drumming keeps time for Charles's melancholy piano and horn fills. Glover's extended metaphor comprises the entire lyric: I'm missing you so much that my tears come down like rain, so copious it threatens to drown me. Charles's voice, a thing of wonder, worries key words brokenheartedly and turns pronouns into tormented shrieks: *I'm* becomes *AAAAAHHHM*. Marsh refers to Charles's "half-exhausted, half-exultant 'Why can't *you*,' where he floats into his upper register for the final word...."[13] Charles caps this great record with a female chorus, a girl group from Brooklyn called the Cookies, which he renamed the Raelets in 1958 when they became his full-time backups. They come in at the 2:40 mark for a drive straight out of gospel, repeatedly chanting the title phrase over which Charles improvises his final plea. The striking contrast in the quality of the voices intensifies the repetition of the bereft lover's apparent fate. A powerful finale to the gospelized blues-and-rhythm of a mid-fifties masterpiece.

Ray Charles continued churning out phenomenal music right to the end of the century. Highlights from 1959 to 1963 alone, all top ten R&B *and* Pop, include "What'd I Say," "Georgia on My Mind," "One Mint Julep," "Hit the Road Jack," "Unchain My Heart," "I Can't Stop Loving You," "You Don't Know Me," and "Busted." All of them were built on the brilliant musical synthesis he developed during the crucial postwar decade.

Pounding the piano and screaming the lyrics, **Little Richard** Penniman (1932–2020) exploded onto the rock 'n' roll scene with an incredible string of loud, fast hits: "Tutti Frutti" (1955), "Long Tall Sally" (1956), "Slippin' and Slidin'" (1956), "Ready Teddy" (1956), "Rip It Up" (1956), "Lucille" (1957), "Jenny Jenny" (1957), "Keep A-Knockin'" (1957), "Good Golly Miss Molly" (1958). On his way to becoming one of the first and greatest rock 'n' roll stars, Richard traveled some of African America's most well-trodden musical paths: gospel, medicine and minstrel shows, rhythm & blues. An unapologetic out gay man, he also took more circuitous routes. Catching Richard and his band at a Houston club in 1953, Johnny Otis observed this "outrageous person, good-looking and very effeminate," and his "beautiful, bizarre, and exotic" act. He introduced himself, Otis reported, as "Little Richard, King of the Blues. And the Queen, too!"[14]

Growing up in Macon, Georgia, Richard sang gospel with his family, the Penniman Singers, and attended the Pentecostal church. In 1957, at the height of his fame, and again in the 1970s, he would leave rock 'n' roll for the church and sing only gospel. His major influences included some artists we have previously met. His favorite singer, Sister Rosetta Tharpe, invited him on stage to perform at age ten. Rejected by his father for his effeminacy, Richard left home at fourteen to join Dr. Hudson's Medicine Show where he peddled snake oil and sang "Caldonia"—Louis Jordan's showmanship would prove seminal. He left Dr. Hudson for Sugarfoot Sam from Alabam, the first in a series of minstrel shows in which he performed in dresses as a female impersonator. Traveling across the South—Birmingham, Atlanta, Nashville—Richard found models in other over-the-top showmen and women: flamboyant singer Billy Wright, who curled his hair and wore make-up; gay singer and pianist Esquerita, who shaped Richard's frantic piano style; gospeler Marion Williams, whose *high who* became a Little Richard trademark. By the time he made his first records, in 1951 for RCA-Victor, Little Richard had absorbed myriad influences. Billy Vera hears "shades of Roy Brown and Clyde McPhatter, but the biggest, most unmistakable influence is Little Esther" with her "signature vocal licks and filigrees...."[15]

Richard doesn't sound much like Little Esther as he rocks jazz critic Leonard Feather's composition **"Get Rich Quick"** (1952) from that first RCA session. Richard's biographer, Charles White, thinks he's imitating Billy Wright, whose session men provided the backing band. Other critics hear "an optimistic jump blues, very much in the Roy Brown style," or "an old-school R&B act in the manner of Wynonie Harris or The Treniers." Like Wynonie or Roy Brown, Richard shouts his lyrics above the three saxes, Roy Mays's trumpet, and Julius Wimby's boogie woogie piano.[16] Singing about his lucky day and how he's gonna get rich quick, he displays the kind of energy and positivity that will make him very rich down the road apiece. Fred Jackson's lengthy tenor sax break, almost a full minute of the song's 2:15, suggests the label's relative lack of enthusiasm for Richard's vocal. Though not so unique as the Little Richard music we will come to know, this hot record augurs the future rocker.

Little commercial success or recognition came of that first session or a second for RCA. Richard found himself back in Macon, washing dishes at the Greyhound bus station until he joined Nashville vocal group the Tempo Toppers and began touring again. In Houston, Peacock Records' Don Robey signed them for a session in 1953. One release, "Fool at the Wheel" with husband-wife team the Deuces of Rhythm got some regional action, but Richard left the Tempo Toppers in less than a year. He recorded once more for Peacock, backed by Johnny Otis' band, but by 1954 it was time to move on.[17] Richard's year with Peacock landed one song on my playlist, the A-side of "Fool at the Wheel," **"Ain't That Good News"** (1953). The label credits Duces (sic) of Rhythm & Tempo Toppers, with "Little Richard" (in quotes) as lead singer. Songwriter Raymond Taylor played keyboards for the Deuces.

Cash Box gave the record its Rhythm 'n' Blues Award o' the Week and described "Ain't That Good News" as "an infectious item that opens slow beat.... Changes to fast tempo about midway with a rocking rhythm. This side has life, excitement and appeal. Should be a big one."[18] Maybe it should have been big, but it wasn't. Though the review never mentions Little Richard, the recording owes its infectiousness and appeal primarily to his bluesy melisma. A curious song with no connection to the gospel suggested by its title, its good news consists of everyone, including the singer, being crazy about the blues. He and his baby have the blues for each other. Why exactly is that good news? Never mind. A heavy rhythm section and funky piano accompany Richard, and the Tempo Toppers provide classic harmony background: *oooh oooh oooh oooh* during the slow first half, and echoes of Richard's lyrics in the up-tempo second. Richard puts on a show. He gives us a taste of the balladeer we never got to hear once he became a rock 'n' roller. Listen to what he does with words like *blu-u-ues* and *ba-a-a-a-by*. When the song changes tempo, Richard swings the lyrics and takes it out with a series of gentle falsetto *hoo hoo hoo*s, as if rehearsing the high who shrieks that will become his rock signature.

After leaving the Tempo Toppers and Peacock, Richard put together a hot new band, the Upsetters, with New Orleans musicians who had been working with Shirley and Lee. Passing through Macon, Specialty recording star Lloyd Price heard the band and convinced Richard to send a tape to Art Rupe, who was looking for someone to compete with B.B. King and Ray Charles. Specialty A&R man Bumps Blackwell listened to Richard's tape: "I could tell by the tone of his voice and all those churchy turns that he was a gospel singer who could sing the blues." In September 1955, Rupe brought Little Richard to New Orleans to record at Cosimo Matassa's studio with Fats Domino's band that had Lee Allen on tenor sax and Earl Palmer on drums.[19]

These sessions produced "Tutti Frutti" (1955) and made Little Richard an instant rock star. The story has been retold many times. During a break from recording, Richard starts banging on the piano and singing the gay anthem he had been performing for years as part of his club act: "Tutti frutti, good booty—if it don't fit, don't force it—a-wop-bop-a-loo-mop-a-good goddamn." Blackwell knows it will be a hit, but not with those lyrics. So he asks local songwriter Dorothy La Bostrie to rewrite it. She does on the spot. Instead of anal sex Little Richard sings of girls named Sue and Daisy driving him crazy. Tutti frutti, aw-rootie!

Critics tend to dismiss the other songs Richard recorded at those sessions. The ballad **"I'm Just a Lonely Guy"** (1955), another La Bostrie composition, released as the B-side of "Tutti Frutti," David Kirby calls "more snoozy than bluesy."[20] But I consider it Little Richard's last best effort as a rhythm & bluesman. Ignore the version included on the 1958 Specialty album *The Fabulous Little Richard*, which overdubs

Little Richard and His Band performing in the movie *Mister Rock and Roll*, 1957. Everett Collection Inc./Alamy Stock Photo.

the song with a female chorus singing *da da da dum da dum* in the background. Listen to the sparer Specialty single featuring horn fills, Justin Adams' undistinguished guitar solo, and Richard singing his heart out. Though it lacks the Dionysian fervor of "Tutti Frutti" and his other rock hits, "I'm Just a Lonely Guy" captures Richard at his most impassioned, exploring the deep gospely blues side of R&B. Singing about being so alone in the *wo-o-o-o-rld*, he'll go drown himself in the river if he can't find his baby. You can hear echoes of Ray Charles, and of screamers Clarence Fountain and Archie Brownlee, as Richard taps into his gospel roots, rasping and flaying his voice, letting loose a sanctified *YEAH!!* near the end. You can hear on this record how, in another life, if he had not become a rock 'n' roll star, Little Richard might have become a master of soul music.

The undisputed Godfather of Soul, Soul Brother Number One, the father of funk, dynamic **James Brown** (1933–2006) began recording in 1956. But his career didn't take off until after our postwar decade with the single "Try Me" (1958) and his album *Live at the Apollo* (1963). Beginning with the iconic "Papa's Got a Brand New Bag" (1965), he topped the R&B chart sixteen times between 1965 and 1974 with "I Got You (I Feel Good)" (1965), "It's a Man's Man's Man's World" (1966), "Cold Sweat" (1967), "Say It Loud—I'm Black and I'm Proud" (1968), "Make It Funky" (1971), "Get on the Good Foot" (1972), "Papa Don't Take No Mess" (1974), and more. Even at its height Brown's musical fame was primarily an African American phenomenon. Of his 43 R&B top tens from 1965 to 1974, only six crossed over to *Billboard*'s Pop top ten, none higher than #3. Despite his remarkable musical innovations and rhythmic inventions, James Brown remained essentially a rhythm & blues artist to the end.

Like Ray Charles, soul music's other First Cause, Brown had a sufficiently mythic life to warrant a major biopic, with Chadwick Boseman playing him in *Get on Up* (2014). Yet his early life and recordings are still little known. Born in South Carolina, Brown was four when his mother left him to be raised by his father, who worked in turpentine camps. In 1938, five-year-old James went to live with his Aunt Honey, who ran a brothel and bootlegging operation in Augusta, Georgia. He started singing and learned some instruments in school but dropped out in early adolescence and spent most of his time in the streets. In 1949, Brown got caught stealing clothes from a car and got sentenced to eight-to-sixteen years in Georgia's state penitentiary. Fortunately, the state sent him to a juvenile facility instead. At the Georgia Boys Industrial Institute at Toccoa, Brown excelled at sports and formed a gospel quartet. Townie Bobby Byrd, who had his own gospel group, heard about this kid in juvie, met Brown and heard him sing. Byrd convinced his mother to petition the warden to release Brown and let him live with their family. Paroled in 1952, Brown sang gospel with Byrd for a while, but soon they started a secular R&B group. They called themselves the Flames, and later the Famous Flames.

The Flames all played multiple instruments and took turns singing lead until Brown gradually usurped that spot. In 1955, they had the good fortune of performing in front of Little Richard in a Toccoa club. Sufficiently impressed, Richard sent the Flames to audition for his manager, Clint Brantley. Brantley agreed to manage them, and the band moved to Macon where they tore up the local joints. As James McBride describes it,

> Five country boys from a no-place town would mount the stage of those small joints and howl at the moon, guitarist Nafloyd Scott playing behind his back, pianist Bobby Byrd hammering the keys like his life depended on it, and the lead guy, James Brown, dancing on the tables, leaping off the piano, daring anybody to outdo him.

Brantley had them cut a demo of a song they developed called "Please, Please, Please" and sent it to record companies. Federal's Ralph Bass heard it and signed the Flames to a contract.[21]

In February 1956, James Brown and the now Famous Flames—though not famous for anything yet—drove to Cincinnati to record **"Please, Please, Please"** (1956) in the King studio. Credited to Brown and Johnny Terry, a Flame who had been in the Toccoa facility with him, the song radically adapts Big Joe Williams' old Delta blues, "Baby Please Don't Go" (remember Big Bill Broonzy in our blues chapter), as redone by Sonny Til and the Orioles in 1952 and filtered through a couple of other versions. Brown and the Flames sound nothing like Big Joe, Big Bill, the Orioles, or anyone else. They reduce the lyric to its emotional core—the singer imploring his beloved not to go—with a strong emphasis, as the title indicates, on the pleading. King Records boss Syd Nathan, enraged at hearing the tape, reamed out Ralph Bass, calling it "the worst piece of shit I ever heard in my life. Sounds like someone stuttering on a record, all he says is one word." Yet Nathan released the record, which spent nineteen weeks on the R&B chart. Brown sings more than one word but does repeat *please* 26 times. The Flames with their "smooth gospel harmonies" repeat it 28 more. Philip Gourevitch argues that the "repetitions, elongations, and elisions of the singer's phrasing make of these words not a lament but a rhapsody, even an ecstasy. ... Feeling is stripped to its essence, and the feeling is the whole story." Dave Marsh hears Brown's "growly pleadings shake and quiver in an unholy cross between sexual passion and religious ecstasy."[22]

Brown's voice sounds hoarse from the start, as if he has already been pleading for a long time. He accuses her of doing him wrong, taking his love and leaving him. But reminding himself that she's gone only makes him beg her harder not to go—*please PLEASE*. This persona differs substantially from the man's man we would come to know at the height of Brown's funky fame, the papa who don't take no mess. Here he plays a sensitive, heartbroken doo wop lover stubbornly refusing to give up. His gruff hard gospel voice throws in a "Great God A'mighty!" late in the song. The Flames provide support, echoing Brown's begging her not to go. Fats Gonder's piano triplets and Edison Gore's drumbeat drive the tune with no instrumental break.

Watch Brown's famous live version of "Please, Please, Please," the conclusion to his exhausting 17-minute performance on the *T.A.M.I.* show in 1964, which left the Rolling Stones, who had to follow him, shaking their heads: https://www.youtube.com/watch?v=vruy2GRUsV8. The Hardest Working Man in Show Business drives his audience to a frenzy, punctuating his highly stylized, somewhat cheesy choreography with gospel screams. In what became the standard finale to his live performances, Brown drops to the floor, is picked up, led offstage in weak-kneed despair with a cape over his shoulders, comes back, throws off the cape and falls again, only to rise again and conclude with another sequence of lacerating screams.

Please is not the only word repeated in "Please, Please, Please." Brown repeats the first-person pronoun sixteen times. Compare that to **"I Feel That Old Feeling Coming On"** (1956), recorded at the same session, where he sings "I" 52 times. Flames Nash Knox and Nafloyd Scott wrote this up-tempo 12-bar shuffle. More than just one of Brown's "occasional nods back to the jump blues of the previous decade," it's a great record full of sparkling, mysterious contradictions and radical, unapologetic subjectivity.[23] The lyrical theme appears to be the bad luck the singer has suffered since he was born, made a fool by his woman, 'buked and scorned. Even being a seventh son, normally a sign of special powers and good fortune, in his case means being unlucky. Is *that old feeling* he feels coming on the anticipation of more bad luck? Maybe. But often the case in the blues, the vocal and musical performance tells a different story than the lyrics. Brown sings and swings the tune as if he has just won the lottery, with triumph and enthusiasm, throwing in *Yeah*'s and *Whoo*'s, and a series of celebratory shouts during the zingy tenor sax break by either Wilbert "Lee Diamond" Smith or Ray Felder.

And what about those I's? Reinforced by the Flames singing "I, I" and "I feel" in the background, Brown lets loose a torrent of I's after the second and fourth verses, fifteen in the first case, nineteen in the second. He doesn't stutter "I–I–I" out of weakness, defeat, or inadequate personal resources. He doesn't make the anguished sound "ay yi yi," aghast at his lack of luck. No, as in "Please, Please, Please," Brown unequivocally sings about his feelings. And he feels *good*. He's conjuring his personhood, fetishizing himself, getting on the good foot in a ritual of persistence and self-naming. Valorizing his own emotions, his Black life, the dreamer knows he will live the dream: Unlucky I may have been born, but I can have a better life, a brand new bag. I can feel it, that old can-do feeling. I-I-I can change my luck by saying it loud, Black and proud, over and over.

Brown tried out various styles in a series of recording dates for Federal, looking for that unique James Brown sound. Or at least something that would sell as many records as "Please, Please, Please." In March 1956, in a good try that failed to dent the charts, he admitted emulating the New Orleans–style rock 'n' roll of his old pal Little Richard with the raucous **"Chonnie-On-Chon"** (1956), co-written by Brown, Flames Byrd and Scott, and saxman Lee Diamond Smith.[24] Byrd pounds the high keys in his best Little Richard–style piano assault, while Smith leads the way with his New Orleans-rooted tenor, blowing his brains out in the break alongside Brown's Richard-like shrieks. The lyrics conjure a rock 'n' roll party à la Roy Brown's "Good Rockin' Tonight": Bigfoot Lizzie, Aunt Fanny, and Annie will be there. It also echoes Richard's "Long Tall Sally," recorded only a month earlier, as Brown sings about Aunt Maud and a man who got so drunk he didn't know where he had been. (The lyrics in the first two stanzas are difficult to make out, but DO NOT trust any of the online lyrical transcriptions, all identically, ridiculously wrong.) The title phrase, repeated a few times in the chorus, echoes Richard's "Awop-Bop-a-Loo-Mop." No doubt, James Brown could reinvent his rhythm & blues as rock 'n' roll. But he didn't really want to.

The Famous Flames' background voices are inaudible on "Chonnie-On-Chon," and the record label credits only James Brown. By the end of the year Brown would sign with Ben Bart's Universal Attractions and the Flames would quit, the solidarity of the group betrayed by Brown's bid for individual stardom. Later, Brown would put together a different group of Famous Flames to back him, and Byrd, Scott, and Terry would rejoin. Bobby Byrd stayed with James Brown until 1973, a living legacy of the early years of rhythm & blues music that shaped the Godfather of Soul and soul music itself.

Chapter Notes

Introduction

1. Johnny Otis, *Upside Your Head! Rhythm & Blues on Central Avenue*, 117; Amiri Baraka, *The Autobiography of LeRoi Jones*, 79; Peter Guralnick, *Looking to Get Lost: Adventures in Music & Writing*, 4; David Mitchell, *Utopia Avenue*, 49.

2. I use the terms *Black* (with a capital B) and *African American* (without a hyphen) interchangeably throughout this work. Where *black* is not capitalized in quotations, I have preserved original spelling. *R&B* is capitalized and *doo wop* spelled as two words with no hyphen. Information about *Billboard* chart positions comes from Joel Whitburn, *Top R&B Singles, 1942–1988*.

3. Bob Rolontz and Joel Friedman, "Teen-Agers Demand Music with a Beat, Spur Rhythm-Blues," *Billboard*, April 24, 1954, 1; "1955: The Year R.&B. Took Over Pop Field," *Billboard*, Nov. 12, 1955, 126; "R&B Spreads Wings," *Billboard*, Feb. 4, 1956, 53; John A. Jackson, *Big Beat Heat: Alan Freed and the Early Years of Rock & Roll*, 142–43; Albin J. Zak III, *I Don't Sound Like Nobody: Remaking Music in 1950s America*, 177, 139.

4. Ruth Brown with Andrew Yule, *Miss Rhythm: The Autobiography of Ruth Brown, Rhythm & Blues Legend*, 76; Bo Diddley qtd in Ruth Padel, *I'm a Man: Sex, Gods and Rock 'n' Roll*, 161; Preston Lauterbach, *The Chitlin' Circuit and the Road to Rock 'n' Roll*, 162–63.

5. On lynching and the blues, see Adam Gussow, *Seems Like Murder Here: Southern Violence and the Blues Tradition*, ch. 1. Isabel Wilkerson doubts that lynchings and changes in the cotton economy were primary motivators for migration, *The Warmth of Other Suns: The Epic Story of America's Great Migration*, 690–93; Henry Louis Gates, Jr., "New Negroes, Migration, and Cultural Exchange" in Elizabeth Hutton Turner, ed., *Jacob Lawrence: The Migration Series*, 18.

6. Mike Rowe, *Chicago Blues: The City & the Music*, 27–28; Ed Ward, "The Fifties and Before" in Ed Ward, et al., eds., *Rock of Ages: The Rolling Stone History of Rock & Roll*, 60.

7. Otis, 46. For the transition from big band to R&B, see Nelson George, *The Death of Rhythm & Blues*, 25–26; Ted Fox, *Showtime at the Apollo*, 133–35; and Lauterbach, 114–18.

8. Viv Broughton, *Black Gospel: An Illustrated History of the Gospel Sound*, 46.

9. Denby qtd in Stuart L. Goosman, *Group Harmony: The Black Urban Roots of Rhythm and Blues*, 33.

10. Zak, 18. For disc jockeys and radio, see George, 40–54; Arnold Shaw, *Honkers and Shouters: The Golden Years of Rhythm & Blues*, 508–10; and Jackson, *Big Beat Heat*, 40–42.

11. Shaw, 128–40. Charlie Gillett points out the huge gap in postwar recording between the independents serving the African American market and the six major labels. *The Sound of the City: The Rise of Rock and Roll*, 2nd ed., 7.

12. See Marv Goldberg, "The Chords," *Marv Goldberg's R&B Notebooks*, 2009, https://www.uncamarvy.com/Chords/chords.html; and James Salem, "'Sh-Boom' and the Bomb: A Postwar Call and Response." *Columbia Journal of American Studies* 7 (2006), 1–31, http://www.columbia.edu/cu/cjas/print/shboom.pdf. Goldberg and Salem cite each other, but Salem's article and the online journal in which it appeared can no longer be found. See also Bob Groom, "Beyond the Mushroom Cloud: A Decade of Disillusion in Black Blues and Gospel Song" in David Evans, ed., *Ramblin' on My Mind: New Perspectives on the Blues*, 328–49.

13. For a comprehensive overview of these events, see Carson Claybourne, et al., *Civil Rights Chronicle: The African-American Struggle for Freedom*. See also Richard Gergel, *Unexampled Courage: The Blinding of Sgt. Isaac Woodard and the Awakening of President Harry S. Truman and Judge J. Waties Waring*.

14. LeRoi Jones, *Black Music*, 17; Ann Powers, *Good Booty: Love and Sex, Black & White, Body and Soul in American Music*, 117.

15. King qtd in Harold Steinblatt, "Blues Is King" in Richard Kostelanetz, ed., *The B.B. King Reader: 6 Decades of Commentary*, 140; Richard J. Ripani, *The New Blue Music: Changes in Rhythm & Blues, 1950–1999*, 66–67; Otis qtd in Charlie Lange, liner notes to *Roy Milton and His Solid Senders*, 7.

16. Jim Dawson, *Nervous Man Nervous: Big Jay McNeely and the Rise of the Honking Tenor Sax*, 4–5; George Lipsitz, *Midnight at the Barrelhouse: The Johnny Otis Story*, 35.

17. Albert Murray, *The Omni-Americans*, 58–59 and *Stomping the Blues*, 45. See also 69, 82, 86.

18. Humes qtd in Whitney Balliett, *American Singers: Twenty-Seven Portraits in Song*, 53; LeRoi Jones [Amiri Baraka], *Blues People: Negro Music in White America*, 170; Peter Guralnick, *Sweet Soul Music: Rhythm and Blues and the Southern Dream of Freedom*, 4–5; Samuel A. Floyd, Jr., "Toward a Philosophy of Black Music Scholarship," in Laurie Matheson, ed., *Music in Black American Life: 1600–1945*, 12.

19. Dorsey qtd in Michael W. Harris, *The Rise of Gospel Blues: The Music of Thomas Andrew Dorsey in the Urban Church*, 99, 97; Hooker qtd in Paul Oliver, *Conversations with the Blues*, 168; Tucker qtd in Jerry Zolten, *Great God A' mighty! The Dixie Hummingbirds: Celebrating the Rise of Soul Gospel Music*, 53.

20. Mark Burford, *Mahalia Jackson & the Black Gospel Field*, 305; Teresa L. Reed, *The Holy Profane: Religion in Black Popular Music*, 111.

21. Anthony J. Gribin and Matthew M. Schiff, *The Complete Book of Doo-Wop*, 9; Brian Ward, *Just My Soul Responding: Rhythm and Blues, Black Consciousness, and Race Relations*, 56; Glenn C. Altschuler, *All Shook Up: How Rock 'n' Roll Changed America*, 56.

22. Ike Turner with Nigel Cawthorne, *Takin' Back My Name: The Confessions of Ike Turner*, 4.

23. Lawrence W. Levine, *Black Culture and Black Consciousness*, 269–70.

24. Greil Marcus, *Mystery Train: Images of America in Rock 'n' Roll Music*, 29.

25. Theodore Gracyk, *Listening to Popular Music Or, How I Learned to Stop Worrying and Love Led Zeppelin*, 112; Questlove with Ben Greenman, *Music Is History*, 12; Guralnick, *Looking to Get Lost*, 479.

26. Allan F. Moore, ed., *Analyzing Popular Music*, 3; Crawford qtd in Guthrie P. Ramsey, Jr., *Race Music: Black Cultures from Bebop to Hip-Hop*, 20, Crawford's italics; Guralnick, *Looking to Get Lost*, 5, his italics; Bob Dylan, *The Philosophy of Song*, 9.

27. Qtd in John Michael Runowicz, *Forever Doo-Wop: Race, Nostalgia, and Vocal Harmony*, 51. Also known as the "Blue Moon" changes: see Jim Dawson and Steve Propes, *What Was the First Rock 'n' Roll Record*, 160.

28. B. Ward, 8.

29. Gussow, *Seems Like Murder Here*, 202; Angela Y. Davis, *Blues Legacies and Black Feminism: Gertrude "Ma" Rainey, Bessie Smith and Billie Holiday*, 29, 33. Paul Garon argues against a sociological approach to the blues: "The essence of the blues is not to be found in the daily life with which it deals, but in the way such life is critically focused on and imaginatively transformed." *Blues and the Poetic Spirit*, 65–71.

30. See Jacqueline Warwick, *Girl Groups, Girl Culture: Popular Music and Identity in the 1960s*.

31. Julio Finn, *The Bluesman: The Musical Heritage of Black Men and Women in the Americas*, 230, Finn's italics. "The term *blues*," writes LeRoi Jones, "relates directly to the Negro and his *personal* involvement in America," 94. For a nuanced study of this issue, see Adam Gussow, *Whose Blues? Facing Up to Race and the Future of the Music*.

Chapter One

1. Baraka, 77; Richard Wright, "Foreword" in Paul Oliver, *Blues Fell This Morning: Meaning in the Blues*, xv; Ralph Ellison, *Shadow and Act*, 78.

2. Robert Palmer, *Deep Blues*, 17. Boyd and Hooker qtd in *The Voice of the Blues: Classic Interviews from* Living Blues Magazine, Jim O'Neal and Amy Van Singel, eds., 254, 224; Waters qtd in Peter Guralnick, *Feel Like Going Home: Portraits in Blues and Rock 'n' Roll*, 67. Mississippi remains one of the poorest states with low literacy levels and life expectancy. See Jesmyn Ward, *Men We Reaped*, 236–37; and Anthony Walton, *Mississippi: An American Journey*.

3. Charles Keil, *Urban Blues*, 61–62.

4. For Paul and Beth Garon, "the pseudonymous tendency in the blues" is a "refusal ... wherein the blues singers assume a new stance beyond the range of white Christian authority." *Woman with Guitar: Memphis Minnie's Blues*, 173.

5. For comprehensive histories of the blues, see William Barlow, *Looking Up at Down: The Emergence of Blues Culture*; Giles Oakley, *The Devil's Music: A History of the Blues*; Paul Oliver, *The Story of the Blues*. For histories of Delta blues, see Palmer, *Deep Blues*; and Ted Gioia, *Delta Blues: The Life and Times of the Mississippi Masters Who Revolutionized American Music*.

6. Barlow, 325–28.

7. Helen Oakley Dance, *Stormy Monday: The T-Bone Walker Story*, 3; Witherspoon qtd in Kevin and Peter Sheridan, "T-Bone Walker: Father of the Blues," *Guitar Player* (Mar. 1977), rpt. in *The Pop, Rock, and Soul Reader*, David Brackett, ed., 35; Otis, 85; Robert Santelli, *The Best of the Blues: 101 Essential Albums*, 67.

8. See Kelly Schrum, *Some Wore Bobby Sox: The Emergence of Teenage Girls' Culture, 1920–1945*.

9. Walter Mosley, *Devil in a Blue Dress*, 27. Cf. Otis: "Black performers throughout the country, and especially in the South, perceived Los Angeles as a kind of promised land," 4.

10. Santelli, 70.

11. Santelli, 121; Michael Hall, "Let There Be Lightnin'," *TexasMonthly* (June 2007), https://www.texasmonthly.com/articles/let-there-be-lightnin/.

12. Stephen Galt's *Barrelhouse Words: A Blues Dialect Dictionary* defines *rat* as "a woman's hairpiece; more commonly, a pad used in hair styling to make hair appear thicker," 193; Alan Govenar, *Lightnin' Hopkins: His Life and Blues*, 47–48.

13. Erika Schiche, "Lightnin' Hopkins, Mance Lipscomb and the Legend of Tom Moore's Farm" *Houston Press*, Mar. 15, 2016, https://www.houstonpress.com/music/lightnin-hopkins-mance-lipscomb-and-the-legend-of-tom-moores-farm-7702841; Lipscomb qtd in Yank

Thornton, "The Secret History of Texas Music: 'Tom Moore's Farm' (1930s)," *TexasMonthly*, https://www.texasmonthly.com/list/the-secret-history-of-texas-music/tom-moores-farm-1930s/, retrieved Jan. 29, 2023; Coy Prather, "Story Behind the Song: 'Tom Moore's Farm,'" *Texas Music*, Sept. 5, 2021, https://txmusic.com/story-behind-the-song-tom-moores-farm/.

14. Gioia, 330.

15. See Nadine Cohodas, *Spinning Blues into Gold: The Chess Brothers and the Legendary Chess Records*; and John Collis, *The Story of Chess Records*.

16. Waters qtd in O'Neal and Van Singel, 172. See Bob Riesman, *I Feel So Good: The Life and Times of Big Bill Broonzy*; and Kevin D. Greene, *The Invention and Reinvention of Big Bill Broonzy*.

17. Greene, 122–23; see David M. Oshinsky, *"Worse Than Slavery": Parchman Farm and the Ordeal of Jim Crow Justice*.

18. Memphis Slim, Big Bill Broonzy and Sonny Boy Williamson as told to Alan Lomax, *Blues in the Mississippi Night*; Greene, 138–39.

19. Santelli, 134; William Broonzy as told to Yannick Bruynoghe, *Big Bill Blues*, 138; Langston Hughes, "Happy New Year with Memphis Minnie," *Chicago Defender*, Jan. 9, 1943, rpt. in *Martin Scorsese Presents the Blues: A Musical Journey*, Peter Guralnick, Robert Santelli, et al., eds., 202.

20. "Bricks in My Pillow: The Robert Nighthawk Story," http://nighthawk.sundayblues.org/index.htm, retrieved April 19, 2023; Palmer, *Deep Blues*, 118, 145–46, 192–95.

21. Presley qtd in Larry Birnbaum, *Before Elvis: The Prehistory of Rock 'n' Roll*, 4; Crudup qtd in Lawrence N. Redd, *Rock Is Rhythm and Blues (The Impact of Mass Media)*, 130–31.

22. Guido Van Rijn, *The Truman & Eisenhower Blues: African-American Blues and Gospel Songs, 1945-1960*, 94.

23. Alan Lomax, *The Land Where the Blues Began*, 405–18; Robert Gordon, *Can't Be Satisfied: The Life and Times of Muddy Waters*, 35–68.

24. Waters qtd in Gordon, 89.

25. Palmer, *Deep Blues*, 161.

26. Gordon, 99.

27. The blues commonplace, "I woke up this morning," Gioia writes, "brings with it half-remembered dreams and nightmares, and the sleepless anxieties of many, many long and lonely nights," 14. Examining hundreds of songs that use some version of that phrase, Michael Taft concludes that it connotes "waking up to a realization that there has been a change in the situation … almost always for the worse." *The Blues Lyric Formula*, 195; Anthony Heilbut, *The Gospel Sound: Good News and Bad Times*, xvi; Gordon, 100; Sandra B. Tooze, *Muddy Waters: The Mojo Man*, 96.

28. Dawson & Propes, 68.

29. Gioia, 218. See Max Haymes, "Catfish Blues (Origins of a Blues)," https://www.earlyblues.com/essay_catfish.htm, retrieved May 30, 2020.

30. Palmer, *Deep Blues*, 164.

31. For High John the Conqueror, see Davis, 156–57. The nameless Black protagonist of Ralph Ellison's *Invisible Man*, published two years earlier, shares Muddy's insistence on being seen and known. One of his revelations, "I am what I am," might serve as epigraph to Muddy's "Hoochie Coochie Man." See Ch. 13.

32. Wayne Everett Goins, *Blues All Day Long: The Jimmy Rogers Story*, 86; Santelli, 110.

33. Discography courtesy of Stefan Wirz, *Wirz's American Music*, https://www.wirz.de/music/jonesfl.htm, retrieved June 4, 2021. David Evans, *Big Road Blues: Tradition and Creativity in the Folk Blues*, 277.

34. Lenoir qtd in Oliver, *Conversations*, 152; Van Rijn, 105–07.

35. See Françoise N. Hamlin, *Crossroads at Clarksdale: The Black Freedom Struggle in the Mississippi Delta after World War II*.

36. Otis Rush interviewed by Jas Obrecht in *Rollin' and Tumblin': The Postwar Blues Guitarists*, Jas Obrecht, ed., 226; Obrecht, 223; Palmer, *Deep Blues*, 265.

37. Willie Dixon with Don Snowden, *I Am the Blues: The Willie Dixon Story*, 106.

38. Shaw, *Honkers and Shouters*, 302; Palmer, *Deep Blues*, 232–33.

39. James Segrest and Mark Hoffman, *Moanin' at Midnight: The Life and Times of Howlin' Wolf*, 39–41; Palmer, *Deep Blues*, 231; Peter Guralnick, *Sam Phillips: The Man Who Invented Rock 'n' Roll*, 118.

40. Mark A. Humphrey, "Bright Lights, Big City: Urban Blues" in Lawrence Cohn, ed., *Nothing But the Blues: The Music and the Musicians*, 189; Gioia, 287; Gillett, 137; Guralnick, *Sam Phillips*, 125; Palmer, *Deep Blues*, 234.

41. Palmer, *Deep Blues*, 234.

42. Santelli, 5. For a careful analysis of Johnson's song, see Elijah Ward, *Escaping the Delta: Robert Johnson and the Invention of the Blues*, 135–38.

43. Robert Palmer, liner notes to *The Sky Is Crying: The History of Elmore James*, 6; Gioia, 313.

44. The only site I have found with *accurate* lyrics for this song is Jas Obrecht, "'Dust My Broom'—Elmore James (1951)," Library of Congress, https://www.loc.gov/static/programs/national-recording-preservation-board/documents/Dust-My-Broom.pdf, retrieved June 19, 2022; Galt, *Barrelhouse Words*, 81; Palmer, *Deep Blues*, 214–15.

45. Palmer, *Deep Blues*, 185. For discussions of both Sonny Boys, see Rowe, 120–25, 140–44.

46. Santelli, 71, 15. See Lawrence Hoffman, "The Blues Harp: The Classic Era," *Living Blues* 167 (Mar.–May 2003), 120–21.

47. Rowe, 91.

48. Tony Glover, Scott Dirks & Ward Gaines, *Blues with a Feeling: The Little Walter Story*, 82–83.

49. Glover, Dirks & Gaines, 141.

50. Donald E. Wilcock with Buddy Guy, *Damn Right I've Got the Blues: Buddy Guy and the Blues Roots of Rock-and-Roll*, 76.

51. Colin Escott with Martin Hawkins, *Good*

Rockin' Tonight: Sun Records and the Birth of Rock 'n' Roll, 52.

52. Evelyn Johnson qtd in James M. Salem, *The Late Great Johnny Ace and the Transition from R&B to Rock 'n' Roll*, 57; Thornton qtd in Michael Spörke, *Big Mama Thornton: The Life and Music*, 19.

53. Alice Walker's short story "Nineteen Fifty-Five" imagines a Big Mama-like character and an Elvis clone who buys her song and later confides in her: "I've sung it and sung it, and I'm making forty thousand dollars a day offa it, and you know what, I don't have the faintest notion what that song means." She prompts him to finally figure it out. Alice Walker, *You Can't Keep a Good Woman Down: Stories*.

54. Thornton qtd in Spörke, 4; Maureen Mahon, *Black Diamond Queens: African American Women and Rock and Roll*, 38; *Cash Box*, May 30, 1953, qtd in Robert Palmer, *Baby, That Was Rock 'n' Roll: The Legendary Leiber & Stoller*, 33.

55. *Billboard* qtd in Peter Guralnick, *Dream Boogie: The Triumph of Sam Cooke*, 104; Guralnick, *Sweet Soul Music*, 24.

56. Leach qtd in Todd R. Baptista, *Group Harmony: Echoes of the Rhythm & Blues Era*, 240; Aretha Franklin with David Ritz, *Aretha: From These Roots*, 66.

57. Santelli, 360; Peter Grendysa, liner notes to *Big Maybelle: The Complete Okeh Sessions, 1952-55*.

58. Dawson and Propes, 134; Etta James and David Ritz, *Rage to Survive: The Etta James Story*, 43.

59. James & Ritz, 48; Buzzy Jackson, *A Bad Woman Feeling Good: Blues and the Women Who Sing Them*, 146.

60. Charles Shaar Murray, *Boogie Man: The Adventures of John Lee Hooker in the American Twentieth Century*, 120.

61. John Milward, *Crossroads: How the Blues Shaped Rock 'n' Roll*, 18; Murray,131-35; Buddy Guy with David Ritz, *When I Left Home: My Story*, 15-16, 22-23.

62. Murray, 145; Adam Gussow, *Beyond the Crossroads: The Devil and the Blues Tradition*, 49.

63. Reed, 78.

64. Galt, 231; Garon and Garon, 103-11. For the blues permutations of "Sugar Mama" and "Queen Bee," see Jerry Wasserman, "Queen Bee, King Bee: *The Color Purple* and the Blues," *Canadian Review of American Studies* 30.3 (2000), 308-11.

65. Guy, *When I Left Home*, 41; King qtd in Jeff Hannusch, "Eddie 'Guitar Slim' Jones," in Obrecht, ed., *Rollin' and Tumblin'*, 354; Palmer, *Deep Blues*, 247-48.

66. Hannusch, 356; Santelli, 302-03.

67. Thomas qtd in *Martin Scorsese Presents the Blues*, ed. Guralnick, et al., 147.

68. Santelli, 95.

69. Charles Sawyer, *The Arrival of B.B. King*, 58-67, 71-72; Daniel de Visé, *King of the Blues: The Rise and Reign of B.B. King*, 103-18, 132-36; Guralnick, *Sam Phillips*, 87-93.

70. de Visé, 144.

71. de Visé, 157.

72. Colin Escott, "Notes on Selected Recordings," in Richard Kostelanetz, ed., *The B.B. King Reader: 6 Decades of Commentary*, 286; Sawyer, 71.

73. Charles Farley, *Soul of the Man: Bobby "Blue" Bland*, 53; Keil, 67.

Chapter Two

1. Ray Charles & David Ritz, *Brother Ray: Ray Charles' Own Story*, 178; Jones, 171; Altschuler, 71.

2. Chip Deffaa, *Blues Rhythms: Six Lives in Rhythm and Blues*, 7.

3. "The Boys Who Sell 'Em See Combos Hogging Theaters." *Billboard*, Aug. 10, 1946, 39; Fox, 133-34. A later *Billboard* survey revealed the major record labels' growing irrelevance to R&B. Of the fifty best-selling R&B records from 1949-53, the majors released only two. Arnold Shaw, *The World of Soul*, 104.

4. Jones, 172; Gillett, 10-11; James Miller, *Flowers in the Dustbin: The Rise of Rock and Roll, 1947-1977*, 29.

5. Brian Ward, 40; David Evans, "The Development of the Blues," in Allan Moore, ed., *The Cambridge Companion to Blues and Gospel Music*, 37.

6. Qtd in Jackson, 3, 73; qtd in Pearson, 338-39; Shaw, *Honkers and Shouters*, xxvi-xxvii.

7. Ed Ward, "The Fifties and Before," 91, 105; Amy Absher, *The Black Musician and the White City: Race and Music in Chicago, 1900-1967*, 102, 111; "A Warning to the Music Business," *Variety*, Feb. 23, 1955, rpt. in Brackett, ed., *The Pop, Rock, and Soul Reader*, 79.

8. Alan Freed, *Down Beat*, April 20, 1955, qtd in Rick Coleman, *Blue Monday: Fats Domino and the Lost Dawn of Rock 'n' Roll*, 99.

9. Peter Silvester, *A Left Hand Like God: The Story of Boogie-Woogie*, 5; Johnson qtd in Silvester, 174.

10. Jones, 172, his italics; Dawson, 41; Baraka, 79.

11. Shaw, *Honkers and Shouters*, 349; George, 68-69.

12. Tony Collins, *Rock, Mr. Blues: The Life and Music of Wynonie Harris*, 115.

13. Richard Middleton, "The Sophisticated Tradition: Urban Styles, the Second Move Towards America and the Development of Soul," in Kostelanetz ed., *The B.B. King Reader*, 40; Nick Tosches, *Unsung Heroes of Rock 'n' Roll*, 34; Jordan qtd in Shaw, *Honkers and Shouters*, 74, his italics.

14. Coleman, 44-45; Jordan qtd in Shaw, *Honkers and Shouters*, 67; John Chilton, *Let the Good Times Roll: The Story of Louis Jordan and His Music*, 144-45; Lauterbach, 103.

15. Jordan qtd in Chilton, 177.

16. Korsha Wilson, "Celebrating the Fish Fry, a Late-Summer Black Tradition," *New York Times*, Sept. 11, 2018, https://www.nytimes.com/2018/09/11/dining/fish-fry-black-tradition.html.

17. Coleman, 45-47.

18. Murray, *Stomping the Blues*, 82.
19. Chilton, 157; "Louie, Louie—Louis Armstrong Meets Louis Jordan," *The Wonderful World of Louis Armstrong*, https://dippermouth.blogspot.com/2010/09/louie-louie-louis-armstrong-meets-louis.html?m=0, retrieved July 12, 2020.
20. Will Friedwald, *A Biographical Guide to the Great Jazz and Pop Singers*, 246.
21. Friedwald, 245.
22. Balliett, 52.
23. Friedwald, 248.
24. Linda Dahl, *Stormy Weather: The Music and Lives of a Century of Jazzwomen*, 153; Shaw, *Honkers and Shouters*, 145–46.
25. Jim Haskins, *Queen of the Blues: A Biography of Dinah Washington*, 40; *Billboard*, Mar. 30, 1946, 160. For voot see "The Roots Canal: Voot Detective," *Tuwa's Shanty and the Roots Canal*, http://tuwa.blogspot.com/2006/06/roots-canal-voot-detective.html, retrieved July 15, 2020. Washington herself managed to find the right man over and over, marrying seven times in her short, troubled life.
26. Shaw, *Honkers and Shouters*, 276.
27. Dahl, 71; Balliett, 35–36.
28. Billy Vera, liner notes to *The Best of Nellie Lutcher*.
29. Silvester, 119; Lauterbach, 84; David Evans, "Early Deep South and Mississippi Valley Blues" in Oliver, ed., *Blackwell Guide to Recorded Blues*, 40.
30. Broonzy, 136; Silvester, 254.
31. Dixon, 64.
32. For every show at Harlem's Apollo, 1934–60, see Marv Goldberg, "Apollo Theater Shows," *Marv Goldberg's R&B Notebooks*, 2019, http://www.uncamarvy.com/ApolloTheaterShows/apollo.html.
33. Tosches, 54.
34. Sampson, "Amos Milburn: 'Chicken Shack Boogie,'" *Spontaneous Lunacy: The History of Rock 'n' Roll—Song by Song*, June 11, 2017, https://www.spontaneouslunacy.net/amos-milburn-chicken-shack-boogie-aladdin-3014/.
35. Fats Domino said, "I first heard triplets on an Amos Milburn record. ... He and Little Willie Littlefield, they both had the same style. ..." qtd in Coleman, 63–64; Miller, 65–66; Palmer, *Baby, That Was Rock & Roll*, 4.
36. Gillett, 135.
37. In Ralph Ellison's *Invisible Man*, ch. 9, the narrator meets a blues musician in Harlem who sings the frog verse.
38. Tosches, 52; Eugene Chadbourne, "Rufus Gore Biography," *AllMusic*, https://www.allmusic.com/artist/rufus-gore-mn0001599628/biography, retrieved July 30, 2022.
39. Bradshaw's drummer, Calvin "Eagle Eye" Shields, a key session man at King, "may have been the first black drummer to record country music." "Calvin Shields—Musical Pioneer," *Zero to 180—Three Minute Magic*, May 3, 2018, https://www.zeroto180.org/?p=31595.
40. Murray, *Stomping the Blues*, 166; Shaw, *Honkers and Shouters*, 48.
41. Tosches, 20–21; Balliett, 43.
42. Galt, *Barrelhouse Words*, 114.
43. Sampson, "Big Joe Turner: 'Low Down Dog,'" *Spontaneous Lunacy: The History of Rock 'n' Roll—Song by Song*. July 18, 2017, https://www.spontaneouslunacy.net/big-joe-turner-low-down-dog-aladdin-3013/.
44. Sherley A. Williams, "The Blues Roots of Contemporary Afro-American Poetry" (1979) in *Write Me a Few of Your Lines: A Blues Reader*, ed. Steven C. Tracy, 449.
45. Garon, *Blues and the Poetic Spirit*, 183, 189.
46. Dawson and Propes, 130; Tosches, 16.
47. Collins, 77, 10.
48. Miller, 27; Dawson and Propes, 30; Robert L. Campbell, et al., *The Tom Archia Discography*, http://campber.people.clemson.edu/archia.html, retrieved Oct. 14, 2021.
49. Collins, 71.
50. John Broven, *Rhythm & Blues in New Orleans*, 23; Lauterbach, 144; Hugh Gregory, *The Real Rhythm and Blues*, 77.
51. Jon Hartley Fox, *King of the Queen City: The Story of King Records*, 38.
52. Witherspoon qtd in Shaw, *Honkers and Shouters*, 212, 215.
53. Davis, 31; Jerry Leiber recounts hearing Witherspoon's "Ain't Nobody's Business" on the radio: "Maybe it was the power and absolute confidence of his voice. Maybe it was the lyrics. ... Whatever it was, I was never the same again." Jerry Leiber and Mike Stoller with David Ritz, *Hound Dog: The Leiber and Stoller Autobiography*, 25.
54. Shaw, *Honkers and Shouters*, 92–93; Ed Ward, *The History of Rock & Roll, Vol. One, 1920–1963*, 63; Gillett, 142.
55. Sampson, "Percy Mayfield, 'Please Send Me Someone to Love,'" *Spontaneous Lunacy: The History of Rock 'n' Roll—Song by Song*, June 30, 2021, https://www.spontaneouslunacy.net/percy-mayfield-please-send-me-someone-to-love-specialty-375/; Mayfield qtd in Lee Hildebrand, *Stars of Soul and Rhythm & Blues*, 147.
56. Shaw, *Honkers and Shouters*, 481; Salem, 67, 72.
57. Dawson and Propes, 172; Salem, 156, 3.
58. James and Ritz, 65; Glover qtd in Susan Whitall with Kevin John, *Fever: Little Willie John's Fast Life, Mysterious Death and the Birth of Soul*, 56–57.
59. Whitall, 59. For "Need Your Love So Bad" covers, see https://secondhandsongs.com/work/12075/versions#nav-entity, retrieved Aug. 30, 2022.
60. Dave Marsh, *The Heart of Rock & Soul: The 1001 Greatest Singles Ever Made*, 38; Joe McEwen, "Little Willie John" in Greil Marcus, ed. *Stranded: Rock and Roll for a Desert Island*, 98.
61. Marsh, 81; Whitall, 75.
62. Brian Ward, 78.
63. Brian Ward, 79.
64. Bass qtd in Shaw, *Honkers & Shouters*, 237; Lipsitz, 41.
65. Dawson and Propes, 13.

66. Davonia "Dee" Williams, who also plays on Little Esther's "Double Crossing Blues," was "one of the first great pianists of rock, and the first great female instrumentalist." "Dee Williams," *Spontaneous Lunacy: The History of Rock 'n' Roll—Song by Song*, https://www.spontaneouslunacy.net/artists-dee-williams/, retrieved Nov. 16, 2020.

67. Hildebrand, 29; Robert Greenfield, *The Last Sultan: The Life and Times of Ahmet Ertegun*, 59; Ruth Brown, 41.

68. Ertegun qtd in Greenfield, 63; Ed Ward, "The Fifties and Before," 54; Sampson, "Ruth Brown: 'So Long,'" *Spontaneous Lunacy: The History of Rock 'n' Roll Song by Song*, July 31, 2018, https://www.spontaneouslunacy.net/ruth-brown-so-long-atlantic-879/.

69. Ertegun qtd in Shaw, *Honkers & Shouters*, 373.

70. Brown qtd in Peter Grendysa, liner notes to *Jump Blues Classics*.

71. Jerry Wexler and David Ritz, *Rhythm and the Blues: A Life in American Music*, 87–88; Marv Goldberg, "Lavern Baker," *Marv Goldberg's R&B Notebooks*, 2020, http://www.uncamarvy.com/LavernBaker/lavernbaker.html.

72. B. Ward, 155; "Dandy Jim from Caroline" (1844), *Uncle Tom's Cabin & American Culture*, http://utc.iath.virginia.edu/minstrel/dandyjimfr.html, retrieved Nov. 20, 2022.

73. Bass qtd in Broven, 4; Mac Rebennack (Dr. John) qtd in Broven, 13.

74. Sampson, "Fats Domino: 'The Fat Man,'" *Spontaneous Lunacy: The History of Rock 'n' Roll—Song by Song*, Jan. 21, 2020, https://www.spontaneouslunacy.net/fats-domino-the-fat-man-imperial-5058/; Miller, 97; Gillett, 139.

75. Bartholomew qtd in Broven, 31; Dawson and Propes, 64; Coleman, 52–54.

76. Rupe qtd in Dawson and Propes, 109; Coleman, 73, his italics.

77. Broven, 43.

78. Sampson, "Wild Bill Moore: 'We're Gonna Rock,'" *Spontaneous Lunacy: The History of Rock 'n' Roll—Song by Song*, June 7, 2017, his italics, https://www.spontaneouslunacy.net/wild-bill-moore-were-gonna-rock-savoy-666/; Tosches, 6; Jackson, 82.

79. Dawson, 27.

80. Dawson and Propes, 53; Graeme M. Boone, "Twelve Key Recordings," in *The Cambridge Companion to Blues and Gospel Music*, ed. Moore, 71–72; Dawson, 44.

81. Sampson, "Chris Powell and The Five Blue Flames: 'Rock the Joint,'" *Spontaneous Lunacy: The History of Rock 'n' Roll—Song by Song*, Mar. 1, 2019, https://www.spontaneouslunacy.net/chris-powell-and-the-five-blue-flames-rock-the-joint-columbia-30175/.

82. Sampson, "Goree Carter: Rock Awhile," *Spontaneous Lunacy: The History of Rock 'n' Roll—Song by Song*, Feb. 6, 2018, https://www.spontaneouslunacy.net/goree-carter-rock-awhile-freedom-1506/. See John Nova Lomax, "Roll Over, Ike Turner," *TexasMonthly* (Dec. 2014), https://www.texasmonthly.com/the-culture/roll-over-ike-turner/.

83. See Barry Lee Pearson, "One Day You're Gonna Hear About Me: The H-Bomb Ferguson Story," *Living Blues* 69 (1985), 17.

84. Sampson, "Jimmy Liggins: 'Cadillac Boogie,'" *Spontaneous Lunacy: The History of Rock 'n' Roll—Song by Song*, April 7, 2017, https://www.spontaneouslunacy.net/jimmy-liggins-cadillac-boogie-specialty-521/. For Cadillac-themed blues and R&B tunes, see "You Call Yourself a Cadillac, You Ain't Nothin' but a T-Model Ford—Automobile Blues," *Big Road Blues Radio*, July 28, 2019, https://sundayblues.org/?p=17982.

85. Tosches, 107–8; see Bill Vance, "1949 Oldsmobile 'Rocket' 88," *Canadian Driver*, Oct. 19, 2004, http://autos.ca/articles/bv/rocket88.htm; Palmer, *Deep Blues*, 220–24; Guralnick, *Sam Phillips*, 103–07; Dawson and Propes, 88–91.

86. John Battles, "Rockin' Is Their Business: The Treniers," *Flying Saucers Rock 'n' Roll: Conversations with Unjustly Obscure Rock 'n' Roll Eccentrics*, ed. Jake Austen, 190–93.

Chapter Three

1. Angelou qtd in Zolten, 80; Sharpton qtd in *Summer of Soul (... or When the Revolution Could Not Be Televised)*, dir. Questlove; Rupe qtd in Guralnick, *Dream Boogie*, 69; Tucker qtd in Zolten, 67.

2. Horace Clarence Boyer, *The Golden Age of Gospel*, 50.

3. Gayle F. Wald, *Shout, Sister, Shout: The Untold Story of Rock-and-Roll Trailblazer Sister Rosetta Tharpe*, 10; Boyer, 29–30, 41–43.

4. Dorsey qtd in Harris, 96–97, 210; Harris, 239; Robert M. Marovich, *A City Called Heaven: Chicago and the Birth of Gospel Music*, ch. 6–7.

5. Opal Louis Nations, *Sensational Nightingales: The Story of Joseph 'Jo Jo' Wallace and the Early Days of the Sensational Nightingales*, 21–22; Boyer, 117, 49. Gage Averill points out terminological inconsistencies in classifying quartets as *jubilee*, *spiritual*, *jazz*, or *gospel*. *Four Parts, No Waiting: A Social History of American Barbershop Harmony*, 196 n.60.

6. Opal Louis Nations, Liner notes to *The Five Blind Boys of Mississippi*, Acrobat CD, 2006, http://opalnations.com/files/Five_Blind_Boys_of_Miss_Acrobat_CD_3003_Liner_Notes.pdf, retrieved Feb. 21, 2021. Du Bois qtd in Henry Louis Gates, Jr., *The Black Church: This Is Our Story, This Is Our Song*, 101–02; Zolten, 29.

7. Heilbut, *The Gospel Sound*, 78.

8. Glenn Hinson, *Fire in My Bones: Transcendence and the Holy Spirit in African American Gospel*, 280, 293–94, 367 n.26; Zolten, 209. Ann Powers discusses the erotically charged passions of gospel in *Good Booty*, ch. 3.

9. Heilbut, 57; Burford, 319–20; Bil Carpenter, *Uncloudy Days: The Gospel Music Encyclopedia*, 206.

10. Boyer, 90, 85; Jackson qtd in Broughton, 53.

11. Jackson qtd in Burford, 147; Bernice Johnson Reagon, "William Herbert Brewster: Rememberings," *We'll Understand It Better By and By: Pioneering African American Gospel Composers*, ed. Bernice Johnson Reagon, 201; Robert F. Darden, "'Move on Up a Little Higher'—Mahalia Jackson (1947)," National Registry, 2005, https://www.loc.gov/static/programs/national-recording-preservation-board/documents/MoveOnUpALittleHigher.pdf.

12. J. Lowe quoted in Carpenter, 102; Opal Louis Nations, Liner notes to *The Greatest Recordings of Madame Edna Gallmon Cooke*. http://opalnations.com/files/Madame_Edna_Gallmon_Cooke_AVI_Nashboro_CD_4008_Liner_Notes.pdf. Retrieved Jan. 5, 2021.

13. Lauterbach, 152; Charles White, *The Life and Times of Little Richard: The Quasar of Rock*, 17; "Sister Rosetta Tharpe," Rock & Roll Hall of Fame, https://www.rockhall.com/inductees/sister-rosetta-tharpe, retrieved Dec. 21, 2021; Robert Darden, *People Get Ready! A New History of Black Gospel Music*, 197.

14. Heilbut, 191; Wald, 42.

15. Wald, 86–87; "Sister Rosetta Tharpe—Up Above My Head on Gospel Time TV Show," https://www.youtube.com/watch?v=JeaBNAXfHfQ. For some of her best guitar work, see "Sister Rosetta Tharpe guitar solos (in motion picture)," https://www.youtube.com/watch?v=gELe5Rj_tXU, retrieved Dec. 21, 2021.

16. Wald, 102. For the 1963 civil rights adaptation and Wilson Pickett's soul version, see "99 1/2 Just Won't Do: Brown-Eyed Has Got to 100!" *Brown Eyed Handsome Soul*, Oct. 18, 2007, http://browneyedhandsomeman.blogspot.com/2007/10/99-12-just-wont-do-brown-eyed-has-got.html.

17. Carpenter, 348.

18. Dave Marsh, "Prof. Alex Bradford Artist Biography," AllMusic, https://www.allmusic.com/artist/prof-alex-bradford-mn0000620491/biography, retrieved Dec. 27, 2022.

19. Marovich, 242; Carpenter, 54.

20. Boyer, 25.

21. Broughton, 63; Van Rijn, 31–32.

22. Boyer, 171–72. See Opal Louis Nations, Liner notes to The C.B.S. Trumpeteers, *Milky White Way*, http://opalnations.com/files/CBS_Trumpeteers_AVI_Nashboro_CD_4534_1995__Liner_Notes.pdf.

23. Boyer, 179; Opal Louis Nations, Liner notes to *The Bells of Joy*, http://opalnations.com/files/Bells_of_Joy_Acrobat_CD_4207_Liner_Notes.pdf, retrieved Jan. 3, 2021.

24. Opal Louis Nations, Liner notes to *The Radio Four, 1952-54*, http://opalnations.com/files/Radio_Four_1952-1954_Heritage_CD_42_1999_.pdf.

25. Tony Fletcher, *In the Midnight Hour: The Life & Soul of Wilson Pickett*, 27. See Opal Louis Nations, "The Fantastic Violinaires," *Blues & Rhythm* 300 (June 2015), http://opalnations.com/files/Violinaires_The_Fantastic_Violinaires_B_R_300_June_2015.pdf.

26. Guralnick, *Dream Boogie*, 119–20; Marovich, 215. The traditional African American complaint "I've been 'buked and I've been scorned" appears frequently in song. Mahalia Jackson sang the spiritual of that title at the 1963 March on Washington.

27. Opal Louis Nations, "From 'Prayer of Death' to 'Uncloudy Day': The Staple Singers' Early Days," *Blues & Rhythm* 128 (April 1998), http://opalnations.com/files/Staple_Singers_Early_Days_Blues_Rhythm_128_April_1998.pdf; James Miller, Liner notes to The Staple Singers, *Faith and Grace: A Family Journey, 1953–1976*, https://www.youtube.com/watch?v=58IA32AJm84, retrieved Aug. 10, 2021.

28. Welding qtd in Greg Kot, *I'll Take You There: Mavis Staples, the Staple Singers, and the Music that Shaped the Civil Rights Era*, 78.

29. Kot, 45–46.

30. Allan F. Moore, *Song Means: Analysing and Interpreting Recorded Popular Song*, 163; Anthony Heilbut, *The Fan Who Knew Too Much: Aretha Franklin, the Rise of the Soap Opera, Children of the Gospel Church, and Other Meditations*, 5.

31. Billy Vera, *Rip It Up: The Specialty Records Story*, 19; Heilbut, *Gospel Sound*, 83–84.

32. Van Rijn, 34–35.

33. Jason Ankeny, "Golden Echoes Biography," AllMusic, https://www.allmusic.com/artist/golden-echoes-mn0000953229, retrieved Feb. 25, 2023. See Stephan Pennington, "Willmer Broadnax, Midcentury Gospel, and Black Trans/Masculinities," *Women & Music*, 22 (2018), 117–25; and Heilbut, *Fan Who Knew Too Much*, 29–30.

34. Opal Louis Nations, Liner notes to Spirit of Memphis, *Happy in the Service of the Lord*, http://opalnations.com/files/Spirit_of_Memphis_Acrobat_CD_3007_Liner_Notes.pdf, retrieved Jan. 31, 2021; Broughton, 67; Kip Lornell, "Happy in the Service of the Lord": Afro-American Gospel Quartets in Memphis, 109, 145–46.

35. Opal Louis Nations, "The Harmonizing Four of Richmond, Virginia: The Early Years," *Goldmine*, July 8, 1994, 56, http://opalnations.com/files/Harmonizing_Four_Goldmine_July_1994.pdf; Marovich, 155; Burford, 115.

36. Nations, "The Harmonizing Four," 58.

37. Zolten, 174.

38. Heilbut, *Gospel Sound*, 273; Boyer, 112; Opal Louis Nations, Liner notes to Angelic Gospel Singers, *Touch Me Lord Jesus*, http://opalnations.com/files/Angelic_Gospel_Singers_Heritage_CD_11_Liner_Notes.pdf, retrieved Feb. 2, 2021.

39. Nations, Liner notes to *Touch Me Lord Jesus*.

40. Boyer, 121; Zolten, 183.

41. Taft, 195–96.

42. Zolten, 199–200; Tucker qtd in Heilbut, *Gospel Sound*, 49.

43. See Boyer, 204, for lists and definitions of sweet and hard quartets.

44. Zolten, 219.

45. Zolten, 228; Heilbut, *Gospel Sound*, 50.

46. Heilbut, *Gospel Sound*, 108; Heilbut, *Fan Who Knew Too Much*, 136; Burford, 375–76;

Robert Santelli, "Marion Williams: The Genius of Gospel," *Gadfly*, Nov./Dec. 1999. http://www.gadflyonline.com/home/archive/NovDec99/archive-marionwilliams.html.

47. Boyer, 107–08; Heilbut, *Gospel Sound*, 225–26. Aretha's powerful performance of the song for Nelson Mandela in 1990 ended with an equally exciting flurry of *Surely's*: https://www.youtube.com/watch?v=MvVfLIR7BlI. Retrieved Feb. 14, 2023.

48. Horace Clarence Boyer, "William Herbert Brewster: The Eloquent Poet," in Reagon, ed., *We'll Understand It Better By and By*, 214, 217.

49. Heilbut, *Gospel Sound*, 75; Broughton, 94; Guralnick, *Dream Boogie*, 61.

50. Guralnick, *Dream Boogie*, 33; Heilbut, *Gospel Sound*, 81–82. Tindley's earlier song, "I'll Overcome Some Day," gained renewed popularity during the civil rights movement. See Horace Clarence Boyer, "Charles Albert Tindley: Progenitor of African American Gospel Music," in Reagon, ed., *We'll Understand It Better By and By*, 58.

51. Boyer, *Golden Age*, 196; George, 79; Lee Hildebrand, Liner notes to *Sam Cooke with the Soul Stirrers*.

52. Guralnick, *Dream Boogie*, 72 (his italics).

53. Guralnick, *Dream Boogie*, 103. Hildebrand's liner notes identify the guitarist as Bob King, but Guralnick references an anonymous "steel guitar player, who might have wandered in off the street ..."; Robert Palmer, "Liner notes for Sam Cooke's *Night Beat*" rpt. in *Blues and Chaos: The Music Writing of Robert Palmer*, ed. Anthony DeCurtis, 190–91.

54. Heilbut, *Gospel Sound*, 121, 125.

55. Guralnick, *Dream Boogie*, 110.

56. Guralnick, *Dream Boogie*, 124–25.

57. Guralnick, *Dream Boogie*, 125–27.

58. Heilbut, *Gospel Sound*, 159; Carpenter, 92; Boyer, *Golden Age*, 217.

59. Boyer, *Golden Age*, 214.

60. Boyer, *Golden Age*, 215–17.

61. Broughton, 74; Santi Elijah Holley, "Remembering Clarence Fountain, a Gospel Legend," *The Atlantic*, June 6, 2018, https://www.theatlantic.com/entertainment/archive/2018/06/remembering-clarence-fountain-blind-boys/562061/.

62. Lee Hildebrand and Opal Nations, Liner notes to the Original Five Blind Boys of Alabama, *The Sermon*.

63. Boyer, *Golden Age*, 199; Zolten, 210; Broughton, 68; Fountain qtd in Carpenter, 142; Heilbut, *Gospel Sound*, 47.

64. Robey qtd in Ray Funk, "Let's Go Out to the Programs (The Peacock Gospel Years)" in Galen Gart & Roy C. Ames, *Duke/Peacock Records: An Illustrated History with Discography*, 38; Zolten, 210.

65. Opal Louis Nations, Liner notes to *The Five Blind Boys of Mississippi*, Acrobat CD, 2006, http://opalnations.com/files/Five_Blind_Boys_of_Miss_Acrobat_CD_3003_Liner_Notes.pdf, retrieved Mar. 19, 2021.

66. Heilbut, *Gospel Sound*, 256; Broughton, 74.

67. Harris qtd in Opal Louis Nations, Liner notes to *Davis Sisters, 1949-1952*, 3, http://opalnations.com/files/Davis_Sisters_1949-1952_Heritage_CD_47_2003__Liner_Notes.pdf.

68. Carpenter, 112.

69. See Heilbut, *Gospel Sound*, 117–20; Boyer, *Golden Age*, 175–78; Fox, *King of the Queen City*, 117–18; Vera, *Rip It Up*, 54–55.

70. Robert Christgau, Review of Swan Silvertones, *Love Lifted Me/My Rock*, https://www.robertchristgau.com/get_album.php?id=15684, retrieved Jan. 31, 2023; Broughton, 66.

71. Broughton, 68; Nations, *Sensational Nightingales*, 44, 89.

72. Nations, *Sensational Nightingales*, 90–91.

73. Nations, *Sensational Nightingales*, 94; Anthony Heilbut, Liner notes to *The Gospel Sound of Spirit Feel*.

74. Nations, *Sensational Nightingales*, 100; Heilbut, *Gospel Sound*, 126–27.

75. Lee Hildebrand, Liner notes to The Chosen Gospel Singers, *The Lifeboat*.

76. Horace Clarence Boyer, "Tracking the Tradition: New Orleans Sacred Music." *Black Music Research Journal*, 8.1 (1988), 139; Peter A. Grendysa, "Atlantic's Gospel Series," *Vocal Group Harmony*, https://www.vocalgroupharmony.com/ROWNEW2/3000Series.htm, retrieved Oct. 15, 2022.

77. Opal Louis Nations, "Salesmen for the Lord: The Kansas City Gospel Singers (Soul Revivers)," *Real Blues* 15 (Oct./ Nov. 1998), http://opalnations.com/files/Kansas_City_Gospel_Singers_Soul_Revivers__Real_Blues_15_1998.pdf; *Billboard*, Nov. 10, 1956, 136.

Chapter Four

1. Carroll qtd in Runowicz, 32; King qtd in Gerri Hirshey, *Nowhere to Run: The Story of Soul Music*, 36, her italics; Denby qtd in Goosman, 20.

2. "Rhythm and Blues Notes," *Billboard*, Sept. 22, 1951, 38; Bill Millar, *The Drifters: The Rise and Fall of the Black Vocal Group*, 111.

3. B. Ward, 88; George, 35–36.

4. Runowicz, 51; Wexler and Ritz, 89; E. Ward, "The Fifties and Before," 125.

5. B. Ward, 65.

6. Goosman, 194, 42–43, 195; Runowicz, 61.

7. Gribin and Schiff, 19; Runowicz, 61–62.

8. B. Ward, 56, 80.

9. Gribin and Schiff, 20; Altschuler, 57.

10. B. Ward, 81; Powers, 117.

11. Goldberg, "The Ravens—Part 1," *Marv Goldberg's R&B Notebooks*, 2009, http://www.uncamarvy.com/Ravens/ravens01.html; Runowicz, 37.

12. Gribin and Schiff, 42–43; *Billboard*, July 12, 1947, 114.

13. Goldberg, "The Orioles—Part 1: The Early Jubilee Years, 1948-1951," *Marv Goldberg's R&B Notebooks*, 2009, http://www.uncamarvy.com/

Orioles/orioles1.html; Goosman, 10; Shaw, *Honkers & Shouters*, 136.

14. Greil Marcus, "The Deborah Chessler Story," *The Dustbin of History*, 235; Sampson, "The Orioles: 'It's Too Soon to Know.'" *Spontaneous Lunacy: The History of Rock 'n' Roll—Song by Song*, June 14, 2017, https://www.spontaneouslunacy.net/the-orioles-its-too-soon-to-know-jubilee-5000/.

15. Goldberg, "The Orioles—Part 1"; Galen Gart, ed., *First Pressings: The History of Rhythm & Blues, Volume 1: 1951*, 6.

16. Guralnick, *Sweet Soul Music*, 25.

17. Hildebrand, *Stars of Soul*, 151; Hirshey, 37–38.

18. Dawson and Propes, 95. For Lovin' Dan and his predecessors, see Dawson and Propes, 92–93; Gribin and Schiff, 219–21; and Mark J. Zucker, "The Saga of Lovin' Dan: A Study in the Iconography of Rhythm & Blues Music of the 1950s." *Journal of Popular Culture* 16 (Fall 1982): 43–51.

19. Philip Groia, *They All Sang on the Corner: A Second Look at New York City's Rhythm and Blues Vocal Groups*, 30; E. Ward, "The Fifties and Before," 84.

20. Goldberg, "The Larks," *Marv Goldberg's R&B Notebook*, 2009, http://www.uncamarvy.com/Larks/larks.html.

21. Jay Warner, *American Singing Groups: A History from 1940 to Today*, 237; Baptista, 142.

22. Hildebrand, *Stars of Soul*, 74–75; Robert Palmer, review of "Monkey Hips and Rice: The '5' Royales Anthology (Rhino)," *Rolling Stone* (Aug. 11, 1994), rpt. in *Blues and Chaos: The Music Writing of Robert Palmer*, 200.

23. Gillett, 157.

24. Warner, 183; Gribin and Schiff, 153. See Goldberg, "The 5 Keys," *Marv Goldberg's R&B Notebook*, 2009, http://www.uncamarvy.com/5Keys/5keys.html, retrieved May 5, 2021.

25. Groia, 21–22.

26. Ertegun qtd in Greenfield, 132.

27. Millar, 19; Murray, *Stomping the Blues*, 41–42.

28. Marsh, 511.

29. Gribin and Schiff, 124, 132.

30. Goosman, 25.

31. Baptista, 28.

32. Goosman, 180–82; Goldberg, "The Swallows," *Marv Goldberg's R&B Notebooks*, 2009, http://www.uncamarvy.com/Swallows/swallows.html.

33. Goldberg, "The Clovers—Part 1," *Marv Goldberg's R&B Notebooks*, 2009, http://www.uncamarvy.com/Clovers/clovers1.html; Tosches, 97.

34. Warner, 121.

35. Groia, 103–04; Goldberg, "The 5 Crowns," *Marv Goldberg's R&B Notebooks*, 2009, http://www.uncamarvy.com/5Crowns/5crowns.html.

36. Goldberg, "The Harptones," *Marv Goldberg's R&B Notebooks*, 2009, http://www.uncamarvy.com/Harptones/harptones.html; Jackson, *Big Beat Heat*, 117–18; Groia, 42–45.

37. Thirty-nine groups recorded "Over the Rainbow," thirty "Gloria" and twenty-four "Sunday Kind of Love." See Douglas E. Friedman and Anthony J. Gribin, *Who Sang Our Songs? The Official Rhythm & Blues and Doo-Wop Songography*, 318–19, 130, 386; Marsh, *Heart of Rock & Soul*, 420; E. Ward, "The Fifties and Before," 95; Warner, 215.

38. Warner, 215–16.

39. Groia, 106; Warner, 317–18.

40. Robert Pruter, *Doowop: The Chicago Scene*, 106; Richard G. Carter, *Goodnight Sweetheart, Goodnight: The Story of The Spaniels*, 9; Vivian Carter qtd in Goldberg, "The Spaniels," *Marv Goldberg's R&B Notebooks*, 2009, http://www.uncamarvy.com/Spaniels/spaniels.html.

41. Pruter, 109.

42. Warner, 193; Cohodas, 128; Nelson qtd in Pruter, 30.

43. Hildebrand, *Stars of Soul*, 77; Todd R. Baptista, *The Flamingos: A Complete History of the Doo-Wop Legends*, 46, 49.

44. Baptista, *The Flamingos*, 78.

45. "The Blue Jays (1)," *Doo-Wop: Groups, Biography & Discography*, http://doo-wop.blogg.org/blue-jays-1-c29949084, retrieved Nov. 1, 2022; Gribin and Schiff, 116.

46. Rolonz and Friedman, 1; Jackson, *Big Beat Heat*, 65; Ben Cosgrove, "'The Luckiest Generation': Teenagers in the '50s," LIFE.com, https://www.life.com/history/the-luckiest-generation-life-with-teenagers-in-1950s-america/. Retrieved Mar. 16, 2023.

47. Jackson, *Big Beat Heat*, 61; Powers, 114. See Dawson and Propes, 124–27.

48. Goldberg, "The Chords," *Marv Goldberg's R&B Notebooks*, 2009, http://www.uncamarvy.com/Chords/chords.html.

49. Dawson and Propes, 139; Goldberg, The Chords"; see Salem, "'Sh-Boom' and the Bomb: A Postwar Call & Response," 16–17.

50. Miller, *Flowers in the Dustbin*, 77.

51. Warner, 108–11; Goldberg, "The Jewels," *Marv Goldberg's R&B Notebooks*, 2012, http://www.uncamarvy.com/Jewels/jewels.html.

52. Dawson and Propes, 132; E. Ward, "The Fifties and Before," 85; Warner, 73–74.

53. Goldberg, "The Royals," *Marv Goldberg's R&B Notebooks*, 2009, http://www.uncamarvy.com/Royals/royals.html; Bass qtd in Dawson and Propes, 133; Fox, *King of the Queen City*, 102; Dawson and Propes, 136.

54. Warner, 261; Pruter, 36.

55. Pruter, 60; Nick Talevski, *Rock Obituaries: Knocking on Heaven's Door*, 310.

56. Pruter, 62.

57. See Warner, 272–75; Dawson and Propes, 158–64.

58. Greil Marcus, "In the Secret Country: Walter Mosley, Doo-wop, and '50s L.A." *Los Angeles* (August 2002), 102.

59. Warner, 86–87. For the backstory of the Cadillacs' "Gloria," see Gribin and Schiff, 211–13; Runowicz, 48–50; and Goldberg, "'Gloria'—A Short History," *Marv Goldberg's R&B Notebooks*,

2010, http://www.uncamarvy.com/Gloria/gloria.html.

60. Groia, 71–72.

61. Weiss qtd in Shaw, *Honkers and Shouters*, 467; Goldberg, "The Solitaires," *Marv Goldberg's R&B Notebooks*, 2009, http://www.uncamarvy.com/Solitaires/solitaires.html.

62. Marsh, *Heart of Rock & Soul*, 48–49; Warner, 153. See Gary Johnson, "MRRL Hall of Fame: Nolan Strong and the Diablos," *Michigan Rock and Roll Legends*, 2019, https://michiganrockandrolllegends.com/index.php/mrrl-hall-of-fame/396-nolan-strong-and-the-diablos.

63. Palmer, *Baby, That Was Rock & Roll*, 22.

64. Gribin and Schiff, 97–98; Warwick, 19–27.

65. "Top Names Now Singing the Blues," *Variety*, Feb. 23, 1955, in Brackett, ed., *Pop, Rock, and Soul Reader*, 77; Gribin and Schiff, 100.

66. Gribin and Schiff, 100; "The Hearts (2)," *Doo-Wop Groups: Biography & Discography*, http://doo-wop.blogg.org/hearts-2-c26505320. "Lonely Nights," https://www.vocalgroupharmony.com/lonely_n.htm. Retrieved Jan. 14, 2023.

67. Gribin & Schiff, 102; Goldberg, "The Mellows," *Marv Goldberg's R&B Notebooks*, 2009, http://www.uncamarvy.com/Mellows/mellows.html; Baptista, *Group Harmony*, 241.

68. "Sure Cure for the Blues," https://www.vocalgroupharmony.com/4ROWNEW/SureCure.htm; "The Four Jacks," *Bear Family Records*, https://www.bear-family.com/listing/manufacturer/sSupplier/127233, retrieved July 3, 2021.

69. "Top Names Now Singing the Blues," in Brackett, ed., 77.

70. B. Ward, 51; Altschuler, 56; Gillett, 34.

71. Warner, 275–76; Zak, 171; B. Ward, 51.

72. Goldberg, "The Platters," *Marv Goldberg's R&B Notebooks*, 2008, http://www.uncamarvy.com/Platters/platters.html, his italics; Dylan, 184.

73. See Matthew F. Delmont, *The Nicest Kids in Town: American Bandstand, Rock 'n' Roll, and the Struggle for Civil Rights in 1950s Philadelphia*, esp. Ch. 1, for the ways Black teens were gradually eliminated from *Bandstand*; Goldberg, "The Turbans," *Marv Goldberg's R&B Notebooks*, 2009, http://www.uncamarvy.com/Turbans/turbans.html.

74. Goldberg, "The El Dorados," *Marv Goldberg's R&B Notebooks*, 2009, http://www.uncamarvy.com/ElDorados/eldorados.html.

75. Warner, 173; Pruter, 113.

76. Greil Marcus, *The History of Rock 'n' Roll in Ten Songs*, 63.

77. Goldberg, "The Del Vikings," *Marv Goldberg's R&B Notebooks*, 2011, http://www.uncamarvy.com/DelVikings/delvikings.html.

78. Goldberg, "The Cleftones," *Marv Goldberg's R&B Notebooks*, 2009, http://www.uncamarvy.com/Cleftones/cleftones.html; Warner, 117–18.

79. Groia, 99; Warner, 218–19; Goldberg, "The Heartbeats," *Marv Goldberg's R&B Notebooks*, 2009, http://www.uncamarvy.com/Heartbeats/heartbeats.html.

80. Marsh, *Heart of Rock & Soul*, 531–33. "Daddy's Home" was the original title and theme song of the 1987 movie *Look Who's Talking*, starring Kirstie Alley, John Travolta, Bruce Willis, and featuring me as Mr. Anal, one of Alley's bad dates.

81. Junior qtd in Pruter, 122; Goldberg, "The Dells," *Marv Goldberg's R&B Notebooks*, 2009, http://www.uncamarvy.com/Dells/dells.html.

82. Baptista, *Group Harmony*, 89–93.

83. B. Ward, 82–83; Powers, 121.

84. Gribin and Schiff, 53; Powers, 119; Miller, *Flowers in the Dustbin*, 117.

85. Goldberg, "The Mello-Moods," *Marv Goldberg's R&B Notebooks*, 2009, http://www.uncamarvy.com/MelloMoods/mellomoods.html; Warner, 256; Todd Baptista, "Meet the Mello-Moods, the teen doo-wop group that started it all," *Goldmine*, July 19, 2011, https://www.goldminemag.com/articles/meet-the-mello-moods-the-teen-doo-wop-group-that-started-it-all.

86. Groia, 112; Marsh, *The Heart of Rock & Soul*, 84; Bruce Eder, "Artist Biography: The Schoolboys," *AllMusic*, https://www.allmusic.com/artist/the-schoolboys-mn0000422822/biography, retrieved Aug. 22, 2021.

87. Goldberg, "The Teenagers," *Marv Goldberg's R&B Notebooks*, 2009. http://www.uncamarvy.com/Teenagers/teenagers.html; Warner, 242–43.

88. Zak, 96.

89. Marsh, *The Heart of Rock & Soul*, 581, 623–24; E. Ward, "The Fifties and Before," 128.

90. Doug Owram, *Born at the Right Time: A History of the Baby Boom Generation*, 144.

91. Art Peters, "Comeback of a Child Star," *Ebony* (Jan. 1967), 43.

92. Goldberg, "The Teenchords," *Marv Goldberg's R&B Notebooks*, 2008, http://www.uncamarvy.com/Teenchords/teenchords.html.

93. Warner, 267.

94. Goldberg, "The Meadowlarks," *Marv Goldberg's R&B Notebooks*, 2009, http://www.uncamarvy.com/Meadowlarks/meadowlarks.html; Goldberg, "The Jaguars," *Marv Goldberg's R&B Notebooks*, 2009, http://www.uncamarvy.com/Jaguars/jaguars.html; Warner, 229.

95. *Billboard* review qtd in "Previous vocal group record of the week #764," https://www.vocalgroupharmony.com/4ROWNEW/MyHeartsDesire.htm, retrieved July 19, 2022.

96. References to "Rubber Biscuit" invariably have Johnson attending the Warwick School for Delinquent Teenagers, but the Warwick facility was actually called the New York State Training School for Boys. See https://abandonedonline.net/location/warwick-state-training-school-for-boys/; Gribin and Schiff, 215; Groia, 129; Paul Laurence Dunbar, "We Wear the Mask" (1895), https://www.poetryfoundation.org/poems/44203/we-wear-the-mask, retrieved Nov. 10, 2022.

Chapter Five

1. Charles and Ritz, 178.
2. Heilbut, *The Gospel Sound*, 277.

3. Broughton, 100; George, 70; Charles and Ritz, 120–21, 178.

4. Charles and Ritz, 65; Robert Palmer, Liner Notes for *Ray Charles: The Birth of Soul* (Atlantic, 1991) rpt. in Palmer, *Blues & Chaos*, 166–67.

5. Charles and Ritz, 128 (his italics), 336, 117; Bill Dahl, Liner notes to *The Very Best of Ray Charles*, 4.

6. Wexler qtd in Guralnick, *Sweet Soul Music*, 61; Greenfield, 77.

7. Charles and Ritz, 148; Palmer, *Blues & Chaos*, 181.

8. Charles and Ritz, 148–49; Guralnick, *Sweet Soul Music*, 63; Greenfield, 102; Palmer, *Blues & Chaos*, 175; Hirshey, 50.

9. Hirshey, 50; Guralnick, *Looking to Get Lost*, 37.

10. Charles and Ritz, 151; Guralnick, *Sweet Soul Music*, 64; Palmer, *Blues & Chaos*, 177; Whitburn, 81–82.

11. Charles and Ritz, 177.

12. B. Dahl, 5.

13. Marsh, *Heart of Rock & Soul*, 110.

14. Otis qtd in Charles White, 36.

15. Ch. White, 16–30; David Kirby, *Little Richard: The Birth of Rock 'n' Roll*, 38–45; Vera, *Rip It Up*, 107.

16. Ch. White, 27; Penny, 181; Mark Deming, review of Little Richard, *Get Rich Quick: The Birth of a Legend, 1951-1954*. AllMusic, https://www.allmusic.com/album/get-rich-quick-the-birth-of-a-legend-mw0000765727, retrieved Sept. 28, 2021; Liner notes to Little Richard, *Little Richard—Rocks*, Bear Family Records, https://www.bear-family.com/little-richard/, retrieved Oct. 4, 2022.

17. "The Tempo Toppers," *Doo-Wop Groups: Biography & Discography*, 2014, http://doo-wop.blogg.org/the-tempo-toppers-a116518060; Ch. White, 37, 235.

18. "Award o' the Week," *The Cash Box*, June 13, 1953, 30.

19. Ch. White, 39–47; Blackwell qtd in Ch. White, 46; Vera, *Rip It Up*, 109–10.

20. Kirby, 111.

21. James McBride, *Kill 'Em and Leave: Searching for James Brown and the American Soul*, 82. For Brown's early life and first professional forays, see Smith, 7–71; Guralnick, *Sweet Soul Music*, 221–26; Lauterbach, 245–55; and Fred J. Hay, "Music Box Meets the Toccoa Band: The Godfather of Soul in Appalachia," *Black Music Research Journal*, 23 (Spring-Autumn 2003), 103–33.

22. Nathan qtd in Fox, 90; Philip Gourevitch, "Mr. Brown." *The New Yorker*, July 29, 2002, https://www.newyorker.com/magazine/2002/07/29/mr-brown; Guralnick, *Sweet Soul Music*, 225; Marsh, *The Heart of Rock & Soul*, 192–93.

23. James Sullivan, *The Hardest Working Man: How James Brown Saved the Soul of America*, 66.

24. Sullivan, 66; Cliff White, Liner notes to James Brown, *Roots of a Revolution*.

Bibliography

Absher, Amy. *The Black Musician and the White City: Race and Music in Chicago, 1900–1967*. Ann Arbor: U of Michigan P, 2014.

Altschuler, Glenn C. *All Shook Up: How Rock 'n' Roll Changed America*. New York: Oxford UP, 2003.

Ankeny, Jason. "Golden Echoes Biography." *AllMusic*. https://www.allmusic.com/artist/golden-echoes-mn0000953229.

Averill, Gage. *Four Parts, No Waiting: A Social History of American Barbershop Harmony*. New York: Oxford UP, 2003.

"Award o' the Week." *The Cash Box*, June 13, 1953. 30.

Balliett, Whitney. *American Singers: Twenty-Seven Portraits in Song*. New York: Oxford UP, 1988.

Baptista, Todd R. *The Flamingos: A Complete History of the Doo-Wop Legends*. Jefferson, NC: McFarland, 2019.

———. *Group Harmony: Echoes of the Rhythm & Blues Era*. Narberth, PA: Collectables, 2007.

Baraka, Amiri. *The Autobiography of LeRoi Jones*. Chicago: Lawrence Hill, 1997.

Barlow, William. *Looking Up at Down: The Emergence of Blues Culture*. Philadelphia: Temple UP, 1989.

Battles, John. "Rockin' Is Their Business: The Treniers." *Flying Saucers Rock 'n' Roll: Conversations with Unjustly Obscure Rock 'n' Roll Eccentrics*. Ed. Jake Austen. Durham, NC: Duke UP, 2011. 190–208.

Birnbaum, Larry. *Before Elvis: The Prehistory of Rock 'n' Roll*. Lanham, MD: Scarecrow, 2012.

Boone, Graeme M. "Twelve Key Recordings." *Cambridge Companion to Blues and Gospel Music*. Ed. Allan Moore. New York: Cambridge UP, 2002. 61–88.

Boyer, Horace Clarence. "Charles Albert Tindley: Progenitor of African American Gospel Music." *We'll Understand It Better By and By: Pioneering African American Gospel Composers*. Ed. Bernice Johnson Reagon. Washington, D.C.: Smithsonian Institution, 1992. 53–78.

———. *The Golden Age of Gospel*. Urbana: U of Illinois P, 2000.

———. "Tracking the Tradition: New Orleans Sacred Music." *Black Music Research Journal* 8.1 (1988), 135–47.

———. "William Herbert Brewster: The Eloquent Poet." *We'll Understand It Better By and By: Pioneering African American Gospel Composers*. Ed. Bernice Johnson Reagon. Washington, D.C.: Smithsonian Institution, 1992. 211–32.

"The Boys Who Sell 'Em See Combos Hogging Theaters." *Billboard*, Aug. 10, 1946. 39.

Brackett, David, ed. *The Pop, Rock, and Soul Reader: Histories and Debates*. New York: Oxford UP, 2005.

"Bricks in My Pillow: The Robert Nighthawk Story." http://nighthawk.sundayblues.org/index.htm.

Broonzy, William, as told to Yannick Bruynoghe. *Big Bill Blues*. New York: Da Capo, 1992.

Broughton, Viv. *Black Gospel: An Illustrated History of the Gospel Sound*. Poole, Dorset: Blandford, 1985.

Broven, John. *Rhythm & Blues in New Orleans*. Gretna, LA: Pelican, 1988.

Brown, Ruth, with Andrew Yule. *Miss Rhythm: The Autobiography of Ruth Brown, Rhythm & Blues Legend*. New York: Donald I. Fine, 1996.

Burford, Mark. *Mahalia Jackson & the Black Gospel Field*. New York: Oxford UP, 2019.

"Calvin Shields—Musical Pioneer." *Zero to 180—Three Minute Magic*, May 3, 2018. https://www.zeroto180.org/?p=31595.

Campbell, Robert L., Leonard J. Bukowski, and Armin Büttner. *The Tom Archia Discography*. http://campber.people.clemson.edu/archia.html.

Carpenter, Bil. *Uncloudy Days: The Gospel Music Encyclopedia*. San Francisco: Backbeat, 2005.

Carter, Richard G. *Goodnight Sweetheart, Goodnight: The Story of The Spaniels*. Sicklerville, NJ: August, 1994.

Chadbourne, Eugene. "Rufus Gore Biography." *AllMusic*. https://www.allmusic.com/artist/rufusgore-mn0001599628/biography.

Charles, Ray, and David Ritz. *Brother Ray: Ray Charles' Own Story*, 3rd ed. New York: Da Capo, 2004.

Chilton, John. *Let the Good Times Roll: The Story of Louis Jordan and His Music*. Ann Arbor: U of Michigan P, 1997.

Christgau, Robert. Swan Silvertones, *Love Lifted*

Me/My Rock. https://www.robertchristgau.com/get_album.php?id=15684.

Claybourne, Carson, et al. *Civil Rights Chronicle: The African-American Struggle for Freedom.* Lincolnwood, IL: Legacy, 2003.

Cohodas, Nadine. *Spinning Blues into Gold: The Chess Brothers and the Legendary Chess Records.* New York: St. Martin's, 2000.

Coleman, Rick. *Blue Monday: Fats Domino and the Lost Dawn of Rock 'n' Roll.* New York: Da Capo, 2006.

Collins, Tony. *Rock, Mr. Blues: The Life and Music of Wynonie Harris.* Milford, NH: Big Nickel, 1995.

Collis, John. *The Story of Chess Records.* London: Bloomsbury, 1998.

Cosgrove, Ben. "'The Luckiest Generation': Teenagers in the '50s." *LIFE.com.* https://www.life.com/history/the-luckiest-generation-life-with-teenagers-in-1950s-america/.

Dahl, Bill. Liner notes to *The Very Best of Ray Charles.* Rhino CD, 2000.

Dahl, Linda. *Stormy Weather: The Music and Lives of a Century of Jazzwomen.* New York: Pantheon, 1984.

Dance, Helen Oakley. *Stormy Monday: The T-Bone Walker Story.* New York: Da Capo, 1987.

"Dandy Jim from Caroline" (1844). *Uncle Tom's Cabin & American Culture.* http://utc.iath.virginia.edu/minstrel/dandyjimfr.html.

Darden, Robert F. "'Move on Up a Little Higher'—Mahalia Jackson (1947)." National Registry, 2005. https://www.loc.gov/static/programs/national-recording-preservation-board/documents/MoveOnUpALittleHigher.pdf.

——. *People Get Ready! A New History of Black Gospel Music.* New York: Bloomsbury, 2005.

Davis, Angela Y. *Blues Legacies and Black Feminism: Gertrude "Ma" Rainey, Bessie Smith and Billie Holiday.* New York: Pantheon, 1998.

Dawson, Jim. *Nervous Man Nervous: Big Jay McNeely and the Rise of the Honking Tenor Sax.* Milford, NH: Big Nickel, 1994.

——, and Steve Propes. *What Was the First Rock 'n' Roll Record?* London: Faber, 1992.

"Dee Williams." *Spontaneous Lunacy: The History of Rock 'n' Roll—Song by Song.* https://www.spontaneouslunacy.net/artists-dee-williams/.

Deffaa, Chip. *Blues Rhythms: Six Lives in Rhythm and Blues.* Urbana: U of Illinois P, 1996.

Delmont, Matthew F. *The Nicest Kids in Town: American Bandstand, Rock 'n' Roll, and the Struggle for Civil Rights in 1950s Philadelphia.* Berkeley: U of California P, 2012.

Deming, Mark. Review of *Little Richard, Get Rich Quick: The Birth of a Legend, 1951–1954.* AllMusic. https://www.allmusic.com/album/get-rich-quick-the-birth-of-a-legend-mw0000765727.

de Visé, Daniel. *King of the Blues: The Rise and Reign of B.B. King.* New York: Atlantic Monthly, 2021.

Dixon, Willie, with Don Snowden. *I Am the Blues: The Willie Dixon Story.* New York: Da Capo, 1989.

Dunbar, Paul Laurence. "We Wear the Mask" (1895). https://www.poetryfoundation.org/poems/44203/we-wear-the-mask.

Du Sautoy, Marcus. *The Creativity Code: Art and Innovation in the Age of AI.* Cambridge: Harvard UP, 2019.

Dylan, Bob. *The Philosophy of Modern Song.* New York: Simon & Schuster, 2022.

Ellison, Ralph. *Shadow and Act.* New York: Vintage, 1972.

Escott, Colin. "Notes on Selected Recordings." *The B.B. King Reader: 6 Decades of Commentary*, rev. ed. Ed. Richard Kostelanetz. Milwaukee: Hal Leonard, 2005. 283–305.

Escott, Colin, with Martin Hawkins. *Good Rockin' Tonight: Sun Records and the Birth of Rock 'n' Roll.* New York: St. Martin's, 1991.

Evans, David. *Big Road Blues: Tradition and Creativity in the Folk Blues.* Berkeley: U of California P, 1982.

——. "The Development of the Blues." *Cambridge Companion to Blues and Gospel Music.* Ed. Allan Moore. New York: Cambridge UP, 2002. 20–43.

——. "Early Deep South and Mississippi Valley Blues." *Blackwell Guide to Recorded Blues.* Ed. Paul Oliver. Oxford: Blackwell, 1991. 31–58.

Farley, Charles. *Soul of the Man: Bobby "Blue" Bland.* Jackson: U of Mississippi P, 2011.

Finn, Julio. *The Bluesman: The Musical Heritage of Black Men and Women in the Americas.* New York: Interlink, 1992.

Fletcher, Tony. *In the Midnight Hour: The Life & Soul of Wilson Pickett.* New York: Oxford UP, 2016.

Floyd, Samuel A., Jr. "Toward a Philosophy of Black Music Scholarship." *Music in Black American Life, 1600–1945.* Ed. Laurie Matheson. Urbana: U of Illinois P, 2022.

"The Four Jacks." *Bear Family Records.* https://www.bearfamily.com/listing/manufacturer/sSupplier/127233.

Fox, Jon Hartley. *King of the Queen City: The Story of King Records.* Urbana: U of Illinois P, 2009.

Fox, Ted. *Showtime at the Apollo.* New York: Da Capo. 1993.

Franklin, Aretha, with David Ritz. *Aretha: From These Roots.* New York: Villard, 1999.

Friedman, Douglas E., and Anthony J. Gribin. *Who Sang Our Songs? The Official Rhythm & Blues and Doo-Wop Songography.* West Long Branch, NJ: Harmony Songs, 2003.

Friedwald, Will. *A Biographical Guide to the Great Jazz and Pop Singers.* New York: Pantheon, 2010.

Funk, Ray. "Let's Go Out to the Programs (The Peacock Gospel Years)." *Duke/Peacock Records: An Illustrated History with Discography.* Ed. Galen Gart and Roy C. Ames. Milford, NH: Big Nickel, 1990. 37–50.

Galt, Stephen. *Barrelhouse Words: A Blues Dialect Dictionary.* Urbana: U of Illinois P, 2009.

Garon, Paul. *Blues and the Poetic Spirit*, rev. ed. San Francisco: City Lights, 1996.

——, and Beth Garon. *Woman with Guitar:*

Memphis Minnie's Blues. New York: Da Capo, 1992.

Gart, Galen, ed. *First Pressings: The History of Rhythm & Blues, Volume 1: 1951.* Milford, NH: Big Nickel, 1991.

_____, and Roy C. Ames. *Duke/Peacock Records: An Illustrated History with Discography.* Milford, NH: Big Nickel, 1990.

Gates, Henry Louis, Jr. *The Black Church: This Is Our Story, This Is Our Song.* New York: Penguin, 2021.

_____. "New Negroes, Migration, and Cultural Exchange." *Jacob Lawrence: The Migration Series.* Ed. Elizabeth Hutton Turner. Emeryville, CA: Rappahannock, 1993.

George, Nelson. *The Death of Rhythm & Blues.* New York: Penguin, 1988.

Gergel, Richard. *Unexampled Courage: The Blinding of Sgt. Isaac Woodard and the Awakening of President Harry S. Truman and Judge J. Waties Waring.* New York: Sarah Crichton, 2019.

Gillett, Charlie. *The Sound of the City: The Rise of Rock and Roll,* 2nd ed. New York: Da Capo, 1996.

Gioia, Ted. *Delta Blues: The Life and Times of the Mississippi Masters Who Revolutionized American Music.* New York: Norton, 2008.

Glover, Tony, Scott Dirks, and Ward Gaines. *Blues with a Feeling: The Little Walter Story.* New York: Routledge, 2002.

Goins, Wayne Everett. *Blues All Day Long: The Jimmy Rogers Story.* Champaign: U of Illinois P, 2014.

Goldberg, Marv. "Apollo Theatre Shows." *Marv Goldberg's R&B Notebooks,* 2019. http://www.uncamarvy.com/ApolloTheaterShows/apollo.html.

_____. "The Chords." *Marv Goldberg's R&B Notebook,* 2009. http://www.uncamarvy.com/Chords/chords.html.

_____. "The Cleftones." *Marv Goldberg's R&B Notebooks,* 2009. http://www.uncamarvy.com/Cleftones/cleftones.html.

_____. "The Clovers—Part 1." *Marv Goldberg's R&B Notebook,* 2009. http://www.uncamarvy.com/Clovers/clovers1.html.

_____. "The Del Vikings." *Marv Goldberg's R&B Notebooks,* 2011. http://www.uncamarvy.com/DelVikings/delvikings.html.

_____. "The Dells." *Marv Goldberg's R&B Notebooks,* 2009. http://www.uncamarvy.com/Dells/dells.html.

_____. "The 5 Keys." *Marv Goldberg's R&B Notebook,* 2009. http://www.uncamarvy.com/5Keys/5keys.html.

_____. "'Gloria'—A Short History." *Marv Goldberg's R&B Notebooks,* 2010. http://www.uncamarvy.com/Gloria/gloria.html.

_____. "The Harptones." *Marv Goldberg's R&B Notebooks,* 2009. http://www.uncamarvy.com/Harptones/harptones.html.

_____. "The Heartbeats." *Marv Goldberg's R&B Notebooks,* 2009. http://www.uncamarvy.com/Heartbeats/heartbeats.html.

_____. "The Jaguars." *Marv Goldberg's R&B Notebooks,* 2009. http://www.uncamarvy.com/Jaguars/jaguars.html.

_____. "The Jewels." *Marv Goldberg's R&B Notebooks,* 2012. http://www.uncamarvy.com/Jewels/jewels.html.

_____. "The Larks." *Marv Goldberg's R&B Notebook,* 2009. http://www.uncamarvy.com/Larks/larks.html.

_____. "Lavern Baker." *Marv Goldberg's R&B Notebooks,* 2020. http://www.uncamarvy.com/LavernBaker/lavernbaker.html.

_____. "The Meadowlarks." *Marv Goldberg's R&B Notebooks,* 2009. http://www.uncamarvy.com/Meadowlarks/meadowlarks.html.

_____. "The Mellows." *Marv Goldberg's R&B Notebooks,* 2009. http://www.uncamarvy.com/Mellows/mellows.html.

_____. "The Orioles—Part 1: The Early Jubilee Years, 1948–1951." *Marv Goldberg's R&B Notebooks,* 2009. http://www.uncamarvy.com/Orioles/orioles1.html.

_____. "The Platters." *Marv Goldberg's R&B Notebook,* 2008. http://www.uncamarvy.com/Platters/platters.html.

_____. "The Ravens—Part 1." *Marv Goldberg's R&B Notebooks,* 2009. http://www.uncamarvy.com/Ravens/ravens01.html.

_____. "The Royals." *Marv Goldberg's R&B Notebooks,* 2009. http://www.uncamarvy.com/Royals/royals.html.

_____. "The Solitaires." *Marv Goldberg's R&B Notebooks,* 2009. http://www.uncamarvy.com/Solitaires/solitaires.html.

_____. "The Spaniels." *Marv Goldberg's R&B Notebooks,* 2009. http://www.uncamarvy.com/Spaniels/spaniels.html.

_____. "The Swallows." *Marv Goldberg's R&B Notebooks,* 2009. http://www.uncamarvy.com/Swallows/swallows.html.

_____. "The Teenagers." *Marv Goldberg's R&B Notebooks,* 2009. http://www.uncamarvy.com/Teenagers/teenagers.html.

_____. "The Teenchords." *Marv Goldberg's R&B Notebooks,* 2008. http://www.uncamarvy.com/Teenchords/teenchords.html.

_____. "The Turbans." *Marv Goldberg's R&B Notebooks,* 2009. http://www.uncamarvy.com/Turbans/turbans.html.

Goosman, Stuart L. *Group Harmony: The Black Urban Roots of Rhythm and Blues.* Philadelphia: U of Pennsylvania P, 2013.

Gordon, Robert. *Can't Be Satisfied: The Life and Times of Muddy Waters.* New York: Little, Brown, 2002.

Gourevitch, Philip. "Mr. Brown." *The New Yorker,* July 29, 2002. https://www.newyorker.com/magazine/2002/07/29/mr-brown.

Govenar, Alan. *Lightnin' Hopkins: His Life and Blues.* Chicago: Chicago Review, 2010.

Gracyk, Theodore. *Listening to Popular Music Or, How I Learned to Stop Worrying and Love Led Zeppelin.* Ann Arbor: U of Michigan P, 2007.

Greene, Kevin D. *The Invention and Reinvention of*

Big Bill Broonzy. Chapel Hill: U of North Carolina P, 2018.

Greenfield, Robert. *The Last Sultan: The Life and Times of Ahmet Ertegun*. New York: Simon & Schuster, 2011.

Gregory, Hugh. *The Real Rhythm and Blues*. London: Blandford, 1998.

Grendysa, Peter A. "Atlantic's Gospel Series." *Vocal Group Harmony*, https://www.vocalgroupharmony.com/ROWNEW2/3000Series.htm.

_____. Liner notes to *Big Maybelle: The Complete Okeh Sessions, 1952–55*. Sony CD, 1994.

_____. Liner notes to *Jump Blues Classics*. Rhino CD, 1992.

Gribin, Anthony J., and Matthew M. Schiff. *The Complete Book of Doo-Wop*. Iola, WI: Krause, 2000.

Groia, Philip. *They All Sang on the Corner: A Second Look at New York City's Rhythm and Blues Vocal Groups*. West Hempstead, NY: Phillie Dee, 1983.

Groom, Bob. "Beyond the Mushroom Cloud: A Decade of Disillusion in Black Blues and Gospel Song." *Ramblin' on My Mind: New Perspectives on the Blues*. Ed. David Evans. Urbana: U of Illinois P, 2008. 328–49.

Guralnick, Peter. *Dream Boogie: The Triumph of Sam Cooke*. New York: Little, Brown, 2005.

_____. *Feel Like Going Home: Portraits in Blues and Rock 'n' Roll*. New York: Harper & Row, 1989.

_____. *Looking to Get Lost: Adventures in Music & Writing*. New York: Little, Brown, 2020.

_____. *Sam Phillips: The Man Who Invented Rock 'n' Roll*. New York: Little, Brown, 2015.

_____. *Sweet Soul Music: Rhythm and Blues and the Southern Dream of Freedom*. New York: Little, Brown, 1999.

_____, et al., eds. *Martin Scorsese Presents the Blues: A Musical Journey*. New York: Amistad, 2003.

Gussow, Adam. *Beyond the Crossroads: The Devil and the Blues Tradition*. Chapel Hill: U of North Carolina P, 2017.

_____. *Seems Like Murder Here: Southern Violence and the Blues Tradition*. Chicago: U of Chicago P, 2002.

_____. *Whose Blues? Facing Up to Race and the Future of the Music*. Chapel Hill: U of North Carolina P, 2020.

Guy, Buddy, with David Ritz. *When I Left Home: My Story*. New York: Da Capo, 2012.

Hall, Michael. "Let There Be Lightnin.'" *Texas Monthly* (June 2007). https://www.texasmonthly.com/articles/let-there-be-lightnin/.

Hamlin, Françoise N. *Crossroads at Clarksdale: The Black Freedom Struggle in the Mississippi Delta After World War II*. Chapel Hill: U of North Carolina P, 2012.

Hannusch, Jeff. "Eddie 'Guitar Slim' Jones." *Rollin' and Tumblin': The Postwar Blues Guitarists*. Ed. Jas Obrecht. San Francisco: Miller Freeman, 2000. 353–60.

Harris, Michael W. *The Rise of Gospel Blues: The Music of Thomas Andrew Dorsey in the Urban Church*. New York: Oxford UP, 1992.

Haskins, Jim. *Queen of the Blues: A Biography of Dinah Washington*. New York: William Morrow, 1987.

Hay, Fred J. "Music Box Meets the Toccoa Band: The Godfather of Soul in Appalachia." *Black Music Research Journal* 23, no. 1–2 (Spring–Autumn 2003), 103–33.

Haymes, Max. "Catfish Blues (Origins of a Blues)." https://www.earlyblues.com/essay_catfish.htm.

"The Hearts (2)." *Doo-Wop Groups: Biography & Discography*. 2013. http://doo-wop.blogg.org/hearts-2-c26505320.

Heilbut, Anthony. *The Fan Who Knew Too Much: Aretha Franklin, the Rise of the Soap Opera, Children of the Gospel Church, and Other Meditations*. New York: Knopf, 2012.

_____. *The Gospel Sound: Good News and Bad Times*, 6th ed. New York: Limelight, 2002.

_____. Liner notes to *The Gospel Sound of Spirit Feel*. Spirit Feel CD, 1991.

Hildebrand, Lee. Liner notes to The Chosen Gospel Singers, *The Lifeboat*. Specialty CD, 1992.

_____. Liner notes to *Sam Cooke with the Soul Stirrers*. Specialty CD, 1991.

_____. *Stars of Soul and Rhythm & Blues*. New York: Billboard, 1994.

_____, and Opal Nations. Liner notes to The Original Five Blind Boys of Alabama, *The Sermon*. Specialty CD, 1993.

Hinson, Glenn. *Fire in My Bones: Transcendence and the Holy Spirit in African American Gospel*. Philadelphia: U of Pennsylvania P, 2000.

Hirshey, Gerri. *Nowhere to Run: The Story of Soul Music*. New York: Random House, 1984.

Hoffman, Lawrence. "The Blues Harp: The Classic Era." *Living Blues* 167 (2003), 111–23.

Holley, Santi Elijah. "Remembering Clarence Fountain, a Gospel Legend." *The Atlantic*, June 6, 2018, https://www.theatlantic.com/entertainment/archive/2018/06/remembering-clarence-fountain-blind-boys/562061/.

Hughes, Langston. "Happy New Year with Memphis Minnie." *Chicago Defender*, Jan. 9, 1943. *Martin Scorsese Presents the Blues*. Ed. Peter Guralnick, et al. New York: Amistad, 2003. 202–03.

Humphrey, Mark A. "Bright Lights, Big City: Urban Blues." *Nothing But the Blues: The Music and the Musicians*. Ed. Lawrence Cohn. New York: Abbeville, 1993. 151–203.

Jackson, Buzzy. *A Bad Woman Feeling Good: Blues and the Women Who Sing Them*. New York: Norton, 2005.

Jackson, John A. *Big Beat Heat: Alan Freed and the Early Years of Rock & Roll*. New York: Macmillan, 1991.

James, Etta, and David Ritz. *Rage to Survive: The Etta James Story*. New York: Da Capo, 1998.

Johnson, Gary. "MRRL Hall of Fame: Nolan Strong and the Diablos."

Michigan Rock and Roll Legends, 2019. https://michiganrockandrolllegends.com/index.php/mrrl-hall-of-fame/396-nolan-strong-and-the-diablos.

Jones, LeRoi [Amiri Baraka]. *Black Music.* New York: Akashic, 2010.

―――. *Blues People: Negro Music in White America.* New York: William Morrow, 1963.

Keil, Charles. *Urban Blues.* Chicago: U of Chicago P, 1966.

Kirby, David. *Little Richard: The Birth of Rock 'n' Roll.* New York: Continuum, 2009.

Kostelanetz, Richard, ed. *The B.B. King Reader: 6 Decades of Commentary,* rev. ed. Milwaukee: Hal Leonard, 2005.

Kot, Greg. *I'll Take You There: Mavis Staples, the Staple Singers, and the Music That Shaped the Civil Rights Era.* New York: Scribner's, 2014.

Lange, Charlie. Liner notes to *Roy Milton and His Solid Senders.* Specialty CD, 1989.

Lauterbach, Preston. *The Chitlin' Circuit and the Road to Rock 'n' Roll.* New York: Norton, 2011.

Leiber, Jerry, and Mike Stoller with David Ritz. *Hound Dog: The Leiber and Stoller Autobiography.* New York: Simon & Schuster, 2009.

Levine, Lawrence W. *Black Culture and Black Consciousness.* New York: Oxford UP, 1977.

Liner notes to Little Richard, *Little Richard—Rocks. Bear Family Records.* https://www.bear-family.com/little-richard/.

Lipsitz, George. *Midnight at the Barrelhouse: The Johnny Otis Story.* Minneapolis: U of Minnesota P, 2010.

Lomax, Alan. *The Land Where the Blues Began.* New York: Delta, 1993.

―――. "Memphis Slim, Big Bill Broonzy and Sonny Boy Williamson." *Blues in the Mississippi Night.* Rykodisc CD, 1990.

Lomax, John Nova. "Roll Over, Ike Turner." *Texas Monthly* (Dec. 2014). https://www.texasmonthly.com/the-culture/roll-over-ike-turner/.

"Lonely Nights." https://www.vocalgroupharmony.com/lonely_n.htm.

Lornell, Kip. *"Happy in the Service of the Lord": Afro-American Gospel Quartets in Memphis.* Urbana: U of Illinois P, 1988.

"Louie, Louie—Louis Armstrong Meets Louis Jordan." *The Wonderful World of Louis Armstrong.* https://dippermouth.blogspot.com/2010/09/louie-louie-louis-armstrong-meets-louis.html?m=0.

Mahon, Maureen. *Black Diamond Queens: African American Women and Rock and Roll.* Durham, NC: Duke UP, 2020.

Marcus, Greil. *The Dustbin of History.* Cambridge: Harvard UP, 1995.

―――. *The History of Rock 'n' Roll in Ten Songs.* New Haven: Yale UP, 2014.

―――. "In the Secret Country: Walter Mosley, Doo-wop, and '50s L.A." *Los Angeles* (August 2002), 98–104.

―――. *Mystery Train: Images of America in Rock 'n' Roll Music,* 3rd rev. ed. New York: Dutton, 1990.

Marovich, Robert M. *A City Called Heaven: Chicago and the Birth of Gospel Music.* Urbana: U of Illinois P, 2015.

Marsh, Dave. *The Heart of Rock & Soul: The 1001 Greatest Singles Ever Made.* New York: NAL, 1989.

―――. "Prof. Alex Bradford Artist Biography." *AllMusic.* https://www.allmusic.com/artist/prof-alex-bradford-mn0000620491/biography.

McBride, James. *Kill 'Em and Leave: Searching for James Brown and the American Soul.* New York: Spiegel & Grau, 2016.

McEwen, Joe. "Little Willie John." *Stranded: Rock and Roll for a Desert Island.* Ed. Greil Marcus. New York: Da Capo, 1996. 93–99.

Middleton, Richard. "The Sophisticated Tradition: Urban Styles, the Second Move Towards America and the Development of Soul." *The B.B. King Reader: 6 Decades of Commentary,* rev. ed. Ed. Richard Kostelanetz. Milwaukee: Hal Leonard, 2005. 35–51.

Millar, Bill. *The Drifters: The Rise and Fall of the Black Vocal Group.* London: November, 1971.

Miller, James. *Flowers in the Dustbin: The Rise of Rock and Roll, 1947–1977.* New York: Simon & Schuster, 1999.

―――. Liner notes to The Staple Singers, *Faith and Grace: A Family Journey, 1953–1976.* Concord CD, 2015. https://www.youtube.com/watch?v=58IA32AJm84.

Milward, John. *Crossroads: How the Blues Shaped Rock 'n' Roll.* Boston: Northeastern UP, 2013.

Mitchell, David. *Utopia Avenue.* Toronto: Knopf Canada, 2020.

Moore, Allan, ed. *The Cambridge Companion to Blues and Gospel Music.* New York: Cambridge UP, 2002.

Moore, Allan F. *Song Means: Analysing and Interpreting Recorded Popular Song.* New York: Routledge, 2012.

―――, ed. *Analyzing Popular Music.* Cambridge: Cambridge UP, 2003.

Mosley, Walter. *Devil in a Blue Dress.* New York: Pocket Books, 1990.

Murray, Albert. *The Omni-Americans.* New York: Vintage, 1983.

―――. *Stomping the Blues.* New York: Da Capo, 1976.

Murray, Charles Shaar. *Boogie Man: The Adventures of John Lee Hooker in the American Twentieth Century.* New York: St. Martin's, 2000.

Nations, Opal Louis. "The Fantastic Violinaires." *Blues & Rhythm* 300 (June 2015). http://opalnations.com/files/Violinaires_The_Fantastic_Violinaires_B_R_300_June_2015.pdf.

―――. "From 'Prayer of Death' to 'Uncloudy Day': The Staple Singers' Early Days." *Blues & Rhythm* 128 (April 1998). http://opalnations.com/files/Staple_Singers_Early_Days_Blues_Rhythm_128_April_1998.pdf.

―――. "The Harmonizing Four of Richmond, Virginia: The Early Years." *Goldmine,* July 8, 1994. http://opalnations.com/files/

Harmonizing_Four_Goldmine_July_1994.pdf.

———. Liner notes to Angelic Gospel Singers, *Touch Me Lord Jesus*. Heritage CD, 1992. http://opalnations.com/files/Angelic_Gospel_Singers_Heritage_CD_11_Liner_Notes.pdf.

———. Liner notes to *Davis Sisters, 1949–1952*. Heritage CD, 2003. http://opalnations.com/files/Davis_Sisters_1949-1952_Heritage_CD_47_2003__Liner_Notes.pdf.

———. Liner notes to Spirit of Memphis, *Happy in the Service of the Lord*. Acrobat CD, 2005. http://opalnations.com/files/Spirit_of_Memphis_Acrobat_CD_3007_Liner_Notes.pdf.

———. Liner notes to *The Bells of Joy*. Acrobat CD, 2006. http://opalnations.com/files/Bells_of_Joy_Acrobat_CD_4207_Liner_Notes.pdf.

———. Liner notes to The C.B.S. Trumpeteers, *Milky White Way*. Nashboro CD, 1995. http://opalnations.com/files/CBS_Trumpeteers_AVI_Nashboro_CD_4534_1995__Liner_Notes.pdf.

———. Liner notes to *The Five Blind Boys of Mississippi*. Acrobat CD, 2006. http://opalnations.com/files/Five_Blind_Boys_of_Miss_Acrobat_CD_3003_Liner_Notes.pdf.

———. Liner notes to *The Greatest Recordings of Madame Edna Gallmon Cooke*. Nashboro CD, 1995. http://opalnations.com/files/Madame_Edna_Gallmon_Cooke_AVI_Nashboro_CD_4008_Liner_Notes.pdf.

———. Liner notes to *The Radio Four, 1952–54*. Heritage CD, 1999. http://opalnations.com/files/Radio_Four_1952-1954_Heritage_CD_42_1999_.pdf.

———. "Salesmen for the Lord: The Kansas City Gospel Singers (Soul Revivers)." *Real Blues* 15 (Oct./Nov. 1998). http://opalnations.com/files/Kansas_City_Gospel_Singers_Soul_Revivers__Real_Blues_15_1998.pdf.

———. *Sensational Nightingales: The Story of Joseph 'Jo Jo' Wallace and the Early Days of the Sensational Nightingales*. n.p.: Black Scat, 2014.

"Need Your Love So Bad." https://secondhandsongs.com/work/12075/versions#nav-entity.

"1955: The Year R.&B. Took Over Pop Field." *Billboard*, Nov. 12, 1955. 126.

"99½ Just Won't Do: Brown-Eyed Has Got to 100!" *Brown Eyed Handsome Soul*, Oct. 18, 2007. http://browneyedhandsomeman.blogspot.com/2007/10/99-12-just-wont-do-brown-eyed-has-got.html.

Oakley, Giles. *The Devil's Music: A History of the Blues*, rev. ed. London: BBC, 1983.

Obrecht, Jas. "'Dust My Broom'—Elmore James (1951)." Library of Congress. https://www.loc.gov/static/programs/national-recording-preservation-board/documents/Dust-My-Broom.pdf.

———, ed. *Rollin' and Tumblin': The Postwar Blues Guitarists*. San Francisco: Miller Freeman, 2000.

Oliver, Paul. *Conversations with the Blues*. New York: Horizon, 1965.

———. *The Story of the Blues*, rev. ed. London: Pimlico, 1997.

———, ed. *The Blackwell Guide to Recorded Blues*. Oxford: Blackwell, 1991.

O'Neal, Jim, and Amy Van Singel, eds. *The Voice of the Blues: Classic Interviews from* Living Blues *Magazine*. New York: Routledge, 2002.

Oshinsky, David M. *"Worse Than Slavery": Parchman Farm and the Ordeal of Jim Crow Justice*. New York: Free Press, 1996.

Otis, Johnny. *Upside Your Head! Rhythm & Blues on Central Avenue*. Hanover, NH: Wesleyan UP, 1993.

Owram, Doug. *Born at the Right Time: A History of the Baby Boom Generation*. Toronto: U of Toronto P, 1997.

Padel, Ruth. *I'm a Man: Sex, Gods and Rock 'n' Roll*. London: Faber, 2000.

Palmer, Robert. *Baby, That Was Rock 'n' Roll: The Legendary Leiber & Stoller*. New York: Harcourt, Brace, 1978.

———. *Blues and Chaos: The Music Writing of Robert Palmer*. Ed. Anthony DeCurtis. New York: Scribner's, 2009.

———. *Deep Blues*. New York: Penguin, 1981.

———. Liner notes to *The Sky Is Crying: The History of Elmore James*. Rhino CD, 1993.

Pearson, Barry Lee. "One Day You're Gonna Hear About Me: The H-Bomb Ferguson Story." *Living Blues* 69 (1985).

Pennington, Stephan. "Willmer Broadnax, Mid-century Gospel, and Black Trans/Masculinities." *Women & Music* 22 (2018), 117–25.

Peters, Art. "Comeback of a Child Star." *Ebony* (Jan. 1967): 42–50. https://books.google.ca/books?id=6iZkedjSfZoC&printsec=frontcover&source=gbs_ge_summary_r&redir_esc=y#v=onepage&q&f=false.

Powers, Ann. *Good Booty: Love and Sex, Black & White, Body and Soul in American Music*. New York: Dey Street, 2017.

Prather, Coy. "Story Behind the Song: 'Tom Moore's Farm.'" *Texas Music* (Sept. 5, 2021). https://txmusic.com/story-behind-the-song-tom-moores-farm/.

Pruter, Robert. *Doowop: The Chicago Scene*. Urbana: U of Illinois P, 1996.

Questlove, with Ben Greenman. *Music Is History*. New York: Abrams, 2021.

"R&B Spreads Wings." *Billboard*, Feb. 4, 1956. 53.

Ramsey, Guthrie P., Jr. *Race Music: Black Cultures from Bebop to Hip-Hop*. Berkeley: U of California P, 2003.

Reagon, Bernice Johnson. "William Herbert Brewster: Rememberings." *We'll Understand It Better By and By*, ed. Bernice Johnson Reagon. Washington, D.C.: Smithsonian Institution, 1992. 185–210.

———, ed. *We'll Understand It Better By and By: Pioneering African American Gospel Composers*. Washington, D.C.: Smithsonian Institution, 1992.

Redd, Lawrence N. *Rock Is Rhythm and Blues (The Impact of Mass Media)*. East Lansing: Michigan State UP, 1974.

Reed, Teresa L. *The Holy Profane: Religion in Black

Popular Music. Lexington: UP of Kentucky, 2003.
Riesman, Bob. *I Feel So Good: The Life and Times of Big Bill Broonzy.* Chicago: U of Chicago P, 2011.
Ripani, Richard J. *The New Blue Music: Changes in Rhythm & Blues, 1950–1999.* Jackson: UP of Mississippi, 2006.
Rolontz, Bob, and Joel Friedman. "Teen-Agers Demand Music with a Beat, Spur Rhythm-Blues." *Billboard,* April 24, 1954. 1.
"The Roots Canal: Voot Detective." *Tuwa's Shanty and the Roots Canal.* http://tuwa.blogspot.com/2006/06/roots-canal-voot-detective.html.
Rowe, Mike. *Chicago Blues: The City & the Music.* New York: Da Capo, 1975.
Runowicz, John Michael. *Forever Doo-Wop: Race, Nostalgia, and Vocal Harmony.* Amherst: U of Massachusetts P, 2010.
Salem, James M. *The Late Great Johnny Ace and the Transition from R&B to Rock 'n' Roll.* Urbana: U of Illinois P, 1999.
———. "'Sh-Boom' and the Bomb: A Postwar Call and Response." *Columbia Journal of American Studies* 7 (2006), 1–31. http://www.columbia.edu/cu/cjas/print/shboom.pdf.
Sampson. "Amos Milburn: 'Chicken Shack Boogie.'" *Spontaneous Lunacy: The History of Rock 'n' Roll—Song by Song.* June 11, 2017. https://www.spontaneouslunacy.net/amos-milburn-chicken-shack-boogie-aladdin-3014/.
———. "Big Joe Turner: 'Low Down Dog.'" *Spontaneous Lunacy: The History of Rock 'n' Roll—Song by Song.* July 18, 2017. https://www.spontaneouslunacy.net/big-joe-turner-low-down-dog-aladdin-3013/.
———. "Chris Powell and The Five Blue Flames: 'Rock the Joint.'" *Spontaneous Lunacy: The History of Rock 'n' Roll—Song by Song,* Mar. 1, 2019. https://www.spontaneouslunacy.net/chris-powell-and-the-five-blue-flames-rock-the-joint-columbia-30175/.
———. "Fats Domino: 'The Fat Man.'" *Spontaneous Lunacy: The History of Rock 'n' Roll—Song by Song,* Jan. 21, 2020. https://www.spontaneouslunacy.net/fats-domino-the-fat-man-imperial-5058/.
———. "Goree Carter: 'Rock Awhile.'" *Spontaneous Lunacy: The History of Rock 'n' Roll—Song by Song,* Feb. 6, 2018. https://www.spontaneouslunacy.net/goree-carter-rock-awhile-freedom-1506/.
———. "Jimmy Liggins: 'Cadillac Boogie.'" *Spontaneous Lunacy: The History of Rock 'n' Roll—Song by Song,* April 7, 2017. https://www.spontaneouslunacy.net/jimmy-liggins-cadillac-boogie-specialty-521/.
———. "The Orioles: 'It's Too Soon to Know.'" *Spontaneous Lunacy: The History of Rock 'n' Roll—Song by Song,* June 14, 2017. https://www.spontaneouslunacy.net/the-orioles-its-too-soon-to-know-jubilee-5000/.
———. "Percy Mayfield, 'Please Send Me Someone to Love.'" *Spontaneous Lunacy: The History of Rock 'n' Roll—Song by Song,* June 30, 2021. https://www.spontaneouslunacy.net/percy-mayfield-please-send-me-someone-to-love-specialty-375/.
———. "Ruth Brown: 'So Long.'" *Spontaneous Lunacy: The History of Rock 'n' Roll Song by Song,* July 31, 2018. https://www.spontaneouslunacy.net/ruth-brown-so-long-atlantic-879/.
———. "Wild Bill Moore: 'We're Gonna Rock.'" *Spontaneous Lunacy: The History of Rock 'n' Roll—Song by Song,* June 7, 2017. https://www.spontaneouslunacy.net/wild-bill-moore-were-gonna-rock-savoy-666/.
Santelli, Robert. *The Best of the Blues: 101 Essential Albums.* New York: Penguin, 1997.
———. "Marion Williams: The Genius of Gospel." *Gadfly,* Nov./Dec. 1999. http://www.gadflyonline.com/home/archive/NovDec99/archive-marionwilliams.html.
Sawyer, Charles. *The Arrival of B.B. King.* New York: Doubleday, 1980.
Schiche, Erika. "Lightnin' Hopkins, Mance Lipscomb and the Legend of Tom Moore's Farm." *Houston Press,* Mar. 15, 2016. https://www.houstonpress.com/music/lightnin-hopkins-mance-lipscomb-and-the-legend-of-tom-moores-farm-7702841.
Schrum, Kelly. *Some Wore Bobby Sox: The Emergence of Teenage Girls' Culture, 1920–1945.* New York: Palgrave Macmillan, 2004.
Segrest, James, and Mark Hoffman. *Moanin' at Midnight: The Life and Times of Howlin' Wolf,* rev. ed. New York: Thunder's Mouth, 2005.
Shaw, Arnold. *Honkers and Shouters: The Golden Years of Rhythm & Blues.* New York: Macmillan, 1978.
———. *The World of Soul.* New York: Cowles, 1970.
Sheridan, Kevin, and Peter Sheridan. "T-Bone Walker: Father of the Blues." *Guitar Player* (Mar. 1977).
Silvester, Peter. *A Left Hand Like God: The Story of Boogie-Woogie.* New York: Omnibus, 1988.
"Sister Rosetta Tharpe." Rock & Roll Hall of Fame. https://rockhall.com/inductees/sister-rosetta-tharpe/.
"Sister Rosetta Tharpe guitar solos (in motion picture)." https://www.youtube.com/watch?v=gELe5Rj_tXU.
"Sister Rosetta Tharpe—Up Above My Head on Gospel Time TV Show." https://www.youtube.com/watch?v=JeaBNAXfHfQ.
Smith, RJ. *The One: The Life and Music of James Brown.* New York: Gotham, 2012.
Spörke, Michael. *Big Mama Thornton: The Life and Music.* Jefferson, NC: McFarland, 2014.
Steinblatt, Harold. "Blues Is King." *The B.B. King Reader: 6 Decades of Commentary,* rev. ed. Ed. Richard Kostelanetz. Milwaukee: Hal Leonard, 2005. 136–42.
Sullivan, James. *The Hardest Working Man: How James Brown Saved the Soul of America.* New York: Gotham, 2008.
Summer of Soul (... or When the Revolution Could Not Be Televised). Dir. Questlove. Searchlight Pictures, 2021.
"Sure Cure for the Blues." https://www.vocal

groupharmony.com/4ROWNEW/SureCure.htm.

Taft, Michael. *The Blues Lyric Formula.* New York: Routledge, 2006.

Talevski, Nick. *Rock Obituaries: Knocking on Heaven's Door.* London: Omnibus, 2006.

"The Tempo Toppers." *Doo-Wop Groups: Biography & Discography,* 2014. http://doo-wop.blogg.org/the-tempo-toppers-a116518060.

Thornton, Yank. "The Secret History of Texas Music: 'Tom Moore's Farm' (1930's)." *Texas Monthly.* https://www.texasmonthly.com/list/the-secret-history-of-texas-music/tom-moores-farm-1930s/.

Tooze, Sandra B. *Muddy Waters: The Mojo Man.* Toronto: ECW, 1997.

Tosches, Nick. *Unsung Heroes of Rock 'n' Roll.* New York: Charles Scribner's Sons, 1984.

Turner, Ike, with Nigel Cawthorne. *Takin' Back My Name: The Confessions of Ike Turner.* London: Virgin, 1999.

Van Rijn, Guido. *The Truman & Eisenhower Blues: African-American Blues and Gospel Songs, 1945–1960.* New York: Continuum, 2004.

Vance, Bill. "1949 Oldsmobile 'Rocket' 88." *Canadian Driver,* Oct. 19, 2004. http://autos.ca/articles/bv/rocket88.htm.

Vera, Billy. Liner notes to *The Best of Nellie Lutcher.* Capitol Jazz CD, 1995.

———. *Rip It Up: The Specialty Records Story.* Los Angeles: BMG, 2019.

Wald, Gayle F. *Shout, Sister, Shout: The Untold Story of Rock-and-Roll Trailblazer Sister Rosetta Tharpe.* Boston: Beacon, 2007.

Walker, Alice. "Nineteen-Fifty-Five." *You Can't Keep a Good Woman Down: Stories.* New York: Harcourt Brace, 1981.

Walton, Anthony. *Mississippi: An American Journey.* New York: Vintage, 1996.

Ward, Brian. *Just My Soul Responding: Rhythm and Blues, Black Consciousness, and Race Relations.* Berkeley: U of California P, 1998.

Ward, Ed. "The Fifties and Before." *Rock of Ages: The Rolling Stone History of Rock & Roll.* Eds. Ed Ward, Geoffrey Stokes and Ken Tucker. New York: Rolling Stone, 1986. 17–224.

———. *The History of Rock & Roll, Volume One, 1920–1963.* New York: Flatiron, 2016.

Ward, Elijah. *Escaping the Delta: Robert Johnson and the Invention of the Blues.* New York: Amistad, 2004.

Ward, Jesmyn. *Men We Reaped.* New York: Bloomsbury, 2013.

Warner, Jay. *American Singing Groups: A History from 1940 to Today.* Milwaukee: Hal Leonard, 2006.

"A Warning to the Music Business." *Variety,* Feb. 23, 1955. *The Pop, Rock, and Soul Reader.* Ed. David Brackett. New York: Oxford UP, 2005. 79–80.

Warwick, Jacqueline. *Girl Groups, Girl Culture: Popular Music and Identity in the 1960s.* New York: Routledge, 2007.

Wasserman, Jerry. "Queen Bee, King Bee: *The Color Purple* and the Blues," *Canadian Review of American Studies* 30.3 (2000), 301–16.

Wexler, Jerry, and David Ritz. *Rhythm and the Blues: A Life in American Music.* New York: Knopf, 1993.

Whitall, Susan, with Kevin John. *Fever: Little Willie John's Fast Life, Mysterious Death and the Birth of Soul.* London: Titan, 2011.

Whitburn, Joel. *Top R&B Singles, 1942–1988.* Menomonee Falls, WI: Record Research, 1988.

White, Charles. *The Life and Times of Little Richard: The Quasar of Rock.* New York: Da Capo, 1994.

White, Cliff. Liner notes to James Brown, *Roots of a Revolution.* Polydor CD, 1989.

Wilcock, Donald E., with Buddy Guy. *Damn Right I've Got the Blues: Buddy Guy and the Blues Roots of Rock-and-Roll.* San Francisco: Woodford, 1993.

Wilkerson, Isabel. *The Warmth of Other Suns: The Epic Story of America's Great Migration.* New York: Penguin Random House, 2010.

Williams, Sherley A. "The Blues Roots of Contemporary Afro-American Poetry." *Write Me a Few of Your Lines: A Blues Reader.* Ed. Steven C. Tracy. Amherst: U of Massachusetts P, 1999. 445–55.

Wilson, Korsha. "Celebrating the Fish Fry, a Late-Summer Black Tradition." *New York Times,* Sept. 11, 2018. https://www.nytimes.com/2018/09/11/dining/fish-fry-black-tradition.html.

Wirz, Stefan. *Wirz's American Music.* https://www.wirz.de/music/jonesfl.htm.

Wright, Richard. "Foreword." *Blues Fell This Morning: Meaning in the Blues* by Paul Oliver, 2nd ed. Cambridge: Cambridge UP, 1990. xiii–xvii.

"You Call Yourself a Cadillac, You Ain't Nothin' but a T-Model Ford—Automobile Blues." *Big Road Blues Radio,* July 28, 2019. https://sundayblues.org/?p=17982.

Zak, Albin J., III. *I Don't Sound Like Nobody: Remaking Music in 1950s America.* Ann Arbor: U of Michigan P, 2010.

Zolten, Jerry. *Great God A'mighty! The Dixie Hummingbirds: Celebrating the Rise of Soul Gospel Music.* New York: Oxford UP, 2003.

Zucker, Mark J. "The Saga of Lovin' Dan: A Study in the Iconography of Rhythm & Blues Music of the 1950s." *Journal of Popular Culture* 16 (Fall 1982), 43–51.

Index

Numbers in **_bold italics_** indicate pages with illustrations

a cappella 9, 16, 118, 133–35, 138–39, 142, 146, 158, 182
"The ABCs of Love" 207
Abrams, Lawrence **_154_**
Abramson, Herb 90
AC/DC 31
Ace, Johnny 63, 100–2, **_101_**; see also Alexander, John
Ace Records 109
The Aces 49, 51
Acuff, Roy 123
Adams, Faye 21, 55; see also Tuell, Fanny
Adams, Justin 220
"Adorable" 177
Aerosmith 31
"Aged and Mellow" 105
"Ain't Nobody Here but Us Chickens" 71, 73
"Ain't Nobody's Business" 11, 98, 229n53
"Ain't That a Shame" 109–10
"Ain't That Good News" 218
"Ain't Times Hard" 40
Aladdin Records 10, 29, 75–76, 84, 86, 91, 109, 111, 128, 174
Alexander, Alger "Texas" 28–29, 41
Alexander, John 100; see also Johnny Ace
"All Aboard" 156
"All I Could Do Was Cry" 58
"All Right Now" 147, 211
Allen, Lee 86, 147, 219
Allison, Margaret 136–38
"Alone and Motherless" 153
"Along Came Jones" 109
Altschuler, Glenn C. 66, 166
"Amazing Grace" 119
Amazing Grace 141, 213
American Bandstand 199, 201; see also _Bandstand_
American Federation of Musicians 66
American Graffiti 166, 183, 202
Ammons, Albert 69

Ammons, Gene "Jug" 69, 185
"Amos' Blues" 84
Amos Milburn and the Aladdin Chickenshackers 86
Anderson, Cat 95
Anderson, Rudy 210
The Angelic Gospel Singers 136–38, 156
Angelou, Maya 117
"Annie Lee Blues" 33
"Annie's Aunt Fanny" 57
"Another Soldier Gone" 130
Anthony, Little 205
Anthony, Ray 169
"Anytime Is the Right Time" 83
Apollo Records 78, 121–22, 172–73
Apollo Theater 53, 71, 106, 155n32, 170, 174, 177, 180, 182, 186, 201, 220
Archia, Tom 94
"Are You Ready?" 2
Aristocrat Records 33, 35–36
Armstrong, Louis 71, 74, 215
"Around the Clock" 93
artificial intelligence (AI) 19
ASCAP 9
"At Last" 58
"At My Front Door" 199
Atkins, Alex 84
Atkins, Cholly 192, 201, 207
Atlanta 214, 217
Atlantic Records 10, 27, 90, 92, 103, 106–8, 161, 164, 174, 174–75, 178–79, 214–15
Atlas Records 114
"Atom and Evil" 128
Augusta, GA 220
Austin, TX 129
Autrey, Gene 189

Babasin, Harry 80
Babb brothers 129–31; see also The Radio Four
"Baby Don't Do It" 173
Baby Face Leroy Trio 36–37, 59

"Baby Get Lost" 79
"Baby It's You" 183
"Baby Let Me Hold Your Hand" 214
"Baby, Please Don't Go" 31, 221
"Back Door" 50
"Back to the Dust" 137
"Bad, Bad Whiskey" 84
Bagby, Doc 137
Bagsby, Jonathan 114
Bailey, Buddy **_179_**–80
Bair-Bey, Vincent 94
Baker, Bea 108; see also Baker, Dolores LaVern
Baker, Dolores LaVern 103, 108–9, 196, 207, 212; see also Baker, Bea; Sharecropper, Little Miss
Baker, Mickey 56, 92, 107, 175, 178, 187, 195, 211, 214
"Ball and Chain" 55
Ballard, Hank 76, 189, 197
Balliett, Whitney 76, 81–82, 90
Baltimore, MD 9, 172, 165, 167–68, 177–79, 184
"Bambalam" 91
Bandstand 199; see also _American Bandstand_
Banks, Al 199
Baptista, Todd 172, 185, 195
Baraka, Amiri 5, 11, 13, 23, 25, 66, 69; see also Jones, Leroi
Baranco, Wilbert 79
Barber, Keith 133–34
Barksdale, Chuck 202
Barksdale, Freddy 193
Barlow, William 25
Barnes, Earle 96
Barnes, Prentiss 190–91
"Barnyard Boogie" 73
barrelhouse 32, 37, 61, 82, 120
Bart, Ben 97, 223
Bartholomew, Dave 74, 109–11
Bartley, Dallas 88
Basie, William "Count" 67, 75, 87, 90, 113, 124

245

Index

Bass, Ralph 21, 26, 104–5, 109, 171, 189, 197, 221
Baton Records 195
B.B. King Orchestra 62
"Be-Baba-Leba" 12, 75–76, 90, 112
"Be with Me Jesus" 147–48, 161
Beal, Eddie 100
Beale Street 62–63, 83
The Beale Streeters 63, 65, 100
"Beams of Heaven" 124
"Beat Me Daddy Eight to the Bar" 85
The Beatles 1, 66, 111
Bee Bee's Jeebies 63
Bell, Leard "Kansas City" 54
"The Bells" 172
The Bells of Joy 129
"The Bells of St. Mary's" 176
Below, Fred 14, 35, 38, 48–51
Bennett, Tony 180
Bennett, Wayne 42
Benton, Brook 79
Berry, Chuck 14, 26, 70, 82, 91, 113–14, 189, 207, 212
Berry, Richard 57
"Beside You" 179
Besman, Bernard 58, 60
Bethea, James 204
Bibb, Leon 159
big bands 8, 33, 35, 85, 90–91, 96, 101, 103, 117–18, 153, 213
Big Bill Broonzy and His Fat Four 32
"Big Fat Mama" 54
"Big Fat Mama Blues" 54
"Big Road Blues" 39, 161
"Big Ten-Inch Record" 80
Biggs, Howard 195
Bihari brothers 45, 63–64
Bill Doggett Octet 75–76
Bill Haley and the Comets 69, 122; see also Haley, Bill
Bill Moore's Lucky Seven Band 90; see also Moore, Wild Bill
Billboard 6–7, 13, 26, 28–30, 40, 44–45, 49, 55, 57, 64–67, 71, 75, 78, 83, 86, 96, 98–99, 101, 103, 113, 127, 155, 162–63, 167, 169–70, 179, 182, 186, 195, 202–3, 210, 215, 220
Billy Ward and His Dominoes 16, 105, 170, 174; see also The Dominoes
"Bim Bam Boom" 199
bird groups 167
Birmingham, AL 149, 151, 217
Bivens, Cliff 48
Black & White Records 26–27
"Black Angel Blues" 33, 64; see also "Sweet Little Angel"
"Black, Brown and White" 31
"Black Diamond Express to Hell" 127

Black Lives Matter 22
Blackwell, Bumps 148, 219
Blake, Paul 30
Blakemore, Amos Wells, Jr. 51; see also Wells, Junior
Blanchard, Edward 97
Bland, Bobby "Blue" 16, 27, 63, 65, 96, 100, 212
Bledsoe, Jet 135
Blind Boys of Alabama 16, 19, 119–20, 126, 146, 151–54
Blind Boys of Mississippi 146, 152, 158; see also Five Blind Boys of Mississippi
"Blood Done Signed My Name" 130
"Blow Your Brains Out" 94
The Blue Jays 164, 167, 185
"Blue Monday" 109
Blue Moon changes 221; see also '50s progression; ice cream changes
"Blue Velvet" 180
"Blueberry Hill" 109
Bluebird Records 30, 46, 111
The Blues Brothers 141, 210
"The Blues Had a Baby and They Named It Rock 'n' Roll" 212
Blues in the Mississippi Night 83
Blues Jubilee 75–76, 99; see also Bull, Frank; Norman, Gene
"Blues with a Feeling" 50
BMI 9
Board, Johnny 116
The Bobbettes 194
"Bobby Sox Blues" 26
Bobo, Willie **137**–38, 140
Bogan, Lucille 33, 64
"Boogie at Midnight" 97
"Boogie Chillen" 59, 86
boogie woogie 21, 44, 69, 73–77, 80, 82, 84–85, 93, 95, 99, 110, 112, 114, 167, 181, 214, 218
"Boogie Woogie Country Girl" 93
"Boogie Woogie (I May Be Wrong)" 87
Boone, Graeme 113
Boone, Pat 187, 199
Boseman, Chadwick 220
Bossard, Henry 158
"'Bout the Break of Day" 52
Bowers, John 52
Boyd, Eddie 11, 23–24, 36, 40–41, 46; see also Eddie Boyd and His Chess Men
Boyer, Horace Clarence 122, 128–29, 141, 149, 151
Bradford, Alex 126–27, 152, 157
Bradford Specials 126–27
Bradley, Oscar Lee 27
Bradshaw, Myron Tiny 55, 67, 80, **88**–89

Branker, Rupert 187
Brantley, Clint 220–21
Brenston, Jackie 84, 115; see also Jackie Brenston and His Delta Cats
Brewster, the Rev. William 122, 141–42
"Bricks in My Pillow" 33
bridge 101, 103, 105, 129, 150, 165, 168, 173–74, 177–78, 180, 182–84, 186–87, 190–93, 195, 200–1, 209, 216; see also channel
Broadnax, Wilmer "Little Axe" 134–35
Brocken, Warren 11, 91
Bronx, NY 8, 56, 187, 195
Brooklyn, NY 172, 210, 217
The Broomdusters 45–46
Broonzy, Big Bill 24, 30–32, 46, 49, 51, 83, 221
Brothers, Prince 177
Broughton, Viv 135, 142, 158, 213
Broven, John 96, 111
Brown, Bill 171, 185
Brown, Billy **181**–82
Brown, Charles 99, 213–14
Brown, James 11, 51, 70, 96, 102, 117, 121, 141–42, 158, 188, 212, 220–23; see also Famous Flames; James Brown and His Famous Flames
Brown, Jimmy 106
Brown, John 75
Brown, J.T. 46, 83
Brown, Roy 74, 89, 94–98, 109, 111–12, 114, 215, 217–18, 222
Brown, Ruth 5, 7, 21, 103, 106–8; see also Weston, Ruth
Brown, Willie 23
"Brown-Eyed Handsome Man" 82
Brown v. Board of Education 7, 10, 186
Brownlee, Archie 146, **154**–56, 159, 213, 215, 220
Bruce Records 182
Bruster, Thomas L. **143**
Buckner, Milt 116
Buckner, Teddy 27
"Build Me a Cabin" 123; see also "Lord Build Me a Cabin in Glory"
"Build Myself a Cave" 35; see also "I'm Gonna Dig Myself a Hole"; "The World's in a Tangle"
Bull, Frank 75, 99; see also Blues Jubilee; Norman, Gene
"Bumble Bee" 32, 60
Bumble Bee Slim 46, 60; see also Easton, Amos
Bunn, Allen 209; see also Slim, Tarheel

Burnett, Chester 42; *see also* Wolf, Howlin'
"Burnin' Hell" 59–60, 105
Burns, Eddie 59
Burroughs, Alvin 82
"Burying Ground" 160
"Busted" 217
"by and by" 120, 140, 144, 150, 157
"By and By, Pt. 1 & Pt. 2" (Davis Sisters) 157
"By and By" (Tindley) 142–43, 150, 157
Byrd, Bobby 220–23
Byrd, Eddie 71, *72*
Byrd, Roy 96; *see also* Longhair, Professor

"Cadillac Baby" 97, 114
"Cadillac Boogie" 114–15
The Cadillacs 163, 192, 201
Café Society 75, 90
"Cain't No Grave Hold My Body Down" 124
Caiola, Al 182
"Caldonia" 217
Caldonia 72
Calhoun, Charles 92, 180; *see also* Stone, Jesse
call and response 9, 71, 85, 87, 122, 124, 129–30, 136, 140–41, 161, 164, 201
"Call It Stormy Monday" 27; *see also* "Stormy Monday Blues"
"Calling Me" 132
Calloway, Cab 26, 87, 124
"Camille's Boogie" 81
Campbell, Lucie E. 145
Canned Heat 60
"Can't We Be Sweethearts" 201
Capitol Records 27, 79, 81, 174
The Cardinals 167, 177–78
Carey, Jake 184
Carey, Zeke 184
Carpenter, Bil 123, 126
Carroll, Earl 163, 192
Carroll, Gregory 170
Carroll, Howard *137*, 140
Carter, Benny 6, 80
Carter, Calvin 202
Carter, Goree 113–14
Carter, John 184
Carter, Vivian 183, 202
Cash, Johnny 6, 43, 123
Cash Box 14, 54, 218
Casimir, Bill 41, 83
Cat Records 187
"Catfish Blues" 37
The Cats and the Fiddle 169
Cavalcades of Jazz 78, 99
Cavanaugh, Dave 80
Champagne Records 189
Chance Records 183–85, 189

Chaney, Sonny 209
"A Change Is Gonna Come" 15, 145, 148
channel 165, 173, 188, 193, 203; *see also* bridge
The Channels 164, 180, 203
The Chantels 21, 186, 194–95, 205
Charles, Ray 29, 61–62, 66, 86, 99, 117, 212–17, *216*, 219–20
Charlie Ferguson and His Orchestra 173
Charlie Singleton Orchestra 114
The Charms 188, 196
Chase, Lincoln 108
Chatman, John 83; *see also* Memphis Slim
Chatman, Peter 83
"Cheating and Lying Blues" 20
Checker Records 30, 49, 185, 202
The Checkers 185
Cheeks, Julius "June" 146–47, 159–60
Chess, Leonard 30, 36–38
Chess brothers 21, 30, 33, 35, 45
Chess Records 10, 14, 30, 33, 36–38, 41, 43–44, 53, 58, 84, 115, 190
Chessler, Deborah 168–69
Chicago 8–11, 15, 23–24, 28, 30–42, 44–46, 48–49, 53, 58, 68, 78, 83, 89, 108–9, 115, 118, 120, 122, 124, 130–31, 142, 145, 160, 167, 177, 183–85, 189, 202
"Chicago Bound" 39, 84
"Chicken Shack Boogie" 85–86
The Chips 11, 210–11
chitlin' circuit 18, 63, 65, 117, 179
"Chonnie-On-Chon" 222–23
"Choo Choo Ch'Boogie" 71–72
The Chords 10, 163, 186–88
Chosen Gospel Singers 126, 131, 160–61
Chris Powell and the Five Blue Flames 113
Christgau, Robert 158
Christland Singers 126, 145
Chudd, Lew 109
"Church Bells May Ring" 183
Cincinnati 10, 58, 68, 80, 89, 97, 109, 132, 188, 221
Cita, Raoul 181–82
civil rights 1, 10–11, 109, 120, 122, 125–26, 131, 143, 149, 161, 165
Clapton, Eric 30, 42, 48
The Clara Ward Singers 188; *see also* The Famous Ward Singers; The Ward Singers
Clark, James "Papa" 180
Clark, Nicky *181*

Clarke, Frank 26
Clarksdale, MS 33, 35–36, 40, 115, 145
Clayton, Buck 76
Clayton, Doctor 20
The Cleftones 201
Cleveland, James 141–42, 160
Cleveland, OH 68, 80, 186, 189
Clinkscales, J.T. *154*, 156
"Close Your Eyes" 174
"The Closer You Are" 164, 203
The Clovers 163, 171, *179*–80, 186
The Coasters 109, 195
Coates, Carl 199, 160
Coates, Dorothy Love 17, 19, 125, 132, 148–51, *149*, 160; *see also* Dorothy Love Coates and the Gospel Harmonettes
Coates, the Rev. J.M. 127
Cobra Records 42
"Coffee Blues" 28
Colb, Vera 150–51
"Cold Sweat" 220
Cold War 10, 187
Cole, Bernice 138
Cole, Nat King 99, 170, 213–14
Coleman, Rick 110–11
Coleman Records 152, 155
The Colgate Comedy Hour 116, 186
Collins, Tony 93, 95
Coltrane, John 6
The Colts 177
Columbia Records 55, 68, 107, 113, 121, 128, 137
"Come and Go to That Land" 146
"Come Go with Me" 200–1
Comet Records 27
Completely Well 64
Condon, Eddie 106
"Confession Blues" 214
Cook, Lorenzo 210
Cooke, Madame Edna Gallmon 122–23, 129
Cooke, Sam 10, 14, 40, 91, 117, 130–31, 142, 144–48, *145*, 159–61, 163, 212
The Cookies 217; *see also* The Raelets
Cooper, Lee 41
Corbin, Warren 201
Cosey, Antonio 32
Cotton, Ernest 41, 84
Cotton, James 52, 115
Cotton Blossom Singers 154; *see also* Five Blind Boys of Mississippi
Cotton Club 123
"Cotton Crop Blues" 52
"Count Every Star" 168
"Country Blues" 35
cover versions 6, 16, 24, 30–31,

33, 40, 42, 54, 67, 70, 76, 100, 102–3, 126, 128, 134, 168–69, 177, 179–80, 183, 185, 187–88, 190–91, 193, 195–96, 199, 204, 209
Cox, Herb 201
Crain, S.R. 142, *143*, 145
Crawford, Ernest "Big" 15, 36–37, 39
Crawford, Richard 18
"Crazy for You" 201–2
Crenshaw, the Rev. Robert 158
The Crew-Cuts 187–88, 190, 195–96, 209
Crosby, Bing 80, 106
"Cross Over the Bridge" 187
The Crows 163, 167, 186–87
Crudup, Arthur "Big Boy" 24, 30, 34–35, 39
"Crying in the Chapel" 163, 170
"Crying Won't Help You" 64
The Crystals 21
Culley, Frank 95
"Cupid's Boogie" 105
Curtis, King 203, 211
"Cut That Out" 51

"Daddy's Home" 202
Dahl, Bill 214, 216
Dahl, Linda 78, 81
Dallas, TX 25, 30
"Dance to the Music" 116
"Dance with Me, Henry" 57, 67
"Dandy Jim from Caroline" 108–9
Darden, Robert 122–23
"Dark Road" 39
Darling, James 135
Davenport, Cow Cow 214
Davenport, Wallace 96
Davis, Angela 20, 98
Davis, Bill 186
Davis, Blind John 110
Davis, Eddie "Lockjaw" 28
Davis, James *137*–38
Davis, Jimmy 97
Davis, John W. 27
Davis, Larry 30
Davis, Maxwell 46, 57–58, 64, 76, 84–86, 100, 195
Davis, Miles 6
Davis, Ruth "Baby Sis" 156–57
Davis, Wild Bill 71, *72*
The Davis Sisters 126, 156–57; *see also* The Famous Davis Sisters
Dawson, Jim 17, 37, 69, 84, 92, 105, 112–113, 171, 187, 189, 254
Day, Doris 190, 204
"The Deacon Moves In" 105
"Dearest" 178
"Death Cell Blues" 41
"Death's Black Train Is Coming" 127

Decca Records 71, 74, 124, 127
Dedmon, James 114
Deep Blues 24
Delgarde, Mario 54
The Dell-Vikings 200–1
The Dells 202
Delmark Records 33
(Mississippi) Delta 8, 14, 23–24, 33, 36–37, 39–40, 43, 61–62, 115, 131, 221
De Luxe Records 96–97, 109, 188
Dempsy, William *181*
Denby, Al 200
Denby, Herman "Junior" 9, 163, 178–79
Detroit 8, 24, 58–60, 86, 102, 112, 127, 130, 160, 167, 173, 177, 188, 193, 212
The Deuces of Rhythm 218
Devil in a Blue Dress 37
"Devil or Angel" 180
de Visé, Daniel 63–64
The Diamonds 183
Diddley, Bo 5, 7, 59, 212; *see also* McDaniel, Elias
Dion and the Belmonts 204
disc jockey 10, 109, 163, 186, 201
Discovery Records 76–77
Dismukes, Holly 96
The Dixie Hummingbirds 14, 16, 65, 117, 119, *137*–40, 158–59, 163
Dixon, Willie 14, 33, 35, 38, 42, 44, 48, 50, 52, 84
"Do Something for Me" 171
Dr. Daddy-O 109
Dr. Hudson's Medicine Show 217
Doggett, Bill 74–75; *see also* Bill Doggett Octet
Domino, Antoine "Fats" 54, 74, 83, 109–11, 196, 212, 219, 229n35
The Dominoes 17, 105, 163–64, 170–72, 174, 178, 180, 186; *see also* Billy Ward and His Dominoes
Don Julian and the Meadowlarks 209
Donaldson, Bobby 94
"Don't Leave Me Baby" 26
"Don't Start Me Talkin'" 48
"Don't You Lie to Me" 110
Dootone Records 26, 162, 190, 209
Dorothy Love Coates and the Gospel Harmonettes 16, 125, 132, 148–51, *149*; *see also* Coates, Dorothy Love
Dorsey, Thomas A. 9, 13, 31, 118, 122, 139, 146, 149–50, 155, 213; *see also* Georgia Tom
Dorsey, Tommy 67, 80

Dot Records 200
"Double Crossing Blues" 104, 194
Douglas, Lizzie 44; *see also* Minnie, Memphis
Doulphin, Edward 203
Down Beat 68
"Down Home Girl" 32
"Down the Road Apiece" 85
Downbeat Records 214
Downchild Blues Band 48
The Drifters 163, 166, 170, 174–77, *175*, 180, 186, 212
The Drifters 235
"Drinkin' Hadacol" 96
the drive 120, 129–30, 132, 135–36, 140, 147, 153, 156, 158, 161, 217
"Driving Wheel" 83
"Drown in My Own Tears" 216–17
Drummond Records 130
The Du Droppers 91
Dublin, Curtis 156–57
Du Bois, W.E.B. 119, 166
Duke Records 10, 65, 100, 188
Dunbar, Paul Laurence 210
Duncan, Al 42
Duncan, Billy 86, 101
Duncan, Cleveland 17, 190
Dunham, Herman 193
Durham, NC 172
Du Sautoy, Marcus 19
"Dust My Blues" 45
"Dust My Broom" 45–46, 48, 92
Dylan, Bob 1, 17–18, 37, 198

"E-Baba-Leba" 75
"Eagle Rock" 51
Earl M. Barnes Orchestra 96
Earle Warren Orchestra 105
"Early in the Morning" 52
"Earth Angel" 17, 26, 163, 190, 192, 196, 209
East Monroe, LA 46
East St. Louis, MO 39, 84
Easton, Amos 60; *see also* Bumble Bee Slim
Ebony magazine 142, 208
Eckstine, Billy 67
The Ed Sullivan Show 121
Eddie Boyd and His Chess Men 41; *see also* Boyd, Eddie
Edwards, David "Honeyboy" 35
Edwards, Ricky 187
"Eisenhower Blues" 40
The El Dorados 199–200
elevation 120, 129, 132, 135–36, 146–47, 153, 155
Ellington, Edward "Duke" 90
Ellison, Ralph 2, 23, 25, 166, 227n31, 229n37

Ely, Claude 124
Ember Records 200
End Records 186
Ernie Fields Orchestra 87
Ertegun, Ahmet 90–91, 106–7, 174, 176–77, 179, 214; *see also* Jernet; Nugetre; Nuggy
Escott, Colin 64
Esquerita 217
Esther, Little 103–6, 111, 194, 196, 218; *see also* Phillips, Esther; Washington, Esther Mae
Evans, David 83
"Every Beat of My Heart" 188
"Every Day of the Week" 207
"Every Day Will Be Sunday" 149–50
"Every Time I Feel the Spirit" 135
"Every Time I Think of You" 54–55
"Everyone's Laughing" 177
"Evil Is Goin' On" 44
Exkano, the Rev. Paul 120, 152–53
"Eyesight to the Blind" 38, 48

The Fabulous Little Richard 219
The Fairfield Four 126, 149
"Faith and Grace" 144
falsetto 13, 53, 57–58, 64, 85, 117, 120, 126, 129–31, 133, 139, 144, 152, 155–56, 158, 164, 167–68, 171–72, 174–75, 178, 182, 184, 190–93, 196, 198–99, 202–3, 210, 215, 218
The Famous Davis Sisters 156–57; *see also* The Davis Sisters
The Famous Flames 220–23; *see also* The Flames; James Brown and His Famous Flames
The Famous Hokum Boys 31; *see also* Georgia Tom
The Famous Ward Singers 140–41; *see also* Ward Singers
"Fare Ye Well" 129
Farley, Jesse 143–145, 193
"Farther on Up the Road" 65
"Fat Daddy" 54
"The Fat Man" 54, 109–10
Feaster, Carl 187
Feather, Leonard 218
Federal Records 10, 86, 105–6, 171, 178, 188, 197–98, 221–22
"Feel Like My Time Ain't Long" 143–44
Felder, Ray 103, 222
Ferguson, Robert "H-Bomb" 114
"Fever" 103
Fields, Frank 111
'50s progression 164; *see also* Blue Moon changes; ice cream changes
"Fine Brown Frame" 82
Fire Records 45
First Annual Mid-Summer Festival of Gospel Music 47
Fisk Jubilee Singers 118, 128
Fitzgerald, Ella 6, 71, 75, 88, 170, 194
The Five Blind Boys of Mississippi 136, 144, *154*–56, 163; *see also* The Blind Boys of Mississippi
The Five Crowns 180–81
The Five Keys 163, 173–74, 181, 186, 193, 196
"Five Long Years" 40–41
The "5" Royales 172–73, 189
The Five Satins 200, 209
"5-10-15 Hours" 107
The Five Willows 183; *see also* The Willows
Flair Records 45, 195
The Flames 220; *see also* The Famous Flames; James Brown and His Famous Flames
"Flames of Jive" 83
The Flamingos 12, 167, 184–85, 187, 207
The Florida Playboys 213
Floyd, Buddy 87
Floyd, George 21–22
Floyd, Samuel A., Jr. 13
Fontane Sisters 188, 195
Fontenette, Johnny 97
"Fool at the Wheel" 218
"Fool Fool Fool" 179–80
A Fool for You" 216
"Fool That I Am" 58
Forest, Earl 86, 101
Fortune Records
"44 Blues" 83
Foster, Baby Face Leroy 36–37
Foster, Paul 134–35, 142–48, *143*, 161
Fountain, Clarence 19, 120, 146, 152–54, 220
The Four Barons 230; *see also* The Larks
The Four Jacks 195–96
Fowler, T.J. 112
Fox, John Hartley 129
Foxx, Jamie 213
Foxx, Redd 190
Francis, David Albert "Panama" 56, 211, 216
Francis, James "Blind" 122
Frankie Lymon and the Teenagers 11, 204–9, *206*; *see also* Lymon, Frankie
Franklin, Aretha 56, 102, 117, 121, 127, 141–42, 212–13
Franklin, the Rev. C.L. 127, 212
Freed, Alan 7, 14, 68–69, 112, 182, 184, 186, 189–90, 198, 201, 207
Freedom Records 113
Freeman, Ernie 6
Freeman, Jim 200
Friedwald, Will 75, 77
From Spirituals to Swing 69, 90–91, 124, 128; *see also* Hammond, John
Fulson, Lowell 24, 29–30, 63, 214
Fulson, Martin 29–30
Funches, Johnny 202
Fuqua, Harvey 189–90
Fury Records 183, 208

Gaines, Roy 65
Gaither, Tommy 168–*169*
Gaither, William 81
"Gal from Kokomo" 97
Galloway, Dicey *181*
Galt, Stephen 61
Gamble, Renaldo 205
Gamble & Huff 208
Gant, Cecil 99
Garnes, Sherman 205–8, *206*
Garon, Paul 92
Gary, IN 183
Gaston, Stacy 162
The Gaston Brothers 161; *see also* Kansas City Soul Revivers
Gates, Henry Louis, Jr. 8
"Gee" 163, 186, 189–90
Gee Records 186, 201, 205
gender 20–21, 71, 134, 179, 194, 215
Gene Gilbeaux Quartet 99, 116
George, Karl 79
George, Nelson 70, 164
"Georgia on My Mind" 217
Georgia Tom and the Famous Hokum Boys 42, 118; *see also* Dorsey, Thomas
"Get It" 189
"Get on the Good Foot" 220
Get On Up 220
"Get Rich Quick" 218
Gibbs, Georgia 57, 67, 187
Gilbeaux, Gene 99, 116
Gillespie, Dizzy 67, 79
Gillett, Charlie 67, 87, 100, 109, 197
Gilmore, Willie 162
Gioia, Ted 30, 37
The Girl Can't Help It 116
girl groups 5, 28, 194–95
Gladys Hampton Blues Boys 116
Gladys Knight and the Pips 188
"The Gleam in Your Eyes" 203
Glenn, Artie 170
Glenn, Darrell 170

Glenn, Lloyd 27
The Gliders 108
"Gloria" 182, 192, 233n59
"The Glory of Love" 174
Glover, Henry 88, 102, 178, 216
Go Johnny Go! 184
"Goin' Down Slow" 16
"Goin' Down to Eli's" 20
Gold Star Records 28–29
Goldberg, Doc 85
Goldberg, Marv 108, 168, 187, 189, 198, 205
The Golden Echoes 134–35, 142
The Golden Gate Quartet 128, 132
Golden Gospel Classics: The Dixie Hummingbirds 139
"Golden Teardrops" 184
Goldner, George 186, 201–2, 205, 207
Gonder, Fats 221
Gone Records 186
Gonna Take a Miracle 193
"Good Daddy Blues" 79
"Good Golly Miss Molly" 217
"Good Lovin'" 180
"Good Luck Darlin'" 180–81
"Good Morning Mr. Blues" 93
"Good Morning, School Girl" 46
"Good News" 133
"Good Rockin' Daddy" 57
"Good Rockin' Tonight 93–97, 112, 222
Goodfellas 166, 182
Goodman, Benny 67, 174
Goodman, Shirley 111–12
"Goodnite Sweetheart, Goodnite" 163, 183–84, 186
Goosman, Stuart 165, 168, 178
Gordon, Dexter 6, 77
Gordon, Robert 36
Gordon, Roscoe 63, 65
Gore, Edison 103, 221
Gore, Rufus 89, 103
Goree Carter & His Hepcats 113–14; *see also* Carter, Goree
The Gospel Harmonettes 25, 132, 148–51, 159; *see also* Dorothy Love Coates and the Gospel Harmonettes
Gospel Highway 14, 117, 165
Gospel Nostalgia 139
Gospel Pearls 118
Gotham Records 136–37, 141, 156–57
"Gotta Gimme Whatcha' Got" 79
Gourevitch, Phillip 221
Gracyk, Theodore 17
Graves, Pete 190–91
Grease 166
Great Migration 8, 23, 41, 68, 73, 160, 167

The Great 1955 Shrine Concert 147
"The Great Pretender" 166, 198, 210
Greatest Hits (Aretha Franklin) 213
Green, Al 1–2, 13, 158
Green, Tucker 99
Greene, Imogene 156–57
Greer, Big John 54
Gregory, Gerald 183–84
Gribin, Anthony 14, 165–67, 177, 194–95, 204, 210
Griffin, Bessie 126
Griffin, Leroy 209
Groia, Philip 171, 174, 183, 192, 201, 205, 210
Gunter, Shirley 195
Guralnick, Peter 5, 13, 18, 43, 55, 131, 142, 145–48, 170, 215
Gussow, Adam 20, 60
Guthrie, Woody 31
Guy, Buddy 40, 42, 51, 59, 61–62
"The Gypsy" 164

H-bomb 14, 151
"Hadacol Bounce" 96
"Hadacol That's All" 96
Hadnott, Billy 27, 74, 82
Haley, Bill 93, 113; *see also* Bill Haley and the Comets
Hall, Michael 28
Hall, Orrington 95
Hallelujah, I Love Her So 215–16
"Hallelujah, I Love Her So" 216
Hamilton, Gerald 186
Hammond, John 69, 90, 124; *see also From Spirituals to Swing*
Hampden, Larry 203
Hampton, Lionel 78, 116
Handy, W.C. 62
Hank Ballard and the Midnighters 49, 57, 197; *see also* Ballard, Hank; The Midnighters
The Happyland Singers 152; *see also* The Blind Boys of Alabama
"Hard Driving Mama" 77
"Hard Times" 40
Hardesty, Herb 111
Hardy, Leon 178
Hare, Pat 20, 52
"Harlem" 11
"Harlem Bound" 39, 84
Harlem, NY 39, 53, 84, 123, 167, 180, 183, 186, 192, 203–4, 208
The Harmonizing Four 16, 135–36, 156
The Harptones 164, 180–83, *181*, 186, 203, 208
Harris, Bill *179*

Harris, Chizz 75
Harris, LeRoy 95
Harris, R.H. 142–45, *143*, 154, 157–58
Harris, Wynonie 17, 77–78, 89, 93–96, *94*, 97, 112, 114, 116, 215, 218
Harrison, Wilbert 86
Harvey, Bill 55, 65
Harvey & the Moonglows 190, 207
"Have Mercy Baby" 171
Haven, Shirley 260–61
Hawkins, Jamesetta 57; *see also* James, Etta
Hayes, Eloise 126
Hayes, Ernie 56
Hayes, Linda 197
"He May Be Yours" (aka "He May Be Your Man") 76; *see also* "I'm Gonna Let Him Ride"
"He Won't Deny Me" 158
heart ballad 101, 103
The Heartbeats 201–2
The Hearts 195, 201
"Hearts of Stone" 188
"Heaven and Paradise" 209
Hefflin, Leon 99
Heilbut, Anthony 18, 36, 121, 124, 133, 141–43, 147–48, 154, 159–60, 213
Helena, AK 24, 33, 38, 47, 49, 69, 82–83
"Helen's Advice" 77
"Hello Little Boy" 107–8
"Help Me Somebody" 173
Hendrix, Jimi 62
Henry, Haywood 92, 107
Henry, Shifty 27, 91, 99
Herald Records 55, 199, 209
Herman, Woody 67
"He's a Real Gone Guy" 82
"He's My Rock" 155, 158
"Hey Senorita" 190
Heyward, Louis 168
high who 119, 126, 133, 135, 141, 142, 144, 151, 217
The Highway QCs 16, 129–31, 193, 159–60
Hill, Don 99, 116
Hill, Raymond 115
Hinson, Glenn 120
Hinton, Milt 195
Hirshey, Gerri 171, 215
"Hit the Road Jack" 217
Hite, Les 26
"Hobo Blues" 59
Hogan, Carl *72*
hokum 31, 79, 118
Holliday, Billie 6, 75, 98, 106, 148
Holloway, Red 42, 190
Holly, Buddy 88

The Honey Bears 194
"Honey Bee" 38
"Honey Love" 176, 186
"Honey Hush" 20
"Honey in the Rock" 172
"The Honeydripper" 83, 114
"Hoochie Coochie Man" 38–39, 44, 96
"Hoodoo Man" 51
Hoodoo Man Blues 51
Hooker, Earl 51
Hooker, John Lee 13, 24, 33, 35, 40, **58**–61, 65, 86, 105, 212
Hootenany 142
Hopkins, Herman 112
Hopkins, Lightnin' 24, 28–29, 58, 80
Horton, Big Walter 42
Hot Harlem Revue 53
"Hound Dog" 53–55
House, Son 13, 23, 35
"The House of Blues Lights" 21
The House Rockers 83
Houston 10, 24, 27–28, 53, 55, 65, 84, 86, 89, 101, 109, 113, 116, 126, 133, 154, 160, 217–18
"How Long" 144
"How Many More Years" 44
Howard, Camille 77, 81, 87–88
Hudson, James "Pookie" 183–84
Hughes, Langston 11, 32, 98
Hull Records 201-2
Humes, Helen 6, 12–**13**, 21, 75–77, 79, 81, 87, 90, 99, 106, 112
Hunter, Ivory Joe 99
"Hurry On Down" 82
"The Hustle Is On" 28
"Hypin' Woman Blues" 27

"I Believe" 45–46
"I Believe I'll Dust My Broom" 45
"I Be's Troubled" 20, 35
"I Can See Everybody's Mother But Mine" 152
"I Can't Be Satisfied" 15, 20, 30, 36–37, 52
"I Can't Put You Down, Baby" 65
"I Can't Quit You Baby" 42
"I Can't Stop Loving You" 217
"I Can't Walk This Highway" 161
"I Don't Need No One Else" 162
"I Don't Stand a Ghost of Chance" 164, 192–93
"I Dreamed Heaven Was Like This" 131
"I Feel Like Going Home" 36
"I Feel That Old Age Coming On" 95–96
"I Feel That Old Feeling Coming On" 222
"I Got My Discharge Papers" 10
"I Got You (I Feel Good)" 220
"I Have a Right to the Tree of Life" 144
"I Just Wanna Make Love to You" 38
"I Like 'Em Fat Like That" 54
"I Like My Baby's Pudding" 93
"I Love You So" 186
"I Miss You So" 169–70
"I Only Have Eyes for You" 185
"I Pity the Fool" 65
"I Promise to Remember" 206
"I Want You to Be My Girl" 206
"I Wouldn't Mind Dying" 150–51
ice cream changes 19, 164, 190; *see also* '50s progression
"I'd Be Satisfied" 16
Ike Turner's Rhythm Kings 115
"I'll Be Forever Loving You" 199–200
"(I'll Be Glad When You're Dead), You Rascal You" 74
"I'll Be Home" 185, 187
"I'll Be Satisfied" (Dixie Hummingbirds) 16, 138
"I'll Be Satisfied" (Jackie Wilson) 17
"I'll Drown in My Tears" 216
"I'll Fly Away" 16
"I'm a Royal Child" 127–28
"I'm a Soldier" 127
"I'm Determined to Run This Race" 160
"I'm Going Back with Him" 160–61
"I'm Gone" 111, 183
"I'm Gonna Dig Myself a Hole" 34–35; *see also* "Build Myself a Cave"; "The World's in a Tangle"
"I'm Gonna Get Married" 110
"I'm Gonna Have Myself a Ball" 88–89
"I'm Gonna Let Him Ride" 76–77; *see also* "He May Be Your Man"
"I'm Gonna Move in the Room with the Lord" 16, 144
"I'm Gonna Murder My Baby" 20
"I'm in Love Again" 109
"I'm Just a Lonely Guy" 219–20
"I'm Not a Juvenile Delinquent" 11, 207–8
"I'm Not a Know It All" 207
"I'm Ready" 38
"I'm Sealed" 149
"I'm So Happy" 276
"I'm the Fat Man" 54, 145
"I'm the Father of Annie's Baby" 57
Imperial Records 28, 61, 109
The Impressions 2
"In My Diary" 190
"In My Lonely Room" 172
"In My Real Gone Rocket" 115
"In the Morning" 137–39
"In the Still of the Nite" 200
"In the Wilderness" 156
The Ink Spots 164, 167, 179, 188, 197–98
Invisible Man 166, 227n31, 229n37
Isley, Ronnie 132
The Isley Brothers 117, 132–33
"It Ain't the Meat" 178–79
"It Hurts Me Too" 46
"It's a Man's Man's Man's World" 220
It's a Natural Records 168
"It's Later Than You Think" 17, 88
"It's Tight Like That" 79
"It's Too Soon to Know" 168–70, 177–78
iTunes 2, 15, 139, 152
"I've Got a Right" 144, 192
"I've Got a Woman" 215–16
Izenhall, Aaron 71, **72**, 74

Jack McVea and His All Stars 26; *see also* McVea, Jack
Jackie and the Starlites 172
Jackie Brenston & His Delta Cats 115; *see also* Brenston, Jackie
Jackson, Benjamin "Bull Moose" 80
Jackson, Earl Sumner 81
Jackson, Fred 218
Jackson, Gator 102
Jackson, Jimmy 77
Jackson, John 7
Jackson, Josh 71, **72**, 73–74
Jackson, Jump 83
Jackson, Mahalia 14, 117–18, **121**–24, 126, 161, 213
Jackson, Michael 193, 205
Jackson, Milt 6, 78–79
Jackson, Rudy 188
Jackson, Willie C. 183
Jackson, Willis "Gator Tail" 69, 135
Jackson, MS 45, 48, 154, 161
The Jackson Five 205
The Jackson Gospel Singers 161
The Jackson Harmoneers 152, 205; *see also* The Five Blind Boys of Mississippi
Jacobs, Little Walter 24, 48, 65; *see also* Little Walter
Jacquet, Illinois 69
The Jaguars 209
James, Colin 30
James, Elmore 24, 45–46, 51, 92
James, Ernest 138–39, 159–160

James, Etta 21, 53, 57–58, 67, 102, 121, 187, 212; *see also* Hawkins, Jamesetta
James, Harry 67
James, Joyce 195
James, Skip 5
James Brown and His Famous Flames 173; *see also* Brown, James
Jay-Dee Records 195
The Jay McShann Sextet 20; *see also* McShann, Jay
jazz 1, 6, 8, 13, 31, 66–68, 70, 73, 76, 79, 81, 90, 98, 109, 122, 124, 167, 187, 213–14, 218
Jefferson, Blind Lemon 26, 28
Jefferson, John 159
Jenkins, Charles 84
Jennings, Bill 103
"Jenny Jenny" 217
Jernet 108; *see also* Ertegun, Ahmet
"Jesus Gave Me Water" 145
"Jesus Hits Like the Atom Bomb" 134
"Jesus Is a Rock in a Weary Land" 155
"Jesus Is Waiting" 2
Jeter, Claude 158, 213
The Jewels 188
"Jim Dandy" 108–9
The Jimmy Cotton Blues Quartet 115; *see also* Cotton, James
Jimmy Liggins and His Drops of Joy 114; *see also* Liggins, Jimmy
Jimmy Preston and the Prestonians 113; *see also* Preston, Jimmy
"Jingle Bells" 150, 168, 176
J.O.B Records 32, 39–40
Joe, Kansas 44; *see also* McCoy, Joe
Joe, Little Son 44; *see also* Lawler, Ernest
Joe Liggins and His Honeydrippers 114
The Joe Scott Orchestra 55
John, Little Willie 102–3
John, Mertis 102
"Johnny Has Gone" 101
Johnny Otis Orchestra 101, 106; All Stars 93; Quintet 104; *see also* Otis, Johnny
"Johnny's Still Singing" 101
Johnson, Billy 190
Johnson, Bubber 102
Johnson, Buddy 82
Johnson, Charles 210–11
Johnson, Conrad O. 113
Johnson, Harold 195
Johnson, Jack 178
Johnson, Joseph 128–29

Johnson, Merline 108
Johnson, Pete 69, 83, 86, **90**–91, 93
Johnson, Robert 23, 35–36, 43, 45–46, 83, 114
Johnson, Tommy (blues singer) 23, 33, 39, 54
Johnson, Tommy (Harmonizing Four) 136
Johnson, Willie 43–44
Jones, Charles Price 150
Jones, Chet 199
Jones, Deacon 79
Jones, Eddie 61–62; *see also* Slim, Guitar
Jones, Floyd 39–40, 51
Jones, Hank 108
Jones, Isaiah 130
Jones, Jo 76
Jones, Johnny 46, 51, 92
Jones, LeRoi 8, 11, 13, 32, 66–67, 69; *see also* Baraka, Amiri
Jones, Ruth 105; *see also* Washington, DInah
"The Jones Girl" 200
Joplin, Janis 55
Jordan, Louis 8, **9**, 17, 49, 51, 54, 67, 70–74, **72**, 76, 82, 85, 87–88, 116, 217
"Joshua Fit de Battle of Jericho" 128
Josie Records 192, 210
"Joy in the Beulah Land" 130
jubilee 9, 13, 119, 128–29, 135–36, 143, 159
Jubilee Records 168
"Juiced" 84
"Juke" 49
Juke Box Records 87; *see also* Specialty Records
The Jukes 49
Julia Lee and Her Boyfriends 79; *see also* Lee, Julia
Julian, Don 209
jump/jump blues 1, 12, 32–33, 36, 39, 41, 50, 65, 67, 70–71, 83–84, 99–100, 103, 105, 165, 171, 184–85, 190, 199, 218, 222
"Jump Children" 12, 184
"Jumpin' Tonight" 12
Junior, Marvin 202
Junior Wells and His Eagle Rockers 51; *see also* Wells, Amos "Junior"
"Junker's Blues" 109
"Just Another Day" 146
Just Jazz 99
Justis, Bill 5–6

Kahn, Tommy 26
"Kansas City" 86
"Kansas City Blues" 86
Kansas City Bill & Orch 54; *see also* Otis, Johnny

Kansas City, MO 68, 79, 86, 89–90, 93, 162
Kansas City Soul Revivers 162
Kaufman, Murray 163
Kay, Connie 92–93, 107, 214
"K.C. Loving" 86
Keels, James 128
"Keep A-Knockin'" 217
"Keep on Churnin' (Till the Butter Comes)" 93
Keil, Charles 24
Kelly, Red 27
Kelsey, the Rev. Samuel 127–28, 135, 141
Kelso, Jackie 88
Kern, Jerome 209
Keyes, Jimmy 187
Kimble, Sam 182
King, Albert 27, 175
King, B.B. 6, 10, 12, 24–25, 27, 29–30, 33, 35, 43, 59, 62–65, **63**, 70, 96, 114, 175, 212, 214, 219
King, Ben E. 163, 174, 177, 180; *see also* Nelson, Benjamin
King, Bob 145, 148
King, Earl 61
King, Martin Luther, Jr. 10, 121, 127
King Biscuit Time 63
King Records 10, 80, 86, 88, 93, 96–97, 102, 105, 108, 135, 158, 171, 173, 178, 188, 216, 221
"King Size Papa" 80
Kirby, David 219
Kirkland, Leroy 74
"A Kiss from Your Lips" 185
"Kissa Me Baby" 214
"Kissing in the Dark" 32
Kizart, Willie 115
Knight, Joe 94
Knight, Madame Marie 124–**125**
Knowling, Ransom 34–35
Knox, Nash 222
Knoxville, TN 158
Korean War 10, 34, 91, 100, 130, 139, 144, 156, 185
Kot, Greg 132

Labelle 193
Labelle, Patti 121
La Bostrie, Dorothy 219
Lacey, Jimmy 83
Lambert, Eddie 113
Land, Harold 114
Lane, Ernest 33
Langford, William 128
The Larks 167, 172–74, 210
Latifah, Queen 124
Lauterbach, Preston 18, 71, 82, 96, 123
"Lawdy Miss Clawdy" 110–11
Lawler, Ernest 32; *see also* Joe, Little Son

Index

Leach, Lillian 55, 195
Lead Belly 31
"Leak in This Old Building" 129
Leake, Lafayette 42
Led Zeppelin 42
Lee, George 79
Lee, James 164
Lee, Julia 17, 79–80, 103
Lee, Laura 160
Lee, Leonard 111–12
Lee, Peggy 103
"leer-ics" 68, 80, 171, 188
Leiber, Jerry 71, 98, 229n53
Leiber & Stoller 21, 53, 86, 98, 193–94
Lenoir, J.B. 40
Leroy, Baby Face 36; see also Foster, Baby Face Leroy
Lester, Bobby 189–91
"Let Me Go Home Whiskey" 84
"Let Me Play with Your Poodle" 28–29, 80
"Let the Good Times Roll" (Louis Jordan) 8, 17, 71–73
"Let the Good Times Roll" (Shirley & Lee) 111–12
Let the Good Times Roll 70
"Levee Camp Moan Blues" 41
Lewis, Earl 203
Lewis, Jerry 116
Lewis, Jerry Lee 6, 43, 113, 166
Lewis, John 107
Lewis, Meade Lux 69
Lewis, Pete 54, 105
Lewis, the Rev. Samuel K. 152–53
Lewis, Smiley 109
Lewis Lymon and the Teenchords 204, 208
"Life Is But a Dream" 182–83
The Lifeboat 161
Liggett, Ellsworth 41
Liggins, Jimmy 114–15
Liggins, Joe 114
Lillian Leach and the Mellows 195; see also The Mellows
Lipscomb, Mance 29
Little, David 208
Little Anthony and the Imperials 205
"Little Boy" 127
"Little Girl of Mine" 201
"Little Miss Love" 199
Little Miss Sharecropper 143; see also Baker, LaVern
Little Walter and His Night Caps 49; see also Walter, Little
Littlefield, A.C. 129
Littlefield, Little Willie 86, 96, 229n35
Live at the Apollo 220

Livingston, Ulysses 109
Lockwood, Robert Jr. 35, *47*, 49–50
"Lollipop Mama" 94
"Lolly Pop Mama" 94
Lomax, Alan 20, 31, 35–36, 83, 154
"Lonely Nights" 195, 201
"Long About Midnight" 97
"Long Distance Call" 38
"Long Tall Sally" 217, 222
Longhair, Professor 96, 109; see also Byrd, Roy
Look Down Upon Me, Lord: The Dixie Hummingbirds 139
"Lord, Build Me a Cabin in Glory" 123
Los Angeles 8, 10, 24, 26–27, 29–30, 53, 57, 64, 68, 75–76, 78, 81, 84, 86–87, 89–90, 98–99, 104, 109, 114–16, 133, 145, 147, 161–62, 167, 177, 185, 190, 194, 197, 209, 214
Louis Jordan and His Tympany Five 8, 71–74, *72*
Louisville, KY 75, 189
Love, Billy 84
Love, Milton 193
Love, Willie 48, 149
"Love Lifted Me" 158
Love Lifted Me/My Rock 158
"Lover's Island" 185
Lovett, Sam "Baby" 79
"Lovey Dovey" 180
"Lovin' Blues" 65
"Lovin' Machine" 96
"Low Down Dog" 91
Luandrew, Albert 44; see also Slim, Sunnyland
"Lucille" (Clyde McPhatter) 175
"Lucille" (Little Richard) 217
Lucky Thompson's All Stars 78; see also Thompson, Lucky
"Ludella" 39
Lunceford, Jimmy 116
Lutcher, Joe 96
Lutcher, Nellie 17, *81*–82, 96, 103, 111
Lymon, Frankie 205–9, ***206***
Lymon, Lewis 208
Lynch, Dave ***197***
lynching 8, 31, 225n5
Lyons, Lonnie 113

Mack, Norris "Bunky" 178
Macon, GA 217–18, 221
Madonna 123
The Magnificent Four 203
Mahalia Jackson: The Original Apollo Sessions 122
Mahon, Maureen 54
"Mailman's Sack" 89
"Make It Funky" 220
Mallard, "Sax" 41, 83

Malone, Earl D. 135
"(Mama) He Treats Your Daughter Mean" 107
"Mamma Talk to Your Daughter" 40
Marcus, Greil 16, 169, 190, 200
Marion Williams and the Stars of Faith 142; see also Williams, Marion
Marks, Rose 170
Marsh, Dave 17, 102–3, 126, 177, 193, 202, 205–7, 217, 221
Marshall, Joe 107
Marshall, Maithe 167–68
Martha and the Vandellas 21
Martin, Bill 95
Martin, Dean 116
Martin, Ed 200
Martin, Joe 183
Martin, Leslie 205
Martin, Ralph 183
Martin, Sallie 78, 118
The Marvelettes 21
Matassa, Cosimo 144, 146, 219
"Maybe" 194
Maybelle, Big 21, 32, 55–57, 112; see also Smith, Big Maybelle
"Maybelle's Blues" 56
Mayfield, Curtis 100
Mayfield, Percy 100, 102
Mays, Roy 218
Mazzetta, Vinnie 200
McBride, James 221
McClennan, Tommy 60
McCollum, Robert Lee 33; see also Nighthawk, Robert
McCoy, Joe 32; see also Joe, Kansas
McDaniel, Elias 212; see also Diddly, Bo
McDaniel, Willard 27, 46
McDowell, Josephine 137
McDowell, Mississippi Fred 46, 153
McElroy, Sollie 184–85
McFadden, Ruth 208
McGhee, Brownie 24, 56
The McGuire Sisters 190, 195
McKinley, Ray 85
McNeely, Big Jay 12, 69
McNeil, David 171
McNeil, Leroy 209
McPhatter, Clyde 13, 16–17, 19, 170, 173–78, ***175***, 189, 193, 205, 217
McQuater, Matthew ***179***
McShann, Jay 28, 67, 98
The McSon Trio 213; see also Charles, Ray
McTell, Blind Willie 24, 41
McVea, Jack 26, 50, 91
"Me and My Chauffeur Blues" 32
The Meadowlarks 167, 209

"Mean Old World" 49–50
Mean Streets 210
The Meditation Singers 126, 160
Medlock, James 144–45
Melba Records 183
melisma 42, 64, 79, 102, 108, 136, 139, 143, 145–46, 171, 176, 218
The Mello-Moods 204
The Mellows 56, 195
Melrose, Lester 30, 46
Memphis 5, 8, 10, 24, 32, 36, 39, 47, 51–52, 55, 58, 62–63, 65, 68, 83, 100, 115, 122, 154, 212
"Memphis Blues" 62
Merchant, Jimmy 205, **206**
Mercury Records 32, 76, 78–79, 197–98
Merritt, Maurice 65
"Mess Around" 214
Meteor Records 45
Middleton, Tony 183
The Midnighters 65, 74, 173, 189; *see also* Ballard, Hank
"Mighty, Mighty Man" 96
The Mighty Mighty Men 97; *see also* Brown, Roy
Milburn, Amos 17, 84–86, 93, 106, 112, 214, 229n35
"Milky White Way" 128–29
Millar, Bill 176
Miller, Aleck "Rice" 38, 43, 45, **47**–48; *see also* Williamson, Sonny Boy II
Miller, Glenn 198
Miller, James 67, 86, 94, 109, 188, 204
Miller, Mildred 149
Millinder, Lucky 67, 80, 93, 106, 124
"Million Dollar Secret" 77, 99, 106
The Mills Brothers 164, 166–67
Milton, Roy 17, 54, 75–77, 81, 87–89
"Milton's Boogie" 87
Milward, John 59
Mingus, Charles 6, 78–79
Minnie, Memphis 21, 24, 30, 32, 52–53, 60–61, 108, 124; *see also* Douglas, Lizzie
Miracle Records 83–84
"Mr. Blues Is Coming to Town" 93
"Mr. Blues Jumped the Rabbit" 93
"Mr. Down Child" 48
"Mr. Lee" 194
Mister Rock and Roll **219**
Mitchell, Billy **179**–80
Mitchell, David 5
Mitchell, Freddie 214
"Moanin' at Midnight" 43–44

Modern Records 10, 29, 45, 57–58, 63, 65, 76–77, 86, 99
"Money Honey" 175–76, 180
Monroe, Bill 123
Montgomery, Little Brother 32
The Moonglows 186, 189–91, 196, 207
Moore, Alfred 75
Moore, Allan 18, 133
Moore, Fleecie 72
Moore, Johnny 177
Moore, Wild Bill 75, 90–91, 112
Morganfield, McKinley 48; *see also* Waters, Muddy
"Morning at Midnight" 44
Morris, Billy 203
Morris, Joe 55
Morrison, Toni 2
Morrison, Van 31
Morse, Ella Mae 21
Morton, Johnny 83
Moses, Pirkle Lee 199–200
Mosley, Walter 2, 27
"Most of All" 190
"Mother Bowed" 133–34
Motown 1, 127, 160, 192, 205
Mount Lebanon Singers 170, 174
"Move in the Room with the Lord" 144
"Move On Up a Little Higher" 122, 124
Muddy Waters Sings Big Bill Broonzy 31
Muldaur, Maria 179
Mumford, Eugene 172
Murray, Albert 13, 16, 25, 74, 89, 176
Murray, Charles Shaar 59
Murray, Louise Harris 195
"My Babe" 50
"My Gal's a Jockey" 90–91
"My Heart's Desire" 209–10
"My Love Will Never Die" 42
"My Man Rocks Me with One Steady Roll" 15
"My Memories of You" 164, 182
"My Own Fault, Darlin'" 63
"My Prayer" 198
"My Reverie" 172
"My Road's So Rough and Rocky" 134
"My Rock" 158
"My Song" 100–2
Myers, Bumps 27
Myers, Dave 49
Myers, Louis 49–50, 52
Myles, John 158

Nackel, Billy 116
Nashville 118, 123, 129, 217–18
Nathan, Syd 97, 221
National Records 90, 108, 167

Nations, Opal Louis 119, 122, 129, 135–37, 155, 159–62
Navarro, Esther 192
NBC Television Orchestra 140
"Nearer My God to Thee" 13, 197
"Nearer to Thee" 147–48
"Need a Little Sugar in My Bowl" 60
"Need Your Love So Bad" 102–3
Negroni, Joe 205, **206**
Nellie Lutcher and Her Rhythm 82; *see also* Lutcher, Nellie
Nelson, Benjamin 180; *see also* King, Ben E.
Nelson, George 168–70, **169**
Nelson, Nate 184–85
"Never Turn Back" 155
New Haven, CT 200
New Orleans 24, 49, 61–62, 71, 73–74, 86, 89, 91, 94, 96–97, 109–11, 122, 161, 214, 218–19, 222
"New Orleans Woman" 99
New York 8, 10, 53, 55, 71–72, 75, 81, 88–90, 102, 109, 114, 124, 132, 164, 167, 171–73, 177, 181–82, 192–93, 195, 201, 209
Newark, NJ 10, 55
Newbern, Hambone Willie 36–37
Newman, David "Fathead" 214
Newport News, VA 173
"Night Time Is the Right Time" 83
Nighthawk, Robert 10, 20, 24, 30, 33–34, 38, 46, 64; *see also* McCollum, Robert Lee
"Nine Below Zero" 48
1950s Southern Gospel 139
"99 ½ Won't Do" 125, 155
"Ninety-Nine and a Half Won't Do" 151
Nix, the Rev. A.W. 127
Nix, Willie **47**, 63
"No Hiding Place" 150–51, 159
"No More Trouble Out of Me" 56
"No Rollin' Blues" 99
"No Room at the Hotel" 126
"No Room at the Inn" 126
"No Voot No Boot" 78
Noel, Orville Fats 97
Nolan Strong and the Diablos 193
Norman, Gene 75, 99
Norris, Ella Mae 137–38
Norton, Sonny 186–87
"Now You Know" 203
Nubin, Katie Bell 124–25
Nugetre 91, 176; *see also* Ertegun, Ahmet
Nuggy 214; *see also* Ertegun, Ahmet

Nunn, Bobby 104–5
The Nutmegs 209
Nyro, Laura 193

The Oakaleers 178; *see also* The Swallows
Oakland, CA 29
Obrecht, Jas 42
Oden, St. Louis Jimmy 16
"Oh Baby Don't" 201
Oh Lord—Stand by Me 152–53
"Oh Lord, What Then" 139
"Oh Mary Don't You Weep" 158
"Oh What a Nite" 202
Okeh Records 55–56, 108, 116, 137, 205
"Ol' Man River" 164, 167–68
"The Old Landmark" 141–42
"Old Maid Boogie" 78, 95
Old Town Records 180, 182, 192, 208
Oliver, Jimmy 177
Oliver, Paul 23, 40
Omaha, NE 68, 93
"On the Judgement Day" 159
"One Bad Stud" 194
"One Day" 137–39
"One Mint Julep" 217
"One Mistake" 173
"One Monkey Don't Stop No Show" 56
"One Scotch, One Bourbon, One Beer" 84
"Only Sixteen" 91
"Only You" 196, 198
"Only You (and You Alone)" 198
"Oop Shoop" 195
Orendorff, George 27
The Orioles 5, 17, 163, 167–70, 174, 177–78, 180, 190, 221
Otis, Johnny 5, 8, 12, 25, 53–54, 57, 67, 102, 104–5, 116, 188, 217–18
"Our Father" 155
"Over the Rainbow" 182
Owens, Paul 138, 158–59

Pacific Gas & Electric 2
"Packin' Up" 142
Page, Hot Lips 76, 93–94
Page, Jimmy 42
Page, Patti 187–88
Palmer, Earl 86, 110–11, 219
Palmer, Robert 18, 23, 36, 42–46, 61, 86, 146, 173, 215
"Papa Don't Take No Mess" 220
"Papa's Got a Brand New Bag" 220
Paradise Records 182
Parchman Farm 31
Parham, Chuck 82

Parker, Charlie 25, 67
Parker, Frank 97
Parker, Junior 63, 65
Parker, Sonny 115–16
Parks, Rosa 10
Parkway Records 36–37
Parris, Fred 200
Parrot Records 40, 185
Parton, Dolly 123
Patton, Charlie 23, 43–44, 131
Paul, Wilbur "Yonkie" 180–81
Pauling, Loman 172–73
Payne, Odie Jr. 46
"Peace in the Valley" 146
The Peaches 57
Peacock Records 10, 53, 55, 116, 126, 129, 137, 139–40, 154–55, 159, 188, 218
The Penguins 17, 26, 163, 167, 190, 196, 209
Penniman, Little Richard 217; *see also* Richard, Little
Penniman Singers 217
"People Get Ready" 2, 100
Perkins, the Rev. Percell **154**–56
"Personality" 110
Petrillo, James 66–67, 133
Petway, Robert 37
Philadelphia 8, 71, 113, 136–37, 141, 156, 159, 167, 177, 199
Phillips, Bobby 192
Phillips, Earl 44
Phillips, Little Esther **104**; *see also* Esther, Little; Washington, Esther Mae
Phillips, Sam 6, 21, 43, 63, 84, 115
Phillips Records 5–6
Philo Records 75–76
Pickett, Wilson 1, 117, 125, 130, 159
Pierce, Maryland 174
The Pilgrim Travelers 16, 133–34, 138, 160, 213
"Pink Champagne" 114
Pinkney, Bill **175**–77
Pittsburgh Courier 68
Plater, Bobby 116
The Platters 14, 166, 187, 196–99, **197**, 212
"Please Find My Baby" 45
"Please, Please, Please" 221–22
"Please Say You Want Me" 205
"Please Send Me Someone to Love" 100, 102
"Pleasing Man Blues" 76
"Pledging My Love" 101–2
Pomus, Doc 93
"Poor Boy" 45
"Poor Boy Long Ways from Home" 45, 78
Porter, Arthur 189
Powell, Chris 113

Powell, Jesse 192
Powell, Vance 155
"Power of the Lord" 119–20
Powers, Ann 12, 167, 204
"Precious Lord, Take My Hand" 9, 213; *see also* "Take My Hand, Precious Lord"
Premium Records 209
Presley, Elvis 6, 30, 34, 43, 53, 94, 111, 123, 128, 170
Preston Jimmy 113
Price, Lloyd 109–11, 212, 218
Price, Sam 124
Pride, Charlie 123
Prima, Louis 182
Propes, Steve 17, 37, 84, 92, 105, 113, 171, 187, 189, 254
"Prowling Nighthawk" 33
Pruter, Robert 184
Pryor, Snooky 40
Prysock, Red 80, 185
pumping bass 121, 128–31, 140, 145, 158, 162

"Queen Bee" 60
Queens, NY 201
Questlove 17
Quick, Clarence 200–1

R&B Records 188
The Radio Four 123, 129–31, 138
The Raelets 217
"Rain Is a Bringdown" 106
Rainbow Records 180
Rainey, Ma 26, 60, 81, 118, 122
Raleigh, NC 172
Ram, Buck 166, 196–98
Rama Records 186, 202
Ramey, Hurley 82
Ramirez, Ram 76, 182
Randall, J.B. 161
Ratley, J.T. 161
"Raunchy" 5–7
The Ravens 5, 164, 166–68, 171–72, 174, 176, 180
Rawls, Lou 130, 160–61
Ray 213
Ray Charles 215–16
Ray Charles Trio 213
Raye, Don 85
RCA-Victor Records 30, 34, 41, 83, 108, 217–18
"Ready Teddy" 217
"Real Gone Mama" 190
"Reconsider Baby" 30
"Record Ban Blues" 133
Red, Tampa 28, 30, 33, 60, 64, 79, 110, 118; *see also* Whittaker, Hudson
Red Robin Records 183, 204
Redd, Gene 108
Redding, Otis 121
Reed, Clem J. 129
Reed, Herb **197**

Reed, Johnny 168–*169*
Reed, Lula 216
Reese, Della 160
Reet, Petite and Gone 73
Regal Records 32
Renfro, Sister Jessie Mae 126, 129
Republic Records 123, 129
Rhodes, Todd 96
Rich, Eddie 178
Richard, Little 13, 58, 109, 111, 117, 119, 123, 128, 142, 212, 216–20, *219*, 222; *see also* Penniman, Little Richard
Richard, Renald 215
Ricks, Jimmy 134, 167–68, 171
"Ride Daddy Ride" 97
Riley, Judge 34
Ripani, Richard 12
Ritz, David 214
"R.M. Blues" 87
Robeson, Paul 167
Robey, Don 53–54, 65, 116, 155, 218
Robi, Paul *197*
The Robins 91, 104, 167, 194
Robinson, Bobby 183, 203, 208
Robinson, Jimmy 80
Robinson, Ray Charles 213; *see also* Charles, Ray
Robinson, R.B. *143*
Robinson, Smokey 193
Rock Around the Clock 198
"Rock Awhile" 150
"Rock H-Bomb Rock" 114
"Rock Me Daddy" 81
"Rock Mr. Blues" 93
Rock, Rock, Rock 189, 207–8
"Rock the Joint" 113, 137
"Rocket '88'" 2, 14, 115
"Rockin' at Midnight" 97
"Rockin' Is Our Bizness" 116
"Rockin' the House" 83
Rogers, Jimmy 24, 35–36, 38–39, 48–49, 84
Rogers, Junior 77, 88
Roker, Wally 201–2
"Roll and Tumble Blues" 36
"Roll Over Beethoven" 13
"Roll with Me, Henry" 57, 67; *see also* "The Wallflower"
"Rollin' and Tumblin'" 36–37, 60
"Rollin' Stone" 19, 37–38
Rolling Fork, MS 38
The Rolling Stones 1, 24, 35, 153, 221
The Ronettes 21, 205
"Roomin' House Boogie" 86
Roots of a Revolution 212
"Rosa Lee Swing" 41
Ross, Diana 205
Rowe, Hadie 172

Rowe, James 158
Royal, Ernie 80
Royal, Marshall 76
Royal Sons Quintet 172; *see also* The "5" Royales
The Royals 173, 188–89; *see also* The Midnighters
RPM Records 44, 63
"Rubber Biscuit" 11, 210–11
Rundless, Ernestine 160
Rundless, Laura Lee 160; *see also* Lee, Laura
Runowicz, John Michael 164–67
Rupe, Art 87, 110–11, 117, 134, 219
Rush, Otis 41–42
Rushing, Jimmy 87
Ruth, Thermon 172
Ruth McFadden and the Harptones 208

"Sad Hours" 49
Sailes, Jesse 86
St. Augustine, FL 213
St. Louis 8, 39, 82–83
Salem, James 100, 102
Sam, Magic 42
Sam, Washboard 50
Sam Price Trio 124
Sampson 85, 112–13
Samuels, Clarence 94
Sanders, Zell 195
Santana, Carlos 42
Santelli, Robert 17, 27–28, 32, 38, 45, 49, 61–62, 141
Santiago, Herman 205–206
Sapp, Hosea 87
"Satisfied with Jesus" 16
"Saturday Night Fish Fry" 73–74
Saunders, Red 92
Savoy Records 10–11, 104–5, 141, 157
"Sax Shack Boogie" 86
"Say a Word" 16, 136
"Say It Loud—I'm Black and I'm Proud" 11, 220
Schiff, Matthew 14, 165–67, 177, 194–95, 204, 210
"School Boy" 46
"School Girl Blues" 91
"Schoolboy" 208
The Schoolboys 204–5
Schubert Swanston Trio 204
Score Records 128
Scott, George 152–53
Scott, Nafloyd 221–23
Scott, Phillip 129
Seattle, WA 213
"Secret Love" 190
Sedaka, Neil 183
"See Saw" 190
Seeger, Pete 31

Selah Jubilee Singers 172, 209; *see also* The Larks
The Sensational Nightingales 131, 138, 146–47, 149, 159–60, 162
Sepia Swing Club 63
The Sermon 152–53
"Sexy Ways" 189
"Shadrack" 128
"Shake a Hand" 55
"Shake, Rattle and Roll" 2, 20, 69, 92–93
Sharecropper, Little Miss 108; *see also* Baker, LaVern
Sharp, Alexander *169*–70
Sharpton, the Rev. Al 117
Shaw, Arnold 18, 43, 71, 78, 80, 89, 98, 100, 168
"Sh-Boom" 10, 163, 186–88, 190
"She Moves Me" 38
"She Sets My Soul on Fire" 116
Shep and the Limelites 202
Sheppard, James "Shep" 201–2
"She's Nineteen Years Old" 91
Shields, Calvin "Eagle Eye" 89
"Shipyard Woman Blues" 20
Shird, Lucille 137
The Shirelles 21
"Shirley" 205
Shirley & Lee 109, 111–12, 183, 218
Shirley Gunter and the Queens 195, 197
Shirley Haven and the Four Jacks 195–96
"Short Haired Woman" 28
"Shotgun Blues" 28
"Shouldn't I Know" 177–78
"Shout" 132–33
Sievers, Vernon 201
Sim, Willie 115
Simpkins, Jesse 71, *72*
Sinatra, Frank 26, 99
"Sincerely" 190
Singer, Hal "Oklahoma" 94–96
Singleton, Charlie 114; *see also* Charlie Singleton Orchestra
"Sinner Man" 159
"Sinner's Prayer" 214
"Sit Down Servant" 153
"Sittin' on It All the Time" 78, 95
"16 Candles" 91
"Sixty Minute Man" 164, 171, 178
"The Sky Is Crying" 46
Slack, Freddie 21, 26, 85
Slim, Bumble Bee 33, 80; *see also* Easton, Amos
Slim, Guitar 12, 24, 61–62, 109, 214; *see also* Jones, Eddie
Slim, Memphis 31, 39, 83–84; *see also* Chatman, John

Slim, Sunnyland 32, 36, 39–40; see also Luandrew, Albert
Slim, Tarheel 209; see also Bunn, Allen
"Slippin' and Slidin'" 217
Sly and the Family Stone 116
Smith, Arlene 205
Smith, Bessie 60, 75, 98, 122
Smith, Dickie 174
Smith, Lonnie 136
Smith, Mabel 55; see also Maybelle, Big
Smith, Pinetop 214
Smith, Trixie 15
Smith, Wilbert "Lee Diamond" 222
Smith, Willie 76
Smith, Wilson "Thunder" 28–29
"Smoke from Your Cigarette" 195
"Smokestack Lightning" 44–45
"Snatch and Grab It" 17, 80
"So Long" 106–7
The Solid Senders 81, 87–88
The Solitaires 164, 192–93, 204
"Someday You'll Want Me to Want You" 176–77
"Somebody Done Hoodooed the Hoodoo Man" 51
"Somebody Touched Me" 123
"Somewhere to Lay My Head" 131, 159–60
Songs of Faith 212
"Soul on Fire" 108
The Soul Stirrers 16, 120, 134, 142–48, **143**, 157, 159, 163
Southern Harmonaires 172
The Spaniels 163, 183–84, 186
Spann, Otis 35, 38–39, 44, 48, 52, 115
Spark Records 258
Spartanburg, SC 159
Specialty Records 10, 61, 81, 87, 100, 109–10, 114, 117, 126, 133–34, 142–43, 149, 152, 158, 160–61, 219–20
Spector, Phil 111
Spector, Ronnie 205
"Speedoo" 192
Speiginer, Louis 98
Spirit of Memphis Quartet 16, 134–35
Spo-de-ode 72; see also Theard, Sam
Spotify 2, 15, 139
Stackhouse, Houston 33
Stagger Lee" 109–10, 146
"Standing at the Crossroads" 45–46
Staples, Mavis 126, 131–32
Staples, Roebuck "Pops" 131–32
The Staples Singers 131–32
Starks, Evelyn 149

States Records 51
Steel, Willie 43
Steele, Silas, Jr. 135
Stewart, Curtis 123
Stewart, Teddy 79
Stone, Jesse 92, 175, 177–80, 187, 214; see also Calhoun, Charles
"Stop the Wedding" 58
"Stormy Monday Blues" 27, 65; see also "Call It Stormy Monday"
"The Story of My Life" 61–62
"Story Untold" 209
"Strange Things Happening Every Day" 124
Strong, Nolan 257
The Students 204, 207
"Such a Night" 176
"Sugar Mama" 60
Sugarfoot Sam from Alabam 217
Sullivan, Ed 116, 163
Sumlin, Hubert 44
Sun Records 6, 10, 43, 52
"A Sunday Kind of Love" 58, 182
"Sunny Land" 46
"Super Fly" 100
Supreme Records 98, 100
The Supremes 21, 205
"Sure Cure for the Blues" 195–96
"Surely God Is Able" 141–42
Sutton, Charles 188
The Swallows 9, 163, 167, 178–79
The Swan Silvertones 16, 138, 155, 158, 163
"Sweet Home Chicago" 23
"Sweet Little Angel" 33, 64; see also "Black Angel Blues"
"Sweet Little Sixteen" 26, 91
"Sweet Sixteen" 91
"Swing Down Chariot" 128, 132
swing orchestras 8, 66–67, 75
switch lead 20, 120, 125, 129, 135, 142–43, 146, 152–53, 156, 158, 161, 164, 176, 196
Sykes, Roosevelt 82–83

"T-Bone Shuffle" 27
"T-Model Blues" 28
"'Tain't Nobody's Business If I Do" 98
"Take My Hand, Precious Lord" 118; see also "Precious Lord, Take My Hand"
The T.A.M.I. Show 221
Tanner, Johnny 173
Tarrant, Rabon 26, 50
Tatum, Robbie 201
"Tax Payer Blues" 40
Taylor, Eddie 40
Taylor, Johnnie 130–31, 159
Taylor, Raymond 218

Taylor, Sam "The Man" 56–57, 92, 107–8, 175–76, 178, 180, 187, 193, 195, 203
Taylor, Zola **197**
"Teardrops from My Eyes" 107
"A Teenager in Love" 204
"Tell Me Mama" 50
Tempo-Tone Records 40
The Tempo Toppers 218
The Temptations 37
"Ten Commandments of Love" 190, 207
"Terraplane Blues" 114
Terry, Johnny 221, 223
Terry, Sonny 24
Tharpe, Sister Rosetta 13, 123–26, **125**, 127–28, 135, 151, 170, 217
"That's All Right" (Big Boy Crudup) 34
"That's All Right" (Jimmy Rogers) 39
"That's What You're Doing to Me" 171
Theard, Sam 71–72, 74
"There in the Night" 199
"These Foolish Things Remind Me of You" 171
"They Call Me Big Mama" 54
"They Raided the House" 73, 76
"They Raided the Joint" 76
"The Things That I Used to Do" 61–62, 214
"Third Degree" 11, 40–41
"This Little Girl of Mine" 216
"This May Be the Last Time" 152–53
"This Train" 50
Thomas, Charles 98
Thomas, Rufus 10, 62
Thomas, Sam 161
Thompson, Beachey **137**–38, 140
Thompson, Lucky 78; see also Lucky Thompson's All Stars
Thompson, Sonny 178, 189, 216
Thornton, Willie Mae Big Mama 21, 32, 46, 53–55, **54**, 101
"A Thousand Miles Away" 201–2
Thrasher, Andrew **175**
Thrasher, Gerhart **175**, 177
"Three Hours Past Midnight" 30
"Three O'Clock Blues" 29–30, 63
"The Thrill Is Gone" 64
"Thrill Me" 81
Til, Sonny 17, 168–70, **169**, 178, 184, 205, 221; see also Tilghman, Earlington
Tilghman, Earlington 168; see also Til, Sonny

Till, Emmett 12, 183, 192
"Tim Moore's Farm" 29
Tindley, Charles Albert 16, 142–43, 150
Tisbey, Dexter 190
Toccoa, GA 220–21
"Toll the Bell Easy" 135
Tom, Georgia 31, 79, 159; see also Dorsey, Thomas A.
"Tom Moore's Farm" 29
"Too Close" 126
"Too Close to Heaven" 126–27, 152, 155, 157
"Too Soon to Know" 17
Tooze, Sandra 37
Toscano, Eli 42
Tosches, Nick 71, 84, 89–90, 92, 112, 115, 179
"Touch the Hem of His Garment" 145, 147
"Tough Lover" 57–58
"Treasure of Love" 170
Trenier, Claude 77, 116
The Treniers 96, 116, 218
Trotman, Lloyd 107
"Trouble at Midnight" 97
Trouble in My Way" 140, 158
Truman, Harry 10
Trumpet Records 45, 48
The Trumpeteers 128–29
"Trust in Me" 58
"Try Me" 220
Tucker, Alonza 189
Tucker, Ira 14, 16, 65, 117, *137*–40, 159, 213
Tuell, Fanny 55; see also Adams, Faye
Tulsa, OK 29, 87
Tupelo, MS 34
The Turbans 199
"Turn on Your Love Light" 65
Turner, Big Joe 10–12, 17, 20, 69, 86–87, 89–93, **90**, 96, 98, 108, 112
Turner, Danny 113
Turner, Ike 14, 40, 44–45, 63, 115
Turner, Kylo 133–34
Turner, Tina 55, 115
Turrentine, Stanley 214
"Tutti Frutti" 144, 216–17, 219–20
"T.V. Mama" 92
12-bar blues 11–12, 19, 25–28, 30, 32–33, 42, 46, 52–53, 61, 65, 75–77, 79, 84, 88, 90–92, 96–97, 153; ballad 76–77, 99, 175; boogie 81, 83–84, 87, 94, 116; shuffle 46, 49, 222
"24 Hours" 40–41
"Twilight Time" 196
"Two Years of Torture" 100

"Unchain My Heart" 217
"Uncloudy Day" 132
United Records 33–34
"Up Above My Head" 124–25
The Upsetters 218
Upshaw, George 201

"Valerie" 172
Variety 68, 195–96, 203
Vaughan, Sarah 6
Vaughan, Stevie Ray 42, 62
Vee-Jay Records 10, 40, 131–32, 152, 158, 183, 188, 199, 202
Vera, Billy 82, 217
Verdell, Jackie 157
Vinson, Eddie "Cleanhead" 78, 89, 95
The Violinaires 130, 138
Vogue Records 31
Von Streeter, James 54, 102
"The Vow" 185

Waddy, Henrietta 141
"Wade in the Water" 128
"Wading Through Blood and Water" 139–40
Wald, Gayle 118, 124–25
Walker, Aaron Thibodeaux T-Bone 12–13, 24–28, **26**, 29–31, 46, 49, 61–62, 97, 113, 123
Walker, Alice 2, 228n53
Walker, James *137*
Walker, Mel 105
"Walking Along" 193
"Walking Blues" 36
Wallace, Albert 95
Wallace, Jo Jo 159
Waller, Fats 109
"The Wallflower" 57, 67, 187; see also "Roll with Me Henry"
Walls, Harry Van "Piano Man" 91, 93, 107, 180
Walsh, Ellis 73
Walter, Little 10, 35–39, 49–51; see also Jacobs, Little Walter
Ward, Billy 170–71, 174
Ward, Brian 18–19, 68, 103, 108, 164–66, 197, 203
Ward, Clara 141–42, 147, 156, 213
Ward, Ed 8, 106, 165, 171, 189
Ward, Gertrude 141–42
The Ward Singers 119, 137, 140–42; see also The Famous Ward Singers
"Warm Your Heart" 176
Warner, Jay 172, 174, 182, 184, 204
Warren, Earle 105
Warren, Ernest 178, 183
Warwick, Jacqueline 194
Warwick, NY 210
Washington, Booker T. 41
Washington, Dinah 5–6, 21, 54, 78–79, **78**, 103–4, 106, 133; see also Jones, Ruth

Washington, Esther Mae 104; see also Esther, Little
Washington, D.C. 121, 123, 127, 159, 167, 177, 179
"Watch Ye Therefore" 161
Waters, Benjamin 88
Waters, Ethel 75
Waters, Muddy 5, 14–16, 19–20, 23–24, 30–31, 33–42, **35**, 44, 48–49, 51–53, 58, 62, 91, 96, 114, 212; see also Morganfield, McKinley
Watson, Johnny "Guitar" 12, 29
"The Way I Feel" 176
"The Way You Look Tonight" 209
"We Shall Overcome" 143
"The Weary Blues" 98
Webb, Chick 71
Webster, Ben 6, 106
Weiss, Sam 192
Welding, Pete 132
We'll Never Turn Back 126
Wells, Junior 49, 51–52
"We're Gonna Rock" (aka "We're Gonna Rock, We're Gonna Roll") 112
West, Rudy 174
West Helena, AK 46
West Memphis, AK 24, 43, 52, 62
West Side sound 56
Weston, Ruth 106; see also Brown, Ruth
Wexler, Jerry 21, 108, 164–65, 176, 214
"What Then" 139; see also "Oh Lord, What Then"
"What'cha Gonna Do" (The Drifters) 176
"What'cha Gonna Do" (The Radio Four) 130
"What'd I Say" 215, 217
Wheatstraw, Peetie 60
The Wheels 209–10
When Harry Met Sally 75
"When He Spoke" 156–57
"When I Leave These Prison Walls" 172
"When the Saints Go Marching In" 95, 134–35
"When You Dance" 199
"Where Are You (Now That I Need You)" 204
"Where Shall I Be" 150
Whirlin' Disc Records 183, 203
Whitall, Susan 135
White, Charles 218
White, Charlie 105, 171, 180
White, Ellison 195
"White Christmas" 166–68, 176
"White Cliffs of Dover" 164, 185
Whittaker, Hudson 45; see also Red, Tampa

"Who Can Explain" 205
"Who Threw the Whiskey in the Well" 93
"Why Do Fools Fall in Love" 205–6
"Why, Johnny, Why?" 101
"Wild Wild Young Men" 107
Wilkerson, Don 86, 214–15
Wilkins, Ernie 79
Wilkins, Joe Willie 48
Will Bradley Trio 85
"Will He Welcome Me There" 159
"Will You Be Mine" 178
Williams, Al 11
Williams, Big Joe 31, 221
Williams, Bobby 193
Williams, Cootie 67
Williams, Cora 195
Williams, Curtis 190
Williams, Devonia 105–6, 156n66
Williams, Dootsie 26; see also Dootone Records
Williams, Hank 123
Williams, Jody 44
Williams, Marion 119, 141–42, 147, 217
Williams, Otis 188
Williams, Paul "Hucklebuck" 107, 112
Williams, Ralph 170
Williams, Sherley Anne 91
Williams, Tony 196–98, **197**
Williamson, John Lee "Sonny Boy I" 31, 33, 46–47, 49, 51–52, 60, 83
Williamson, "Sonny Boy II" 10, 24, 38, 43, 45, **47**–49, 51–52, 58, 62; see also Miller, Aleck "Rice"
Willis, Chuck 174, 178
The Willows 180, 183
Wilson, August 2
Wilson, Carl "Flat Top" 94
Wilson, Jackie 17, 96, 121
Wilson, Paul 184–85
Wimby, Julius 218
"The Wind" 193
Winfield, Willie **181**–82
Winley, Harold **179**
Witherspoon, Jimmy 6, 11, 20–21, 25, 55, 89, 98–100, 116
"Without Love (There Is Nothing)" 170
"Without the Help of Jesus" 152
Wolf, Howlin' 6, 10, 16, 24, 35, 39, 42–45, **43**, 52, 58, 60, 131; see also Burnett, Chester
Womack, Solomon 158
Wonder, Stevie 205
"Wonderful Girl" 200
Woodard, Lloyd **154**
Wooten, Buddy 204
"Work with Me" 49
"Work with Me Annie" 49, 57, 188–89, 262
"Working for the Lord" 136
"Working on the Building" 129
"The World's in a Tangle" 35; see also "Build Myself a Cave"; "I'm Gonna Dig Myself a Hole"
Wright, Billy 217–18
Wright, Clifton 203
Wright, Jimmy 201, 205–6
Wright, Norman 200
Wright, Richard 23, 25, 28

The Yardbirds 48
"You Better Cut That Out" 51
"You Can't Get That Stuff No More" 79
"You Could Be My Love" 180–81
"You Don't Know Me" 217
"You Gave Me Peace of Mind" 184
"You Got to Move" 153
"You Must Be Born Again" 151
"You Send Me" 145
"You Upset Me, Baby" 64
Young, Lee 82
Young, Lester 6, 76
Young, Snooky 76
"Young Man's Blues" 77
Youngstown, OH 88
"Your Cash Ain't Nothin' But Trash" 180
"Your Promise to Be Mine" 177
"You're My Inspiration" 180
"You're Sixteen, You're Beautiful, and You're Mine" 91
YouTube 2, 15, 110, 125, 139, 142–43, 152–53, 157, 160, 185, 198, 207, 221
"You've Been Mistreatin' Me" 32

Zak, Albin 205
Zolten, Jerry 119–20, 136, 138, 140, 155

www.ingramcontent.com/pod-product-compliance
Ingram Content Group UK Ltd.
Pitfield, Milton Keynes, MK11 3LW, UK
UKHW062230220426
5349IPUK00006B/87